RED ROSES ON THE VELDT

RED ROSES ON THE VELDT

Lancashire Regiments in the Boer War, 1899–1902

LIEUTENANT-COLONEL JOHN DOWNHAM

Carnegie Publishing

Red Roses on the Veldt

Published by Carnegie Publishing Ltd
Carnegie House, Chatsworth Road,
Lancaster LA1 4SL
01524–840111

Typeset and originated by
Carnegie Publishing

ISBN 1-85936-075-0

Cataloguing-in-Publication data
A catalogue record for this book is available from the British Library

Printed and bound in the UK by
The Alden Press, Oxford

Contents

Illustrations

Introduction

The war in South Africa from 1899 to 1902, the Boer War, has been submerged in British consciousness by two terrible World Wars, and yet at the time it caught the popular imagination in a way that few if any previous conflicts had done. Nowhere was the prevailing patriotic fervour more intense, or more strongly sustained, than in Lancashire, which then as now nurtured a large proportion of the British Army.

One lasting consequence of this surge of interest in military matters was that Lancastrians 'discovered' and, for the first time, identified with their County Regiments, whose names would be familiar in almost every household in the County during the Great War. British Infantry Regiments of the Line had until 1881 borne numerical titles, of which after some two centuries they were fiercely proud, but in 1873 the territorial basis of Army recruiting was reorganised and this was further confirmed on 1 July 1881 when the majority of the old Regiments of Foot were linked in pairs and redesignated as battalions of County Regiments. One battalion would serve overseas while the other remained at home, providing drafts and available for home defence or expeditionary tasks. Each Regiment formed a Depot in the County and had affiliated Militia and Volunteer battalions. My book is concerned with just three of these Regiments, closely related in the past and today combined in The Queen's Lancashire Regiment.

The senior of these was the East Lancashire Regiment, whose 1st and 2nd Battalions were, respectively, the old 30th and 59th Regiments, recruited in the cotton towns and villages around Blackburn and Burnley. The Regimental Depot had been moved in January 1899 from Burnley Barracks to Fulwood Barracks, Preston but the Headquarters of its 3rd (Militia) Battalion and of the 2nd Volunteer Battalion had remained in Burnley, while the 1st Volunteer Battalion was based in Blackburn.

The South Lancashire Regiment (Prince of Wales's Volunteers) had similarly been formed from the 40th and 82nd Regiments of Foot. The Depot was at Orford Barracks, Warrington, and the Headquarters of the Militia and of the 1st Volunteer Battalion were also in that staunch Lancashire town, while the 2nd Volunteer Battalion was at St Helens.

The Loyal North Lancashire Regiment, 47th and 81st, was centred on Preston but drew many recruits from Blackburn, Wigan and Bolton. The Regimental Depot, shared with the East Lancashires, was Fulwood Barracks, while the Headquarters of the Militia and the 1st Volunteer Battalions were also in Preston. The 2nd Volunteer Battalion was based in Bolton.

It is a significant feature of the Boer War that, for the first time, all constituent parts of the Regiment were involved in active service overseas. The three Regular 1st Battalions (the 30th, 40th and 47th) and the three Militia Battalions all took part as complete units, while the Volunteers contributed manpower to a succession of composite Volunteer companies which served in South Africa with their respective 1st Battalions. The Regular 2nd Battalions sent substantial drafts to their 1st Battalions and to serve as Mounted Infantry. For the Volunteers in particular, who had previously been confined to local defence, this first overseas expedition was an important precedent, and today's Territorials, serving with Regular units in the Balkans, Northern Ireland and elsewhere, are following in their foot-steps.

The great majority of the Lancashire soldiers who served in South Africa were not serving professional soldiers but recalled reservists, typically married men in their late twenties and early thirties, or part-time soldiers of the Militia and Volunteers. In their thousands they left civilian occupations, families, friends and work-mates, a local community of interest which followed their progress with a keen sympathy, identifying with triumphs and tribulations alike, in a way which is not so evident when only Regular soldiers are engaged. This intense local involvement with the fortunes of a local Regiment was something quite new in 1899, but would be a common experience in the new century.

The Boers, or Afrikaners, were mainly of severe Dutch Calvinist stock, leavened with French Huguenots and Germans, and had been settled around the Cape of Good Hope since the seventeenth century. In 1795, when the Netherlands were occupied by the armies of the French Republic, a British expedition captured the Cape, holding it until the short-lived Peace of Amiens in 1803. Part of the garrison at that time was the 81st Regiment, later to become the 2nd Loyal North Lancashires. In 1806, during the Napoleonic Wars, Britain took permanent control of the Cape after a brief struggle with the Dutch garrison in which the 59th Regiment, forebears of the 2nd East Lancashires, took part.

The rural Afrikaners depended on the manual labour of Africans, maintained in divinely ordained servitude, and they deeply resented interference by their more liberal British rulers. The abolition of slavery throughout the British Empire in 1834 was the final straw, prompting the Great Trek, a Boer migration north, over the Orange and Vaal rivers, to found the Transvaal and the Orange Free State. There, free from British restraint, bible in one hand and sjambok in the other, the Boers combined a fundamentalist Old Testament devoutness with an absolute determination to keep the Africans in a state of subjection. An attempt in 1877 to bring these anachronistic farming republics under British control was reversed in 1881 when, following the defeat of a small British force at Majuba hill, the Afrikaners regained their independence.

The discovery in 1886 of the world's largest gold deposits on the Witwatersrand, in the heart of the Transvaal, breached the Boer laager as hordes of adventurers flocked into the republic. These newcomers, or Uitlanders, soon paid eighty per cent of the taxes but were denied rights of citizenship or representation by an Afrikaner leadership fearful of losing control. The Uitlanders, many of whom were British, appealed to Britain for support against Afrikaner oppression. Meanwhile, President Kruger of the Transvaal used his growing gold revenues to buy modern arms from France and Germany. Gradually, through a combination of Afrikaner intransigence, imperial pride, and the machinations of the mining magnate Cecil Rhodes, amid diplomatic bickering, Britain and the Boer republics drifted inexorably towards armed conflict.

Indecision and wishful optimism at Cape Town and in London hampered British preparations for war, but it should not be thought that the Army was entirely ignorant of the Boers and of what it would take to beat them. Some three months before the outbreak of war, an article entitled 'Majuba II – A Forecast' appeared in *The XXX*, journal of the East Lancashire Regiment under the pen-name 'En Avant'. It was a regimental officer's prediction of the possible course of the impending conflict and included some quite prescient comments on the military requirement:

'In the Autumn of 18— everything was ready ... and, within one week of the final decision, a fleet of transports with the 1st Army Corps sailed from Southampton and other ports for Delagoa Bay and Durban ... Commanded by a grim old general who had had many years experience of guerilla warfare and was particularly conversant with Boer tactics ... [the Army was] largely composed of Cavalry, Mounted Infantry, Horse and Field Artillery, and machine guns. Each column constituted a mobile force so necessary in a campaign where the quickest movements mean success.' Unfortunately, an expeditionary force constituted along the lines suggested by 'En Avant' was not available.

On the outbreak of war in 1899 there were some 27,500 British troops in South Africa, including the 1st Loyal North Lancashires. The

Boers mobilised over 48,000 men initially, nearly all mounted and armed with the latest high-velocity Mauser rifles, firing smokeless cartridges. They were organised in local commandos, variable in size from a few hundred to two to three thousand men, and supported by 72 guns. They were challenging the whole might of the British Empire, but if they moved fast they might exploit their temporary superiority of numbers, and their central position, to snatch a quick victory before the arrival of British reinforcements.

On 14 October the Boers invaded Cape Colony and Natal, investing the towns of Mafeking and Kimberley, the latter defended by half the Loyal North Lancashires. By the end of the month Ladysmith, with Sir George White's field force, was also besieged. British attempts to raise these sieges are the main theme of the next four months.

In Britain the 1st Army Corps, commanded by Sir Redvers Buller, was mobilised on 7 October, but it was towards the end of the following month before they reached the front in South Africa in sufficient numbers for Buller to advance. His first offensive operations foundered in 'Black Week', defeated on all fronts by a combination of poor intelligence, over-confidence and Boer exploitation of their modern rifles in defensive battles. Lord Roberts, aged but a national hero, was sent out to replace Buller as Commander-in-Chief, with Lord Kitchener as his Chief of Staff. More reinforcements also headed south, including the 1st Battalions of the East Lancashire and South Lancashire Regiments. It is clear from their letters and diaries that these soldiers had little doubt why they were going – to bring freedom and justice to the suffering Uitlanders and to restore the prestige of British arms in Southern Africa.

The difficulties and limitations confronted by the British generals in the early months of the war are often under-estimated, though those who fought under their command, experiencing these same problems at first hand, were less critical. On the Orange River front in particular, British options were severely restricted by lack of artillery and mounted troops, and over-dependence on the railway for supplies, and it was not until these deficiencies had to some extent been remedied that Roberts was able to advance to the relief of Kimberley. On the Tugela front the problem was rather how to break through a formidable natural defensive position to relieve Ladysmith, and there were two further reverses, including the bloody battle of Spion Kop, before Buller combined guns and Infantry in a methodical reduction of the Boer positions.

The Boers, heavily defeated at Paardeberg, were now on the defensive, and the capture of Bloemfontein, capital of the Orange Free State, soon followed. The British now advanced on all fronts, following the strategic railways. Mafeking was relieved, and northern Natal liberated, and when on 5 June Roberts took Pretoria the conventional war was all but over.

The conflict now assumed a completely different complexion, that of guerrilla warfare. As he advanced, Roberts had attempted to win over the Afrikaners by a policy of conciliation, but it was soon clear that there was an irreconcilable element willing to fight to the bitter end.

De Wet, Botha, De la Rey and like-minded 'bitter-enders' evolved an appropriate strategy, aggressive raiding by mobile commandos against the long and vulnerable railway lines of communication and against isolated garrisons, convoys and columns. This activity ranged in scale from sniping and cutting telegraph wires, through railway demolitions and ambushes, to fairly major offensive operations by several commandos, two to three thousand men with artillery support. The commandos could be concentrated for operations and then disperse to their homes, hiding their weapons, only to reappear in strength elsewhere. This strategy depended on support from the farmsteads and hamlets which, in effect, formed a network of Boer supply depots, intelligence agencies and safe houses across the sparsely populated veldt. Anyone who withheld support from the commandos was likely to have his farm burned and his stock confiscated. In response, the British reluctantly resorted to punitive farm burning.

Lord Roberts left South Africa in December 1900, handing over to Kitchener and complacently dismissing the remaining Boer forces as 'a few marauding bands'. Kitchener's strategy, more systematic than Roberts' reactive farm burnings, was to clear the land in disaffected areas while harrying the enemy with mobile columns. At the same time he had to protect his lines of communication and garrison the larger towns and settlements, which would otherwise have been reoccupied by the Boers. Kitchener had some ten times the overall strength of the Boers, but by the time his lines of communication had been secured he had barely more soldiers available for offensive operations than his opponents, perhaps 22,000 to the Boers' 20,000. In consequence, at local level the game of cat and mouse involved frequent role reversals when the 'mice' converged in superior strength. This was often exacerbated by poor co-ordination between British columns, a fault traceable to Kitchener's own staff.

As the war entered its second year, Kitchener realised that he had to deny both logistic support and freedom of movement to the Boers. His draconic farm clearances were largely achieving the first of these requirements, and to achieve the second he began a comprehensive programme of blockhouse building to cordon off great tracts of the country. Within these defended lines, co-ordinated drives by mobile columns cleared area after area. By October 1901 this system was proving its worth, but it was not until May 1902 that the surviving Boer leaders accepted that further resistance was useless.

An unusual feature of the Boer War, and of its guerrilla phase in particular, was the prominence of mounted troops, including Mounted Infantry. There was, indeed, nothing particularly novel about Infantry on horseback. For many years British battalions in South Africa, including the 82nd in 1884–87, had adapted to local conditions by raising Mounted Infantry Companies. But the scale of the requirement was now much greater, and by May 1901 Kitchener had some 80,000 mounted troops in South Africa, of whom 12,000 were Regular Mounted Infantry. The East, South and Loyal North Lancashire Regiments all provided large numbers of Mounted Infantry, including several complete companies. As the cutting edge of the mobile columns the mounted men saw more than their share of the fighting, and there was never any shortage of volunteers for this dashing role.

It is not my intention to enter into the many controversies that still attend discussion of the Boer War, though inevitably some of these must be touched on. Indeed, I have sketched in the larger picture only to the extent necessary for readers to put activities at Regimental level and below in some context. I offer the present work not as a fully rounded history of the war but as an attempt to convey something of the experience of the thousands of Lancashire soldiers who fought in South Africa.

I have, whenever possible, let the participants, young soldiers and officers, speak for themselves, using extracts from their letters, diaries and memoirs, illustrated with their own photographs from collections donated to the extensive Regimental archives.

This was the first war in which many junior officers, as opposed to professional photographers, carried cameras. They photographed what appealed to them, notably their soldiers, each other and their horses, took illuminating vignettes of life in camp and on trek, and attempted to capture something of their exotic surroundings. Whilst the results produced by these enthusiastic amateurs, in carefully annotated sepia-tinted albums, often lack the posed artistry and technical skill of, say, Fenton's Crimean photographs, the best of them have an immediacy and charming spontaneity which, by filling in the physical detail, breaths life into and ideally complements the written word.

The Boer War was, perhaps, the high water mark of letter-writing and diary-keeping in the British Army. There were two good reasons for this. Firstly, thanks to elementary education most soldiers of all ranks were now literate. They were accustomed to letter-writing as the only means of keeping in touch with friends and family at home, and many of them wrote with an easy fluency and considerable powers of expression. Secondly, military censorship was almost non-existent and, unlike the two World Wars, full, frank and sometimes brutally realistic accounts of current operations, written by ordinary soldiers, appeared regularly in their local newspapers at home and were avidly read. These detailed low-level narratives, charged with all the pathos, physical discomfort and mental anxiety, humour and incongruity of war, filled column after column in provincial journals and are a rich human testament and source that has been almost completely ignored by most historians of the Boer War.

Other letters home, some of them almost serialised diaries, were lovingly kept by families, and several of these collections have since been donated to the Regiment. Many soldiers of all ranks also kept diaries, or subsequently committed their reminiscences of the war to paper, and we are fortunate that many of these too survive in the Regimental Archives at Fulwood Barracks, Preston.

I have appended a list of casualties, including the nearly four hundred men who died in South Africa, mostly from disease. The names, good Lancashire names predominantly, could have been taken at random from a nominal roll of The Queen's Lancashire Regiment of today and remind us that young soldiers have always paid the price in blood for the obduracy of politicians.

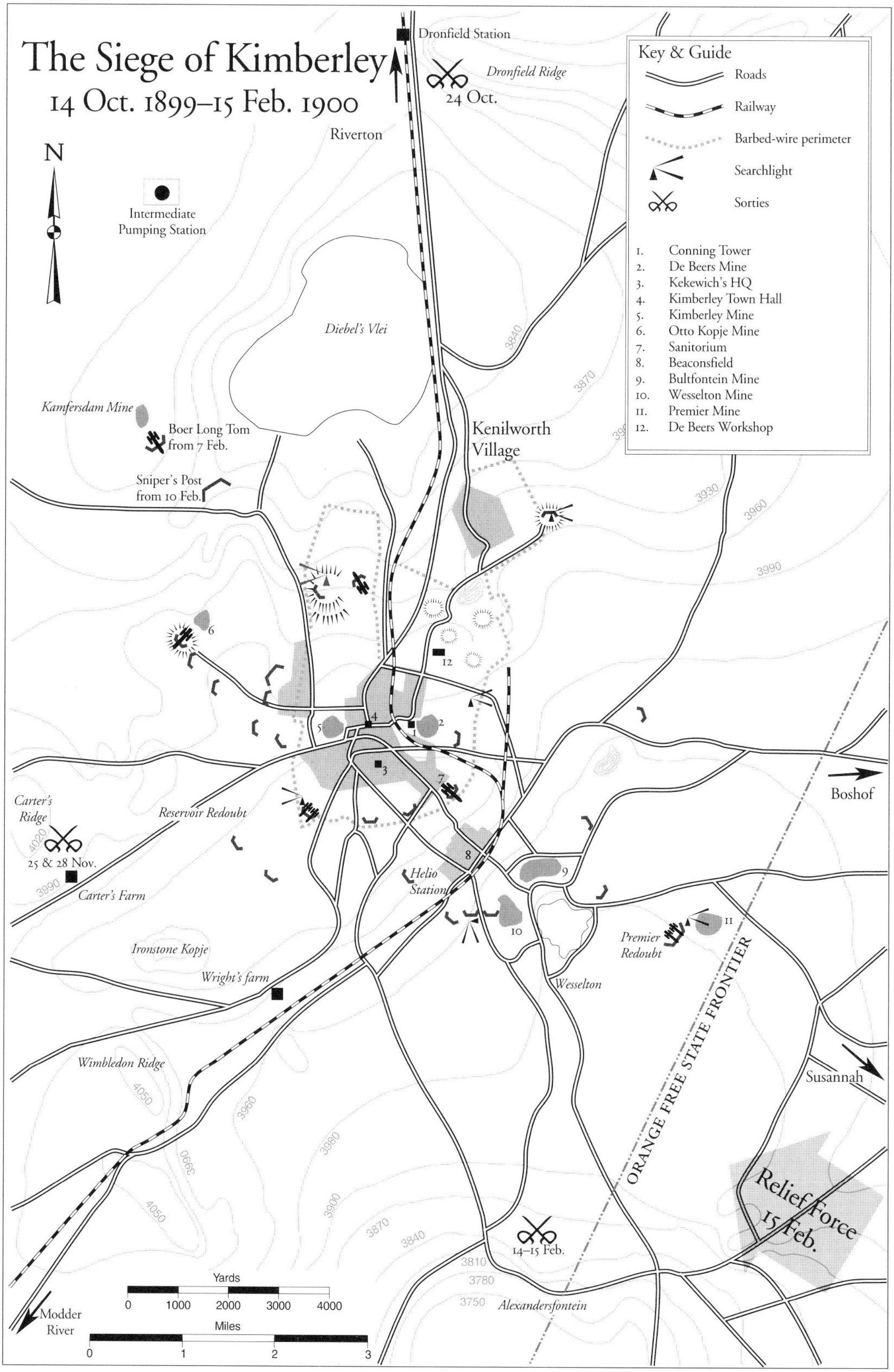
The Siege of Kimberley
14 Oct. 1899–15 Feb. 1900
N
Key & Guide
Roads
Railway
Barbed-wire perimeter
Searchlight
Sorties
1. Conning Tower
2. De Beers Mine
3. Kekewich's HQ
4. Kimberley Town Hall
5. Kimberley Mine
6. Otto Kopje Mine
7. Sanitorium
8. Beaconsfield
9. Bultfontein Mine
10. Wesselton Mine
11. Premier Mine
12. De Beers Workshop
Dronfield Station
Dronfield Ridge
24 Oct.
Riverton
Intermediate Pumping Station
Diebel's Vlei
Kamfersdam Mine
Boer Long Tom from 7 Feb.
Sniper's Post from 10 Feb.
Kenilworth Village
Carter's Ridge
25 & 28 Nov.
Reservoir Redoubt
Carter's Farm
Ironstone Kopje
Wright's farm
Wimbledon Ridge
Helio Station
Premier Redoubt
Wesselton
Boshof
Susannah
ORANGE FREE STATE FRONTIER
Relief Force 15 Feb.
14–15 Feb.
Alexandersfontein
Modder River
Yards
0 1000 2000 3000 4000
Miles
0 1 2 3

PART I

Kimberley

You damned soldiers are so loyal to each other that I verily believe that if God Almighty even was in a fix you would refuse to get Him out of it should the doing so interfere with your damned military situation!

(Cecil Rhodes to Lieutenant Colonel Kekewich)

The Diamond Fields in Danger

At 9 a.m. on 13 September 1899 a balding middle-aged gentleman in civilian clothes alighted from the Cape Town train at Kimberley, centre of the Diamond Fields, and made his way to the Kimberley Club. Lieutenant Colonel Robert Kekewich, Commanding Officer of 1st Battalion The Loyal North Lancashire Regiment, was on a secret mission.

Lying within sight of the border between Cape Colony and an increasingly belligerent Orange Free State, the Diamond City and the adjacent township of Beaconsfield produced some ninety percent of the world's supply of diamonds and were obvious and attractive targets, clearly vulnerable to attack and equally unprepared for defence. Through the town ran the strategically vital railway line from the Cape to Mafeking and the north. A sprawling, ugly, corrugated iron boom-town of some twenty thousand European and thirty thousand African inhabitants, Kimberley was dominated by its diamond mines, by the De Beers Company that owned them, and by its chairman, Cecil Rhodes.

Conscious of their exposed position, the citizens of Kimberley had appealed to the Cape Government for protection. The Cape Ministry, which at that time was anxious to appease the Boer republics, was unsympathetic to the point of obstruction and blocked any move to provide an adequate force for the defence of the Diamond Fields, insisting that the threat was illusory and that in the unlikely event of hostilities the local Volunteers and Cape Police would suffice. Fortunately, in early September the British High Commissioner, Alfred Milner, decided to take the matter in hand himself and sent Kekewich to report on the defence of Kimberley.

On arrival in the Diamond City, Kekewich found a perilously unsatisfactory situation. The Volunteers of the Kimberley Regiment, Diamond Fields Horse and Diamond Fields Artillery were under-strength, had few horses and obsolete artillery, the Cape Police were widely dispersed, and no defence works had been constructed. He soon concluded that a nucleus of imperial troops, British Regulars, would be essential and advised the military authorities at the Cape accordingly. As a result of prevarication in Cape Town and Whitehall, the British garrison in South Africa was dangerously weak, and in the middle of September the only Regular troops in Cape Colony were three and a half battalions of Infantry, two companies of Royal Garrison Artillery and two companies of Royal Engineers. Nevertheless, on 18 September a telegram from Cape Town informed Kekewich that headquarters and four companies of his own Battalion, six guns and a company of Engineers would leave for the Diamond Fields that same night.

The Loyal North Lancashires

The 1st Battalion The Loyal North Lancashire Regiment, the former 47th (Lancashire) Regiment of Foot, had been based at Cape Town, with detachments at Wynberg and Simonstown, since arriving in the

Lieutenant-Colonel Robert George Kekewich.

Commanding Officer, 1st Battalion Loyal North Lancashire Regiment. He assumed command of the 47th in June 1898.

Officers, 1st Loyal North Lancashires, in front of their Mess, Main Barracks, Cape Town, 1899.
Back row, left to right: Capt Jourdain, Lt Bingham, NK, NK, Lt Webster, Capt Wylde-Browne.
Middle row: Capt (QM) Gill, Capt & Adjt Lowndes, Maj Jackson, Lt-Col Kekewich, Maj Murray, Maj. Fielden.
Front row: Lt Clifford, Capt Woodward.

Colony on 9 March 1899. Some re-roling was required to suit local conditions, and on arrival of the Regiment at the Cape immediate steps had been taken to form a Mounted Infantry Company, strength three officers, five sergeants and one hundred and twelve rank and file, from men of all companies with experience of horses.

The Battalion was towards the end of a long foreign tour, having left England in July 1882 for garrison duty in, successively, Gibraltar, India, Ceylon and South Africa. Despite this long period of overseas service the 47th had seen no war service since the Crimea, though its Commanding Officer had considerable experience of colonial campaigns.[1]

Lieutenant Colonel R. G. Kekewich, who assumed command of the 47th on 1 June 1898, aged 44, had enjoyed a modestly successful career as a diligent and capable professional soldier. He was undoubtedly conventional, perhaps a little pedantic, and did not cope easily with exceptional stress, but these traits were outweighed by his many positive characteristics. Lord Baden-Powell later summed up his qualities as 'a clever brain, a human heart, and a cheery spirit; a lovable disposition, unswerving loyalty, and absolute devotion to duty.' Colonel Sir David Harris knew him well during the siege of Kimberley:

1. Robert George Kekewitch was born at Peamore, Devon, on 17 June 1854. Commissioned into the Buffs in 1874, he fought in the Perak expedition of 1875–76, the Sudan campaign of 1888 and operations in Burma, 1892–93.

Sergeants Mess, 1st Loyal North Lancashires. Main Barracks, Cape Town, 1899.

Back row, left to right: CSgt Wilkinson, Sgts Brennan and Hodgson, Cpl Rathbone, Sgts Richardson, Mitchell and (?) Ennis. *Third row*: Sgts Mossop, Bowman and Dorey, Band-Sgt Bray, Sgts Moffat, Jeffreys and Atkinson, CSgt Porter, Provost Sgt Davies, Sgts Holohan and Burton, CSgt Still, Sgts Cotes, Passmore, Wilson, Messent, Hellard and Nelson. *Seated*: Sgt O'Donnell, CSgt Heald, Bandmaster Frayling, RSM Mudge, Maj Jackson, Lt-Col Kekewich, Lt Lowndes, RQMS Hill, Sgt Dmr (Drum Maj) Langton, CSgt Miller, Sgt O'Brien. *Front row*: Sig Sgt Herbert, Sgts Dyar, Watts, Morgan, Morley and Beer, CSgt Carey. Note Mounted Infantry NCOs wearing riding breeches and bandoliers.

'He was fair-minded, painstaking, humorous and devoted to duty, leaving nothing to chance. Despite the fact that he occasionally suffered from neuralgia, he was never away from duty. Often when talking on defence matters he would rest his elbows on the table, put both hands to his head and not utter a word for 10 or 15 minutes. One could see from his flushed and perspiring face that he was suffering untold agony, but he never once complained, and would continue the conversation as if in the best of health. His friends and enemies alike admired him very much. Even in the darkest days he always had a smile and a joke for all.'[2]

The Right Wing of the Battalion (better known later as 'the siege half'), consisting of 'A', 'B', 'G' and 'H' Companies, the Headquarters, Regimental Band, and one Maxim machine gun, with a strength of ten officers[3] and 413 NCOs and men, left Cape Town for Kimberley

2. Colonel Sir David Harris KCMG VD, *Pioneer, Soldier and Politician*, p. 172.
3. Major W. H. E. Murray, Captain T. H. O'Brien, Lieutenants C. H. M. Bingham, C. de Putron, H. J. Gill (Quartermaster), J. G. Lowndes (Adjutant), G. R. Wallace, A. McC. Webster, and Second Lieutenants W. J. C. Fletcher and A. W. Hewett.

On Route to Kimberley.
Soldiers of 1st Loyal North Lancashires stretch their legs at De Aar Station during their 44-hour journey north to the Gold Fields.

at 10 p.m. on the 18th. They travelled in two troop trains, preceded by a pilot engine. 'The necessity for a pilot soon became apparent, for on several occasions (at Beaufort West in particular) we were the objects of hostile demonstrations on the part of the inhabitants. As they confined themselves to hooting and groaning, we treated them with contempt, except that precautions were taken against any act of treachery. We were a mere 'handful' of troops passing through what was, practically, a hostile country, far away from any reinforcements, and at every halt expecting to hear of some act of aggression on the part of the Boer forces, which were massed close to the border. When we arrived at Orange River and skirted the Free State border, the necessity for alertness became even greater than ever; but it is sufficient to say that we arrived at Beaconsfield about 6.0 p.m. on 20 September without mishap.'[4] On that same day Kekewich was placed in command of all British and Colonial forces in Griqualand West and Bechuanaland.

Preparations for a Siege

These developments enabled Kekewitch, who now appeared in uniform for the first time, to press on with more overt preparations for defence. A Town Guard was raised from the citizens of Kimberley and Beaconsfield[5] and, together with the Volunteers, started training

Lieutenant F. W. Woodward left the following day with the mules and transport, while on the 27th Lieutenant W. R. Clifford arrived in Kimberley with a section (22 men) of the Mounted Infantry Company.

4. Letter written by 'One of the Siege Half' shortly after the relief of Kimberley, published in *The Lancashire Lad*, June 1908, p. 13.
5. Authority to raise this force was not received until 29 September, but considerable preparatory work had been done by then and within a week over 1,100 men had been enrolled and officers appointed. The Town Guard eventually totalled some 2,650 all ranks.

Arrival of 1st Loyal North Lancashires at Kimberley, 21 September 1899.

'There was a jolly lot of cheering as we marched through.'

under instructors from the North Lancashires.[6] De Beers provided horses for the artillery and mounted troops, searchlights, telephone communications, and even a welcome cache of rifles, machine guns and ammunition, in store since the ill-fated Jameson Raid of 1896. The Company also made available their workshops and the invaluable services of George Labram, their former chief mechanical engineer. Labram, an American, had elected to remain in Kimberley and assist in its defence, and was to prove one of the true heroes of the siege.

Meanwhile, thousands of African labourers toiled under Royal Engineer supervision to build defence works. The surrounding landscape was generally open sandy veldt, but marked by numerous large mine-spoil heaps, known as tailings, many of which were turned into redoubts. To the east the plain ran four miles to where the Premier Mine stood guard at the wire marking the border of the Orange Free

6. The requirement was for at least sixty instructors, and Kekewich was doubtful that his half-battalion could produce so many, but Colonel Harris, commanding the Town Guard, offered to pay instructors at a rate of two shillings and sixpence for each one and a half hour drill. 'When this information passed through the ranks,' recalled Harris, 'there was no dearth of instructors. Men tumbled over each other to get the jobs, and really good instructors they were.'

State. To the north, some six miles from town the railway passed Dronsfield Ridge and Station before continuing its 220-mile progress to Mafeking. To the south-east, and some three miles from Kimberley centre, rose Carter's Ridge and Ironstone (or Johnstone's) Kopje, while six miles to the south the railway ran over Wimbledon Ridge on its way to the Modder River, 24 miles away.

The main defended area encircled Kimberley and Beaconsfield within a perimeter of some fourteen miles, consisting of sandbagged redoubts, barbed wire and thorn hedge obstacles, remotely-controlled mines and road blocks, with isolated advanced posts at the Premier Mine and Otto's Kopje Mine. Some of the redoubts mounted searchlights, whose beams at night illuminated the approaches.

The Conning Tower.

Kekewich's 155-foot command and observation post, built on the De Beers Mine headgear.

The various posts were linked by telephone to Kekewich's command and observation post, the 155-foot 'Conning Tower', erected by Labram on scaffolding above the headgear of the De Beers Mine. From this precarious vantage point Kekewich was able, with a powerful telescope, to watch the movements of the Boers and to direct his own men by telephone and heliograph. He often slept in a hut at its foot, connected to the duty officer at the top by a speaking tube, and one hour before dawn most mornings he could be found in his lofty crow's nest, scanning the horizon until satisfied that all was well. His presence in the tower, a favoured aiming mark for Boer gunners, was signified by a small blue flag, and later in the siege a red flag was hoisted on the headgear whenever the Boers shelled the town.

Each redoubt had its own garrison, while in reserve Kekewich held two companies of the 47th,[7] commanded by Major William Murray with local rank of Lieutenant Colonel. These reserves were encamped in the Public Gardens near the town centre. For offensive action Kekewich put together a scratch mounted force, supported by the Diamond Fields Artillery with six 7-pounder guns, and an armoured train, prepared in the De Beers workshops and commanded by

7. 1st Battalion The Loyal North Lancashire Regiment at this time was sometimes known by its shortened title, 'North Lancashires', and often by its pre-1881 titles, '47th' and 'Lancashires', but never 'Loyals'.

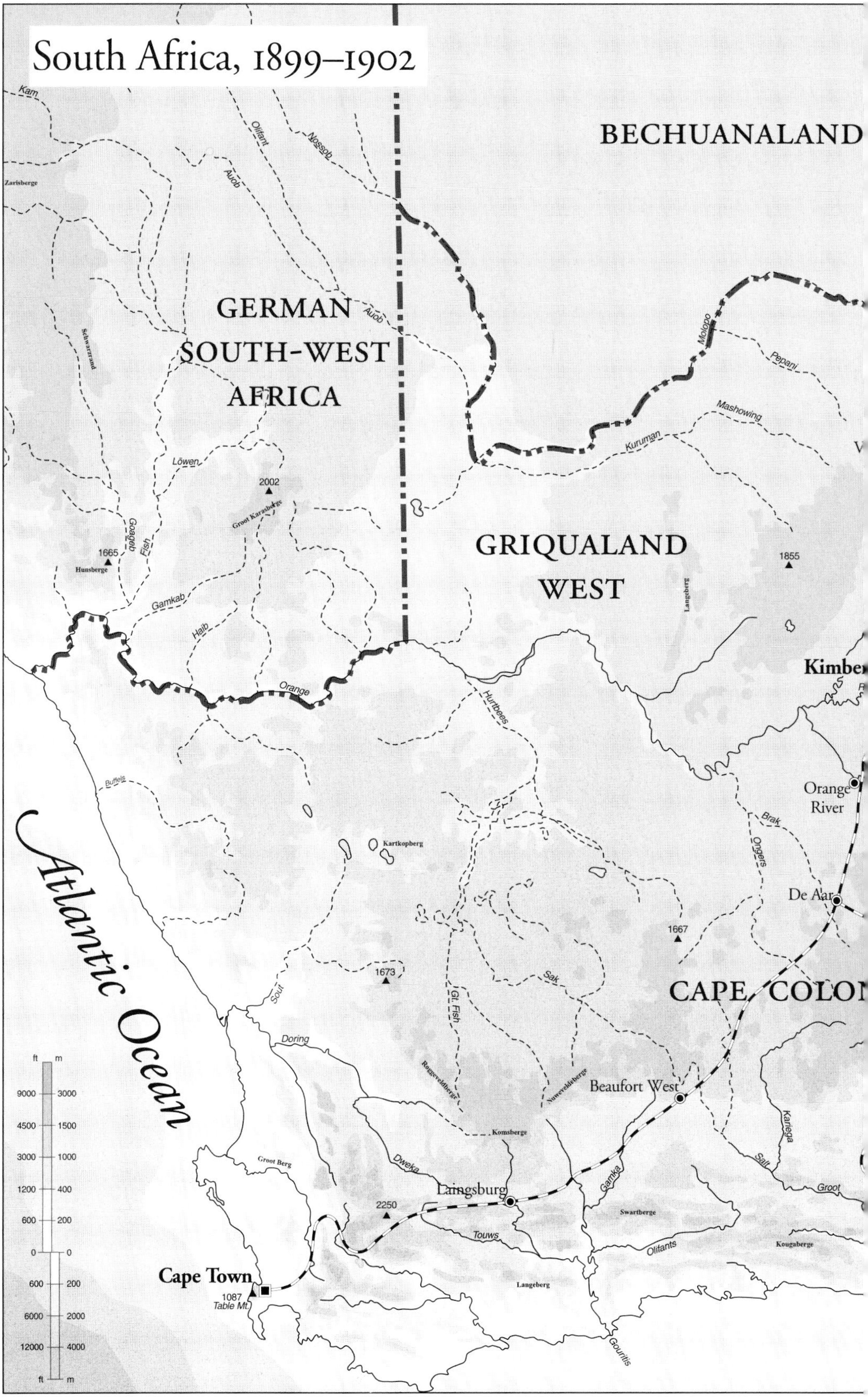

South Africa, 1899–1902

TRANSVAAL
ORANGE FREE STATE
BASUTOLAND
NATAL COLONY
SWAZILAND
ZULULAND
PONDOLAND
TRANSKEI
PORTUGUESE EAST AFRICA
Indian Ocean
Pietersburg
Lydenburg
2285
Mt. Anderson
Komatipoort
Zeerust
Rustenburg
Pretoria
Belfast
Mafeking
Krugersdorp
Carolina
Lichtenburg
Johannesburg
Lourenço Marques
Tweebosch
Bethel
Ermelo
Vereeniging
Klerksdorp
Standerton
Volksrust
Vrede
Vryheid
Kroonstad
Dundee
Harrismith
Itala
Fort Prospect
Ladysmith
Colenso
Estcourt
3299
3482
Pietermaritzburg
Durban
Thaba Nchu
Bethanie
3096
Thaba Putosa
3002
Ben Macohui
Bethulie
Aliwal North
Stormberg Junction
2371
Gt. Winterberg
East London
Port Elizabeth
Lake Sibaya
Lake St Lucia
Kosi-meer
Richard's Bay
Limpopo
Elefantes
Lataba
Olifants
Sand
Hout
Magalakiene
Pangola
Notwani
Marico
Apies
Hey
Elands
Incamati
Komati
Usutuo
Pongola
Mkuze
Mfolzi
Tugela
Mooi
Buffalo
Vaal
Vals
Wilge
Harts
Modder
Riet
Oranje
Tina
Mkomanzi
Mzimkulu
Mtamvula
Mzimvubu
Tsomo
Tarka
Bashee
Gt. Kei
Gt. Fish
Boesmans
Stormberg
Drakensberg
N
State Boundaries
Railways
Rivers
Seasonal Rivers
Kilometres
0 10 30 50 100 150 200
Miles
0 10 20 30 40 50 100 150 200

The Kimberley Garrison Reserves.

'A' and 'H' Companies 1st Loyal North Lancashires, plus Regimental Band, on parade in the Public Gardens near their tented camp. Lieutenant-Colonel William Murray, in command, is the mounted officer on the right.

The Kimberley Armoured Train.

commanded by Lieutenant Webster of 1st Loyal North Lancashires. The armoured trucks at each end mounted Maxim machine guns.

Lieutenant Alexander Webster of the North Lancashires, who has left an interesting account of his unusual command:

'Kekewich told me I was to have charge of an Armoured Train and directed me to learn to drive the engine in case anything happened to the regular driver. Warned me not let anyone know about it as the steps then being taken were secret and only precautionary as war had not yet been declared. I accordingly took lessons in driving on the engine of a goods train and was always in mufti.

'The Armoured Train consisted of an engine and tender completely armoured, except for the funnel, to within nine inches of the ground, together with two armoured trucks, one coupled in front and the other behind the engine and tender. These trucks had loopholes 18″ long and 3″ high, with a steel covering flap outside which was opened and closed at will by the simple expedient of a piece of wire passing

Kekewich Reviews the Garrison.

1st Loyal North Lancashires marching past Kimberley Town Hall on 7 October 1899.

through a small hole in the armour above the loophole. At the outer end of each truck a Maxim gun on a swivel mounting on a horizontal slide was fixed to fire through a porthole, which was similarly covered when not in use. There were wooden benches around both sides of the trucks, and elevated portholes with a seat above and on either side of each Maxim gun for observation purposes.

'I had several trips learning to drive, and I also practised whistle signals for communication from the trucks to the engine driver, who in his cabin had no means of observation. After about twenty such trips ... we managed to perfect these. Of course I always had to travel in the leading truck, according to which direction we were travelling in.'[8]

By 4 October good progress had been made with both defence works and training, and, having received warning of a possible surprise attack on Kimberley without a formal declaration of war, Kekewich decided to test his alarm scheme that night. At 1 a.m. the mine hooters sounded the alarm and the garrison turned out, moving smartly to their defence posts, where they remained on the alert until dismissed at 7 a.m. Kekewich had reason for quiet satisfaction.[9]

The detached Premier Mine Redoubt, overlooking the Free State frontier, had been manned since 2 October by 'B' Company of the North Lancashires, commanded by Captain Tim O'Brien, with two

8. 'Reminiscences of the Kimberley Armoured Train', by Major A. McCallum Webster.

9. By the outbreak of war the Loyal North Lancashires were distributed as follows:
Premier Mine Redoubt: Captain O'Brien with 'B' Company (75 NCOs and men)
Sanitorium Redoubt: Lieutenant Wallace with 'G' Company (78 NCOs and men)
Reserve (Public Gardens): Lieutenant-Colonel Murray with 'A' and 'H' Companies.

guns and a searchlight. On the night of the 6th/7th a single shot was fired from across the border at the sweeping beam of the searchlight, passing harmlessly over the redoubt. This was the first overtly hostile act of the Boer War.

Nevertheless, Kekewich was beginning to feel more comfortable with his defence plans and the state of training of his heterogeneous little army. On the 7th, to further boost morale, he held a review: 'The troops in garrison including the Town Guard paraded this afternoon at the Town Hall, and passed me in column of route. It is wonderful how quickly the Town Guard has become efficient. The divisions are drilled daily by instructors supplied by the 1/Loyal North Lan[cashire] Regt; sections of the Town Guard occupy defence posts at night, and all this is done cheerfully, and I have heard no grumbling of any kind.' [10] Relations with the Town Hall were excellent, the Cape Police were now under command, and Kekewich was receiving full co-operation from De Beers.

Away from the fevered transformation of the Diamond City into a fortress, the political crisis between Britain and the Boer republics was rapidly moving towards war. The Transvaal had mobilized on 28 September and the Orange Free State on 2nd October, and already some thirty-five thousand burghers were poised to invade Natal and Cape Province. On the afternoon of 10 October Kekewich received a telegram from Cape Town informing him that President Kruger had issued an ultimatum to the British Government, demanding compliance with deliberately unacceptable terms by 5 p.m. on the 11th. War was now inevitable.

Cecil Rhodes

Kekewich concluded his diary for the 10th by noting that 'The Rt. Honble. C. J. Rhodes arrived this evening.' The figure of Cecil Rhodes casts a strong and pervasive shadow over the story of the siege of Kimberley. An energetic, vain, ruthlessly piratical and self-advertising egotist, Rhodes was the archetypal pioneering entrepreneur. He habitually confused his own very extensive business interests with those of the British Empire and was petulantly impatient with anyone, politician or soldier, who did not share his megalomanic vision. He had, moreover, an ingrained antipathy to officers of the British Army.[11] Rhodes was ostensibly on his way north to Bulawayo with a party of his cronies, but he had an ulterior motive for allowing himself to be

10. Manuscript diary of Lieutenant Colonel R. G. Kekewich (Regimental Archives).
11. Two of his brothers, with whom he was not on good terms, were Regular Army officers.

The Right Hon. Cecil John Rhodes (1853–1902). Founder of De Beers diamond company, Consolidated Gold Fields and the British South Africa Company, and Prime Minister of Cape Colony 1890–96, he was determined to be 'a factor in the military situation'.

besieged in Kimberley; he was protecting his investment. His priorities, whilst sometimes fortuitously overlapping with the public interest, diverged from the Army's strategic policy to such an extent that there was an almost tragic inevitability about his eventual and grievous friction with the military commander of Kimberley. Robert Kekewich was too honourable and discrete a gentleman to confide his opinion of Rhodes even to his private diary, but Captain O'Meara, who acted as his Chief Staff Officer for most of the siege, had fewer inhibitions. He explained Rhodes' subsequent actions as follows:

'The real cause of the difficulties which arose in Kimberley was due to the fact that Rhodes had, immediately prior to his arrival in Kimberley in October 1899, been in close touch with the military authorities at Cape Town. He had thus obtained information as to the British plan of campaign, which, as regards the Western Theatre, contemplated a direct advance from the Orange River, in the neighbourhood of Norval's Pont and Bethulie, on Bloemfontein. Rhodes entirely disapproved of this plan, which, in his opinion, did not give sufficient prominence to the 'strategical importance' of Kimberley, and, in his interviews with Kekewich, he made no secret of his intention to be a 'factor in the military situation', and to secure a radical change in the foregoing plan, so far as the Western Theatre was concerned. As a soldier, Kekewich could not, and would not, aid and abet Rhodes to force the hands of the superior military authorities. This was Kekewich's great offence in Rhodes' eyes.' [12]

The Kraaipan Incident

Such difficulties were for the future. One of Kekewich's more immediate concerns on 10 October was the over-due despatch by rail to Mafeking of two guns urgently required for the defence of that isolated town by Colonel Baden-Powell. The guns eventually arrived at Kimberley at noon on the 12th and Lieutenant Webster was at once tasked to take them up the line to Vryburg and there transfer them to the Mafeking Armoured Train for onward movement to their destination.

'We arrived at Vryburg about 5 p.m. but found no party from Mafeking. There being nothing to do but wait, I went to the Hotel and whilst having dinner there received a message stating that the railway line from Mafeking had been destroyed at [Kraaipan], a few miles north of Vryburg. At 4 a.m. I received a second message that the [Mafeking] Armoured Train had been derailed at this point and that its crew [were] captured by the Boers. We left Vryburg at 6 a.m., escorting a passenger train which was stranded there, and proceeding cautiously at about five miles per hour in case the Boers had interfered with the line or tampered with any of the many culverts between there and Fourteen Streams. About noon, just about a mile from the bridge at Fourteen Streams, we were fired at several times from a kopje about half a mile east of the railway, but only a few hit us and no damage was done. We crossed Fourteen Streams' bridge soon after noon, and as soon as we were over I released a carrier pigeon saying we were safely across.' [13] Kekewich was immensely relieved, for he too had heard about the disaster at Kraaipan, the first major incident

12. Lieutenant Colonel W. A. J. O'Meara, *Kekewich in Kimberley*, 1926, pp. 10–11.
13. Webster, op. cit. His recollections are not entirely accurate; before it was ambushed the Mafeking train had collected the guns, which were captured.

of the war, and had moreover received a report that six hundred Boers, with guns, had moved up to the railway north of Fourteen Streams.

Two days later, at 6 p.m. on the evening of 14 October, the station master at Modder River telephoned Kimberley to report that Boer officers had arrived there and were demanding supplies of food from his goods depot. Shortly after 10 p.m. Kekewich was waiting in the telegraph office to speak to the G.O.C. Capetown. 'At that moment, the telegraph instruments in the office, which had been clicking away merrily like a lot of noisy crickets, one by one, in rapid succession, ceased their chattering and within a few seconds a dead silence reigned in the room.'[14] Later that night the telegraph lines to the north were also cut. Kimberley was now isolated and would remain so for the next four months.

Opening Rounds at Kimberley

Kekewich was well aware that there were no more than seven thousand British troops in Cape Colony at that time, and that there was no serious prospect of the relief of Kimberley being attempted before December. His concept of operations to carry out this protracted defence was summarised by O'Meara: 'He felt that he would succeed best ... if he could prevent the Boers from closing on to the town defences; this end he hoped to attain by handling his mobile troops with boldness, as the enemy might thus be led to believe that the garrison of Kimberley was really larger than actually was the case. Therefore, from the earliest days of the siege, the mounted troops were constantly sent out, first in one direction and then in another, to harass the Boers and keep them on the move.'[15]

The first of these forays was mounted at first light on the 15th, when the armoured train, supported by some fifty mounted infantry, was sent south towards the Modder River to try and repair the telegraph line. The train reached a point a few miles south of Spytfontein Siding before coming under fire. Webster recalled:

'We reported by carrier pigeon that we had located a Boer commando. A good many shells were fired at the train but no serious damage was done and we got our forward Maxim gun going for the first time, making a party of mounted Boers on the railway about 600 yards away "skidaddle" beautifully. A Lance-Corporal and myself were both looking through the same porthole on the left side of the leading Maxim gun when a 12-pounder shell burst about 50 yards away and a small splinter, about 1″ long and ½″ each way passed

14. O'Meara, op. cit., p. 35.
15. O'Meara, op. cit., pp. 41–2.

Kekewich and his Staff.

The Commander of the Kimberley Garrison (*seated left*) with his staff, *left to right*, Lieutenant MacInnes, Captain O'Meara and Major (local Lieutenant-Colonel) Scott-Turner.

between our heads and buried itself in the woodwork at the other end of the carriage. It just scratched me and made a two-inch scratch in the Lance-Corporal's cheek, which he had to have stitched. After about ten minutes we retired, as Kekewich had instructed us not to run any risk of damage to the train, and picked up the station master of Spytfontein Siding, some gangers and their belongings, and brought them in with us.'

Kekewich now made some final preparations for a state of siege, proclaiming Martial Law, detaining suspected spies (for Kimberley was not without Boer sympathisers), and calling in all outlying detachments of the Cape Police. These were a useful addition to his strength, as was the Kimberley Light Horse, a new volunteer regiment authorised on 13 October, which was rapidly raised and horsed with considerable assistance from Rhodes and his Company.

Second-Lieutenant W. J. C. Fletcher, 1st Loyal North Lancashires.

Died at Kimberley 18 October 1899, the first British officer to die in the Boer War.

On 18 October Second-Lieutenant Fletcher of the Loyal North Lancashires went down with heat sickness, and within hours had the sad distinction of being the first British officer to die in the Boer War.

Food and water supplies were a major concern throughout the siege. In the first week of the siege Kekewich fixed the price of foodstuffs, to prevent speculation, and later introduced rationing. Forage and grazing for horses and cattle remained a problem. The cattle pastures had to be guarded by about 150 mounted men daily to prevent them being 'rustled' by the enemy, and their slaughter was regulated. The town's normal water supply was soon cut off by the Boers, but George Labram connected wells at the Premier Mine to the Kimberley reservoir.

On 19 October Kekewich appointed Major Henry Scott-Turner of the Black Watch to command the mounted troops with the local rank of Lieutenant Colonel. Scott-Turner, whose friendship with Cecil Rhodes went back some years, was a most gallant officer, but dangerously inclined to rashness in action. Young Wigram Clifford of the 47th was to be his Adjutant, and later commanded a squadron of the Kimberley Light Horse. Two days later the mounted force mustered 639 all ranks.[16] The total strength of the garrison at that time was rather less than four thousand, most of whom had received only a few days of military training. Kekewich knew his garrison's military limitations, and in particular was very conscious of his critical shortage of experienced officers. Even his strike force of mounted troops needed time to train and exercise together. In the short term he placed great reliance on Lieutenant Clifford's section of North Lancashire Mounted Infantry and on the armoured train. Some idea of patrol activity at this early stage of the war may be gleaned from the diary entry for 17 October of 'One of the Siege Half':

'Armoured train went about 11 miles towards Modder River at daylight, but did not encounter enemy. Mounted Infantry brought in information that Modder River Bridge was blown up by the Boers at 10 a.m. yesterday ... The armoured train went out about 4–30 p.m. to Dronfield, and brought back a quantity of dynamite. The Adjutant was in charge with 20 selected men, besides the regular escort ... and Lieut. Webster was, as usual, in charge of the Maxim. Got permission to accompany the party, and went myself. Although the Boers were on their way from Riverton, we forestalled them and returned to Kimberley without an encounter after daylight had faded. Got to railway station just after 7 p.m.'

16. Section Loyal North Lancashire Mounted Infantry	22
Diamond Fields Horse	168
Cape Police (mounted)	237
Kimberley Light Horse	212

Over the period 20–23 October the armoured train became even more brazen, deliberately steaming up and down the line to draw enemy fire and locate their gun positions. 'We frequently got them to waste a dozen or more shells from each of their positions,' recalled Lieutenant Webster, 'but none of them ever came too near. We soon got to know the regular places where they would fire at us and if they did not do so we used to stop the Armoured Train and blow off steam or turn some of the men out to fuss about. This was generally successful, especially when they had changed their positions, and then our job was over.'

Kekewich was still concerned about the state of training of his mounted troops, but on the 23rd October Scott-Turner was sent south in the direction of Spytfontein with 135 Cape Police and 40 of the Diamond Fields Horse. Evidently satisfied, Kekewich planned a strong reconnaissance to the north the following day. The object was to ascertain the strength of a Boer commando reported to be at Riverton Road Station, about 16 miles up the railway line from Kimberley, and to deny to the Boers the use of the nearby water pumping plant. The sortie was to be led by Scott-Turner with three hundred horsemen, supported by the armoured train, while another train was to be held in readiness at Kimberley Station to take out infantry reinforcements should they be required.

The Fight at Dronfield

Scott-Turner and his men rode out at 4 o'clock in the morning to Dronfield Siding, and were joined there at 6.45 by the armoured train. He then pushed on through Macfarlane's Farm, where he left part of his force, towards Riverton. Shortly afterwards, about 9 a.m., he made contact with the enemy. After a protracted parley under flag of truce between the Cape Police and the Boers, during which the number of enemy steadily increased, a long-range skirmish started, and Scott Turner decided to retire slowly on Dronfield, drawing the enemy after him. At 10.50 a.m. he flashed a heliograph message from Dronfield to the Conning Tower, requesting Kekewich to reinforce him with two guns and two Maxims.

Two guns of the Diamond Fields Artillery and two horse-drawn Maxims, escorted by seventy mounted Cape Police, were at once sent north by road. 'A' and 'H' Companies of the North Lancashires, under Lieutenant Colonel Murray, were also entrained and steamed up to Macfarlane's, escorted by the Armoured Train. On arriving there, about 600 mounted Boers were seen to be using a covered approach to reach the Dronfield Ridge from a gully to the east of Macfarlane's. The enemy had placed themselves between Scott-

Scene of the Action at Dronfield, 24 October 1899.

Looking west towards the railway line.

Turner's force and Kimberley with the apparent object of cutting off the armoured and troop trains. Scott-Turner advised Murray to fall back along the line to Dronfield and look out for the guns while he retired with his mounted force across the open veldt. The trains withdrew, fired on from bushes near the railway.

As the North Lancashires neared Dronfield, at 1.10 p.m., heavy firing broke out to their rear, and it was seen that the Diamond Fields Artillery were in action near the railway line, about five miles north of Kimberley Station. The guns had been ambushed on the move by the Boers and were hotly engaged with enemy riflemen concealed in the bushes of Dronfield Ridge, some 1,000 to 1,500 yards to the east. Murray halted his train on an embankment south of Dronfield Siding and quickly detrained his companies, who found cover in the track-side ditch. Meanwhile, the mounted troops, moving south towards Dronfield Ridge, had also been ambushed, enfiladed from their left by two hundred Boers behind the stone wall of a dry dam. Having taken casualties, Scott-Turner disengaged and withdrew towards the railway.

The firefight continued with vigour for more than an hour, then Murray launched an assault on the ridge. Lieutenant Charles Bingham's 'A' Company led, accompanied by Murray and his Adjutant, Lieutenant John Lowndes, with Lieutenant Francis Woodward's 'H' Company in support. As the Loyal North Lancashires topped the rise they were met with a heavy fire at a range of 150 yards from enemy concealed in the long grass. Bingham, running forward to see what

Major (local Lieutenant-Colonel) William Murray of 1st Loyal North Lancashire Regiment.

Commanded the wing of the Battalion defending Kimberley and led the charge at Dronfield.

his scouts were doing, was shot through the thigh, and the Adjutant was also hit. Then 'H' Company moved forward in support, and the Lancashire lads, pouring volleys into the bushes, advanced by section rushes until the enemy were driven off the whole ridge. The Boers fled to their horses in the valley, leaving their leader, Field Cornet Botha of the Boshof Commando, dead on the field. Under cover of the Infantry advance, the mounted troops were extricated and the fighting was all over by 3.30 p.m.

The garrison had lost three men killed and nineteen wounded, among the latter being Lieutenants Bingham and Lowndes, and Privates Lee and Milner of the Loyal North Lancashires. 'Reports which came in later,' according to O'Meara, 'show that the Boers were considerably shaken by this encounter and hastened back to Boshof, where they arrived in a demoralized condition.' The Dronfield fight had been watched from vantage points within Kimberley, and when the troops returned to the town they were met with enthusiastic cheers – and a 'pithy little speech' by Rhodes. This little victory both raised the morale of the garrison and civilian population of Kimberley and delayed for some time the close investment of the town.

The Dronfield fight was also noteworthy for several tactical innovations. *The Diamond Fields Advertiser* pointed out that 'It was almost the first time since the battle of Bull Run, in the American Civil War, that reinforcements had been conveyed by rail to the actual scene of fighting, while probably for the first time the wounded had been carried from the field of battle in comfortable saloon carriages. The ordinary heliographic communication was supplemented on this occasion by the telephone, and Colonel Kekewich, standing on the Conning Tower six or seven miles distant, was able to talk over the wires with the officer in charge of the armoured train, and to receive from him constant impressions of the fighting which was proceeding at the moment under his very eyes.'

The Band Plays On

But for the shortage of food, life in Kimberley was at this stage relatively tolerable, and there was indeed a bizarre normality. It was noticed that the Boers, for religious reasons, would never initiate

'Weather and enemy permitting'. The Boers did not fight on Sundays, so the Regimental Bands of the North Lancashire and Kimberley Regiments played for the public and garrison.

hostilities on a Sunday, and advantage was taken of this to hold Sunday afternoon concerts in the park, when the bands of the Loyal North Lancashire and Kimberley Regiments combined to play lively music to a large audience. They played at various venues on other occasions – 'weather and enemy permitting,' according to the invitation cards. Sport was also popular, and there were regular football and cricket fixtures.

On 28 October Private Robert Gregson of 'B' Company wrote a letter home from the Premier Mine redoubt, Wesselton, an account of events in Kimberley which reflects a fairly confident perception of affairs at this early stage in the siege:

> Dear Mother,
>
> I am writing this letter from one of the richest diamond mines in the world. Although I have been in Kimberley and district for the last 6 weeks I have never seen a diamond yet ... By the time you receive this, the siege of Kimberley will be a thing of the past. I don't know how long it will be before we are relieved, but we can hold out for six months. There is no chance of us having to do that as there is a very strong army corps coming in this direction.
>
> There is only four companies of our Regiment in Kimberley at present, counting our company as well, and we are about seven miles out of Kimberley at a diamond mine right on the border of the Orange Free State. We have been in this mine 3 weeks, and we

have erected a big redoubt here as it is looked upon as the key of the Diamond Fields. It is a jolly strong place. I think the men we have here could hold it against 50 times their number, and even if we had to leave it we would blow it up and get in Kimberley all right before anybody knew ... as there are railway lines and small locomotives that are used about the mine that would soon take us out of the road.

We didn't know we were going to leave Cape Town until the Monday morning we got the order to leave at the night, and we didn't know where we were going to until we landed here. We were under the impression we were going to Mafeking until we got out at Beaconsfield, five miles out of Kimberley. We had been two nights on the train then, and we had to sleep in the train again that night, and we marched to Kimberley the day after. There was a jolly lot of cheering as we marched through. The war had not started then, but the Boers had threatened to blow Kimberley up and there was only the Volunteers to stop them until we arrived on the scene, and if it had not been for us they would have done so.

I think the first shots that started the war were fired from men of our company. No. 4 Section of our company were in charge of an armoured train and they went out about a fortnight ago to see where the line had been damaged and to bring a station master and his wife in as they were in a dangerous position, and when they got a few miles out of Kimberley they found that the rails had been taken up on both sides and thrown out of the way. They got out of the train, mended the line and went on to the place they were going to, got the station master and his family on board and started back. As they were going back they were fired on by the Boers' artillery. They fired thirteen shells at the train but only dinged it [a] bit. Our chaps gave them a receipt for it by killing 5 of their men and wounding about a dozen.

Last Wednesday we had a pretty good do. The train went out in the morning, and it, along with the Volunteer horse, were attacked. The Regiment had to turn out, and the remainder of the garrison. The Boers had a jolly good position [and] it was nearly a case with the Volunteers, and the train, only the Regiment got there on time and it finished up with the Boers having to clear off.

If we had the whole of our Regiment here, instead of half, we would fairly wipe them Boers out. We can't afford to leave this place to attack them. We are only waiting for more troops to go up country a lot further. You will have seen the way the Boers have been wiped out at Mafeking. We will do the same here if they only move in a bit closer. They keep out about 8 miles and it takes a good deal of watching to prevent being surprised, but we have 4 searchlights at work, at night we sleep in the trenches, ready with our magazines charged, and ready at a second's notice. We have had a couple of wet nights this week, and it wasn't comfortable at all, but it all comes in, and we had to put up with it.

The country must be in an unsettled state just now, with all the Militia and Reserves out, but I don't think that the Boers will hold out so very long after the defeats they have had in Natal and at Mafeking. There has been no letters or papers up here for about a fortnight, but I think the line will be opened up this week as there were a lot of troops coming up this way and General Buller was supposed to land yesterday.

The Adjutant and a Lieutenant was shot this week and wounded severely, and a couple of men, but up to now there are none of our Regiment killed. I am all right and hope to remain so. John Pilkington was all right up to today, so you can let his mother know. Hoping to hear from you all soon.

This 'phoney war' phase of the siege, during which the garrison continued to mount sorties in all directions, lasted until 4 November, when Captain Tim O'Brien at the Premier Mine reported some six hundred Boers advancing under a flag of truce. Then a small party came forward to deliver an ultimatum, calling upon Kekewich to deliver up the town by 6 p.m. on 6 November. 'I answered,' wrote Kekewich, 'in the usual manner.' On the afternoon of the 6th the Boers were seen to drag a gun into position near Carter's Farm, and at 7 p.m. they signalled the expiry of their ultimatum by firing two shells at the Premier Mine. The bombardment of Kimberley had begun. The shelling was in fact intermittent and largely ineffective, causing few casualties and remarkably little damage. The British 7-pounder guns were no match for the Boer 9 and 15-pounders, and were short of ammunition, but Kekewich countered the enemy artillery by pushing forward small parties of riflemen to harass their gunners.

The Orange River

Meanwhile, over seventy miles to the south of Kimberley, the Left Wing of the Loyal North Lancashires,[17] under Major Spenser Jackson, had been at Orange River, defending the station and bridge, since 21 September. There too was the Mounted Infantry Company, less

17. The wing consisted of 'C', 'D', 'E' and 'F' Companies, with Majors S. Jackson and H. F. Coleridge, Captains C. E. A. Jourdain (acting Adjutant), Lieutenants F. J. Bowen and R. B. Flint, and Second Lieutenant Wells. Captain G. H. Wylde-Browne commanded the Mounted Infantry, with Lieutenant C. C. Wood as his subaltern.

Lieutenant Clifford's section at Kimberley. The main task of this half-battalion for the next seven weeks was to construct and man the defences of the vital rail crossing, a red-painted iron bridge which spanned the muddy waters of the Orange River. Despite rumours and alarms, there was no contact with the enemy during this period. The work was hard, with little rest, but morale was high. They also had their first experience of refugees, for whom they expressed a lively sympathy:

'It is heartrending to see the Kaffirs and Dutch coming here every day for us to protect them – old men and women and children who have been turned out of their homes and farms by the Boers. Their sons have been taken away from them to fight against us, and the Boers have taken all their cattle, set fire to their houses, and sent them away naked to the skin. On arrival at our camp they have been properly "clammed" and we have had to give them a share of our biscuits and corned beef, and given up our old clothes to cover the women. There are about two hundred refugees with us.' [18]

The Mounted Infantry had been first to arrive at Orange River, and were constantly in the saddle. 'I am going with a good heart and as a Lancashire lad,' wrote Private Fred Blackburn to his mother in Blackburn. 'We expect an attack at any time of the night, and we have to be out every morning at 3.30, saddled up ready to mount at any time, till five when we go out, if our turn, and be in the saddle for six hours without rest. We only get two nights sleep a week, and then we are in full dress. I had pulled off my boots to go to bed, but now we have to put them on again.' [19] As the Mounted Infantry scoured the veldt for enemy, there were minor successes, one of which was recounted by Private John Smith to his wife in Blackburn: 'I was out on patrol one day, and we happened to go to a farmhouse. It seems there were Boers there, and we found them armed with six rifles and 300 rounds of ammunition. Of course we took them prisoners and brought them into camp. We have been expecting the Boers attacking the bridge here, but I think they are a bit frightened because of their defeat at Glencoe.' [20]

18. Private Stephen Wilcock, Loyal North Lancashire Mounted Infantry, to his parents in Ribbleton Lane, Preston, published in *The Preston Herald*, 24 February 1900. Contrary to Africaner myth, it was the Boers who, both in Natal and Cape Colony, started to burn farms, driving their occupants to seek food and shelter in British refugee camps.
19. Private F. Blackburn letters from Orange River dated 20 September and 9 October, published in *The Lancashire Daily Post*, 30 December 1899.
20. Private J. Smith letter from Orange River, published in *The Blackburn Times*, 13 January 1900.

Reconnaissance to Belmont

The small British garrison at Orange River was at first very vulnerable to attack, but by early November reinforcements had arrived to the extent that an advance towards Kimberley could at last be contemplated. On 6 November the North Lancashire Mounted Infantry (M.I.) Company went east on a two day reconnaissance patrol. Then at first light on the 9th seven hundred mounted troops rode north on a reconnaissance in force towards Belmont. The column,

Lieutenant-General Lord Methuen, KCVO, CB, CMG, JP. Commander 1st Infantry Division.

A patrician guardsman, tall, taciturn and drooping, Paul Methuen had considerable African experience, in the Gold Coast, in Bechuanaland and on the staff at Cape Town. A painstaking, able but unlucky general, he nevertheless retained the confidence and affection of his troops. He remained closely associated with 1st Loyal North Lancashires throughout the war.

commanded by Colonel Gough, consisted of two squadrons of the 9th Lancers, three companies of mounted infantry, including the North Lancashires, and a half-battery of guns. Two companies of the Regiment were held ready to support them.

Early next morning the Boers were located on a line of kopjes east of Belmont. Determined to feel out the extent and strength of this position, Gough sent the Lancers round to the right and two hundred mounted infantry to the left, while the artillery opened fire. The enemy response was slight, encouraging an impression that the position was but weakly held, so while Orange River was signalled for more troops, the mounted infantry pushed forward to get behind the Boers and cut off their retreat. 'C' and 'F' Companies of the North Lancashires had left for the north by train at 5.45 a.m., and at 3 p.m. 'D' and 'E' Companies were also hurried forward.

Moving round the Boer flank, the mounted infantry were suddenly ambushed. Within moments a hail of fire brought down four officers, conspicuous on account of their swords and accoutrements,[21] including Lieutenant Charles Woods of the 47th, a jovial young officer who was mortally wounded. Privates Beaton and Thompson were also hit. Private Hill reached cover with Lieutenant Wood, who was trying to locate the enemy through his field glasses when he was shot:

'I was against Lieutenant Woods when he fell. He had just told me to fire at one of them, who, he said, was in command of the Boers. I knocked him over, too, or got very close to him, for he bobbed down quick enough. They were too strong for us and we had to retire. There were thousands of bullets whizzing around us. The major said we would never be under so heavy a fire again as long as the war lasted. It is a funny sensation the first few minutes, but you soon get used to it. There were some very narrow escapes. One of our men had his horse shot through the ear, and how it missed him Heaven alone knows. You said "Be brave." Why, you cannot be anything else. Every man's eyes seem to strike fire, and you are mad for the time being, and you feel as strong as a lion.'

Hill had been a week in the saddle on short rations, but his greatest concern was for his beloved horse:

'My poor horse is lame, and will never be any use again, and I have to leave him behind. I could have cried when the captain told me he would have to be left behind. I have had him ten months now, and he can nearly talk. He follows me like a dog, and will shake hands with me. When he was lame we stopped at an ostrich farm. He kept lifting his lame leg up, and rubbing his nose against me, and

21. In Natal officers already carried rifles and dressed exactly the same as their men. As a result of this incident, the practice was extended to Cape Colony.

I took one of my putties off, and bound it round the leg. I came down with him in the train sent for wounded.'[22]

A Non-Essential Civilian

On the same day as the unfortunate skirmish at Belmont, Lieutenant General Lord Methuen, newly-appointed commander of the 1st Division and an experienced Africa hand, landed at Cape Town and was instructed by his Commander-in-Chief, Sir Redvers Buller, to march from Orange River to the relief of Kimberley. His orders were to reinforce and resupply the garrison, and to evacuate all non-essential civilians.

In Kimberley that day, Robert Kekewich was coming to the conclusion that there was at least one civilian too many in the besieged town. Around midnight on 9/10 November there had been a knock on the door of his hut at the foot of the Conning Tower. Outside stood an NCO with an African runner, who had managed to make his way from Orange River with a message from Buller. The code was soon deciphered and read: 'Civilians in Kimberley represent situation there as serious. Have heard nothing about this from you. Send appreciation of the situation immediately.'[23]

Kekewich and his staff were naturally taken aback. Throughout the siege he had taken both Rhodes and the Mayor into his confidence, briefing them on the military situation and consulting them whenever appropriate. There had been minor disagreements, but nothing serious, and in his private diary Kekewich had frequently noted his appreciation of Rhodes' contributions to the defence of the town. Now, it appeared, someone of considerable standing had been sending out alarmist reports behind his back and in clear betrayal of his trust. What Kekewich did not know, and could only begin to guess, was that ever since the start of the siege Rhodes and his friends had been bombarding the High Commissioner and others with orchestrated demands that the relief of Kimberley should receive the utmost priority. In his diary for 10 November, Kekewich wrote:

'Coded messages have been allowed hitherto from De Beers etc. to the High Commissioner and to the Military Authorities, but I must stop this, as I find that all kinds of alarmist reports are being sent. I have always tried to give all details as to the military situation, and have kept back nothing. I only hope all my messages have got through. I have represented in my telegrams the dangers and difficulties, as

22. Private Hill, letter from Orange River dated 14 November, published in *The Preston Herald*, 16 December 1899. Sentence order changed.
23. O'Meara, op. cit., p. 58.

they affect the military situation. With so many rich people here, who can employ special despatch riders and pay them very highly, it is most difficult to control telegrams, letters and newspapers, etc. coming into or leaving the town, but I shall now take stronger action in order that the military situation may not be misrepresented.'[24]

The Battle of Belmont

On 22 November Lord Methuen's column was ready to move forward from the Orange River to Kimberley. He had two splendid Infantry brigades,[25] the Guards and the 9th, which Major Jackson's wing of the 47th had joined on the 20th with a strength of eleven officers and 353 men. There was also an attached Naval Brigade of bluejackets and marines. The division was, however, deficient in other respects. Methuen had only twenty guns, no horse artillery, no more than five hundred mounted men, and insufficient transport to operate away from the railway. But an advance was imperative and so, led by the Guards Brigade, the Division set off before light the following morning.

The country to be crossed was for the most part open plain, dotted with kopjes, though some two-thirds of the way to Kimberley the railway and track crossed the Modder ('Mud') River. There seemed to be three places where the four to five thousand Boers commanded by Commandant Prinsloo might seek to block Methuen's advance; at Belmont, between Graspan and Enslin, and, north of the Modder, in the Magersfontein-Spytfontein area. Methuen had insufficient cavalry and logistic support to turn these positions, so was obliged to advance up the line of the railway.

The battle of Belmont began at first light on the 23rd. Since the Regiment played only a minor role in this engagement, being in charge of the divisional baggage, it will suffice to say that three successive Boer positions were cleared at bayonet point in gallant but costly frontal assaults.[26] Methuen had intended his mounted troops to push forward on the flanks to cut off the enemy withdrawal, but they were too few and exhausted, so most of the Boers escaped.

The North Lancashires did not arrive on the field of battle until 6.30 a.m., when 'E' Company was detailed to relieve a half-company

24. Kekewich Diary, 10 November 1899.

25. The Ninth Brigade consisted of 1st Northumberland Fusiliers, 2nd King's Own Yorkshire Light Infantry, 2nd Northamptons, and the half-battalion of 1st Loyal North Lancashires. The total Infantry strength of the division amounted to some 7,500 men.

26. Lord Methuen had not intended a frontal attack, but the leading battalion of the Guards Brigade lost direction during the night approach march.

of Coldstreams on a kopje to the left of the advance, with orders to prevent the Boers from breaking back that way, and the remaining companies stayed under cover. By ten o'clock the action was over, and the wing took charge of some fifty prisoners and assisted in clearing the battlefield.

The Battle of Graspan

The next enemy position was at Graspan, where four hundred Boers and two guns were reported. In fact some 2,500 of them, with six artillery pieces and two machine guns, were entrenched on a semicircle of five kopjes to the east of the railway, while a further five hundred were lurking out to Methuen's right. The British force advanced north-east from Swinks Pan in the early hours of 25 November, the 47th wing bringing up the rear of the column. In consequence of the heavy losses sustained at Belmont in storming the Boer position without full artillery preparation, Methuen had decided to open the battle with an intensive bombardment. Indeed, he hoped to shell them out the position and to cut off the retreat of the Boer left wing with his small mounted force, the greater part of which was sent well forward on the right for that purpose. For three hours the British artillery plastered the kopjes with shrapnel and duelled with the Boer guns, but to little effect, for the enemy were well protected. By 7 a.m. it had become clear that the Boers were in much greater strength than originally reported, and would not be shifted by firepower alone.

During the artillery duel the 9th Infantry Brigade, with the Naval Brigade under command, had formed up facing the enemy position. Methuen remained determined on an attack against the Boer left, and he now ordered it to be assaulted by the Naval Brigade and the King's Own Yorkshire Light Infantry, while the Northumberland Fusiliers contained the enemy right. The attacking troops were accordingly moved half right until opposite a large kopje on the Boer left flank, then faced uphill and advanced to the assault.

The North Lancashire wing was initially ordered to escort a gun battery, which was deployed well forward on the right to support the attack. 'C' and 'F' Companies moved out as escorts, marching in extended order towards the eastern end of the range of hills held by the Boers. They were followed by the Naval Brigade. 'D' and 'E' Companies were for a while diverted to counter a threat from the open right flank, where some two hundred Boers had occupied a kopje and had opened a heavy fire on the 9th Lancers, but they soon returned to support the guns.

Then Lord Methuen, who was near the guns, personally ordered Major Paul Churchward to take 'C' and 'F' Companies and join the

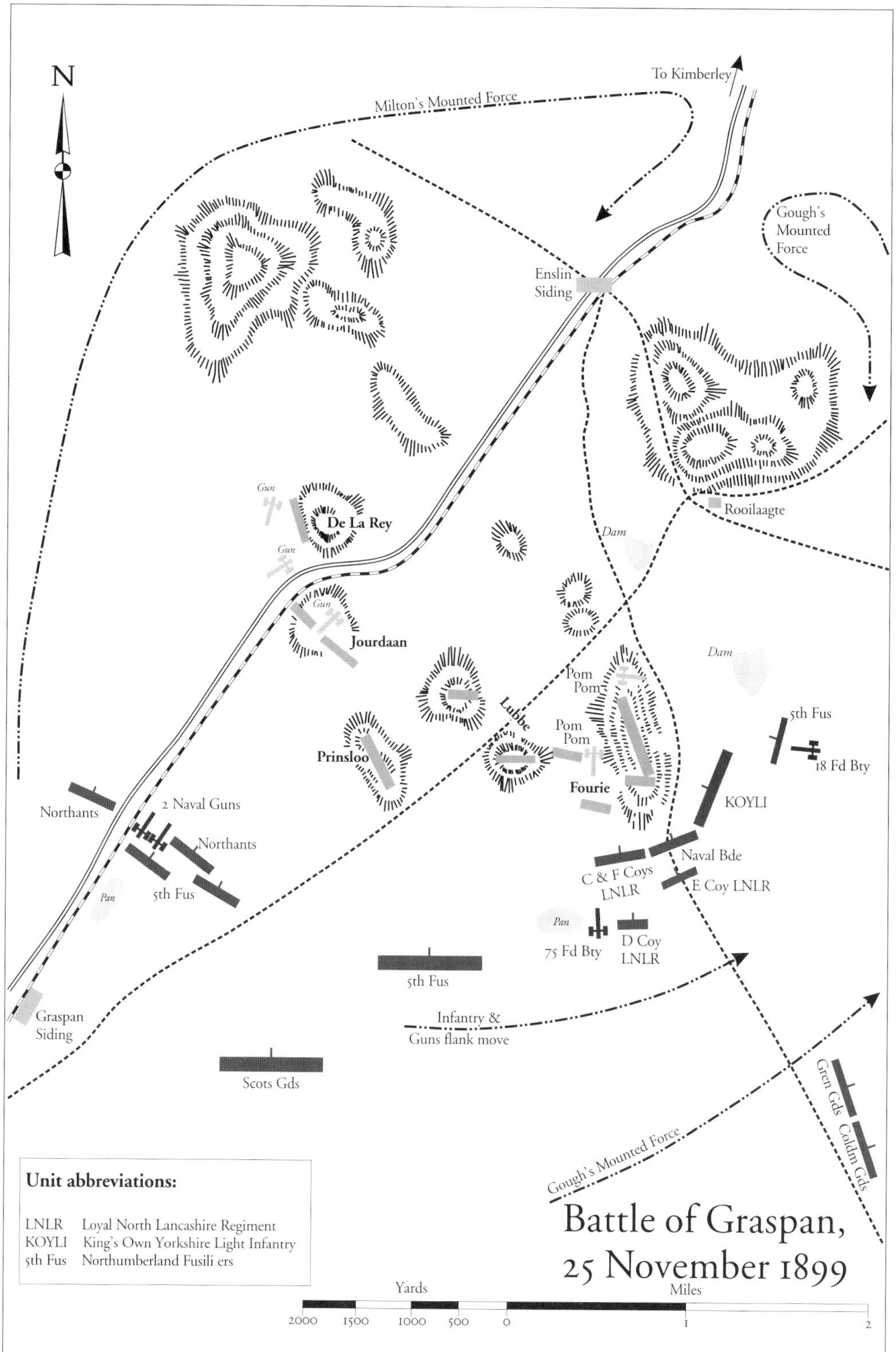
N
To Kimberley
Milton's Mounted Force
Gough's Mounted Force
Enslin Siding
Gun
De La Rey
Gun
Gun
Jourdaan
Rooilaagte
Dam
Dam
Pom Pom
Pom Pom
Lubbe
Prinsloo
Fourie
5th Fus
18 Fd Bty
KOYLI
Northants
2 Naval Guns
Northants
5th Fus
Pan
Naval Bde
C & F Coys LNLR
E Coy LNLR
Pan
75 Fd Bty
D Coy LNLR
5th Fus
Graspan Siding
Infantry & Guns flank move
Scots Gds
Gren Gds
Coldm Gds
Gough's Mounted Force
Unit abbreviations:
LNLR Loyal North Lancashire Regiment
KOYLI King's Own Yorkshire Light Infantry
5th Fus Northumberland Fusili ers
Battle of Graspan, 25 November 1899
Yards
Miles
2000 1500 1000 500 0 1 2

attack on the left of the Boer position.[27] The Royal Marines and seamen led the assault with magnificent gallantry, firing volleys as they advanced, but, moving in too close formation and with insufficient use of cover, they were bowled over by the dozen.[28] For a moment it appeared that the attack might fail, but the Naval Brigade would not be denied and, with the King's Own Yorkshire Light Infantry and Loyal North Lancashires on their right and left respectively, renewed the assault.

Hearing the heavy fire in front, 'E' Company advanced to assist the firing line. 'As it topped a rise the Marines and 'C' and 'F' Companies were seen under a heavy fire. 'E' Company then opened long range volleys over the heads of the firing line, the guns with shrapnel also covering the advance. 'C' Company was under the hottest fire, 'F' Company on its left hardly coming under fire. 'E' Company, then inclining to the right to try and turn the flank, advanced by rushes of one or two men at a time, the whole company being extended over a front of about 500 yards, the fire being 'independent' most of the time. By this time 'C' Company, with Marines and some King's Own Yorkshire Light Infantry, had reached [the] foot of [the] hill and were in dead ground, and, fixing bayonets, were beginning to scale the hill. 'E' Company had to cease fire in this direction now and turned its fire onto the ridges beyond.'[29]

As soon as the attackers reached the top of the blood-spattered hill someone, presumably a Boer, sounded the 'ceasefire', and the enemy could be seen retreating. Some withdrew along the ridge to their right, while others mounted their horses and fled the field amid the long-range volleys of the British Infantry. 'C' and 'F' Companies were consolidating on the far side of the enemy position when Major Churchwood ran into a party of Boers, nineteen strong. He levelled his revolver and called on them to surrender, which they promptly did.[30] Meanwhile, 'D' and 'E' Companies advanced northwards in pursuit of the enemy, moving to the east of the base of the kopje.

The enemy position had been turned and was untenable. 'The heights gained,' wrote Methuen, 'I found I had taken the whole Boer force in flank, and had entirely cut them off from their line of retreat. My guns played on the masses of horsemen, but my few cavalry, dead

27. According to the Regimental Digest of Service, Methuen ordered Churchward 'to attack and take the two kopjes on the right of the range of hills held by the Boers.' This would include a smaller hill to the left of the main objective.

28. The Royal Marines lost three officers and 88 men out of a total strength of 206.

29. Manuscript *Digest of Services of 1st Loyal North Lancashire Regiment, October 1894–August 1914.* The Battalion fired 17,913 rounds in the course of this battle.

30. In 1929 Churchward presented the Mauser rifle carried by the Boer Field Cornet in charge of this party to the newly formed Regimental Museum, of which it was the very first exhibit.

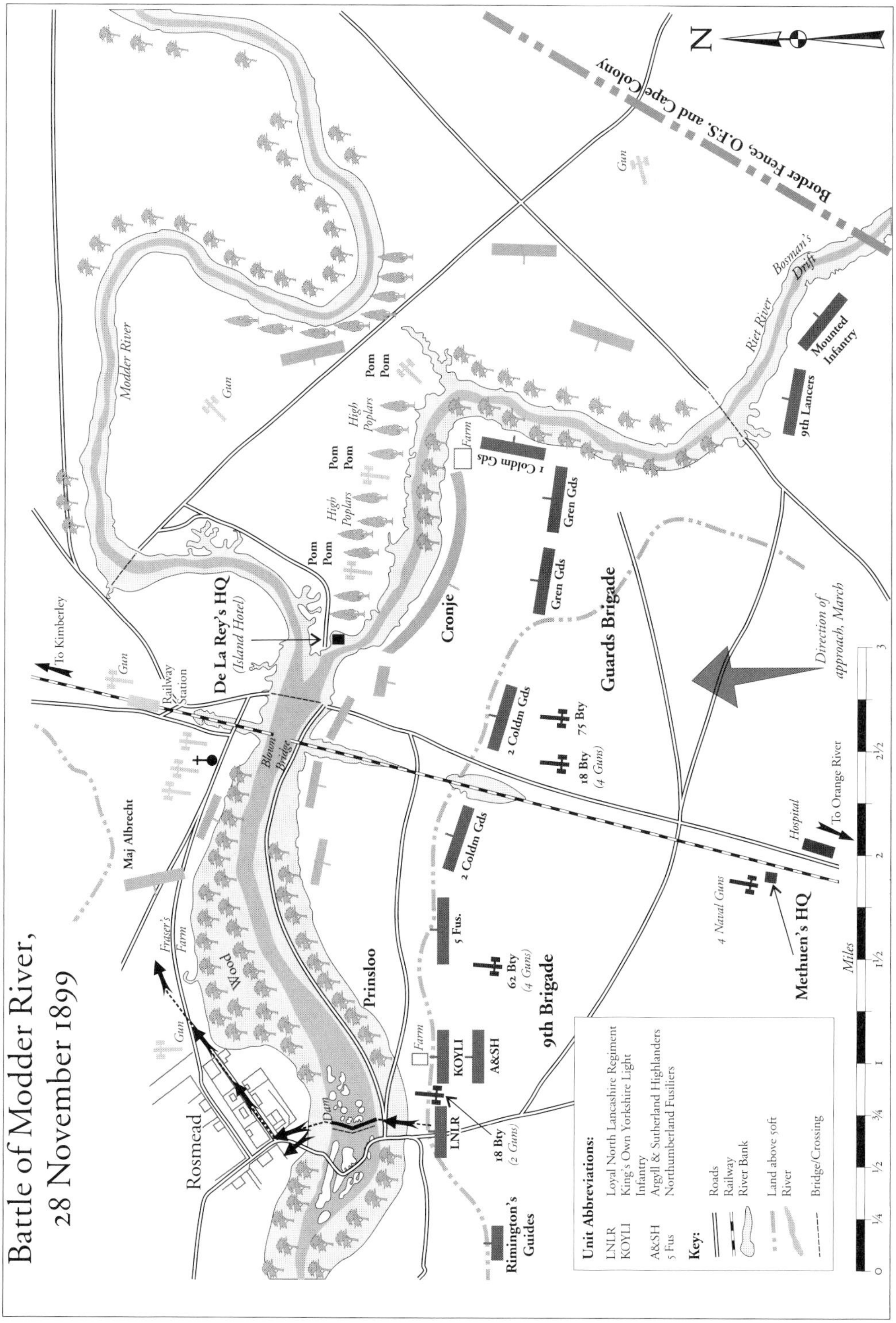
Battle of Modder River, 28 November 1899
N
Border Fence, O.F.S. and Cape Colony
Gun
Bosman's Drift
Riet River
Mounted Infantry
9th Lancers
Modder River
Gun
Pom Pom
High Poplars
Pom Pom
High Poplars
Pom Pom
Farm
1 Coldm Gds
Gren Gds
Gren Gds
Guards Brigade
Cronje
De La Rey's HQ
(Island Hotel)
To Kimberley
Gun
Railway Station
Blown Bridge
2 Coldm Gds
75 Bty
18 Bty
(4 Guns)
2 Coldm Gds
Direction of approach, March
Maj Albrecht
Fraser's Farm
Wood
Prinsloo
5 Fus.
62 Bty
(4 Guns)
9th Brigade
4 Naval Guns
Methuen's HQ
Hospital
To Orange River
Gun
Farm
KOYLI
A&SH
Dam
LNLR
18 Bty
(2 Guns)
Rosmead
Rimington's Guides
Unit Abbreviations:
LNLR Loyal North Lancashire Regiment
KOYLI King's Own Yorkshire Light Infantry
A&SH Argyll & Sutherland Highlanders
5 Fus Northumberland Fusiliers
Key:
Roads
Railway
River Bank
Land above 50ft
River
Bridge/Crossing
Miles
0 ¼ ½ ¾ 1 1½ 2 2½ 3

beat, were powerless, and for the second time I longed for a cavalry brigade and a horse artillery battery to let me reap the fruits of a hard-fought action.'[31]

British losses totalled twenty killed and 154 wounded, two-thirds of whom were of the Naval Brigade. The Loyal North Lancashires' loss was comparatively slight considering the severity of the action, amounting to three men killed and eighteen wounded, almost all in 'C' and 'E' Companies and the Mounted Infantry. The Regiment attributed this to the wide extensions, or spacing between individuals, adopted by the companies. Boer casualties are, as usual, not known, but twenty-one of their dead were buried on the battlefield by the victors. Two soldiers of the 47th were reported for their gallantry during the assault.[32]

'I suppose you have heard about the gallant charges we have been making with the bayonet,' wrote Private J. Snape of 'E' Company to his mother at Witton, Blackburn. 'The General says all England is talking of the gallant Loyal North Lancashires. We are glad we have done something to be proud of at last, for it shows people there are as brave men in Lancashire as anywhere else. We expect heavy fighting again these next few days, and expect to be in Kimberley on Wednesday.'[33]

The Battle of Modder River

On the morning of 28 November Methuen made an early start. He intended to halt his troops for breakfast on the banks of the Modder River, five miles away. True, the previous afternoon there had been reports of Boers, up to four thousand of them, digging in along the river line. Methuen had been forward himself to reconnoitre, but all seemed quiet. The gentle slope down to the poplar and willow-lined river seemed peaceful enough. The railway bridge had been blown, but otherwise there was no sign of untoward activity around the scattered houses and hotels of what was, in normal times, a popular resort for the citizens of Kimberley, and so it was decided to advance. Methuen was convinced that his enemy would next be encountered in strength on the Spytfontein kopjes.

Nevertheless, when the force moved out on the morning of the

31. Despatch from Lieutenant-General Lord Methuen, 25 November 1899.
32. Private Turner of 'C' Company was reported by Lieutenant Bowen, Royal Marines, 'for his cool conduct in close proximity to the Boer position in attending to Private Metcalfe, Royal Marines, who was shot in the stomach'. Private Johnson of 'E' Company was reported by Major Hunt, King's Own Yorkshire Light Infantry, 'for his coolness and gallantry during the attack.'
33. Private J. Snape, letter published in *The Lancashire Daily Post*, 30 December 1899.

The Battle of Modder River.
From a sketch by a British officer showing the view from the right centre of the Guards Brigade firing line across the open ground to the defended river-line. On the left, the Loyal North Lancashires were rather closer to the river, but their situation was otherwise similar.

28th it was in battle formation. The Guards Brigade took the right flank, the 9th Brigade the left, with the 47th wing moving in front as advance guard to the Division. The flanks were extended to right and left by mounted troops, the Loyal North Lancashire Mounted Infantry being among those on the right. The artillery was distributed along the line.

The wing moved off from Witkoplaagte at 5.30 a.m., and about one hour later the mounted troops on the right became engaged with small parties of enemy, who withdrew south-east. 'I hurt myself with getting one of my chums out of the firing line,' wrote Fred Blackburn of the Loyal North Lancashire M.I. to his mother. 'He got shot in the back, but he is getting on all right.'[34]

While the artillery shelled the retiring Boers, the general advance continued astride the railway, towards the Modder River crossing. The Loyal North Lancashires led at first, marching across a perfectly open plain devoid of cover, but as the Division drew closer to the river they halted while the Guards and Northumberland Fusiliers were passed through to form a firing line. Ahead, down along the poplars where the Riet and Modder rivers joined, all remained silent.

The peaceful scene was deceptive, for along both sides of the river line over three thousand riflemen lay in wait, burrowed deep into the sheltering river banks and invisible among the trees and houses. The

34. Private F. Blackburn, letter dated Modder River 1 December 1899, published in *The Blackburn Times*, 20 January 1900.

Modder was some eighty to one hundred yards wide and, in addition to the drift close to the demolished railway-bridge, there were only one practicable ford, some two miles down-stream where the stream had been dammed to form an ornamental lake opposite the small hamlet of Rosmead. Beyond the river the ground sloped up a few hundred yards to a parallel ridge, behind which the Boer artillery was sited, 6–7 Krupp field guns and 3–4 one-pounder Maxim 'pom-poms'. The Boers had decided to halt Methuen's advance at the Modder, and De la Rey, Prinsloo and Cronje had combined their forces for that purpose. Their strongly entrenched position, extending for some five miles, appeared almost impregnable. For maximum effect, the burghers were ordered to hold their fire until the British Infantry were within four hundred yards of their Mauser rifles.

The Boer artillery opened, in a desultory fashion, from behind its protective ridge, but at about 10 o'clock the British advance continued, the troops moving steadily in open order. Opposition appeared to be light, and Methuen was confirmed in his belief that there was no more than a small delaying force before him. He ordered the Loyal North Lancashires forward to support the left flank of the Northumberland Fusiliers, which put them on the extreme left of the Infantry line.

The Guards descended the grassy slope towards the Modder, but were still some thousand yards from the river when Cronje's burghers opened fire prematurely, and their undisciplined but intensive fusillade rattled right along the Boer front. The fire of their flat-trajectory weapons across the open ground was, nevertheless, terrible in its effect. 'The earth seemed to open and vomit a terrible discharge of bullets which whistled through the air and fairly swept the field. The advancing infantry was struck down as if by a sudden blast ... The whole force was compelled to throw themselves flat on the ground to escape annihilation, and the whole day the Guards were compelled to lie prone on the earth.'[35]

On the British left, the North Lancashires were advancing, with 'C' and 'F' Companies leading and 'E' and 'D' in support, when, about one thousand yards from the river, they came under effective fire from their front and right flank. The Boers here were on both sides of the river. 'The General came up to me,' wrote Major Jackson, 'and ordered me to attack the enemy's right on the Modder River, and push my attack home. He didn't know that I should have to cross the open under enfilading fire and then find an unfordable river between myself and the position.'[36] The task seemed quite impossible, but the wing pushed forward towards their unseen enemies.

35. *With Lord Methuen from Belmont to Hartebeestfontein*, p. 26. Klerksdorp, July 1901.
36. Major S. Jackson, letter published in *The Preston Herald*, 24 February 1900.

'C' Company occupied a small ridge or kopje overlooking the river, but came under a heavy and accurate fire that caused many casualties. 'As soon as they saw us we got to know it,' wrote Private Snape of 'C' Company, 'for bullets came flying at us like hail stones, and I had three men shot dead within ten yards of me, all belonging to my company. Private Harris was shot through his thigh, Sergeant Richardson was shot through his chest, and Private Bell was shot dead through his heart.'[37] Major Jackson pulled the Company back to a less exposed position, and 'E' Company came into the line on their left.

The whole wing were now lying down, trying to locate the enemy fire. The Boers were entrenched some seven to eight hundred yards away, but their smokeless cordite ammunition made them very difficult to spot – in contrast to the British Infantry, who were still issued with black powder cartridges. The North Lancashires resorted to firing volleys at likely enemy positions. The Boers replied with cannon, pom-poms, and rifles, but Jackson kept his men down in cover and there were few casualties, though some had narrow escapes. Private Albert Robinson, from Colne, had his haversack blown off his back, whilst Privates Crook and McMann respectively had a helmet clipped and a pouch shot through.

For two awful hours the firing continued, as the sun rose higher and the temperature soared to a reported 110 degrees Fahrenheit. The men were hungry and desperately parched. Owing to the enemy's fire, ammunition had to be thrown along the line from man to man. But in truth most of the Infantry, lying out in the open, were almost impotent, and this stage of the battle became an unequal duel between the British gunners, gallantly firing from exposed positions as near as eight hundred yards from the Boer trenches, and entrenched enemy markmen and artillery.

It was clearly not possible to advance across the open ground to the river without artillery support, so Major Jackson sent Captain Charles Jourdain, his Adjutant, to the nearest artillery officer to ask for guns. Eventually two were sent, coming up under fire. 'Before they could unlimber or fire a shot,' wrote Jackson, 'the Boers ran for it, mounted their horses and went for their lives'. Prinsloo's Free Staters retired in haste to the far side of the Modder. At about this time, the King's Own Yorkshire Light Infantry stormed a farmhouse which dominated the approaches to the Modder in the area of the Rosmead dam. Seizing the opportunity, the 47th now rose and rushed in two lines to the river, where they forced a crossing at and below the dam and weir, which were to their right front. 'About 12 o'clock,'

37. Private J. Snape, letter dated Modder River, 1 December 1899, published in *The Lancashire Daily Post*, 30 December 1899.

recalled Private Hayes of 'C' Company, 'the enemy began to retire, and then we did pepper them with bullets. We then marched along, and came across the river. We drank water till we nearly burst, and we dipped our rifles in the water to cool them.'[38] Paul Churchward's 'C' Company was first across. 'Now, boys,' cried Major Hugh Coleridge as he sprang into the water, 'Who's for otter hunting?'[39]

Claims have been advanced on behalf of other battalions for the honour of being first across the Modder weir, but both the Divisional history and the Regimental Digest of Service are quite clear on this point: 'The river was very full and the [dam] wall submerged, but the men waded through, waist deep in water, on the bank of the dam. Four companies of the Loyal North Lancashires crossed first and turned to their left, down stream, clearing the enemy out of some houses and bushes, and then, turning right about, came up stream to some more houses which they also cleared, under a very heavy fire, and took up a position among some sluits or furrows, which they stuck to, despite all attempts to dislodge them. These companies were greeted during their advance with a discharge of case shot from a Boer gun, delivered at 1000 yards range, probably the only occasion during the war on which such missiles were employed. They were soon followed by General Pole-Carew and Colonel Barter with a mixed force of Argyle and Sutherland Highlanders, Yorkshire Light Infantry, Northumberland Fusiliers and Royal Engineers, and they all remained on the north bank that night. This was a daring act which completely surprised the Boers, who had never contemplated such a performance, and they made room for the reckless fellows, who, with bayonets fixed, appeared to them irresistible and invincible, as no doubt they were.'[40]

This audacious assault crossing of the Modder was witnessed by an incredulous correspondent of *The Times* newspaper: 'That it could even be attempted to cross the river sliding sideways through the rush of water over the paddles along a rickety iron bar one by one, clinging to the short supports in full view of the opposite shore, was an act of reckless heroism against which even the wary Cronje had not provided.'

The appearance of British Infantry on the north bank of the Modder proved decisive, but lack of clear co-ordination with the artillery checked their bold outflanking move and saved the Boers from rout.

38. Private J. Hayes, letter dated Modder River, 5 December 1899, published in *The Blackburn Times*, 13 January 1900.
39. Conan Doyle, *The Great Boer War*, p. 146.
40. With Lord Methuen, pp. 27–8. 'At about 12.30,' records the Regimental Digest of Service, 'some details King's Own Yorkshire Light Infantry and Argyle and Sutherland Highlanders, etc., followed.' 'I got my men over the river,' states Jackson, 'and was joined by crowds of men – Highlanders, Guardsmen, all sorts.'

First the Infantry were unable to advance through Rosmead because their own guns were still shelling it, and then, as they cleared east along the river bank, they were subjected to a heavy bombardment by both British and Boer artillery. The Infantry were checked around Fraser's Farm and obliged to retire, and some were for a time ordered back across the river, but a bridgehead was maintained until darkness put an end to the day's fighting. The Loyal North Lancashires bivouacked for the night on the north bank, protected by their outposts. 'We finished at nine o'clock in the evening,' wrote Private Hayes. 'Our feet were wet through and we had nothing to eat all day. We were told to open our emergency rations, which consisted of ¼lb of beef and another ¼lb of cocoa, and it was welcome and no mistake.'[41]

The next morning it was found that the Boers had evacuated their positions and retired. It was another victory,[42] but a dear-bought one. Methuen had lost 63 dead, and was himself among the 388 wounded. The Loyal North Lancashires had suffered three killed in action and seventeen wounded, of whom two later died. Corporal Hodgson and Private Caddick were brought to notice for rescuing wounded men, Lance-Corporal Smith and Private Harris respectively, and carrying them to a place of safety under fire. Hodgson was awarded the Distinguished Conduct Medal.

Encamped after the battle just south of the Modder, the North Lancashires had some cause for satisfaction: 'Lord Methuen has given us a week's rest,' wrote Private Snape of 'C' Company, on 1 December, to his mother at Witton, Blackburn, 'and I think we have earned one, what with the battle of Belmont,, then the battle of Graspan, near Enslin siding, where we were the first up the hill after driving the Boers from it at the point of the bayonet, then at Modder River we were the first to cross the river and get behind the enemy. The General ... told us we have earned a name which both we and the people of Lancashire ought to be proud of. He says we shall have a great reception when we arrive in Lancashire after the war, for he says we have made a gallant charge and worked magnificently all through.' He concluded with an artful plea: 'I think if this war does not come to an end, or if some good Samaritan doesn't send me some tobacco, there will be a Snape less in this war, for we can't get tobacco for love nor money.'[43]

41. Private J. Hayes, ibid.
42. The Battle Honour 'Modder River' was granted to nine Regiments, but, despite their critical contribution, denied to the Loyal North Lancashires because their headquarters was not present.
43. Snape, ibid.

Carter's Ridge

Meanwhile, some 24 miles to the north the garrison of Kimberley had been far from idle. The town had been completely isolated for nearly a fortnight when, early on the morning of 23 November, a despatch rider managed to get through from the Orange River with a message which, when decoded, read:

> 18th November. No. R98: General leaves here with small force on 21st November, and will arrive Kimberley on 26th, unless detained at Modder River. Look out for signals by searchlight from us, they will be in cipher.

Since the Dronsfield action on 24 October, Kekewich had continued to use his mounted troops and armoured train aggressively for reconnaissance and small-scale sorties. Scott-Turner was always to the fore, as were the Loyal North Lancashire Mounted Infantry. Writing 28 years later, when he was a yeoman warder at the Tower of London, Percy King gave some account of his experience in some of these patrol actions:[44]

> 28/9/1899 – Patrolled Free State border fence mounted with a sergeant and four men of the L.N.L.R., and for about three weeks was engaged nightly with the 'De Beers Patrol' under Lieut. Clifford (L.N.L.R.) in watching the said border, armed with revolvers only. On one occasion we made a reconnaissance to Bisset's Farm at Magersfontein.
>
> 31/10/1899 – Baptism of fire at Susannah. L.N.L.M.I. present [This reconnaissance by Scott-Turner with about 250 men was engaged by the Boers with twenty rounds of shrapnel, without casualties].
>
> 16/11/1899 – Sortie to Carter's Farm. L.N.L.M.I. in advance [On this occasion there were ten casualties].
>
> 17/11/1899 – Brush with Boers at Bulfontein Mine. L.N.L.M.I. began to trot when ordered to retire, but Lieut. Clifford asked if that was how they had been taught to retreat, and made them walk out. One of them took up a comrade, whose horse had been shot, behind him.

Kekewich now decided to assist Methuen's relief column by mounting a larger sortie to the south-west, involving almost one third of his garrison. There were to be two columns, commanded by Lieutenant-Colonels Chamier and Scott-Turner. Chamier's force, about nine

44. Yeoman P. L. King, letter in *The Lancashire Lad*, November 1937.

hundred strong, consisted of 'A' and 'H' Companies of the North Lancashires, under Lieutenant Woodward, four guns, two Maxims and a mounted escort. They were to make a demonstration against Ironstone Kopje and Wimbledon Ridge while Scott-Turner, with some four hundred mounted men, attacked enemy positions on Carter's Ridge. Smaller detachments were to occupy Otto's Kopje and secure the flanks of the advance.

Chamier's column moved off from the Reservoir Redoubt at daybreak on 25 November, and at 4.43 a.m. his guns opened fire on Ironstone Kopje. This cannonade was intended to deceive the Boers as to the real direction of attack, and in addition was the signal for Scott-Turner to launch his attack. As the two companies of North Lancashires advanced, they were met by a fusillade from enemy on two kopjes, 1,100 and 1,500 yards to their front, but successfully occupied a commanding position from which, according to the *Diamond Fields Advertiser*, 'Our infantry fired some admirable volleys at the enemy in the kopjes.' The combined fire of artillery and riflemen neutralised these Boer positions, preventing any interference with Scott-Turner's advance.

Wigram Clifford led the attack with his section of North Lancashire Mounted Infantry and at once surprised a sleeping Boer picqet of six men. Scott-Turner thereupon dismounted his men and skirmished forward to take a row of rocky ridges to his front. These proved to be unoccupied, but, as Scott-Turner's men continued their advance beyond the ridgeline, some fifty Boers opened a sudden and heavy rifle fire on them from a series of four redoubts on the left flank. These entrenchments were stormed by Scott-Turner and about seventy men in a celebrated bayonet charge, 33 prisoners being taken. Meanwhile, the remainder of the mounted troops had pressed on up Carter's Ridge, driving the enemy before them. On gaining the summit, they saw the Boer laager in a hollow some 800 yards away.

'Our men lined the ridge and riddled all the tents with bullets, compelling the enemy to retire in the direction of Carter's Farm. Colonel Scott-Turner, who now rejoined the main body, was informed that Boer reinforcements were coming from the direction of Kamfersdam, and he therefore determined to abandon the idea of taking the camp. About the same time he detected small bodies of the enemy stealing out of the bush at the back of their camp and working towards his right flank.

'Our troops were now in something of a dilemma, as they were almost out of ammunition, and owing to the misty state of the atmosphere it was found impossible to signal by heliograph for fresh supplies to be sent out. At this stage of the fight, Lieutenant Clifford, North Lancashire Mounted Infantry, behaved with great coolness,

The Return from Carter's Ridge.
Scott-Turner's mounted troops ride into Kimberley after their successful sortie of 25 November 1899.

galloping all along the line several times to find out who was short of cartridges, and afterwards returning with bandoliers which he had collected from the dead and wounded and from the men who were holding horses ... Had fresh supplies of ammunition and a couple of field guns arrived upon the scene at this moment the enemy might easily have been driven out of the bushes, from which they were keeping up a constant fire on our men, and the whole camp would have fallen into our hands.'[45]

However, as visibility remained too poor for signalling and Boer reinforcements continued to arrive, Scott-Turner decide to gather his scattered forces and retire on Kimberley with his casualties and prisoners. He completed his withdrawal by about 8 a.m. in perfect order and without loss.

All this time the two North Lancashire companies with Chamier had remained exposed to a heavy fire. Lieutenant Cyril de Putron's 'H' Company was in the firing line, and 'A' Company, under Lieutenant Arthur Hewett, in support. The men were widely extended and lay flat on the ground, most of them behind ant-heaps or some other cover, for any movement attracted fire from the enemy's slightly dominating position. The North Lancashires held their position for three and a half hours, when, following the retirement of Scott-

45. *The Siege of Kimberley, 1899–1900*, pp. 59–60, published by *The Diamond Fields Advertiser*, Kimberley.

Turner's force, they too were ordered to withdraw. This movement was executed with perfect discipline, the men skirmishing slowly back, covered by the guns, and the detachment returned to camp at 9 a.m.

The sortie had cost the garrison seven killed and 29 wounded, the latter including Private J. Walcroft of the North Lancashires. Boer losses are unknown, but were certainly greater. In addition to the 33 prisoners, they admitted to nine killed and seventeen wounded.

Kekewich and Rhodes both watched the fight from the 'Observatory', an elevated observation post in the Reservoir Redoubt, and it may have been on this occasion that a Lancashire soldier, oblivious to the mining magnate's pretensions, assisted him up a ladder, exclaiming: 'Here, old Cockalorum, give us your flapper and I'll help you up.'

The Observatory at Reservoir Redoubt.

This was Kekewich's command and observation post for both the Carter's Ridge sorties.

Following the action on 25 November, the Boers strengthened their works on Carter's Ridge and opened fire with a single gun from the main redoubt in that position. Kekewich, who was now expecting Methuen's relief force to appear at any time, resolved to make another, even bigger, sortie to the south-west 'to relieve the pressure on the relief column by drawing off and holding as many as possible of the enemy opposing its advance.' The demonstration was given specific objectives; first, to capture Ironstone Kopje, and then 'if it could be arranged, for the mounted troops and some of the guns to move at once to Carter's Farm and shell the enemy on the ridge west of Lazaretto [i.e. Carter's Ridge].'[46]

Almost half the garrison was allocated to this sortie, organised in three columns under the overall command of Lieutenant-Colonel Chamier. On the left, the armoured train was to make a sally towards Wimbledon Ridge, supported by three hundred of the Town Guard under Major J. R. Fraser of the North Lancashires. The main column in the centre, commanded by Chamier himself, consisted of 'A', 'G' and 'H' Companies of the Loyal North Lancashires, under Lieutenant-Colonel Murray, two companies of the Kimberley Regiment, six guns, four Maxims, and a detachment of Royal Engineers, 960 officers and men in all. Their initial task was to capture Ironstone

46. Kekewich, 28 November 1899.

Kopje. On their right were 633 mounted men under Scott-Turner, including the North Lancashire Mounted Infantry detachment.

At the conclusion of his orders, according to O'Meara, Kekewich recalled Scott-Turner as he was leaving the room. He had noticed that Scott-Turner seemed particularly keen to storm Carter's Ridge again, having expressed the opinion that the enemy there were few and would clear from the redoubts on the ridge when shelled. He had also been exposing himself and his men to enemy fire rather more than necessary. Kekewich was worried, and explained to Scott-Turner that an all-out attack was not to be undertaken against the Boer position, his final words being: 'My dear chap, remember I do not want you to make an assault on Carter's Ridge or to capture it, unless it is unoccupied by the Boers, or so slightly occupied that there is every prospect of an attempt against it succeeding.'[47]

Operations began at 1.30 p.m. on 28 November when Lieutenant Webster's armoured train steamed northwards to deceive the enemy, then returned to Kimberley. At 3 o'clock Kekewich watched from the 'Observatory' as the infantry advance on Ironstone Kopje began, led by 'A' Company of the North Lancashires, under Lieutenant Hewett, supported by 'G' and 'H' Companies. The artillery were to the right rear of the infantry, while the right of the advance was covered by Scott-Turner's mounted troops. Two Boer guns opened fire, but their range was poor and no harm was done. The Boer outposts having withdrawn, the Kopje was occupied without loss. Chamier then sent a company of the Kimberley Regiment out to his left to secure Wright's Farm, while on the right the mounted troops drove the enemy from Carter's Farm. Meanwhile the armoured train made a demonstration towards Wimbledon Ridge, successfully drawing the fire of the Boer guns in that area, and the Diamond Fields Artillery began to bombard Carter's Ridge. Up to this point, all had gone according to plan.

At 5 p.m. 'A' Company was detached from the centre column to relieve the mounted troops at Carter's Farm, deploying in defensive positions to the north and south of the farm buildings. Standing on the 'Observatory', Kekewich could see a fierce engagement raging at the southern end of Carter's Farm. 'Bullets came over like hail,' wrote Private Brindle of 'A' Company, 'until we commenced to return our fire.'[48]

The arrival of 'A' Company freed the mounted troops for the next phase, but Scott-Turner was becoming impatient and, without waiting for all his squadrons to come up, and contrary to his explicit orders from Kekewich, he launched an almost suicidal assault on Carter's

47. O'Meara, pp. 74–5.
48. Private J. Brindle, manuscript account of 'Carter's Farm Engagement'.

Carter's Farm. Four miles south-west of Kimberley, the buildings were held by 'A' Company 1st Loyal North Lancashires during the action on 28 November 1899.

Ridge with barely one hundred men – Cape Police, Kimberley Light Horse and the Loyal North Lancashire Mounted Infantry section. 'The little body of attackers, small as it was, advanced in loose skirmishing order with wonderful coolness and intrepidity. The distance ahead was about one mile. One group, led by Scott-Turner in person, advancing by rushes of 50 yards under cover of a Maxim, quickly crossed this fire-swept zone and occupied the nearest redoubt, whence Scott-Turner, seeing the weakness of his position, signalled for guns to be sent to Carter's to support his further attack.' [49]

Meanwhile a party of the Diamond Fields Horse, moving west, had rushed the Boer laager, and a sergeant and twenty men of 'A' Company went forward to assist them in the work of destroying the enemy's tents, stores and food supplies. Considerable booty was also removed. 'They had a good supply of cut-up tobbacco, Afrikander,' recalled Private Brindle, 'which we enjoyed after.' [50]

Two guns arrived at 5.30 p.m. and, coming into action north of Carter's Farm, engaged the redoubts on Carter's Ridge at a range of one thousand yards, but their fire was not effective. Despite this, Henry Scott-Turner apparently remained fixed in his determination to carry the remaining redoubts and silence their gun, and at 6.10 p.m. he led a fresh advance. Two more redoubts were captured in

49. *The Siege of Kimberley, 1899–1900*, p. 68, published by *The Diamond Fields Advertiser*, Kimberley.
50. Brindle, ibid.

fine style, but the last one, which dominated the others and sheltered the enemy gun, proved too formidable for the unsupported and depleted little band. Lieutenant Braine of the Diamond Fields Horse took part in this desperate charge and has left a vivid account:

'On we went through a withering fire. I saw fifteen men go down dead and wounded within the 100 yards run. Down we went again, every man prone. I kept an eye on Col. Scott-Turner, and ere long saw him spring up and rush forward. We were now about 200 yards from the redoubt. I and the men about me immediately followed. The sight of the Colonel ahead of us, fearlessly breasting that stream of lead, was magnificent. He ran straight to the enemy's position, and, being a good runner, soon outstripped the best of us. He was now alone, and we could see the dust spitting all around him. Wonderful as it seems, he soon gained what we had thought was the front of the fort ... We were astonished to find only a shallow redoubt. The fort was still some sixty yards ahead. One of the first officers to join the Colonel was Lieut. Clifford, 1st Loyal North Lancashire Regiment ...

'We remained quiet – almost breathless – for a few minutes, then came the misfortune of the day. I noticed the Colonel seize a rifle from a man near him and deliberately take aim and fire several shots, then he sank down, as I thought from fatigue. But it was not so, as we soon knew. A bullet had passed through his head, cutting his hat to pieces. We were staggered at this, but I cannot describe the feeling more particularly. Laying him down, we next thought of the foe. The sand-bagged fort, thoroughly loop-holed, was plainly visible. From it the hail of bullets was incessant, and to show a head meant additional volleys. I ventured a couple of shots from my revolver, and quick as lightning a bullet cut the sand beside my hand.

'Lieut. Clifford now moved round, and, seizing a rifle, leant over the bank and fired three shots. After the last he exclaimed, "I've hit one!" and down the brave little chap fell, as if struck by lightning, a stream of blood flowing from his head. Sorrow deepened in us, for all thought him dead. I got hold of him and held him in a sitting position. He remained quiet a few moments, then gasped, rubbed his fingers into the wound, and exclaiming "It's only a scalp wound," gave the order "Fix bayonets! Charge!" We promptly countermanded that order, for it meant certain death to all.'[51]

The survivors of Scott-Turner's rash attack remained pinned down in the third redoubt, where they were joined by Lieutenant-Colonel Peakman of the Kimberley Light Horse with a handful of men. 'By God,' exclaimed one of his troopers, 'the Colonel's dead!' 'You bloody fool!', retorted Wigram Clifford fiercely, 'Hold your tongue!' The

51. Lieutenant Braine, quoted in *The Siege of Kimberley, 1899–1900*, pp. 71–4.

situation was indeed desperate, for the little band could move neither forward nor back, and any reinforcements attracted a fierce fire which cut most of them down. 'Every now and again,' wrote Lieutenant Braine, 'a man would rush towards us believing we had taken the fort. Our entreaties to such to 'keep down' and 'take cover' had no effect, and all were shot dead or wounded ... One instance impressed itself on my memory very vividly. Two brave fellows – one of the Lancashires and one of the Light Horse – rushed out of their slight cover towards us. The Lancashire came dauntlessly forward, whilst the other came along zig-zag fashion. The soldier was shot – the volunteer escaped, but bandolier and water-bottle were shot off him.'

It appears, indeed, that part of 'A' Company of the North Lancashires was drawn into this heroic assault: 'Then we were on the attack,' recalled Private Brindle, 'and cleared them out of a redoubt they had made, so they retired to a fort stronghold behind, and as we were ready to attack again. Colour Sergt Heald of A [Company] got up, and, as he had just said 'Follow me, lads', he was killed, so we had to carry on. Also, Pte J. Lutner, of A [Company] as well, was killed.' This is confirmed by the Regimental Digest of Services, which records that 'Colour-Sergeant Heald and Private Lutner were killed while leading the section in the rushes on the fort.'

It was not until after 9 p.m. that Kekewich received a report from Carter's Ridge, and he then ordered Peakman to withdraw under cover of darkness. The attackers accordingly retired on Carter's Farm,

After Carter's Ridge.
Soldiers of 1st Loyal North Lancashires firing volleys over the graves of Lieutenant-Colonel Scott-Turner and nineteen other officers and men, including two North Lancashires, killed in the action at Carter's Ridge, 28 November.

whence 'A' Company rejoined Chamier. Early next morning the whole force withdrew into Kimberley.

The sortie, or rather the unfortunate assault on Carter's Ridge, had cost the garrison 22 dead and some 32 wounded, including two of the Loyal North Lancashires killed and seven wounded, of whom three were Mounted Infantry. Rhodes quite wrongly blamed Kekewich for the death of his friend, Scott-Turner. Lieutenant Wigram Clifford was awarded a DSO.

The Lights of Kimberley

The main means of communication between Kimberley and the outside world was now by searchlight beam. The relief column's searchlight signals were first seen on 27 October, and from early December regular communications were maintained between the Wesselton Mine searchlight and the Modder River. The searchlight was manned by Lancashire signallers under Lieutenant Woodward and Sergeant Herbert, from Edgworth, near Bolton, who used a manually operated shutter to flash encoded morse messages into the night sky. Signalling commenced at 8 p.m. each evening, subject to weather, and

The Wesselton Mine Searchlight. Manned by Lancashire signallers, the searchlight was used for nightly communication with the relief force. The first message passed to the beleaguered garrison from the outside world was apparently an enquiry from the Remount Department, Wynberg as to the number marked on the hoof of a horse issued to the garrison!

Major John Fraser. Loyal North Lancashires, who commanded the Beaconsfield Town Guard. His sharp eyes were first to spot the winking heliograph signals of both Methuen's relief force and French's cavalry.

went on till sunrise. Then, on 13 January, Major Fraser happened to be on the headgear of the Bultfontein Mine when he spotted, through a gap in the Spytfontein Hills, the winking beam of a heliograph at Enslin, 44 miles away. Borrowing a looking glass from a nearby house, he flashed a message in the direction of the beam and was gratified to receive an acknowledgement. From that time the Regimental signallers could communicate with the relief force by day as well as by night. Their efforts did not go unrecognised, for on 18 January Kekewich recorded in his diary: 'The Signallers have had very hard work lately, and I was glad to receive a message yesterday praising their good work. Much credit is due to Lts. Woodward and De Putron who have personally superintended every message being sent through.'

Progress of the relief force had, as we have already seen, been somewhat slower than anticipated, but on the morning of the 29th, as Kekewich's men marched back to camp, their comrades were at least across the Modder River. Methuen, having fought and won three battles in less than a week, halted there for a few days to rest his men and horses, and to receive reinforcements. When he did move forward again, early on the rain-swept early morning of 11 December, it was to launch an ill-conceived and badly executed attack against a well-entrenched enemy position at Magersfontein, a mere sixteen miles from Kimberley. The result was disaster. The Highland Brigade, which led the attack, was slaughtered and all hopes of an early relief of Kimberley were dashed. The Loyal North Lancashires were fortunately not involved in this debacle, having been left to guard the Modder River camp, and the only Regimental casualty that day was Private H. White of the Mounted Infantry, wounded.

Kekewich was not aware of Methuen's plans for the Magersfontein attack, for communications with the Modder River were intermittent, but on 5 December 5 he sent a strong reconnaissance force, including three companies of the North Lancashires, towards Wimbledon Ridge. On the 9th he launched another sortie ' in order to draw from other places and hold as many [Boer] troops and guns as possible in the hope of relieving the pressure on the column from Orange River.' Chamier was again in command of the force, which consisted of 225 mounted troops, three companies of the North Lancashires, one hundred of the Town Guard and some Royal Engineers, supported by six guns and four Maxims. The troops deployed towards the Kamfersdam Mine at 4 a.m. and remained out all day while the Diamond Field Artillery duelled with the Boer gunners. Chamier's men had eight casualties, and the Boers nine.

On the 11th the distant rumbling of British guns at Magersfontein was heard in Kimberley, shell-bursts were seen over the Spytfontein hills, and a distant observation balloon was spotted. Relief seemed imminent and hopes ran high; but that evening a cryptic message was flashed by Methuen to Kekewich: 'I am checked.' This was, indeed, the British Army's 'Black Week' of the war, for on the 10th Lieutenant-General Gatacre's column was ambushed at Stormberg, while Sir Redvers Buller's first attempt to relieve Ladysmith failed on the 15th at Colenso.

It was several days before Kekewich was aware of the magnitude of Methuen's bloody reverse, but on 18 December he received orders to make his supplies last until February. Relief was indefinitely postponed.

Kekewich now had to plan for the long term. He had three principal problems which were, in ascending order, the superiority of Boer artillery, famine, and Cecil Rhodes.

Rhodes and Kekewich

Serious confrontation with Rhodes came to a head when, on 3 December, a despatch rider arrived from Methuen with confidential instructions to Kekewich. The burden of Methuen's message was that he had insufficient troops to permanently secure communications from

The Sanitorium. A 'redoubt', manned by 'G' Company of the 1st Loyal North Lancashires, was the residence throughout the siege of Cecil Rhodes, seen here (*left*) about to take his morning ride with his house party. The balcony, strengthened with timber, iron plates and sandbags, mounts a Maxim machine gun.

Kimberley to the south and that accordingly the relief force would reinforce and re-provision the town, and then withdraw to prepare for the planned strategic advance on Bloemfontein. Moreover, in order to reduce the feeding requirement in Kimberley, Kekewich was to plan for the evacuation of all non-essential civilians. Rhodes, who on account of his paramount position in the town continued to enjoy privileged access to military information, was briefed on these sensitive plans by Kekewich, having first been sworn to secrecy. Rhodes was very displeased, for Methuen's intentions would seriously impede his mining operation. His first priorities for transportation north were not troops and ammunition, nor even food for the civilian population, but coal and dynamite for his mines. Despite his word, Rhodes at once divulged the unpalatable plan to the directors and officials of De Beers. The following day a stormy interview took place when Rhodes called on Kekewich's headquarters to see whether there had been any further developments:

'He was told that another message had come in, but, said Kekewich: 'I can only communicate the further information if you will give me a solemn assurance that you will keep whatever I may communicate to you strictly to yourself and not repeat it either to De Beers' directors or the Company officials.' Rhodes completely lost his temper and shouted: 'That is exactly what you told me yesterday and I am not going to be told that by you again.' Kekewich remained unruffled and

Proclamation.

Issued in Kimberley by Lieutenant-Colonel Kekewich on 26 December 1899 regulating the issue of food in the besieged town.

V R

PROCLAMATION NO. 12.

Whereas

It is deemed necessary to regulate the sale and supply of Foodstuffs and Necessaries,

Now, Therefore,

I, ROBERT GEORGE KEKEWICH, Lieutenant-Colonel Commanding Griqualand West and Bechuanaland, do hereby proclaim and make known:—

1. That from and after Thursday, the 28th December, 1899, the allowances to Consumers per head per day shall be as follows:

	SUPPLIES.	EUROPEANS AND COLOURED COLONIALS.	ASIATICS.	NATIVES.
(a)	BOER MEAL	6ozs.	Nil.	Nil.
	FLOUR	4ozs	,,	,,
(b)	or BREAD	14ozs	,,	,,
	MEALIE MEAL	2ozs of either	2ozs of either	6ozs.
	KAFIR CORN MEAL			4 ,,
	SAMP			2 ,,
	RICE	2ozs	8ozs	Nil.
	SUGAR	2 ,,	2 ,,	2ozs.
	TEA	$\frac{1}{4}$,,	$\frac{1}{4}$,, Tea, or	$\frac{1}{4}$,, Tea, or
	COFFEE	$\frac{1}{2}$,,	$\frac{1}{2}$,, Coffee	$\frac{1}{2}$,, Coffee

2. Any European or Coloured Colonist desiring to obtain Food Supplies shall, not later than 3 p.m. on the day prior to that on which such supplies are required, make and forward to the Office of the Issuer of Food Supply Permits regulating the Supplies for the Ward in which such person resides a declaration, in writing, giving full, accurate, and detailed particulars of all or any Supplies in his or her possession or control of any of the Foodstuffs or Necessaries enumerated in Section 1 of this Proclamation.

3. Every such person shall be bound to make and forward to the place and at the time mentioned in the last preceding Section a declaration showing the number of the members of the household of such person, and giving such other information as the Declaration Forms to be issued shall provide.

4. Any duly authorised Issuer of Food Supply Permits may issue a permit for such of the Foodstuffs and Necessaries hereinbefore enumerated as he shall be satisfied is necessary for the requirements of any applicant, but he may refuse to issue any permit should he deem it advisable to do so. In all cases of refusal to issue a permit the Issuer shall make an entry of the grounds of such refusal in a book to be kept for that purpose.

5. Any person applying for Supplies shall make application for a week's Supplies, and such person shall not be entitled to again apply for Supplies until the same day in the following week.

6. The person to whom any Food Supply Permit is issued may purchase and obtain the Foodstuffs and Necessaries mentioned in such permit, on production and handing over of such permit, at any Retail Store or Shop where the same are kept.

7. Every Retail Storekeeper, Dealer or Salesman who owns, possesses, or controls any of the Foodstuffs or Necessaries enumerated in Section 1 of this Proclamation shall be bound on presentation, during business hours, of any Food Supply Permit to sell, supply, and deliver to the holder of such permit the Foodstuffs and Necessaries mentioned therein on payment being made therefor in cash, at the prices already or which may be hereafter fixed in respect thereof by Proclamation or Notice duly published.

8. No Storekeeper, Dealer, Salesman, or other Person shall sell, supply, or deliver any of the Foodstuffs or Necessaries mentioned in Section 1 of this Proclamation to any person other than the holder of a Food Supply Permit.

9. That all Food Supply Permits in respect of which Foodstuffs or Necessaries shall have been supplied by any Storekeeper or Dealer shall be forwarded to the Supply Office, Lennox Street, Kimberley, when such Storekeeper or Dealer sends in his weekly requisition for further supplies.

10. Proprietors, Managers or Keepers of Hotels, Clubs, Cafes, Restaurants, Boarding Houses, or Eating Houses shall only be entitled to obtain supplies for their regular boarders.

11. Asiatics shall only be supplied at the Food Supply Depots specially appointed for the supply of Foodstuffs and Necessaries to Asiatics, and all Asiatics applying for supplies shall be bound to observe and comply with all rules and regulations from time to time exhibited in the Food Supply Depots for Asiatics.

12. Natives shall only be supplied at the Food Supply Depots specially appointed for the supply of Foodstuffs and Necessaries to Natives, and all Natives applying for supplies shall be bound to observe and comply with all rules and regulations from time to time exhibited in the Food Supply Depots for Natives.

13. Notice will be given by advertisement of the offices where Food Supply Permits may be obtained and of the places where Food Supply Depots are established for the supply of Asiatics and Natives.

14. Any Storekeeper, Dealer, Salesman, or other person whosoever who shall fail, neglect, or refuse to observe or comply with any of the provisions of this Proclamation, or who shall make an incorrect or false declaration, or who shall act in any way whatsoever contrary to the terms of this Proclamation, shall be liable to summary arrest, and to such penalties or punishment (including confiscation of goods) as to the Special Court of Summary Jurisdiction shall seem meet.

15. Every Storekeeper or Dealer shall be held liable and responsible for any act of his agent, assistant, or servant in contravention of any of the provisions of this Proclamation, and shall be punishable for the same, as well as such agent, assistant, or servant.

16. Notice No. 3, dated the 3rd day of December, 1899, signed by Major Gorle, is repealed as from the date of the publication of this Proclamation.

17. This Proclamation shall apply to the Districts of Kimberley and Beaconsfield (including Wesselton).

Given under my hand at Kimberley this 26th day of December, 1899.

GOD SAVE THE QUEEN.

R. G. KEKEWICH.

Lieutenant-Colonel, Commanding Griqualand West and Bechuanaland.

a1034

NOTICE NO. 8.

PUBLISHED IN TERMS OF PROCLAMATION No. 12.

It is hereby notified that the undermentioned are the Offices for issue of Food Supply Permits to Europeans and Coloured Colonists:

KIMBERLEY: Town Hall. BEACONSFIELD: Town Hall.

2. Food Supply Depots where food may be obtained by Asiatics and Natives:

KIMBERLEY:—

ASIATICS: No. 6, The Crescent, Malay Camp.

NATIVES: No. 1 Location, Railway Crossing, Transvaal Road; No. 2, Barkly Road; Meyer's Location, No. 3 Halkett Road; Malay Camp, No. 2, The Crescent.

BEACONSFIELD.—

NATIVES and ASIATICS: Dutoitspan and Wesselton, Gregory's Store, Castle Street.

NATIVES: Green Point and Race Course Locations, Capetown Barrier Store, Mankoroane's Location, Boshof Road Crossing Store.

By Order,

H. V. GORLE, Major, A.S.C.

Kimberley, December 26, 1899.

a1035

REDUCED FACSIMILE OF THE PROCLAMATION OF December 26, 1899, Regulating the supply of food in the beleaguered town, as published in the *Diamond Fields Advertiser*.

Ration Issue. Serving bread rations to the Loyal North Lancashires during the siege of Kimberley.

quietly explained that he had learnt that Rhodes had communicated to others the information given to him in confidence on the previous day, and he had to consider the matter not alone from the point of view of a breach of the undertaking expressly given by Rhodes, but also from the point of view of the jeopardy in which military arrangements were placed by the possibility of the Boers obtaining full knowledge of the plans which the military authorities were intending to carry out. Rhodes' answer was that he intended to make whatever use he might think necessary of the information already given to him and refused to be bound in any way as to communications made to him by Kekewich; he left the office in high dudgeon, vowing all kinds of vengeance agaist Buller and Kekewich and his staff. The rupture between the Commandant of Kimberley and the leading citizen in the town was now complete.'[52]

Rhodes now bombarded both the High Commissioner and Kekewich with petulant messages, opposing the 'removal order' and threatening to close down the mines unless he had his way, and before long his words were echoed in the columns of the *Diamond Fields Advertiser*. Rhodes was implacable and made quite clear his intention to ruin Kekewich's career and reputation.

Kekewich had fixed food prices since the early days of the siege, and on 20 December rationing was introduced and livestock slaughter was controlled. The soldiers, who for obvious reasons received more than civilians, were issued one pound of bread a day, and half a pound of meat. Vegetables were very scarce,[53] and dairy products were a rarity. It was becoming difficult to find good grazing for the cattle, but Labram built a 14,000 cubic foot cold storage chamber so that the best of them could be slaughtered before their condition went off. On 8 January horse-meat was first issued to supplement beef supplies, and shortly a 'Siege Soup' kitchen was opened. Nevertheless, hunger

52. O'Meara, pp. 82–3.
53. At a Christmas dinner party for the senior officers of the garrison, fourteen of them shared thirteen potatoes.

began to gnaw at morale and added impetus to Rhodes' querulous and intemperate tirade.

Long Tom and Long Cecil

There was indeed almost more conflict within Kimberley than without. The Boers had no wish to assault the town's defences and were content merely to blockade the place, their offensive action being limited to a desultory long-range cannonade, more inconvenient than destructive.

As has already been mentioned, the Boer guns out-ranged those of the defenders, whose stock of ammunition was limited. Labram, who spent long hours chatting to Kekewich in the Conning Tower, where they hatched many schemes, again came to the rescue. First, on the basis of information from Kekewich's staff and examination of Boer shells, he designed and manufactured 7-pounder shells in the De Beers workshops. Then, on Christmas Eve, Kekewich commissioned him to

'Long Cecil'.

The 28-pounder breech-loading gun manufactured in De Beers workshops during the siege to make up for the relative inferiority of the British artillery in range and calibre. George Labram, the designer, is standing with his arm resting on the wheel. 'Long Cecil' now stands at the Honoured Dead Memorial in Kimberley.

construct a gun to challenge the Boer artillery. Labram consulted such articles on gunnery as were available in Kimberley, and set to work to design and build what was, in all the circumstances, a quite remarkable feat of engineering. The result was 'Long Cecil', a 28-pounder rifled breech-loader which was test-fired, against the enemy, on 19 January. The correspondent in Kimberley of the *Daily Telegraph* and *Liverpool Daily Post,* heliographed the news that same day to Modder River, adding, for the further information of friend and foe, that the new gun 'fired accurately to 8,000 yards range.'

Within days of 'Long Cecil's' debut being reported in the British newspapers the Boers despatched one of their 90-pounder 'Long Tom' siege guns from Pretoria, and this formidable weapon came into action from an emplacement on the Kamfersdam Mine tailing on 7 February. This was an altogether more destructive gun than the Boer field-pieces and caused considerable alarm in Kimberley. Bombproof shelters were hastily excavated, and, in order to provide fifteen seconds warning when the big gun fired, a signaller on the Conning Tower waved a red flag (which is now in the Regimental Museum) and Regimental buglers, stationed in suitable positions, sounded a 'G'. Casualties remained remarkably few, but on 9 February one of 'Long Tom's' six inch shells hit the hotel bedroom which George Labram had just entered and killed him. The only North Lancashire casualty was Private Tom Jones, who lost a foot on the 11th when hit by a shell splinter.

'Long Cecil' engaged his new adversary, with some success: 'Several time we were covered with earth,' wrote a French volunteer with the Boers, 'and I am certain that out of twenty shells, the extreme error was not more than 200 metres. One fortunately fell diagonally on 'Long Tom's' very platform, rebounded, and burst a little way off. Seven men were killed.'[54]

Early on the 10th Kekewich sent out some thirty volunteers, including eighteen selected Lancashire marksmen, under Lieutenant Augustus Wallace, to harass 'Long Tom's' crew. One hour before dawn the 'snipers' had dug in behind a bank, which provided good cover some 1,200 to 1,500 yards south of the big gun's emplacement. Whenever 'Long Tom's' muzzle ran out to the firing position its embrasure was engaged with sustained and effective rifle fire. The 'sniping' party remained out all day, returning after dark. The success of this tactic was so marked that it was repeated daily for the remainder of the siege. On the 12th Kekewich again deployed thirty men, together with a Maxim, who pushed their trenches forward to some 700 to 800 yards from 'Long Tom'. 'It is wonderful nobody has been hit so far,' he remarked to his diary. 'There were some very narrow shaves today,

54. *Ten Months in the Field with the Boers*, 1901, p. 68.

'Long Tom'. Six inch shells from this 100-pounder Boer gun were fired into Kimberley for the last nine days of the siege, but its effectiveness was limited both by the fire of 'Long Cecil' and by snipers of the Loyal North Lancashires, who hit the chief gun-layer.

bullets passing through one man's hat and another's sleeve. The enemy had a large number of riflemen firing all day at our snipers from trenches at the foot of Kamfersdam.' The most notable victim of the North Lancashire marksmen was Leon, the Boer's chief gun layer, from the Creusot factory in France, who was shot through the forehead.

Despite all efforts to silence 'Long Tom', he made life distinctly unpleasant for those whose duties kept them above ground during his hours of work. The Conning Tower was a favourite target, and there were some uncomfortably near misses. One shell passed under its canvas awning and another, while Kekewich was on the tower, went through its supporting bars, and a large splinter struck some five feet below the signalling platform, making the whole structure shudder. Although casualties and damage remained remarkably light,[55] the big gun continued to erode the fragile morale of a vocal element of Kimberley's residents, and a message sent by Kekewich on 10 February betrays his growing anxiety at that time: 'Enemy recommenced bombardment with six inch gun 6 a.m. today. Nerves of inhabitants much shaken by continuous bombardment for three days. Difficulties being experienced by them fetching daily rations. Necessity for relief becoming urgent. Have not sufficient troops for sortie against Kamfersdam, which most strongly entrenched and held.'

55. The total number of civilian casualties from shell-fire during the four month siege amounted to nine killed and about sixteen wounded.

'Why Kimberley Cannot Wait'

The understandable fears of the civilian population were played upon by Rhodes, who now whipped up sustained agitation for the immediate relief of the town and made every effort to force Lord Roberts to subordinate his longer-term plans to that object. Rhodes' high-handed activities, involving direct and contemptuous defiance of the military commander of Kimberley, led inevitably to confrontation with Kekewich, which came to a head on 10 February. On that day the *Diamond Fields Advertiser* carried an hysterical article entitled 'Why Kimberley Cannot Wait' which repeated, almost word for word, many of Rhodes' intemperate views and his demand for immediate relief. Rhodes then presented himself at Kekewich's headquarters and insisted that a message, prepared at a meeting of the leading citizens of Kimberley, which he had convened in defiance of Kekewich, should be flashed to Lord Roberts. Kekewich demurred, pointing out that as his signallers were very busy dealing with military work he could make no promise that Rhodes' long text could be encoded and sent that day, but undertook to send a precis of the views expressed. At this, Rhodes flew into a violent rage, producing a tirade of accusations.

'Rhodes ... made grossly insulting remarks about the British Army and, finally, clenching his fist, made a rush at Kekewich, shouting the meanwhile: "I know what damned rot your signallers are wasting their time in signalling. You low, damned, mean cur, Kekewich, you deny me at your peril." The Mayor and a staff officer were standing in front of Kekewich's desk and Rhodes' doubled fist shot over their shoulders. Kekewich at once rose from his desk; he was ashen pale and the fire of fierce anger shone in his eyes. For a moment it looked as if the two men would come to blows, but Rhodes suddenly turned round and made for the door and was hastily followed out by the Mayor.'[56] It was, according to Kekewich's very restrained diary, 'a most disagreeable interview'.

As promised, later that day Kekewich signalled to Lord Roberts, who had now assumed personal command at the Modder River, a fair summary of the document produced by Rhodes: 'First. Answer required whether immediate effort being made to relieve Kimberley. Second. Duration siege, shortness proper food, hardships endured, disease prevalent strongly represented. Third. Consternation destruction of life, property caused by enemy's siege gun pointed out. Fourth. Their views military situation stated.'

From this, and other febrile messages received direct from Rhodes, Roberts incorrectly, but understandably, inferred that Rhodes was

56. O'Meara, pp. 114–15.

contemplating surrender if his demand for immediate relief was not met, and he accordingly sent two signals to Kimberley. The first of these was intended to be seen by Rhodes:

'I beg you will represent to Mayor and Rhodes as strongly as you possibly can disastrous and humiliating effect of surrendering after so prolonged and glorious defence. Many days cannot possibly pass before Kimberley will be relieved as we commence active operations tomorrow. Our future military operations depend in a large degree on your maintaining your position a very short time longer, and our prestige would suffer severely if Kimberley were to fall into hands of enemy. Those, therefore, who counsel surrender should now carefully consider the very serious responsibility they incur from National point of view.'

The second signal was for Kekewich, urging robust action against any dissidents:

'As I understand Kimberley is under Martial Law, you have full authority to prohibit, by force if necessary, any public meeting you consider undesirable under present circumstances, and also to arrest any individual, no matter what his position may be, who may act in manner prejudicial to National interests. I desire you to exercise to the full, if necessary, yours power as defined above, and you will have my fullest support in so doing. You can assure all who are now apprehensive that we shall strain every nerve to relieve you, which will I hope be in a few days time.'

Realising that he had over-played his hand, Rhodes responded (after Kekewich had refused to send his original, abusive, reply) with a more conciliatory, if disingenuous, message redirecting his criticism of military operations towards Buller:

'We have never thought or spoken of surrendering, but the endless delay of your predecessor led us to believe that no efforts were being made for our relief and by force of circumstances this community would have been crushed. I thought it right to send you the situation from the principal citizens.'

In his own candid reply to Lord Roberts, Kekewich too sought to defuse the situation, giving Rhodes his due and explaining the precarious internal balance of power in Kimberley:

'Rhodes during siege has done excellent work for welfare town and defenders; and also, when his views on military questions have coincided with mine, he has readily assisted me, but he desires to control the military situation. I have refused to be dictated to by him; on such occasions he has been grossly insulting to me, and in his remarks on British army. More can be explained when we meet. I have put up with insults so as not to risk safety of defence. Key of military situation here in one sense in Rhodes' hands for large majority Town Guardsmen, Kimberley Light Horse and Volunteers are De Beers employees. Fully realise powers conferred on me by existence Martial Law, but have not sufficient military force to compel obedience. Conflict between few Imperial troops here and local levies has been and must continue to be avoided at all costs.'

Typhoid at the Modder

In the days immediately following the disastrous battle of Magersfontein the left wing of the Loyal North Lancashires was several times sent out to make demonstrations towards the Boer positions, coming under enemy shell-fire without loss. On 19 and 20 December the companies were inspected by Lord Methuen, who complimented them on being the smartest unit in his force and on their sharpness in turning out. On 21 December 'D' and 'F' Companies marched to Klokfontein, where in mid-January they were joined by the rest of the wing. Private H. Ashworth, a newsagent's son from Nelson, wrote home:

'The North Lancashires are formed in two parties, namely two companies at the old reservoir, near where there is a river flowing, and from where our men were drinking, and in which they were washing and getting their drinking water, until some horses were taken to water. The horses, however, refused to drink, and then they stampeded, thus loosening some bodies, which were found to be those of dead Boers. The engineers then sent a dragging party and found about 107 bodies, all Boers, besides horses, so you can see the reason we can't get any accurate account of the Boers' killed. All the bodies had a rope with a stone attached, so that they would sink. Our men – I mean a percentage – are stricken down with typhoid fever, and the General is going to relieve them from the place, which I think will not be too soon.

'Where I am stationed, with the other two companies, is about five miles from the reservoir at a place called Klokfontein, which also has a history. We are all lively here, and to get a wash we have to walk about three miles, and then we can't go individually; we have to go in parties of about twenty or thirty men, and have our rifles and 50 rounds of ammunition. We have not had the pleasure of a wash every morning, and you would be surprised to see a group of men waiting for their turn to wash in about two pints of water, and even that is a luxury, so you see it is not all what the public of England think. We have to rough it, and pretty hard at times, but thank God we all know what we are doing. We know that God is good, and we hope to say we have relieved our downtrodden countrymen.'[57]

57. Letter dated Klockfontein, January 1900, published in the *Nelson Chronicle*, 16 February 1900.

The Relief of Kimberley

At 6 a.m. on the morning of 14 February John Major Fraser of the North Lancashires, who commanded at Beaconsfield, received a report that the Boers had evacuated Alexandersfontein, some seven miles south-east of Kimberley, apparently alarmed at the anticipated approach of British cavalry. Fraser at once dashed out with about one hundred of the Town Guard and occupied the place, capturing some prisoners and a quantity of food and ammunition in what had been a Boer supply depot. Later that morning Fraser was relieved by Captain O'Brien, who was tasked to hold Alexandersfontein with a force of some three hundred men, two guns and a Maxim, including 'A' and 'B' Companies of the Loyal North Lancashires. The enemy were all about and kept up a heavy artillery and small arms cross-fire on the defenders all day. The fight was renewed with warmth the following morning and lasted until about 2.30 p.m., when Tim O'Brien saw, amid a mighty cloud of dust, a large body of horsemen bearing down on his post from the south-east. Despatching a bicycle orderly, pedalling furiously towards Beaconsfield with an urgent request for reinforcements, O'Brien prepared to make a stand against the advancing host. At Beaconsfield, however, Fraser had already seen heliograph signals far out on the veldt, and just before 4 p.m. the defenders received a heliograph message from Lieutenant-General French, who was rapidly approaching with his cavalry division – some five thousand mounted men. After four months, Kimberley was relieved.

Seeing that the Boers were retreating, Kekewich ordered Murray to take all available troops and move north at once in hot pursuit to cut off the retreat of 'Long Tom' and take as many prisoners as possible. Murray quickly collected some four hundred mounted men, four guns and two horsed Maxims, together with 'A' and 'H' Companies of the Loyal North Lancashires, who at 6 p.m. marched out towards Kamfersdam. This force soon occupied positions stretching on a wide north–south front from the Intermediate Pumping Station to opposite

Alexandersfontein. Occupied by Major Fraser on the morning of 24 February, then held by Captain O'Brien under heavy fire until the following afternoon when French's relieving Cavalry Division rode in from the south-east.

the Kamfersdam tailing, but as it was getting dark and enemy strength was unknown the troops were ordered to stand fast until dawn. That night Boer ox-wagons were heard on the move, and shots were exchanged between outposts. At first light the enemy position was rushed, but 'Long Tom' had vanished. The great gun had somehow been spirited away and was, indeed, never seen again.

About 5 o'clock Kekewich rode towards Alexandersfontein, where he hoped to meet French, but somehow missed the commander of the relief force, who was instead welcomed by the Mayor of Kimberley. Kekewich met Rimington's Tigers, and then conducted the 1st Cavalry Brigade to its bivouac area, and it was evening before the victorious Commandant of Kimberley headed back to his headquarters. He decided to call in at the Sanitorium Hotel, where Rhodes had been resident throughout the siege, on the off-chance of meeting French there.

'As we approached the building,' wrote O'Meara, 'we heard sounds of merriment and many voices in the hall, and a few minutes later we entered the hotel. Tables were laid in the hall, laden with all manner of luxuries, champagne was flowing freely, and to us, who had seen nothing but the meagre rations served daily at the Kimberley Club for many weeks past, this display of dainties came as a great surprise. Rhodes was now entertaining French and his staff, who, we learnt, had been invited to stay at the hotel as his guests during their halt at Kimberley. Rhodes was in the hall when Kekewich arrived; the two men had not met since the stormy interview of the afternoon of 10th February, and Kekewich naturally wished to avoid any altercation, so he remained by the door by which he had entered. Fortunately, a staff officer came along and Kekewich went forward

Kekewich meets the Relief Force outside Beaconsfield. Not for him, however, the public and military accolades which were heaped on White of Ladysmith and Baden-Powell of Mafeking. While the victorious Garrison Commander dutifully conducted the cavalry to their bivouac areas, Rhodes was entertaining French and poisoning his perception of Kekewich's successful defence.

The Honoured Dead Memorial, Kimberley.

On this monument to those who fell in the siege are the following lines by Rudyard Kipling:

> This is a charge to our children in sign of the price we paid, / The price that we paid for freedom that comes unsoiled to our hand, / Read, revere and uncover, here are the victors laid, / They that died for their country – being sons of the land.

and told him that he wished to see General French. Rhodes observed this and, rushing forward, attempted to block the stairway, shouting: "You shan't see French; this is my house, get out of it." Kekewich took no notice of Rhodes' ill-mannered conduct, but accompanied the staff officer upstairs.

'Kekewich went into the room occupied by French and saw him alone; the interview was extremely short, and the former at once returned to the Kimberley Club. The conclusions, if any, the Cavalry Commander had then come to as to the conduct of Kekewich during the siege must have been founded alone on information derived from *ex parte* statements made by Rhodes. On the ride back to the Club Kekewich said little, but from that little it was not difficult to draw the inference that he had met with an icy reception.'[58]

At 6 o'clock next morning, the 16th, French, accompanied by Kekewich, rode north towards Dronfield with two cavalry brigades and Alderson's Mounted Infantry. Murray also advanced, and opened the day's activities by attacking a Boer position at Dronfield Siding. French's cavalry joined the engagement, which continued all day as

58. O'Meara, pp. 133–4.

the retreating Boers fought a stubborn rearguard action to protect their wagons; but the unacclimatised British cavalry horses, still out of condition from their sea voyage, were exhausted after their four-day advance, and the veldt was soon littered with dead and dying animals. Late in the afternoon French broke off the engagement. 'A' and 'H' Companies of the North Lancashires, who had been out all the previous night, were in action on the left flank till evening and had a sergeant and three privates wounded.

The following morning Kekewich arrived at his headquarters to find that he had been replaced as Commandant in Kimberley. Rhodes' poison had done its intended work. Indeed, although Kekewich was promoted to brevet-colonel and awarded a CB, he was returned to Regimental duty and it was not until July 1901, after the Mayor of Kimberley had interceded with the War Office on his behalf, that the defender of the Diamond Fields was given command of a column.

Presentation of the Kimberley Memorials.

On 26 June 1908, at the Curragh Camp near Dublin, massive silver replicas of the Honoured Dead Memorial were presented to the Officers' and Sergeants' Messes of the 1st Loyal North Lancashires. The presentation was made, on behalf of the citizens of Kimberley and Beaconsfield, by Colonel Sir David Harris, commanding the Kimberley Regiment. These two fine centrepieces remain on display to the present day in the respective messes of The Queen's Lancashire Regiment, now allied to the Kimberley Regiment.

The defence of Kimberley had cost 1st Battalion The Loyal North Lancashire Regiment two killed in action, thirteen wounded and six died of disease or by accident, while in the course of operations for its relief a further ten were killed in action or died from their wounds, thirteen had died of disease and thirty-six had been wounded.

Rhodes had his moment of triumph, but by his insistence on priority being given to the relief of Kimberley he had unwittingly brought about the virtual destruction as an effective fighting force of the Cavalry Division, the one formation in Roberts' army which had the mobility to out-manoeuvre the mounted Boers. He thereby made a major contribution towards lengthening the war that his own overweening ambitions had in large part unleashed.

The town of Kimberley was generous towards its defenders. Every member of the garrison was presented with the semi-official Mayor's Siege Medal, otherwise known as the Kimberley Star.[59] This unusual civic medal is a six-pointed star surmounted by a chased bar and a ribbon of dark blue, white, blue and orange. On the obverse is the Kimberley coat-of-arms and its motto, 'Spero Meliora', with the word 'Kimberley' inscribed above and the date '1899–1900' below, while on the reverse the words 'Mayor's Siege Medal, 1900' are engraved. On 9 July 1902 a grand reception was held in Kimberley for Colonel Robert Kekewich, at which he was presented with a sword of honour by the citizens and diamonds by their ladies.

Over the resting place in Kimberley of some of the fallen, the Honoured Dead memorial was raised, a classical monument with the famous gun 'Long Cecil' on its pediment, and on 26 June 1908 a pair of massive silver replicas of this memorial were presented by the citizens of Kimberley and Beaconsfield to the Officers' and Sergeants' Messes of 1st Battalion The Loyal North Lancashire Regiment. To the present day these imposing centrepieces are proudly displayed in the Messes of 1st Battalion The Queen's Lancashire Regiment, constant and very visible reminders of one of the Regiment's unique Battle Honours.

59. These medals were stuck in England at the expense of the Town Council and first distributed on 15 April 1901, though it was not until 17 July that year that the War Office grudgingly conceded that they could be issued, but not worn.

Pride of the Regiment.

Regimental Colours and Trophies of the Fighting 40th at Cork, 1895. The latter commemorate actions on four continents and include (*bottom left*) the Drum Major's staff of the French 65th Regiment, captured near Salamanca in 1812, the Maharajpore Drum (*centre*), captured in 1843, and a cabinet including a Germantown Medal, remembering a gallant action in 1777, and a Victoria Cross of 1861 from the Maori Wars. The silver sphinx is a presentation piece of 1871. The Colours are guarded by two Colour Sergeants and supported by two drummer boys, the one on the left being Boy Boast, from a well-known Regimental family.

PART II

The Relief of Ladysmith

'Remember, men, the eyes of Lancashire are watching you today'
(Lieutenant-Colonel W. MacCarthy O'Leary)

'Gentlemen in Khaki Ordered South'

The morning of Thursday 30 November 1899 dawned dull and grey in Preston, Lancashire, but up at Fulwood Barracks the lights were on long before dawn in the old grit-stone buildings ranged solidly around its two squares. Reveille was at five o'clock, and when the bugle sounded the assembly, a little after seven, over eleven hundred officers and men of 1st Battalion South Lancashire clattered over the cobbles and fell in by companies on the front, or Infantry Square, together with a draft of one hundred and fifty reservists destined for 1st Loyal North Lancashires in Kimberley and at the Modder River.

The 1st Battalion South Lancashire Regiment had at last been 'ordered south' to join Buller's army and, despite the pangs of family partings on the square that morning, the men were in excellent spirits and an air of highly charged and barely suppressed excitement pervaded the old barracks.

The South Lancashires were not in Buller's original Corps, mobilised in October, but were ordered out on 11 November as part of Sir Charles Warren's 5th Division. As a Home Service battalion they needed to be brought up to strength with reservists, and some 650 former soldiers of the Regiment, mostly from Warrington, St Helens and the surrounding area of industrial South Lancashire, were mobilised and equipped at the Regimental Depot in Orford Barracks, Warrington. These, together with a first draft of reservists for the North Lancashires, had now rejoined the Colours, and Fulwood was full to overflowing, with men sleeping on the floors and each barrack room accommodating double its normal occupants. Khaki drab uniform was issued, columns of reservists marched out through the Lancashire countryside to blow away the cobwebs of civilian life and to harden their feet, while those unaccustomed to the Lee-Metford rifle were sent for musketry instruction at Fleetwood. 'The reservists and the old hands worked well together,' reported the *Lancashire Daily*

Lieutenant Fred Raphael.

'I only hope it won't all be over before we get there.'

Post, 'considering there have been changes in the mode of drilling since the former left the ranks.'[1] The Colours were sent down to Warrington for safe-keeping, and packing was completed.

'Am awfully busy getting my own fighting kit and fixing up the men,' wrote 29-year-old Lieutenant Fred Raphael to his sister, 'We have a grand body of the latter, and ought to carry everything before us with them.'[2] Frederick Melchior Raphael, strongly built and six foot one inch tall, was educated at Wellington and joined the South Lancashires from the Militia in 1891. Popular with all ranks, a good shot and a keen cricketer, he was a member of a well-known family of Jewish stockbrokers long established in England. After years of peacetime soldiering, he welcomed without reservation the challenge of active service.

The 1st Battalion South Lancashires had been stationed in Fulwood Barracks since earlier that year, and were towards the end of a period of home service, most recently at Birr, Cork and Fermoy in Ireland.

1. *Lancashire Daily Post*, 23 November 1899.
2. Lieutenant F. M. Raphael, 1st South Lancashires, letter from Preston dated 16 November 1899.

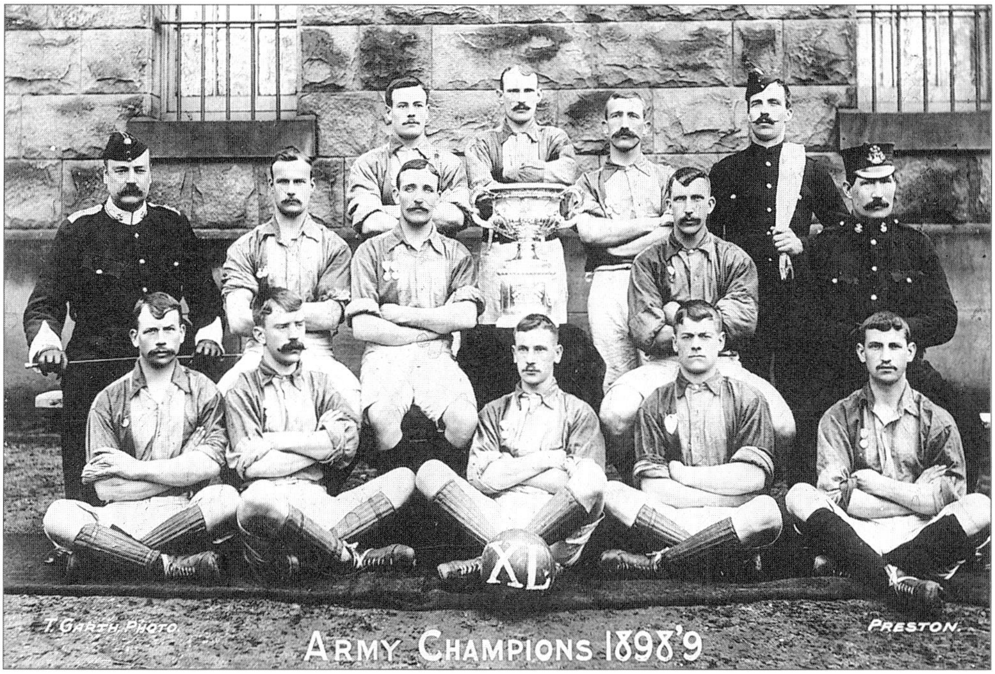

The Army Cup comes to Fulwood.

1st Battalion The South Lancashire Regiment (PWV) Football Team at Fulwood Barracks, Preston, with the Army Football Cup, won on 3 April 1899. Prestonian Colour-Sergeant John Nolan (*seated left of Cup*), the Captain, attributed the victory to the experience and confidence gained in playing against professional teams in Lancashire, including Preston North End and Blackburn Rovers. 'They played a good game,' remarked Lieutenant-Colonel MacCarthy O'Leary (*seated left*), whose enthusiasm for sport had been a major factor in the South Lancashires' success, 'but it is not the only one they can play. They have played on harder fields than football fields.'

Officers and men alike were intensely proud of their history as the old 'Fighting Fortieth'. This nickname was no idle boast, for when, in 1881, the old 40th Regiment became 1st Battalion The South Lancashire Regiment, its Colours carried more battle honours than any other English regiment. Nevertheless, the Battalion had seen no active service since the Maori Wars of the eighteen-sixties.

Lieutenant-Colonel William MacCarthy O'Leary, who had commanded the 40th since November 1896, was in his fifty-first year. A large, warm-hearted Irishman who was proud to hail from 'the dear old County of Cork', he was educated at Stonyhurst College, Lancashire and entered the 82nd Regiment (Prince of Wales's Volunteers) as an ensign in 1869, under the old purchase system. At six foot four inches, 'Big Mick' was the tallest man in the Regiment and his powerfully built figure was a familiar and imposing presence both on the Lancashire scene and in his native Cork, where he was a Justice of the Peace. MacCarthy O'Leary was a keen sportsman, and under his enthusiastic leadership the 40th had brought the Army Football Cup home with them to Preston earlier that year. Loved, admired and respected by all ranks, he was a firm disciplinarian but knew when to temper Queen's Regulations with fatherly forbearance, and his proud, good-humoured but understated spirit pervaded a battalion which he had fashioned in his own robust image. William MacCarthy

Lieutenant-Colonel William MacCarthy O'Leary.

Commanding Officer 1st Battalion The South Lancashire Regiment (PWV) 1896–1900. 'Big Mick', 6 foot 4 inches tall and generous of frame and spirit, was loved and respected by both officers and men, from whom he expected the very best. This photograph was taken at Fermoy, County Cork, where the 40th were stationed in 1897.

O'Leary was a man of few, well-chosen words. Indeed, when asked to speak at a public meeting in Wigan he demurred, replying 'Deeds, not words, are more in our line.' Nevertheless, on the day before departure he called his men together:

'I have paraded you this morning to speak to you for the last time prior to embarking for foreign service. I know you don't care for addresses, and neither do I. However, just a word about the friends we have made here since our arrival. As you are aware, the inhabitants of Preston have made each one of you a present of a pipe and one pound of tobacco. But this is not all. The Mayor would have been here to address you only that this place is out of his jurisdiction. However, he has informed me that he will wave his adieu to us from the Town Hall as we pass by. As regards myself, I can only tell you this is the proudest moment of my life, to be placed in command of a fine old regiment like the 40th. I have spent thirty years and eight months as a soldier in it. I need not say anything to you as regards your conduct in the field. I know that you will all do your best to keep up the name of the old corps – a corps second to none. Your predecessors fought and died for the name which it now bears, and

Officers of 1st Battalion The South Lancashire Regiment at Fulwood Barracks.

Before their departure for South Africa on 30 November 1899. *Front row, left to right*: Maj T. Lamb, Lt Col W. MacCarthy O'Leary, Maj R. H. Hall (2ic), Capt N. M. Lynch. *Middle row*: Lts G. Carlyon, F. M. Raphael and H. R. Kane, Capts E. T. James, B. R. Goren, and C. G. Birch, 2nd-Lt C. H. Marsh. *Third row*: Lts R. C. Trousdale, S. H. Skinner and H. K. Woods, Capt H. A. H. Bailey (Adjt). *Back row*: Capt S. Upperton, Lt E. F. Oakley, an officer of the Hampshire Regiment, 2nd-Lt G. R. Mott.

Fulwood Barracks main gate, *c.* **1900.**
The gateway arch has since been demolished, though the royal arms were preserved and now mark the site. The main range of buildings behind remains intact and now houses the Regimental Headquarters and Museum of The Queen's Lancashire Regiment (open to the public) and, over the massive arch, the Garrison Church.

the honours which you now wear, and I feel sure that one and all will do their best to add to them and to prove that we are still the old "Fighting 40th".'[3]

On the morning of departure the troops wore full foreign service marching order, but in view of the season had their warmer home service uniforms beneath the newly issued, and rather thin, khaki drab. All had Slade-Wallace equipment, but whilst the South Lancashires carried the bolt-action .303 Lee-Metford, the British Army's first magazine rifle, the North Lancashire reservists were issued with the improved Lee-Enfield.

Soon after eight o'clock, the Band of 1st Volunteer Battalion Loyal North Lancashires arrived at the barracks and took up a position near the gate. The first detachment of the South Lancashires prepared to march, some 250 men including the Battalion staff, Band and Drums. 'Just prior to starting,' recorded *The Preston Herald*, 'Colonel MacCarthy O'Leary called for three cheers for the Queen, and the response was very hearty; and a salvo was added for the benefit of Kruger.'[4] Led by the Colonel and his staff, the Fighting 40th swung off under the massive stone entrance arch of Fulwood Barracks and through the

3. *Lancashire Daily Post*, 29 November 1899.
4. *The Preston Herald*, 2 December 1899.

gate, surmounted by the Royal arms, which was picketed by some two to three hundred soldiers of the North and East Lancashire Regiments. The Volunteer Band played them out of the barracks gate with 'The Farewell March' to the rousing cheers of their comrades. At half-past eight the second detachment of the South Lancashires marched out, seven hundred men commanded by Major Hall, as the Regular and Volunteer Bands of the Loyal North Lancashires played 'The Farewell March'. The men, who spent the last few minutes shaking hands and taking leave of their comrades, were again heartily cheered.

There were, according to *The Lancashire Daily Post*, some less conventional departures: 'Several of the men stayed out as late as possible seeing their wives and families and friends, and came running in at the last moment. Considering the liberal way in which the men have been treated to intoxicants by their civilian friends, they have behaved exceedingly well. It was necessary, however, to send one man down in a hansom. He did not wish to proceed in this ignominious fashion, but the only alternative offered him was that of staying behind altogether. This he would not agree to, and drove off amidst the derisive cheers of his fellows. Another feature was the case of Private Grundy. This gallant soldier was kept on hand to fill any vacancy that might occur, and he was hoping that the chance to go would come to him. But the ranks were filled, and as a last resort Private Grundy got in amongst his comrades thinking that he would never be noticed. But he was, and was hauled out. However, just as the detachment had got outside the gates it was found that there was a man missing, and Private Grundy got his chance. He was sent for, and to see him doing the double across the square to catch his comrades was a sight to be remembered.'[5]

A little after nine o'clock the last contingent left Fulwood Barracks. It included a final company of the South Lancashires, with fatigue men, pioneers, servants, and others, and the Loyal North Lancashire reservists. Of the latter it was said that: 'These men belong for the most part to Preston and Blackburn and neighbourhood, and are a well set-up lot of fellows.' The band played 'The Red Rose', the regimental march of the Loyal North Lancashire Regiment, as they passed out of the barracks and marched down Deepdale Road, Church Street and Fishergate, past the old Town Hall, to Central Station. The patriotic demonstration which followed was such as has almost certainly never been seen in Preston before or since.

'Folks were streaming up Deepdale Road before eight o'clock in a never-ending torrent, and when the first detachment passed down,

5. *Lancashire Daily Post*, 30 November 1899.

the roadway was well lined with spectators, who cheered loudly and waved their pocket-handkerchiefs as the "gentlemen in khaki" marched gaily by, headed by their own band playing lustily. At many of the houses flags had been hung from the windows, and numbers of the onlookers had provided themselves with bannerettes. Some 20 minutes elapsed before the second portion of the corps came in sight, and by that time the crowd had greatly increased. It was especially dense near Deepdale Station, where the press was so great that it was almost impossible to pass along the road, and from this point there was a splendid view of the approaching troops as they breasted the hill. Every window was occupied, whilst men, women, and children who were not able to attain that more lofty elevation clung to palisades and railings. Church Street had for once laid aside its accustomed appearance of stolid prosperity, and there was a great display of banners from the shops. As the troops progressed the enthusiasm waxed greater and greater. Men shouted, women laughed and cried, children uttered shrill little screams of delight and surprise, the soldiers waved their hats and cheered, shook hands with their friends, and most of them kissed as many girls as they could. They were in great form, and thoroughly appreciated the demonstration.

'But the great reception was reserved for the third lot [the Loyal North Lancashires, many of whom were local men]. The roads were crammed with people, wedged tighter than the proverbial herrings in a box, and on entering Church Street the men had to adopt a single file and struggle along as best they could ... The hilarity of the men knew no bounds. Most of them were unmistakably glad to get off to the war, and right royally did they enjoy the demonstration in their honour. Pushing and struggling, dragged about, clapped on the back, shaken by the hand, the men gradually forced their way along, but it was nearly half past ten before the small body of officers in the rear passed the Town Hall. One of the bands had to march in couples, and under the circumstances their performance of 'Auld Lang Syne' was very creditable.' [6]

'Some wives clung to their husbands. One private [Boyd, a reservist who in civil life was a popular Preston postman] caught sight of his wife and little baby in the crowd. He broke from the ranks and kissed the child. The crowd cheered, raised him shoulder high with the baby in his arms, and carried him to the station. Another noticed his wife fall back fainting. He stepped out, knelt by her until she came round, and then kissed her goodbye. He, too, was carried shoulder high.' [7]

6. *The Lancashire Daily Post*, 30 November 1899.
7. *The Times*, 1 December 1899.

Departure of the 1st South Lancashires from Preston, 30 November 1899.

'From the Town Hall to the railway station the crowd was just one dense mass of human beings,' wrote Private Neligan, 'all struggling to get a glimpse of the boys in khaki. All along Fishergate the windows and balconies had been requisitioned, and were crowded with people waving flags and bunting of every description, and calling out "good bye" to the soldiers below.'

'The crowd was the densest at the Town Hall and Railway Station. During the early hours of the morning – even before the dawn – people had been streaming from the district around to these common centres. At half past eight the long length of Fishergate, from the Town Hall to the Railway Station, was filled with a dense, swaying, expectant multitude. The windows and balconies were crowded. The Union Jack and British Ensign floated from many a building, and here and there valedictory mottoes were to be seen, such as "Say 'au revoir' but not good-bye", "On to Pretoria!" and "Godspeed!" Some of the tradesmen had the whole frontages decorated with coloured draperies. Such a vast concourse had not been seen in the main thoroughfares since the celebration of the Guild Merchant, nearly twenty years ago, and certainly the enthusiasm, amounting at times to the wildest excitement, no living man has seen the like of in this ancient town.

'The Mayor, the Mayoress, the members of the Town Council, and

Crowds in Church Street, Preston, 30 November 1899.

a large number of ladies and gentlemen – who had been specially invited by his Worship – assembled on the balcony of the Town Hall to give the troops a parting cheer.' Then Colonel MacCarthy O'Leary appeared, marching at the head of the first detachment. 'Turning half-round, he waved his helmet, and called for three cheers for the Mayor, which was responded to most lustily by the soldiers.' Detachment after detachment struggled through the crowd amidst roars of applause while the bands played "The Soldiers of the Queen", "Stanley for Ever" and "Auld Lang Syne".'[8]

'Men and women laughed and wept alternately,' wrote Private

8. *The Lancashire Daily Post*, 30 November 1899.

Thomas Neligan of the South Lancashire Regiment, 'and some of the younger women became quite hysterical. The remarks passed were nearly all relating to President Kruger, and had he been present I don't think he would have enjoyed himself very much. "Don't forget to make 'Owd Kruger' dance when tha' gets to Africa," could be heard from the men, whilst the only appeal from the women, young and old, was "Don't forget to bring 'Owd Kruger's' whiskers back." When the head of the regiment reached the Theatre Royal, as if by common consent, that vast multitude sang the National Anthem, followed by "The Soldiers of the Queen"; in fact, the enthusiasm of the people knew no bounds, and many were the gifts received by the soldiers from stranger as well as friend. Occasionally one heard such a remark as "Cheer up, owd lads, you'll be back agean i' three months; you're only gooing on a picnic." After leaving the barracks in column of fours we arrived at the station one at a time, and about twenty yards apart.'[9]

At the station 'the wives and relatives of some of the soldiers were passed through, and one may fitly draw a veil over the sad and in some cases heartbreaking scenes of saying "Good-bye". The saddest of all was the wife of a sergeant who had four little ones with her, and both the soldier and his wife and children were clinging to one another for some time. However, there were the more humorous aspects of the send-off. Whilst the men were halted the band played lively airs; a group of soldiers grounded arms and kit and treated their comrades to a breezy dance containing some original figures. One tall and muscular dark-moustached private, hailing from East Lancashire, lustily shouted "Cheer up! We'll do you credit. Look bright! Nooan of them sad faces now." ... One of the men shouted for "Three cheers for our grand old Colonel," and a voice replied "Aye, we'll follow him!" Then followed a round of hurrahs given with gusto, the men's faces lighting up with enthusiasm.'

'As the men marched along the platform there was a venerable pensioner of the old 40th, his breast covered with war medals, and many of the men spat on the finger and touched the medals for luck as they passed. They seemed to regard the presence of the old man – and how he got there goodness knows – as a most lucky omen. All the sage old boy said was "Good-bye! Be brave, my lads!" And the invariable exclamation was "Never fear!" The veteran was former Sergeant Kendal of the 40th, described as "a hale old man of 85 years". As a young soldier in India he had fought at the bloody battle of Maharajpore, in 1843, when the red-coated 40th marched boldly across the shell-shot plain to capture three heavily-defended artillery batteries

9. *From Preston to Ladysmith*, pp. 6–7, T. Neligan, Preston.

in succession, and in the arduous New Zealand campaign, and he had served with men who fought at Waterloo. Now he had come up from Tamworth to attend the Sergeants' Mess farewell dinner and to see his old Regiment off to war. Such, as the young soldiers who filed onto Preston Station had instinctively recognised, is the precious continuity of Regimental tradition.

Then the second column arrived, seven hundred men led by the Band of 1st Volunteer Battalion North Lancashires. 'On came the men steadily, six deep, looking every inch armed warriors – real Lancashire die-hards. Then they were halted and were glad to cast off impedimenta and have a smoke. They spoke of the coming fight, and one Hibernian ejaculated, between a white puff from his pipe, "Begorra, we're burrnun for ut." The brass and fife and drum bands meanwhile made the rafters ring with "The Girl I Left Behind Me", "Rule Britannia", and "The Soldiers of the Queen", the men often singing snatches and occasionally waving red, white and blue handkerchiefs with which they made quite gay their helmets, or bunches of fluttering ribbons of the same hue.' [10]

At length the last train pulled out for Liverpool. 'The band played the National Anthem, the coaches move, all heads are bared; cheers again and again renewed fill the air, the train passes over a long line of fog signals, which pepper like the volley which may soon ring from the barrels of these Lancashire lads.' [11]

Along the line to Liverpool, in towns and villages, crowds had assembled to wave farewell as the troop trains rolled through. 'At Lostock Hall', for instance, 'many people eagerly awaited the trains from Preston, and flags were flying, and handkerchiefs waving. The approach of the trains was known by the report of a number of signals, which also had the effect of making the soldiers look through the carriage windows. The men were heartily cheered on their way, and in return they, too, enthusiastically waved handkerchiefs and cheered lustily.' [12]

The scenes in Liverpool were equally extraordinary, with bands and cheering crowds again much in evidence, and the soldiers' wives and sweethearts stormed the dock gates. The Regiment marched behind the Cunard band from the North Mersey railway siding to the Alexandra Dock embarkation shed to board the *S.S. Canada*: 'Here was a scene of greatest excitement, A number of privates, after being marched into the shed, endeavoured to make their exit to bid adieu to their friends, and although the police attempted to keep them back

10. *The Lancashire Daily Post*, 30 November 1899.
11. Ibid.
12. Ibid.

Tommy Atkins was not to be denied. Seeing that the men were resolute the mounted police formed in front of the huge doorway, but with characteristic dogged determination the men flew in a body at the horses, which retired before the onrush, and as the khaki uniforms burst forth into the open a wild cheer burst from the crowd. Many heartrending scenes were witnessed. Mothers followed their sons, and wives their husbands until they were torn away by the hand of the law. So roughly was this done in many instances that the crowd showed their disapproval by hooting loudly.'[13]

The *Canada* was not sailing until the following morning, but once aboard, the soldiers were not allowed to leave the ship, though according to Neligan some daring spirits managed to climb down the sides. 'In attempting to jump from the deck to the landing stage, one of them actually leapt into the water; fortunately he was fished out a sadder, wiser and wetter man, his enthusiastic patriotism being fairly damped.'[14] During the afternoon the Lord Mayor of Liverpool, accompanied by the High Sheriff, came aboard the troopship to bid the men farewell.

Bound for Table Bay

At about 11 a.m. on 1 December the *Canada* weighed anchor and left the Mersey, bound for the Cape. As the ship pulled out into the Mersey there came a final moment of glorious incongruity when the hardened Liverpool dockers lined the quayside to sing 'Auld Lang Syne'.

For Sergeant Hackett of the South Lancashires this was all a great adventure: 'It was a fine voyage, calm, and the further south the more sunny it became and the more pleasurable to us young soldiers. Such excitement, as we watched the dolphins leaping in and out of the water as they kept up for a time with the ship, also the shoals of flying fish leaping twenty to twenty-five yards at a time in a deep blue sea. Other kinds of large fish were seen, and everything stopped to watch the water spout of two whales ... At night it was curious watching the surface of the sea alight with phosphorescence. I have seen much lovely scenery, but a calm moonlight night at sea, with a few light clouds scudding by, takes some beating ... To me everything was new and romantic.'[15]

Private Neligan, more prosaically, recorded the daily routine of sea trooping: 'Reveille was sounded at 5.30 a.m.; all hammocks and blankets had to be given in by 6 a.m.; and breakfast was had at 7 a.m. After breakfast the men commenced to clean the ship; all guards and

13. Ibid.
14. Neligan, op. cit. p. 8.
15. Sergeant E. Hackett, *A Sea Voyage* (part one of his South African War memoirs).

watches were mounted at 8 a.m.; and at 10 a.m. [there was] Commanding Officer's parade. An hour later two companies paraded for physical drill and two for rifle practice, targets being in the shape of boxes and barrels, etc, which were thrown into the water.

'The sleeping accommodation was quite inadequate, consequently when in our hammocks we were packed like sardines, I remember one night, about 10.30 p.m., all was quiet, nothing but the throb of the ship's engines could be heard, when suddenly a string belonging to one of the hammocks broke [and] the occupant came in contact with another's stomach, the owner of which had made his bed on the deck. The ejected, who was half asleep, to the merriment of his mates began shouting "Give me a lifebelt, the ship is sinking," whilst the unfortunate one on the floor afterwards said that he thought he had been hit by a Boer shell.'[16]

In the evening the men held impromptu smoking concerts on deck, singing the popular music hall and parlour songs of the day. Housey Housey, Crown and Anchor, whist, nap, cribbage and other card games were also popular. Lieutenant Fred Raphael recorded his own impressions in letters to his mother in London. 'Our Band is playing on deck now, and the ship looks very picturesque,' he wrote on 5 December. 'The Tommies are lying about all over the place in all sorts of attitudes.' Two days later he noted that: 'The sailors have rigged up a swimming bath on deck, and it is great fun to see about 80 men in it at the same time. They do enjoy it, the poor beggars.'

As the ship headed south, coaling at St Vincent in the Cape Verde Islands, then on past Ascension Island and St Helena, rumours as to the Regiment's eventual destination and the likely progress of the war became more rife. Such information as was available merely served to fuel speculation. 'We have been given four Secret books containing all sorts of information about the Transvaal,' wrote Fred Raphael, 'in fact everything military you can think of and most interesting reading, and not only describes every possible approach, but mentions likely places of attack and defence, water supply, food supply, carts, horses, railways and everything, even where the guns and mines of the forts are, and plans of the forts also ... Our General, Woodgate, is on board with us, but he does not know in the slightest where we are going on arrival at Cape Town.'

Estcourt Camp

On 20 December 1899 the liner *Canada*, carrying 1st Battalion The South Lancashire Regiment and the draft of 150 reservists for the Loyal

16. Neligan, op. cit. p. 9.

General Sir Redvers Buller KCB VC.

Corps Commander in Aldershot at the outbreak of war and Commander-in-Chief in South Africa until superseded by Lord Roberts. A veteran of four previous African campaigns, his early reverses in Natal must be set against the subsequent nine months of unbroken success and the care that he always showed for his troops.

North Lancashires, anchored in Table Bay, her rails lined with excited troops. A former subaltern of the South Lancashires came out in a launch to greet them. 'We shouted "Is the war over?"' recalled Captain Edward Oakeley,[17] 'And the cheering reply was that we had been soundly licked in three engagements and that Buller had wired for us to hurry on to Durban.' Far from being disheartened by this news, Neligan and his comrades 'now saw a medal, always a soldier's ambition, looming in the distance.'

The situation in Natal, as in northern Cape Colony, was indeed critical. The Boers had overrun the northern half of the colony and were besieging a British force of some 12,000 men, under Sir George

17. Captain E. F. Oakeley.

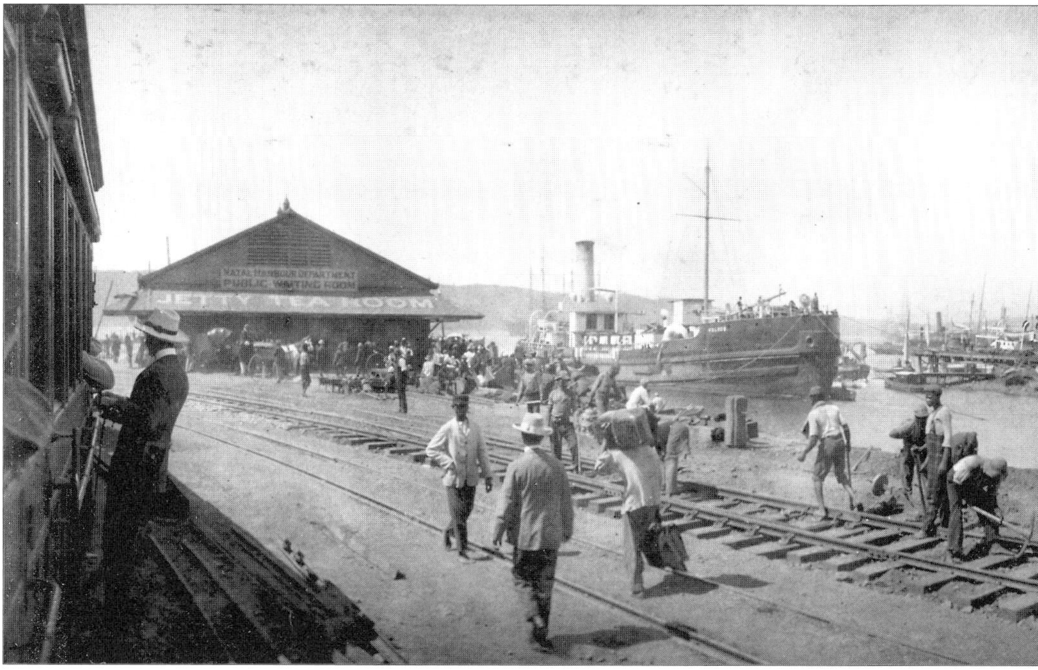

The Docks and Railway Sidings, Durban.

The first glimpse of South Africa for many thousands of British soldiers. The South Lancashires landed here on 23 December 1899 and formed up in a goods shed on the quay, where they were required to leave most of their personal kit before entraining at midnight for the front.

White, in Ladysmith.[18] Sir Redvers Buller had diverted part of his Army Corps to Natal and taken direct command of operations there, but his first attempt to relieve Ladysmith had been bloodily repulsed at Colenso on 15 December.

The Battalion disembarked at Durban on 23 December and entrained at midnight for Estcourt, the 5th Division concentration area. 'We go to the front in the very lightest order,' wrote Lieutenant Fred Raphael, 'carrying only rolled greatcoats, with 1 shirt, 1 pair socks, 1 flannel belt, 1 pair shoes, knife fork and spoon, comb, and 1 emergency ration; that is all we are allowed to take. Our other things will be sent up later if possible, so after tomorrow I start growing a beard.' The officers were to be dressed exactly like the men and all were to carry rifles and bayonets.[19]

Private Neligan remembered without affection his journey north, crouched in an open coal truck: 'The dew was very heavy, and we were soon shivering with the cold, to say nothing of being in a most uncomfortable position all night. We were thankful when we steamed into Estcourt station the following day. A sorry sight we presented to the inhabitants of the place; we were all black with the coal dust, our eyes were swollen and red for the want of sleep, and all our clothing

18. Two officers of the East Lancashire Regiment took part in the defence of Ladysmith: Lieutenants J. E. Green and E. F. Rutter.
19. Raphael letters dated 22 and 25 December 1899. Neligan, op. cit., p. 11.

dirty.'[20] Estcourt, they found, was a cluster of houses and a couple of stores, pleasantly situated in a cultivated valley surrounded by hills. The Battalion pitched camp on Christmas Eve by a small river and all ranks were soon enjoying their first bathe in Africa.

Christmas Day was marked by a church parade, and our friend Neligan recounts an incident that caused some mirth. There was one remarkably slovenly soldier whose section officer had asked him to make a particular effort with his turnout on Christmas Day. On company parade that morning, however, the man confidently appeared in his usual dirty state, to which he was apparently oblivious. Exhortation having failed, his officer decided to shame the dirty one, who was called out to the front and invited to accompany the inspection. Slowly the officer went round the ranks, with the soldier at his heels regarding each man with a critical eye. All were clean and smart. 'Now, my man,' asked the officer, 'what do you think of your comrades?' Without hesitation, he replied: 'Well sir, to tell you the truth, they are the dirtiest lot of beggars I ever inspected, and until they can turn out cleaner I never wish to see them again!'[21]

'I enjoyed my Christmas dinner very well,' wrote Private Jeffreys to his mother in Liverpool. 'We are all happy enough round the camp fire. We had some wild bullock for dinner. It was good food, but not dainty. We went on alright until the monsoon came on at night, and

20. Neligan, op. cit., pp. 11–12.
21. Ibid., 12–13.

lightning illuminated our tents. You could see all the plains for miles, and our tents got flooded out by the rain, and in an hour's time every man in the place was wet to the skin. I hope to get through this alright, but there is no knowing, for there are young fellows who get up in the morning with light hearts, and before sunset they are slaughtered. But British soldiers die with a good heart. I hope you will not fret over me, for I am happy enough, and I hope the next time I embrace you as a son I will have, if I live, the honour of England on my left breast. If we once take Ladysmith we will easily win the day. I have never had a "wet" since the morning I went away, but I am far better off since I have been without it.'[22]

The South Lancashires remained at Estcourt until the 5th Division had concentrated and prepared for the advance. The Battalion formed part of the 11th (Lancashire) Brigade, commanded by Major General Woodgate, which also included 2nd Battalion The King's Own Royal Lancaster Regiment, 2nd Battalion The Lancashire Fusiliers and 1st Battalion The York and Lancaster Regiment. MacCarthy O'Leary made good use of this pause at Estcourt. In addition to outpost duty, the South Lancashires put in some hard field training, skirmishing over the hills in extended order – a useful refresher in particular for the reservists – so that by the time the order came to march the cobwebs of the long sea voyage were blown away and the Battalion was fit for active service.

Conditions in camp were spartan. 'Our bedding consists of one blanket and one waterproof sheet,' wrote Private J. McGuinness of St Helens on the 28th, 'but when you are asleep in the tent at night you run the risk of being bitten by cobras, sand snakes, and scorpions. We are always on the alert in fighting order, that is, with great-coats rolled and 100 rounds of ball ammunition in the pouches. Our company was in this order for 62 hours at one stretch, and as regards our boots and putties, we have not had them off once since we landed on the 23rd, except when you happen to steal away for a bath in a river that runs close by.'[23] On that same day Fred Raphael also wrote home: 'I share a tent with Captain Birch and sleep on the ground. Of course we have no chair or table, nor even a box. Everything lies on the ground and gets filthy, especially in the dust storms which always come before the thunderstorms, and the flies are awful, getting into all the food, which itself is far from appetising. It consists of very salt bacon for breakfast and tea, stewed beef for lunch, and anything you can get, and we get nothing else bar some tea and bread

22. Letter dated Estcourt, 29 December 1899, published in the *Liverpool Courier*, 26 January 1900.
23. Letter dated Estcourt, 28 December 1899, published in the *St Helens Advertiser*, 3 February 1900.

at 5 o'clock, unless we provide it ourselves, which is not always easy to do.'[24] Pineapples were plentiful and could be purchased from nearby farms, albeit at an exorbitant 'war price' of sixpence each.[25] The prime source of off-duty amusement, it appears, was scorpion hunting.

The Home Front

At home in Preston, Mrs O'Leary and the ladies of the South Lancashire Regiment were hard at work collecting and despatching comforts for the troops. In a letter to the *St Helens Reporter*, published on 22 December, the Colonel's wife asked for 'warm clothing, for example, socks, caps, cardigans knitted jackets, cholera belts (knitted),[26] etc., all, if possible, of wool and as light, yet as warm as possible, for the men on service.' The following week she attended a public meeting at Warrington Town Hall, accepting gifts of clothing which included 725 pairs of socks, 500 Balaclava caps and 500 body belts, the first instalment of which would be sent out to the Battalion on 10 January. Apart from clothing, the meeting was told, the men needed tubes of vaseline for their feet (offered by a Chester firm at 1¾ pence each), meat lozenges, and stationery for writing home.

The public response to such appeals was hearty and generous, with numerous and varied local initiatives. In St Helens, for instance, on 1 December the Conservative Club despatched a consignment of half a ton of cake tobacco, 40,000 cigarettes and twenty gross of clay pipes, presents for the men of 1st Battalion The South Lancashire Regiment.

There was also concern for the wives and children left behind by, in the words of the popular music hall song, 'the Absent-Minded Beggar', and many local relief funds were set up to provide practical support. In Preston, for example, at a Town Hall meeting on 15 December of the Mayoress' Clothing Fund it was stated that already about 40 wives and from 110 to 120 children on the strength of 1st Battalion South Lancashire Regiment had received warm flannelette clothing, and it was proposed to extend this assistance to the wives of Reservists of both the North and South Lancashire Regiments. In St Helens there was a seasonal touch when Christmas plum puddings were sent to the families of recalled Reservists.

24. Raphael letter, Estcourt, 28 December 1899.
25. The author recalls paying the same price when the Regiment was in Swaziland in 1965!
26. The cholera belt was an article of clothing issued as a preventative measure to British soldiers serving in the tropics. Basically a waistband or cummerbund made of flannel or silk, the belt was supposed to keep away the cold and damp, the theory being that a chilled abdomen would lead to cholera, dysentery, diarrhoea and other gastrointestinal ailments. This hypothesis was of course incorrect, but the belts continued to be issued until after World War II.

The March to the Tugela

A heavy Boer assault on the defences of Ladysmith was made on 5 January 1900, and although this was eventually repulsed, it very nearly succeeded, considerably heightening Buller's anxiety for the safety of the garrison. He therefore resolved to make a further attempt at relieving the town as soon as possible. In the early hours of 9 January the 5th Division marched out of Estcourt for the Tugela front. Unfortunately the weather had broken.

'We struck camp at 4 a.m., in the dark,' recorded Neligan, 'and commenced to march at 5 a.m., amid a perfect thunderstorm. Anything more dreadful could scarcely be realised. The rain came down in torrents, and the men, being without their great coats, which were carried by the transport wagons, were soon soaked to the skin. The wind howled and seemed to cut one like a knife; the roar of the thunder was deafening, and vivid lightning flashed all round. Still the men trudged on, with the water springing from their boots at every step; all heads were bent down, in order to keep off the rain, which beat mercilessly against them.' [27]

After a march of some four hours the fifteen-mile column of men, horses, ox wagons and mule carts was within sight of its destination at Frere Camp when it was halted by the Blaau Kranz, a small river which was in spate. The ford had risen to some seven feet deep, so, while pontoons were sent for, the troops waited in torrential rain. 'We were allowed to fall out,' wrote Lance-Corporal Chinnery to his parents in Salford, 'and were advised by the doctors to walk about to encourage circulation. Couple all this with the facts that it rained all the time, that we were clothed in khaki, and not a blade of grass to shelter under, and you will be able to form some idea of that day's misery. After remaining in this condition for about seven hours, one of the 'Absent-minded Beggars' asked why the baggage was not thrown off three or four carts, and thus make a bridge. No sooner said than done, and in a couple of hours we were all over. As usual, when the crossing had been effected the pontoons arrived.' The waiting troops, it is said, received the order to march again with three hearty cheers. Four hours later the Battalion reached Frere Camp where, after an issue of tea and biscuits, with a warming peg of rum, the weary soldiers wrapped themselves in their greatcoats and fell asleep on the sodden ground.[28]

---

27. Neligan, op. cit., p. 15.
28. Lance-Corporal J. A. Chinnery, 'D' Company, letter from Chieveley published in the *Northern Whig*, Belfast, 19 February 1900. The writer had by then been killed in action at Spion Kop; Raphael letter, Springfield, 13 January 1900; Neligan, op. cit., p. 16.

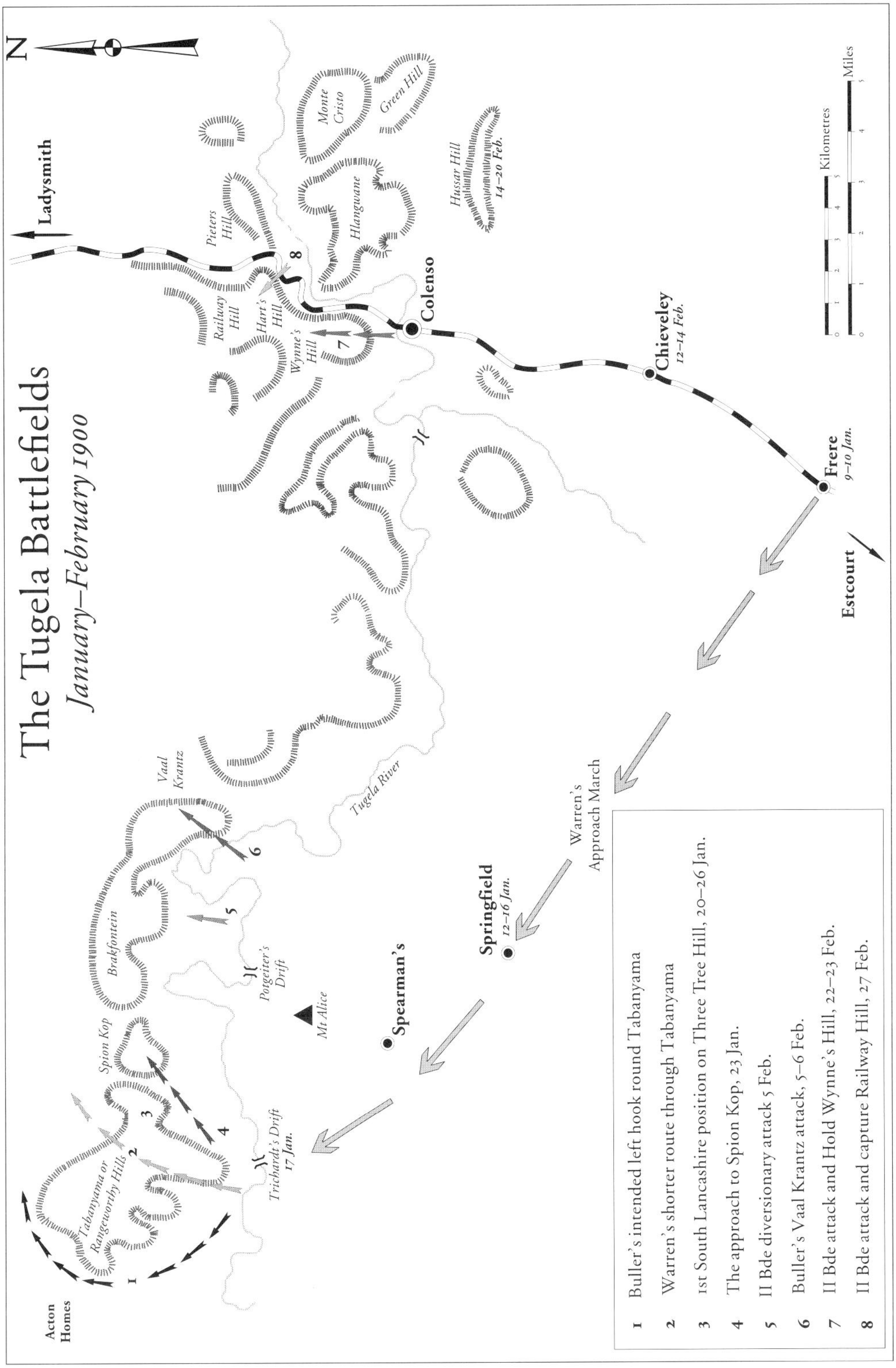
The Tugela Battlefields
January–February 1900
N
Ladysmith
Pieters Hill
Monte Cristo
Green Hill
Hlangwane
Hussar Hill
14–20 Feb.
Railway Hill
Hart's Hill
Wynne's Hill
Colenso
Chieveley
12–14 Feb.
Frere
9–10 Jan.
Estcourt
Vaal Krantz
Tugela River
Brakfontein
Potgeiter's Drift
Mt Alice
Spearman's
Springfield
12–16 Jan.
Warren's Approach March
Spion Kop
Trichardt's Drift
17 Jan.
Tabanyama or Rangeworthy Hills
Acton Homes
Kilometres
Miles
1 Buller's intended left hook round Tabanyama
2 Warren's shorter route through Tabanyama
3 1st South Lancashire position on Three Tree Hill, 20–26 Jan.
4 The approach to Spion Kop, 23 Jan.
5 II Bde diversionary attack 5 Feb.
6 Buller's Vaal Krantz attack, 5–6 Feb.
7 II Bde attack and Hold Wynne's Hill, 22–23 Feb.
8 II Bde attack and capture Railway Hill, 27 Feb.

Next morning the Division remained at Frere and, as the day was hot, the troops soon had their clothes dry. Orders then came for a night march towards Springfield. About 6 p.m. another heavy thunderstorm broke, and by the time the Battalion marched off some two hours later they were once more drenched to the skin. It was a black night and the men trudged silently through the darkness like so many spectres. The track was ankle deep in slimy mud, with numerous deep ruts and holes. Progress was slow and difficult, and the South Lancashires had only moved about seven miles by 3 a.m. Then they were informed that the bridge over Bushman's Spruit had been carried away by the flood. The river had to be forded. Over they went, waist-deep, stooping to drink from the muddy river and replenish their water bottles. The column marched on about half a mile, but the next bridge was also down, and, as the water there was deep, a halt was ordered near Pretorius Farm. 'Such a march,' wrote Lance-Corporal Chinnery. 'I shall never forget it as long as I live. Nothing was known of our destination, at least by Mr. Tommy Atkins. Rain in torrents again, a

11th Lancashire Brigade leaving Frere Camp for Spearman's, 10 January 1900.

A thunderstorm broke as the troops set off on a nightmare night march – 'We started,' wrote Lieutenant Fred Raphael, 'but found the road inches deep in slimy mud with numerous deep ruts and holes. We had the greatest difficulty in getting along at all, as we had only done about 7 miles by 3 a.m. Then we were informed that the bridge had been carried away by the rain, so that we had to wade.'

pitch-like darkness, and wretched roads covered with four inches of mud. It was simply frightful, slipping and stumbling all over the place. I hadn't a watch, so could only guess that we had been marching about six hours when the last halt was given, and, completely exhausted, I threw myself on the ground, not caring about slush or anything else, and before you could say Jack Robinson was fast asleep.' 'We all dropped down in the road', agreed Lance-Corporal Bradley, 'water and mud and all, it made no difference. We were done up and wet through, so down we got, slept just as comfortable as if we were in feather beds until the early morning.'[29]

By 6 a.m. a new bridge had been built. Neligan's account continues: 'At daybreak the men were awakened, and with chattering teeth and shivering limbs again resumed the march. For five more hours we tramped wearily on, scarcely able to keep our eyes open. At 10 a.m. we were again halted, when an ounce of tea and sugar was issued to every three men, together with a ration of biscuits and bully beef, and in a short space of time the veldt became one mass of small twinkling fires. The water that had been procured from the river during the march was poured into the mess tins and placed on the fire to boil. This done, the men began to take off their boots in order to dry their socks and ease their feet ... At last the water began to boil, tea was made, and, as if by magic, the whole force began to assume a cheerful appearance again, laughing, joking, and criticising each other's cooking.'

When the march resumed at twelve the sun was high, and before long the troops were suffering from the heat. 'Scarcity of water was the principal torture,' wrote Neligan, 'and we were so parched with thirst that many of us stooped and drank from pools of water along the road side, certainly not so clean as our English gutters in the rainy season. On we marched in the broiling sun, but towards evening the strain of the march was almost beyond human endurance. Now and again a man would fall insensible on the road side, unable to walk another step. The blood oozed from many a man's boots on that march, and many a shoulder was black and sore with carrying the rifle on the thin khaki coat, still not the slightest suspicion of a word of grumbling was heard.' The South Lancashires reached Springfield that evening, and the following day they crossed the Little Tugela and pitched camp, having completed a march that they would remember as one of the hardest of the whole campaign.[30]

Sergeant G. Welsh wrote home to a friend in St Helens: 'The climate

29. Chinnery, ibid.; Lance-Corporal C Bradley diary; Raphael, ibid.; Neligan, op. cit., p. 17.
30. Raphael ibid.; Neligan, op. cit., pp. 17–19; Colour Sergeant J. T. Pegum diary.

is extremely hot at present, for it is midsummer out here, and not a breath of wind do you get. I can assure you it is as much as a well-trained man can do to stick on marching in this country, which is very rocky and in some places very marshy, and you cannot go above three miles unless you cross a river, not by bridges, but by walking straight through it up to your waist. It is lively, I assure you, and at night it turns into a perfect thunderstorm, and it does come down! Just fancy yourself marching through that lot with only the clothes you stand up in – everything wringing wet and perishing cold. And they stay on until they are dry! We have been like that for at least a dozen times since we came out. That is what causes so many deaths from pneumonia – terrific heat during the day and perishing cold at night, and not a thing to wrap round you only the night air.'[31]

Despite these hardships, the South Lancashires were by now becoming accustomed to living on the veldt. Corporal Ben Tripp, a Maxim gun range finder from Earlestown, described how 'We get together in twos and threes, and cook for ourselves. Bully-beef, biscuits, and tea is our diet. We break the biscuits in pieces, and mince the bully-beef, and boil the lot together; our fireplace being anthills. These hills are about 2 ft high. We cut a hole in the middle, one in front, and another behind, so that the wind can get at it. We then make places for our mess tins on the top, and cook our food in this manner.' Wood was sometimes hard to find, so dried ox dung, 'cow-flap' to the troops, was often used as fuel. Despite the hardships of the recent march, morale remained high. 'We are on the eve of battle,' wrote Corporal Tripp, 'and are all very anxious to meet the Boers ... We are a happy lot; singing and cheering all day long, and making the best of things.'[32]

Buller's Left Hook

Buller's men had no illusions about the formidable task that lay ahead. Between Ladysmith and the relieving force wound the wide, tree-lined Tugela river, and behind it successive tiers of stony, scrub-covered ridges and kopjes rose like rugged ramparts. On these commanding heights some seven thousand of Louis Botha's Boers were posted in well-concealed trenches, sangars and gun emplacements. A direct attack

31. Letter dated Upper Springfield, 14 January 1900, published in *The Lancashire Daily Post* 14 February 1900. In fact the South Lancashires suffered only two deaths from disease between their departure from Estcourt and the Relief of Ladysmith. Sergeant Welsh was wounded in the assault on Pieters Hill on 27 February but rejoined the Battalion and became a Colour-Sergeant.

32. Letter from Corporal (later Sergeant) Tripp to his mother in Earlestown dated Springfield, 13 January 1900, published in *The Liverpool Post*, 14 February 1900.

Lieutenant-General Sir Charles Warren, Commanding the 5th Division in Natal.

Warren's career as an engineer, pioneering archaeologist and colonial soldier included a spell as Commissioner of the Metropolitan Police, in which post he was notable for issuing his orders in verse and failing to catch 'Jack the Ripper'. Buller made the mistake of entrusting the critical turning operation west of Spion Kop to Warren's colourful but untried hands.

across the river had failed at Colenso, so Buller decided on an indirect approach; hence his flank march to Springfield, a move of some twenty miles to the north-west of his former position at Colenso. In his new concentration area he was facing the ford at Potgeiter's Drift, and it was from Mount Alice, overlooking this crossing, that he made his reconnaissance.

Looking northwards over the Tugela, Buller saw a semi-circle of heights, dominated on his right by the Vaal Krantz ridge and to his left by the massive hill known as Spion Kop, beyond which the Tabanyama (Rangeworthy Hills) stretched away to the north-west. In the centre was a lower, undulating ridge, Brakfontein, over which went the track from Potgeiter's Drift to Ladysmith. Buller decided

Buller's View.

A panorama from Mount Alice, looking north across the winding Tugela to Spion Kop, far left, Twin Peaks, the distant Brakfontein Ridge and, far right, Vaal Krantz. In the middle distance on the right can be seen

that a direct assault by the Brakfontein route, enfiladed as it was from both flanks, was impracticable and that the enemy would have to be manoeuvred out of their position by an outflanking move even further to the west. Buller delegated command of this critical turning operation to Sir Charles Warren, GOC 5th Division. His orders, issued on the 15 January, were to cross the Tugela some four miles upstream at Trichardt's Drift, to by-pass the main Boer defences by moving up through the Tabanyama to the west of Spion Kop. 'You will of course act as circumstances require,' Buller continued, 'but my idea is that you should continue throughout refusing your right and throwing your left forward till you gain the open plain north of Spion Kop. Once you are there you will command the rear of the position facing Potgeiter's Drift, and I think render it untenable.' Buller would then advance against the Brakfontein ridge and on to Ladysmith.[33]

The South Lancashires had been encamped at Springfield for four days when, on the evening of 16 January, they set out with Warren's force for Trichardt's Drift. Sergeant Hackett, who revelled in this African adventure, described the march: 'Leaving a party putting a

33. Spion Kop Despatches, HMSO, 1902.

the track from Potgeiter's Drift (in dead ground) towards the Brakfontein Ridge and Ladysmith. The open ground within this river loop was the scene of 11th Lancashire Brigade's successful diversionary attack on 5 February.

lighted candle in each tent (to deceive the Boers who may have been watching) we tailed on to the end of the procession, marching in two ranks, one either side of the line of transport. The transport used the cart track (there were no roads) and we footsloggers trod and stumbled along its sides, likened unto a ploughed field. It gives me a laugh to think how serious that march was. Men stumbled and occasionally cursed. "Stop that talking," was shouted in the intervals of noise created by the transport. Noise! – it was a din. "Umbagi!" shouted the negroes urging on the trek waggons with their 16 span oxen and continually cracking their long whips; "Moo," groaned the oxen. A series of yells from the drivers of the two and four mule cape carts, and noisy replies from the angry mules, and all in pitch dark, and ever in between one heard "No noise!" or "Stop that talking!" That nightmare lasted some ten miles, then we bivouacked in quarter columns behind a rise.'[34]

Warren's force was now at Trichardt's Drift and, with every prospect of action on the morrow, nerves were tense. That night there was what Sergeant Hackett thought was 'a queer happening'. Apparently

34. Hackett, ibid.

Warren's Force massed at Trichardt's Drift. Warren's ponderous lack of urgency after crossing the Tugela allowed Botha time to reinforce the threatened flank and spoilt Buller's plan for an early relief of Ladysmith.

a mounted orderly stumbled upon the sleeping troops and someone raised the panic cry 'The Boers are coming! The Boers are here!' Pandemonium broke out as men grabbed their rifles and equipment, mules stampeded and their drivers shrieked. 'The Division seemed to spring up in a fright and commenced to rush about like mad men,' wrote Sergeant John Pegum in his diary. 'Some men fixed bayonets.' Order was eventually restored in the South Lancashires by Colonel MacCarthy O'Leary, standing in the light of the guard's hurricane lamp and bellowing "Come back, my brave boys! Come back, my 40th!"'[35]

At first light, soaked and shivering from a heavy dew, the men cleaned their rifles and drew an additional fifty rounds each of ammunition. At 7.30 a.m., as the Battalion prepared to advance to the Tugela in battle formation, Fred Raphael scribbled a short note to his mother: 'I can't say I feel any excitement yet, or that I am risking my life and limb, or that there is any danger, but I fancy when the bullets begin to fly I shall feel a bit unpleasant at first, but excitement will soon drive all that away. We shall soon be on the move now, so I shall finish this later if I am able. If not, good-bye, but I hope I shall not be bowled over.'[36] The crossing was in the

35. Hackett, ibid.; Pegum, ibid.
36. Raphael letter, Tugela River, 17 January 1900.

British Infantry Crossing the Tugela River by pontoon at Trichardt's Drift. The South Lancashires crossed without opposition on the morning of 17 January, but were then obliged to remain inactive for two days.

event something of an anticlimax. Buller had estimated enemy strength in front of Warren as at most four hundred with one or two big guns; in fact there was no more than a small picquet, and this were soon dispersed by artillery fire. After the north bank of the Tugela had been thoroughly shelled the Engineers laid a pontoon bridge and the Infantry passed over to secure the bridgehead. The British force now held the tactical initiative.

Had Sir Charles Warren hastened to take the heights north of Trichardt's Drift without giving the Boers time to redeploy there can be little doubt that Buller's plan could have been achieved and the way to Ladysmith opened with little loss. The subsequent battles, from Spion Kop to Pieter's Hill, need never have been fought. But Warren, an engineer, was obsessed with the passage of his baggage train over the Tugela, which he personally supervised, and would not move forward until this movement had been completed more than two days later. Meanwhile he retained his infantry brigades in close defence of the bridgehead and halted the cavalry who were starting to work round the Boers' open right flank at Acton Homes.

The South Lancashires crossed the Tugela on the morning of 17 January and advanced northwards without opposition to occupy the forward slope of a small hill about 2,000 yards north of the drift, part of the protective screen around the crossing. They remained there for the next two days while with sardonic humour the men of Lieutenant Raphael's company employed their enforced idleness in planting trees 'in memory of what they call 'Starvation Hill' as we got nothing to eat yesterday except breakfast at 4 a.m.' [37]

Lieutenant Geoffrey Mott.

Mott, a keen sportsman and an expert shot, served throughout the Boer War and later won distinction with the 6th South Lancashires in the assault on Sari Bair, Gallipoli, in 1915. He survived to celebrate his hundredth birthday with the Regiment.

Warren had never liked Buller's concept of a wide turning movement round the Boer right flank, and having been allowed considerable discretion by his commander he selected a line of advance astride the more direct track which crossed the Tabanyama between Three Tree Hill and Picquet Hill. On 20 January he made his first, belated, move to secure that area. Unfortunately he was by now too late, for the Boers had greatly strengthened and reinforced their defences and Louis Botha had hastened over to take command of the threatened sector.

At 2 a.m. on that morning the South Lancashires, together with 2nd King's Own, were roused and ordered to take the enemy's outlying posts on Three Tree Hill, some two miles to the north. Moving silently uphill in line with fixed bayonets, expecting at any moment to be fired on, the Battalion made their only night attack of the campaign. The Boers had, however, vacated the position during the night and the assault was unopposed. This preliminary operation to clear the lower slopes of the Tabanyama feature was a complete success and provided a gun position from which the upper slopes could be bombarded. The whole of Warren's artillery, six batteries, then moved up to Three Tree Hill to support the main attack. The main body of the South Lancashires remained in this area to protect the guns throughout the six day battle which followed, with two companies deployed a few hundred yards further north on Piquet (known to the Battalion as Coventry) Hill.

The duties of the artillery escort were no sinecure, for the guns were deployed well forward and the position was subjected to both shelling and sniping. The Battalion was required to provide outposts at night and keep under what cover they could find by day, but on the 20th in particular they were, in Fred Raphael's words, 'fairly hotted'. 'As we lay bivouacked in lines some three or four yards apart,'

37. Raphael letter, Tugela River, 18 January 1900.
38. Hackett, ibid.

wrote Sergeant Hackett, 'we had our first casualties from spent bullets fired at the guns. There was a good deal of amusement as a most surprised man here and there cried out "I'm hit," and nobody would at first believe him, until the shout for the Doctor was made and for half an hour he was busy on some twenty wounds – not very serious.'[38]

There were other diversions. Lieutenant Geoffrey Mott recalled how 'during the action a Boer shell fell in a farmyard close by. As a result of this a host of young pigs broke out of the yard and crossed our front to be chased by several men of the Connaught Rangers, bayonets in hand. It was quite an amusing sight.'[39] Towards evening Lieutenant General Sir Francis Clery, the exotically blue-whiskered Commander 2nd Division, appeared with his staff and stood in the open by the guns, using field glasses. Sergeant Hackett noted that Clery, known to all as 'the Dandy', was as always wearing his blue undress uniform with starched white collar and cuffs, kid gloves and a swagger stick. The Boers also noticed this conspicuous group and fired a shrapnel shell which, passing low over them, burst at the rear of the Battalion. The staff scattered as Clery, drawing his sword, shouted 'Damn the Bastards!' – causing much laughter in the ranks. Sergeant Brett, the Pioneer Sergeant, was less fortunate; raising his head from cover, he was wounded by the bursting shrapnel.[40]

Warren's main attack on the Tabanyama heights, on a front of some two miles between Three Tree Hill and Bastion Hill, was launched on the afternoon of 20 January. The Boer entrenchments on the immediate crest were carried in fine style, but it was a false crest. The true crest lay a further thousand yards away across a gently sloping but bare hillside, and there lay the main Boer position. Having lost over three hundred men, Warren called off the attack. The following morning he ordered an assault on the right of the enemy line, which was their weakest sector, but this was unaccountably abandoned when on the verge of success. Warren now determined on a further frontal attack after a lengthy artillery bombardment, but Buller was becoming impatience with his subordinate's lack of progress and on the 22nd he rode over to see him. Buller was still advocating an attack on the Boer right, but reluctantly accepted a bold alternative plan from Warren, a night attack to capture Spion Kop. If this dominating feature could be taken, and held, the whole Boer position would be untenable and the way to Ladysmith would lie open.

Meanwhile, in rear of the South Lancashires' position, Lieutenant Fred Raphael was enjoying his first bath for a week: 'I went down to a small stream, quite close, but at the bottom of a very steep hill. I

---

39. Mott memoirs in *The Lancashire Lad.*
40. Hackett, ibid.; Pegum, ibid.

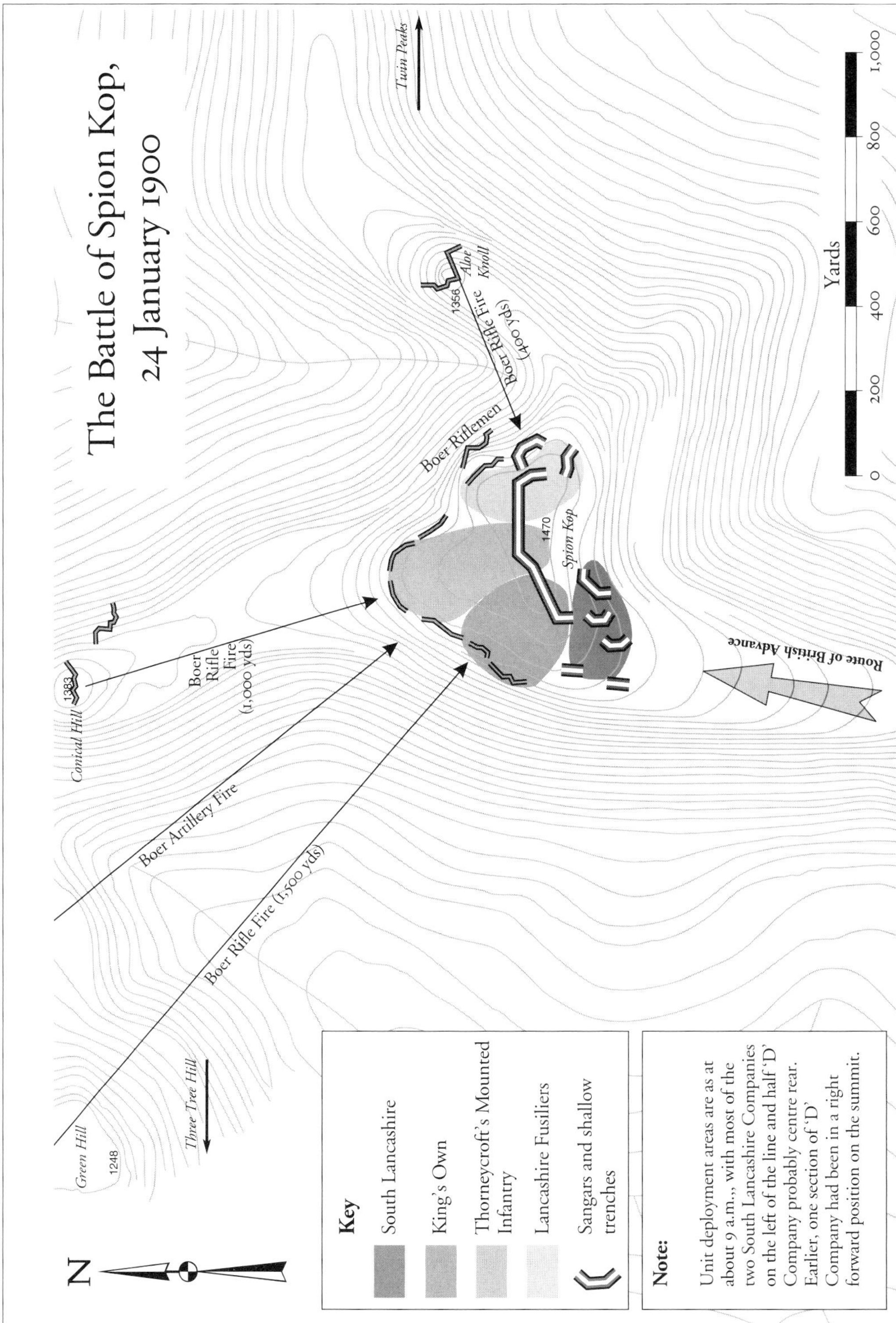
The Battle of Spion Kop,
24 January 1900
N
Twin Peaks
Aloe Knoll
1356
Boer Rifle Fire (400 yds)
Boer Riflemen
1470
Spion Kop
Route of British Advance
Conical Hill
1383
Boer Rifle Fire (1,000 yds)
Boer Artillery Fire
Boer Rifle Fire (1,500 yds)
Green Hill
1248
Three Tree Hill
Yards
0
200
400
600
800
1,000
Key
South Lancashire
King's Own
Thorneycroft's Mounted Infantry
Lancashire Fusiliers
Sangars and shallow trenches
Note:
Unit deployment areas are as at about 9 a.m., with most of the two South Lancashire Companies on the left of the line and half 'D' Company probably centre rear. Earlier, one section of 'D' Company had been in a right forward position on the summit.

blocked the stream with some stones, and simply revelled in it, and washed all my clothes. I have no others here. Whilst bathing, I got a leech on me, which was not very nice, but it is grand to feel clean again. My soap melted in the sun and became like soft soap. What was left, I rolled into a ball and brought back, but that is not much.'[41] It was to be his last bath, and his last letter home.

The Battle of Spion Kop

The looming mass of Spion Kop (1,470 feet) rose about one mile to the east of the South Lancashires' position on Three Tree Hill, from which it was separated by a wide re-entrant. Its summit appeared conical in shape. However, had an accurate map existed it would have revealed a narrow saddle running north from a bare, hog-backed summit some 1,000 yards to Conical Hill (1,383 feet) and a ridge extending to the east, throwing up at about 400 yards a small hump, Point 1356 or Aloe Knoll, and at 2,000 and 2,250 yards respectively the two knolls known as Twin Peaks. Some 1,500 yards to the north-west was Green Hill (1,248 feet), part of the Tabanyama position. All these positions were within long-range rifle fire of Spion Kop. The sides of the hill were generally very steep, almost sheer in places, except towards the south-west where a long spur running down to the south-west offered an arduous but practicable approach from the British lines.

Warren decided to assault Spion Kop on the night 23–24 January with a force of some two thousand men based on Woodgate's Lancastrian Brigade:

2nd King's Own (6 companies);
2nd Lancashire Fusiliers;
1st South Lancashires ('C' and 'D' Companies only);
Thorneycroft's Mounted Infantry (180 men, dismounted);
Half a company of Royal Engineers

This force assembled on the reverse slope of Three Tree Hill at 7.30 p.m. on the 23rd. Extra ammunition was issued, rifles unloaded to avoid giving an accidental alarm, and the password issued – 'Waterloo'. Lieutenant Fred Raphael with half of 'D' Company was towards the end of the column, bringing up the ammunition mules. It was a pitch-black night with a drizzling mist as they filed off towards Spion Kop. The guns on Three Tree Hill stood silent, and all was quiet but for some fitful distant sniping.

'On, on, on we marched in silence,' wrote a Warrington sergeant with the South Lancashires, 'not knowing where we were going, but

41. Raphael, letter dated 'Across Tugela River', 22 January 1900.

Spion Kop from the West.

Showing the bare, rounded summit with Aloe Knoll in the right foreground and Conical Hill behind. The British approach was up the slope from the left of this contemporary photograph, while Boer reinforcements climbed the slopes from the right.

suspecting something desperate was about to happen. We knew we were approaching the enemy's lines when a dog, belonging, I think, to the Lancasters, gave a growl, and commenced howling. Somebody hit it on the head with the butt end of a rifle, and then cut its throat. We lay flat on the ground, not knowing whether we had alarmed the Boers. In about five minutes we crept along as slowly as possible for fear of disturbing these Dutch fiends, until we were at the foot of a hill called Spion Kop. Then we began to realize what was expected of us. We were to attack Spion Kop. It is the highest hill around the district, commanding every other position. It took us two hours and a half to get to the top. Providence favoured us while we were ascending it, as we were enveloped in a thick fog. The Boer sentry shouted out the challenge, but he got his answer by having a bayonet driven through his ribs. Then we heard bullets whizzing past us. 'Fix bayonets and charge' was our order. We rushed along the flat top, yelling like devils, only to find that the Boers had skipped, leaving their tackle behind them. This would be about 3.30 a.m. We gave a good ringing cheer, as we thought we had captured this position without loss of life.'[42]

This cheer was the pre-arranged signal for the artillery on Three Trees Hill to open up, dropping shells beyond the hill to discourage counter-attack. The summit was still shrouded in mist and, according to Colour Sergeant Herbert Cleaver, 'We could not see 10 yards in front.' So far as Woodgate's men could make out in the poor visibility, they occupied a plateau roughly four hundred yards in diameter, sloping away on all sides. They set to work to entrench themselves on the rocky summit, but the ground was hard and there were few tools, so by dawn the 'trenches' amounted to no more than a semi-

42. Letter to the 'Warrington Guardian' dated 29 January 29 1900. The writer was a reservist who until mobilised had been working at Pearson and Knowles Iron Company in Warrington. There were apparently no fewer than 5 reservists from that one Warrington company in action at Spion Kop. Lance-Corporal Mathew Kelly, a Liverpudlian in 'D' Company, noted that they found themselves 'on a flat grassy plateau on which there are three or four trucks filled with blankets and tins of bully meat, field glass[es], a few rifles and a lot of ammunition.'

The Summit of Spion Kop.
This photograph, taken by a Regimental officer within two years of the battle, shows a rough breastwork of boulders and is captioned 'Spion Kop – South Lancashire shelters'.

circle of shallow shell-scrapes and sangars, facing north. The main entrenchment, a flattened V some four hundred yards long, ran along what was believed to be the crest of the hill. Nearly two thousand men were crowded into this confined space. On the right of the line were the Lancashire Fusiliers, then Thorneycroft's Uitlanders in the centre and the King's Own on the left. The two South Lancashire companies, less the ammunition escort, were for the most part at the extreme left of the British position. Throwing out strong covering parties, 'C' and 'D' Companies constructed rough stone breastworks and waited for dawn.

Already, after the night's exertions, men were thirsty. 'A pool was found,' wrote Neligan, 'and those in its vicinity drank eagerly. Oh! what a relief! The water tasted like nectar to the poor fellows, they were so parched, and a good many of them sat close to it for fear of being unable to find it again. Better for them had they left it in the dark, for when daylight appeared, and they saw what they had been drinking, there was not one of them but who was sick. It was a pool of dirty clay-coloured water, covered with green slime.'[43]

Boer retaliation was not long delayed and through the mist the South Lancashire skirmishing line was subjected to Mauser fire from

43. Neligan, op. cit., p. 27.

Left **Captain Mickey Lynch.**

Commanded 'C' Company of the South Lancashires at Spion Kop and when General Woodgate was wounded he led a party of the Regiment to cover his evacuation. Lynch, the only South Lancashire officer to survive Spion Kop, died of disease later that year.

Right **Colour-Sergeant Herbert Cleaver.**

Commanded the remnants of 'D' Company at Spion Kop when both officers were killed.

Conical Hill. 'Myself with twenty men were sent to throw out a line of skirmishers to the right front,'[44] wrote the sergeant, 'and an officer and twenty men to form a similar line to the left front. We had scarcely got into position, when we were greeted with a shower of bullets, which for the moment completely staggered us. I gave the order to my men to keep under cover until we could find out where they were coming from; but it was no use, they were coming as thick as hail stones. We retired to the trenches (poor ones, as they had not

44. The diary of Lance-Corporal Kelly appears to confirm that, contrary to most accounts of the battle, some of the South Lancashires were, at this stage in the action at least, occupying a right forward position on the summit: 'At about 4 a.m. the mist clears off and we find that we are on a very small square shaped plateau fringed with rocks, but it seems to be the highest ground in the vicinity. A few shots are exchanged but no heavy fire. We are separated a bit more. Half my Company being sent to the right of the hill. Gradually the fire increases and we are reinforced by some of the Lancs. Fus. About 7 a.m. the sun breaks through the clouds and we see a long grassy ridge about 1,000 yards in front but commanding our ridge. About 8 a.m. the Boers open a terrific rifle and pom-pom fire from every place except our extreme rear. We take the best cover we can get.'

'C' Company's 'Spion Kop Men'.

A group photograph some months after the battle.

had time to finish them) one by one, creeping along the ground. Up to this time not a shot had been fired by the British, as the fog was too thick. We were waiting to charge the devils. At 5.30 a.m. the fog began to lift and we could see them in trenches, but we had no guns to root them out. Now and again one would show himself, and generally when they did show they soon got a ticket for eternity. The fog had completely lifted at 8 a.m., and from that hour the top of Spion Kop was hell on earth. There we were, perched on the top of a flat hill without a gun to assist us. Shrapnel was bursting all around us, and our men were dying like rotten sheep, and we had nothing but our rifles to help us, and nothing but rocks to aim at. The trenches were soon full of dying and wounded men. Oh, it was horrible, men with pieces of shell in their sides, all ablaze, others with their legs shattered, some with their heads nearly blown off.'[45]

What had gone so terribly wrong? British ignorance of the exact lie of the terrain around Spion Kop was a critical factor. None of Warren's officers had been up Spion Kop before, and there were no accurate maps. It was not until the mist lifted slightly that Woodgate realised that although the ground immediately before his main entrenchment did indeed slope down it did so only very slightly before the true end of the plateau, marked by a fringe of rocks between one and two hundred yards in front of his entrenchments. He sent forward detachments to entrench themselves there, but already Botha's men

45. Warrington Sergeant, ibid.

were climbing through the mist with the same objective in mind. When the mist finally and suddenly lifted, the appalling truth about the British position was abruptly and brutally made apparent. Not only did they occupy only part of the summit, but their exposed position, silhouetted against the skyline, was swept by a storm of fire from three directions over an arc of 120 degrees. Boer riflemen were on Green Hill, Conical Hill, Aloe Knoll and Twin Peaks, while from these heights they were able to direct their artillery with devastating effect. From Aloe Knoll they enfiladed the right of the main British trench so directly that after the battle some seventy men were found dead there with bullets through their right sides. Under cover of this fusillade several hundred gallant burghers, rallied by Louis Botha, clambered up the hill. Despite heavy casualties, they established themselves around the rim of the plateau, some within fifty yards of the British line.

Towards 9 a.m. General Woodgate was mortally wounded whilst locating the cross-fire from Aloe Knoll. His last order, according to Neligan, was: 'Men, fire from where your General fell!' Captain Nicholas ('Mickey') Lynch and Sergeant Price of the South Lancashires led eight of their men forward to cover the General's evacuation. For this and other acts of conspicuous bravery on Spion Kop the Sergeant was later awarded the Distinguished Conduct Medal.[46]

Early in the day Colour Sergeant Herbert Cleaver of 'D' Company was beside his company commander, Captain Charles Birch, sheltering from a very heavy rifle fire behind large stones on the crest of the hill, when the officer was shot though the head. He died as he was carried to the dressing station.[47] His friend Lieutenant Fred Raphael took over the company, but some two hours later he too was killed, struck down by a shell splinter while trying to rescue a wounded man. He had previously been seen sitting on a stone wall in an exposed position taking shots at the enemy.[48]

---

46. His citation reads: 'Sergt. Price showed conspicuous bravery in controlling his section under the hottest fire, and as a volunteer, traversed 200 yards under a heavy fire of shells and bullets to assist a signaller. On his return through same fire he formed one of party employed in covering removal of Gen. Woodgate when wounded. Corpl. Norton, Ptes Ludlow, Lawson, Philbin, Frost, Healy, Brown and Dr[ummer] Johnson (armed with a rifle) were also engaged in the same proceeding under immediate command of Capt. N. M. Lynch.'
47. Cleaver manuscript (brief account of Spion Kop).
48. On 27 January 1900 Colonel MacCarthy O'Leary wrote from Springfield to Raphael's father:

> The captain of your son's company was shot during the first assault – your son then bravely took command and some two hours after his captain's death, was himself instantly killed by shell fire in the head. He had been encouraging his men all morning by word and example, and is reported to have shot five of the

Captain Charles Birch.

Killed in action at Spion Kop, 24 January 1900, commanding 'D' Company.

Private James Humphries, his orderley, was among many members of the Regiment who wrote to Raphael's family: 'We was both in high spirits up to the last after we had taken that never forgotten Spion Kop. Mr Fred and myself had been trench digging when the Boers began sniping on us and we had to seek cover. We both was under a rock for a few minutes, when General Woodgate got wounded and I went to carry him to the hospital, and after that I went back to where Mr Fred and myself had been, but I could not find him, as I learned that he had gone to bring a man out of a trench when a bullet struck him in the head. I tried very hard to get near him, but it was impossible as the bullets got so thick that there was not an inch to spare between them and I was forced to drop back under more cover, just in time too as there came a big shell bursting right in the spot where I had been kneeling. But I managed to get away, wishing my master could have been able to come with me. I retired off that hill with a heavy heart at having lost my best friend.'[49]

As the day wore on and casualties mounted, want of water added to the agony. 'It was a blazing hot day. Men were lying baking in the sun, wounded and crying for water, and we had none to give them.'[50]

Some men had remarkable escapes. Private W. Ollerhead described

> enemy dead before his own noble death. Your dear son, all of him that is mortal, lies decently and reverently buried on that ill-fated ridge surrounded by comrades and friends ... All your late son's brother officers ask me to tell you of their grief and of their sense of loss and sorrow. I loved your dear son whose loyalty and noble qualities I shall never forget and I shall be proud always to know that I commanded the services of such a gallant soldier and such a generous and singleminded gentleman.

Raphael, the only British officer of Jewish parentage killed in the Boer War, left money 'to the officers of my dear old regiment ... for the purpose of buying a picture representing one of the actions in which the regiment has fought. The choice to rest with the officers.' The result was the oil painting of the battle of Pieters Hill by W. B. Wollen which hangs to this day in the Officers' Mess of 1st Battalion The Queen's Lancashire Regiment.

49. Transcript by Raphael family from from Private J. Humphries' undated letter (shortly after Spion Kop).

50. Warrington Sergeant, ibid.

The Scene on Spion Kop, from a sketch by a British officer.

'Shells and bullets of every description rained unmercifully into the trenches, and the enemy seemed to be able to place their fearful Hotchkiss or pom-pom shells anywhere they liked. Some of the sights on that hill were terrible to behold, and one man, who was hit behind the neck with a pom-pom shell that set his clothing on fire, actually simmered where he fell. One might be speaking to the man on his right and left one moment and, after firing a round from his rifle, might turn round the next and find them both dead. Some had their limbs torn clean away, and if a man was only slightly wounded he considered himself extremely lucky.' (Private T. Neligan)

how 'A drummer of ours (his name is Lawrence) was drinking the soup out of his Maconochie's rations – it is a tin of meat and vegetables – when two shots went through it. He picked a rifle off one of the wounded to guard himself, and that got knocked out of his hand; he picked another up with the bayonet fixed, and the bayonet got smashed.'[51]

Down below on Three Tree Hill it was beginning to dawn on anxious spectators that all was not well on Spion Kop. 'As I watched the struggle with my glasses,' wrote Captain Oakeley of the South Lancashires, 'I said to my neighbour, "Things are going badly up there," to which he snapped "That's all you know – we'll be in Ladysmith to-morrow." I turned, and there was Winston Churchill, just escaped from Pretoria!'[52] Churchill left his own painterly impression of the distant battle as seen from the South Lancashires' position: 'It was like a shadow peep-show. Along the mighty profile of the hill a fringe of little black crotchets advanced. Then there were

51. *Black and White*, Vol. II, No. 24, 24 March 1900.
52. Captain E. F. Oakeley, ibid.

brown and red smudges of dust from shells striking the ground and white puffs from shrapnel bursting in the air – variations from the black and white. Presently a stretcher borne by five tiny figures jerks slowly forward, silhouetted on the sky-line; more shells; back goes the stretcher laden, a thicker horizontal line than before. Then – a rush of crotchets rearwards – one leading two mules, mules terrified, jibbing, hanging back – all in silhouette one moment, the next all smudged with dust cloud; God help the driver; shadows clear again; driver still dragging mules – no, only one mule now; other figures still running rearwards. Suddenly reinforcements arrive, hundreds of them; the whole sky-line bristles with crotchets moving swiftly along it, bending forward almost double, as if driving through a hailstorm. Thank heaven for that – only just in time too – and then more smudges on the shadow screen.'[53]

Edward Oakeley was not alone in his concern, for the gunners had found themselves unable to hit the Boer artillery while Buller, on Mount Alice, had received a most alarming message from Colonel Crofton of the King's Own, the senior surviving officer on Spion Kop: 'Reinforce at once or all lost. General dead.' In fact Warren had already ordered up three additional battalions – the Middlesex, Dorsets and Imperial Light Infantry – under Major-General Coke. Then, pressed by Buller to put 'a good hard fighting man in command on the top', he ordered Thorneycroft to supersede Crofton, but without telling either Coke or Crofton. The battle was becoming a classic of incoherent command and bungled communications.

By noon many of the troops on the summit were nearing the limits of their endurance. Apart from the left, they had been forced back to the main trench line and morale was becoming fragile. The Lancashire Fusiliers on the right had suffered more than the other units, particularly from the deadly enfilading fire from Aloe Knoll, losing a high proportion of their officers. At about 1.30 p.m., in the confusion following a feigned Boer surrender, numbers of men on the right were induced to put up their hands. Thorneycroft rushed forward to restore the situation, shouting 'I'm the Commandant here; take your men back to hell, sir! I allow no surrenders.'

At about the same time the Boers on the British left also advanced to take prisoners and called upon Colour Sergeant John Nolan, commanding a detached section of the South Lancashires, to surrender. 'If you don't it will only cost more bloodshed,' said the Boer leader, 'and you are hopelessly beaten already'. Only a few months before, Jack Nolan had captained the victorious regimental team which brought the Army Football Cup home to Preston. Now he was in no

53. W. S. Churchill, *London to Ladysmith via Pretoria*, 1900, p. 336.

mood to accept defeat, and called out: 'When I surrender, it will be my dead body!' [54] Then someone fired a shot and the Boers flew back to their own trenches. Inspired by Nolan's example, the South Lancashires continued to hold their portion of the ridge throughout that terrible day.

The arrival of Coke's reinforcements brought some respite and, despite heavy casualties, stabilised the situation on the summit. Both sides were badly mauled and exhausted. 'It was not infantry we wanted,' wrote our unknown South Lancashire sergeant, 'but artillery, and the hill was too steep to get guns up.' Lance-Corporal Kelly saw that 'some of these officers who have not been up all day try to fire volleys by exposing 10 or 20 men lumped together but the Boers turn the two pom-poms and their big guns on them, often killing or wounding as many as 10 or 20 men at once.' By 5 p.m. a gallant diversionary assault by the 60th had taken Twin Peaks, and Warren was making ponderous plans to reinforce the hill that night; but Buller recalled the 60th at nightfall and Warren did not inform Thorneycroft of his intentions.

After dark Thorneycroft, knowing only that his men had neither the strength nor the means to improve their defences that night, decided on his own initiative to evacuate Spion Kop. 'Better six good battalions safely off the hill,' he argued, 'than a mop-up in the morning.' He asked our Warrington sergeant of the South Lancashires to accompany him round the trenches to give orders for the withdrawal. 'Of course I said "Yes, sir," but before we got half-way round we came to the conclusion it was a warm job. I don't know how we got out of it safe. At that time I didn't care a pin whether I was shot or not. I was so tired and jaded, as I (in fact all of us) had had nothing to eat or drink all day, that I felt as if death would be a relief, but thank God I came out all safe. The retirement was conducted in a marvellous manner ... By Jove! I don't want another day like that. Fighting is all serene when you have guns to help you, but it's a bit off when you haven't.'

At about 11 p.m. the men were fallen in and, carrying as many wounded as they could, they retired down the hill to the Field Hospital. As Thorneycroft neared the foot of the hill he met the relief force sent by Warren – fourteen hundred infantry, with gunners and sappers – but it was too late. The men were exhausted. Colour-Sergeant Cleaver recalled reaching the hospital at about midnight, whereupon he and Sergeant Price were soon fast asleep, their two heads covered by one huge red handkerchief.

The final irony of this catalogue of confusion and missed oppor-

54. Neligan, op. cit., pp. 28–9.

The South Lancashire Regiment Memorial on Spion Kop.
Erected by their comrades, who each contributed a day's pay, and photographed in 1965 during a visit of the battlefield by their Regimental successors.

tunities was that in the face of the protracted British defence, and having themselves lost 335 men, the Boers had also abandoned Spion Kop that evening. They were, however, partly rallied by Louis Botha who persuaded parties to go back up the hill. At 3.30 a.m. came the almost incredible news that the British had evacuated the summit, which was then hastily reoccupied by the Boers.

Meanwhile, at the foot of Spion Kop, Colour-Sergeant Cleaver awoke at 4.30 a.m. and gathered up a handful of his company, for survivors of all units had become hopelessly intermingled in the dark. 'The next thing was to find the Battalion as none of us had any idea which way to go, but we struck a road and after marching for about an hour we came across 2Lt Wood. He had been sent out to look for us and he had a few of 'C 'and 'D' Companies with him that he

The fatal hill-top of Spion Kop.

A Boer propaganda photograph of British dead on the summit.

had picked up. He marched us to camp, about 35 of the two companies. Stragglers [were] coming in all day and it was not until the 26th that we found out our correct list of casualties.'[55] British losses on Spion Kop totalled 243 dead and nearly one thousand wounded or missing. South Lancashire casualties were two officers, two sergeants and seven men killed in action or died of wounds and thirty other ranks wounded or missing. For two days following the fight a truce prevailed on Spion Kop as stretcher-bearers and burial parties toiled to clear the fatal hill-top.

Buller resumed direct command of Warren's force and ordered a retirement to the south bank of the Tugela. This was accomplished without loss by 27 January. The South Lancashires and Connaught Rangers were the last to withdraw, holding Three Tree Hill until 10 p.m. on the 26th. 'G' and 'H' Companies were the most advanced, occupying the outpost on Picquet Hill. It was a nervous time, as Sergeant Hackett recalled: 'It rained torrentially all the night and the day, and soaked through, the water ran down our skins in rivulets from head to foot. Just at dark the sentries reported movement in front and the company formed square where we stood; fell out, another

55. Cleaver manuscript notes compiled on the anniversary of the battle, 1901.

alarm and fell in again.' At 9.30 p.m. orders came to retire. The companies had just fallen in to march off when one of the men accidentally discharged his rifle. The Boers, thinking that they were under attack, opened a terrific fire for some twenty minutes, but without effect. The main body of the South Lancashires, fearing that the two companies had been cut off, were formed up to meet an anticipated Boer attack when Hackett and his comrades marched in. They were met by Colonel MacCarthy O'Leary who, calm as ever, ordered them to 'Just line up here'. Watching the flashes of the Boer rifles, the South Lancashires concluded that two parties of the enemy were firing at each other. The Regiment was left as rearguard and, according to Captain Oakeley, withdrew at about 11.30 p.m., 'wending their rocky way in single file, pitch dark, with a chilling wind cutting through the thin khaki and a steady drizzle. Down we went to the Tugela, quite worn out, and the Boers sent two p.p.c. shells after 'H' Company as it crossed. As I halted the other side, my faithful servant Riley came up with a canteen of hot coffee.' [56]

The Battle of Vaal Krantz

From the banks of the Tugela the Lancashire Brigade retired to Springfield for a week's rest after ten days' hard fighting. Rations remained very restricted – bully beef and biscuits. 'One day,' according to Private Neligan, 'one of the men found a crust of bread on the veldt, which he brought into camp. How the men stared at it! One would have thought it was a curiosity from some museum, and had it been a gold nugget it could not have been handled with greater care.' [57] There was time, too, for letters. Private James Mackin wrote to his mother in Warrington: 'It is an awful sensation to hear the cannons roaring and bullets flying about in all directions, but by the time you receive my letter I shall be in the thickest of the fight, and I hope I shall come out safe. But if I have to die out here I shall die a British soldier's death, and not a coward's. We will let the Boers see what Warrington lads can do.' [58]

'On Sunday, January 28th, Buller inspected the Brigade and praised the men for the excellent manner they had behaved during that trying time. All Lancashire people, he said, would be proud to hear how they had helped to keep the credit of their county to the fore. He also said that we must not suppose that good work had not been done because the force had retired. By the fighting that had taken

56. Oakeley, ibid.
57. Neligan, op. cit., p. 31.
58. Pte J. Mackin, Letter dated Frere Camp, 26 January 1900.

place he had been given the key to Ladysmith, and that the next time we advanced there would be no turning back. He then, read a telegram of sympathy and congratulation from Queen Victoria, for whom three cheers were called and given in a right loyal manner.'[59] Buller had in fact identified what he believed to be the 'key' to Ladysmith, a gap in the hills beyond the Tugela flanked by the heights of Green Hill and Vaal Krantz. If only he could seize these two features, he could march safely through onto the Ladysmith plain. But, as one South Lancashire officer wryly observed after the parade, perhaps the Boers had changed the lock.

Sergeant-Major C. Devlin DCM. (Regimental) Sergeant Major of 1st Battalion The South Lancashire Regiment.

On 3 February The South Lancashires were again on the move towards the Tugela, crossing at Potgeiter's Drift to occupy a group of small kopjes in the bridgehead. The brigade task was to make a feint attack from this area, 'The Kopjes', against the Boer entrenchments on the Brakfontein ridge while the real attack on Vaal Krantz and Green Hill was developed further to the right.

At 6 a.m. on 5 February the 11th Brigade emerged from The Kopjes and deployed as if for an attack, with the South Lancashires and York and Lancasters right and left respectively in front and the King's Own in second line. 'The movement was admirably carried out,' wrote Neligan. 'Each regiment, acting independently, but in line, moved out in skirmishing order, and marched to within a mile or thereabouts of the enemy's position, and then lay down on the open veldt without a vestige of cover. At noon, which was the hour for the attack on the right, the Brigade commenced to retire. The enemy, who had been expecting them to advance, were simply astounded. Then all at once, like so many wild beasts, thinking they were going to be deprived of their prey, [they] suddenly opened a galling fire on the retiring ranks. The shells and bullets began to fall like hail between the lines of skirmishers, who looked like so many brown dots on the green veldt; and it was a magnificent sight to watch the lads from Lancashire enduring that storm of lead without as much as a sign of fear. A thrill of admiration ran through every man present as

59. Neligan, op. cit., p. 32.

Ammunition Mule of the South Lancashire Regiment.
Employed by the Sergeant-Major for immediate re-supply of the firing line.

he saw the tall and manly form of Lieutenant-Colonel MacCarthy O'Leary, retiring slowly and in disdainful silence, without so much as turning his head. The bravery and coolness shewn by this gallant officer during that day was the talk of the whole Division for some time afterwards. Slowly, as if on parade, the Brigade continued to retire, and in about an hour's time the movement was completed, with very little loss.'[60] Lance- Corporal Bradley, too, was impressed by his comrades' discipline under fire: 'It was grand to see our troops retiring with shells dropping at their feet almost, and not a waver out of them, and good order was kept throughout.'[61]

The Battalion had six men wounded in this affair, only three of them serious enough to be listed. Sergeant-Major Devlin marvelled that there were not more casualties: 'A bullet went clean through the helmet of poor old [Colour-Sergeant] Ned O'Brien, and knocked it off his head ... Sergeant Scott was knocked flat by a shell, but did not get a scratch. A shell burst under the feet of a corporal named Carroll, and lifted him clean off the ground, but only just scorched his feet. Another man got a bullet in the heel of his boot, but little

60. Neligan, op. cit.
61. Bradley, ibid.

The Key to Ladysmith.

The NCOs of 'D' Company, 1st Battalion The South Lancashire Regiment in South Africa, 1900. Most of these men fought at the battles of Spion Kop, Vaal Krantz, Wynne's Hill, Pieters Hill and Botha's Pass.

damage was done, and another got a bullet in his heel. One shell burst between the hind legs of my [ammunition] mule, and another under her belly, but we still went on till we reached our bivouac. Sir Charles Warren and General Wynne were watching us all the time, and the Colonel has told me since that both of them said that we retired as if on parade under blank fire, and that that was what saved us. The C.O. has also told me since that he has been told by several that they never saw a retirement carried out like it. Naturally the Colonel is very proud about it, and so are we. It also proved that the Boers are bad shots. Had we been in their place and they in ours, few would have escaped.' [62]

Although this feint by the Lancashire Brigade went entirely according to plan, the main attack was less successful. By the end of the first day only the southern end of Vaal Krantz had been secured and a British observation balloon reported substantial Boer reinforcement of the threatened area. Mindful of the likely cost of continuing this line of assault, on the afternoon of the 6th Buller decided to disengage and led his army once more back across the Tugela. The Lancashire Brigade was pulled back that night to Spearman's Hill, then made a flank march east to Chieveley.

Buller's third attempt to relieve Ladysmith had failed, and well-placed whisperers began to mock 'The Ferryman of the Tugela', but,

62. Sergeant Major (RSM) Devlin, letter from Springfield Camp dated 9 February 1900.

as Sergeant Hackett and others recalled, his popularity with the Lancashire troops was undiminished: 'One very interesting incident occurred as the Brigade, after re-crossing the River, marched back from the rear. Half a mile back, we heard continuous cheering, growing louder and nearer, until looking to our left we saw our Colonel in Chief, General Buller and his staff, riding along at a walk. Our Battalion nearly cheered themselves hoarse as along in front of us the cheering continued. "Good old Buller", he was called. He rode by, chin on chest, looking very sad, and the troops hearts were with him, and it must have helped him to know the men realized what a tough task he had. Two columns smashed at the start, Magersfontein and Stormberg, and geography defying his attempts. The men shouted "Good old Buller; have another go; smash them; we're with you," as they cheered him. He heard the shouts for he looked up and towards us, and seemed to smile, then looked down again as the cheering continued to the head of the column.'[63] This was the real 'key' to Ladysmith, the simple loyalty and undismayed tenacity of the British Infantry.

The South Lancashires pitched camp at Chieveley on 12 February. Here at last they were able to bathe, and enjoy fresh rations – the Battalion had not eaten bread for 35 days or fresh meat for 14 days. This respite did not last long, for at 6 a.m. on the 14th the force marched out of Chieveley in attack formation, heading north once more for the Tugela.

The Tugela Heights

Buller had planned a new offensive, a coordinated series of attacks aimed at forcing a passage through the Tugela Heights, his line of advance being the road and railway from Colenso to Ladysmith, crossing those commanding heights at Pieters Hill. In this area the Boers were entrenched on both sides of the Tugela, and the first phase of Buller's advance involved the methodical reduction of successive enemy positions south of the Tugela. During these actions, the 11th (Lancashire) Brigade occupied the forward slopes of Hussar Hill, acting as left flank guard and as escort to the 34 guns massed in that area. It was a noisy place to be, with naval and artillery guns firing day and night, and some counter-battery fire from the enemy, but the South Lancashires had a ringside seat as the British Infantry turned the Boers off a succession of hills and ridges – Green Hill, Monte Cristo and Hlangwane. From his trench in front of the naval guns, Sergeant Pegum of 'H' Company could see the Boer entrenchments

63. Hackett, ibid.

and tents, but he had a better chance of inspecting them when, on the 19th, he went with a detachment of the Battalion to escort two naval guns forward to a captured position: 'I saw several horses killed and many live ones captured. The tents belonging to the Boers were riddled by our shrapnel shell. Bags containing flour, bread, cakes, lentils and tins of lard were strewn all about. They had not time to take them away. It was glorious to see them running away when a shell from us was sent among them.' Returning to Hussar Hill in the rain, John Pegum received a much-prized, if somewhat belated, Christmas gift, Queen Victoria's Chocolate Box.[64] Other pleasant incongruities enlivened the South Lancashires' time on Hussar Hill. 'While I was in the front trench there,' wrote Captain Oakeley, 'a shell dug itself in just in front, whereupon a naval gunner strolled out, saying 'Where did that b—— pitch, mates? I'll get thirty bob for it at Durban.'[65]

Wynne's Hill

Having captured the heights on the south bank of the Tugela, Buller decided to cross the river to the east of Hlangwane, then clear the hills which rose, tier upon tier, between Colenso and Pieters Hill. About 5 p.m. on the 20th the South Lancashires advanced from Hussar Hill to Hlangwane, where they bivouacked for the night. On the 21st the pontoon bridge was launched and at about 3 p.m. 11th (Lancashire) Brigade crossed, headed by the South Lancashires, and took up positions in the bridgehead of low hills north of Colenso. The South Lancashires occupied a forward line on Hill 244, facing north with the railway and the Tugela to their right and the Onderbrook Spruit to their front. There they remained for some 24 hours, exchanging rifle fire with the Boers to their front.

On the 22nd Buller ordered Major-General Wynne, who now commanded 11th Brigade, to begin the advance northwards along the left bank of the Tugela by capturing the kopje known as Green (or Wynne's) Hill. The South Lancashires were to take the eastern end of the objective, overhanging the railway line and the river, with the King's Own to their left. Wynne was unhappy about the plan as his left flank would clearly be enfiladed by Boer riflemen on the Horse-Shoe and Grobelaar features. He was promised support on this flank from the 4th Brigade, but in the event it was not possible to extricate that brigade from its previous task and so the 11th Brigade attacked unsupported.

The South Lancashires led the advance across the valley of the

64. Pegum, ibid.
65. Oakeley, ibid.

1st South Lancashires in defence, South Africa 1900.

Onderbrook Spruit. 'There was,' according to Sergeant Hackett, 'a large railway bridge to the right below the hill and our C.O. asked the men which they preferred, to go over the top or go round over the bridge. "Over the top," they said, and an hour later (3 p.m.) we fixed bayonets and over we went, covering that half mile at the double. Only one man was hit, the Boers having cleared when they saw the "Rooineks" coming.'[66] Lance-Corporal Bradley was with 'H' Company, providing covering fire for the advance: 'Having located the enemy and got the proper distance, we poured a heavy rifle fire into them over the heads of our Regiment until they were within striking distance and ready to charge, and had to stop firing for fear of shooting our own comrades. As soon as we stopped the enemy opened a heavy fire into our main body but they were too late as our fellows charged and took the hill. The Rifles relieved my Company and we formed support to our Regiment. We were soon called for. We had just got to the Regiment when they shouted "Reinforce", for the Boers were advancing upon them, and we fixed bayonets and with the usual war cry we rushed up the hill.'[67] The enemy's counter-attack was beaten back with bullet and bayonet, and darkness brought an end to the day's fighting. The South Lancashires had lost two sergeants and four men killed in the attack and 22 wounded, including Lieutenant Kane severely wounded twice. 'The bullets here was dropping like rain,' wrote Lance-Corporal Bradley in his notebook, 'and we was surprised

66. Hackett, ibid.
67. Bradley, ibid.

to see such a little list of casualties. I do not think there was half a dozen men thought they would come out of it alive – I know I did not, for one. We buried a couple of men here at the foot of a tree, but they was not the lot.'

During the night 'B' and 'H' Companies were pushed forward to take a small hill where, detached from the main body of the Battalion, they prepared their position for all-round defence with a horseshoe of sangars. At 5.30 a.m. on the 23rd the Boers opened a heavy fire on this exposed position and mounted a counter-attack which pushed back two companies to the left of the Brigade, causing the left flank company of the South Lancashires to fix bayonets and ask the retiring troops 'where the —— they were going to.'

'We had sent a couple of men with our bottles for a supply of water,' recalled Lance-Corporal Bradley, 'but they never returned, because at daybreak we was hard at it and the enemy had a cross-fire upon us from three different directions – in our front, left front and left rear – and they had the correct range. Bullets was flying everywhere if we showed ourselves in the least for less than 5 seconds. The day was a scorcher and we had neither food nor water. The latter we was all greatly in need of. Of course, we had got used to being hungry now and again. Some men had made the attempt to try to get to us, but found it impossible as it was only courting death to try to get anywhere near us.'

The dawn counter-attack by the Boers was repulsed, but fierce fighting continued around Wynne's Hill all day. 'B' and 'H' Companies remained pinned down, returning the fire at every opportunity even though they hardly dared raise their heads. 'Messages and orders had to be delivered,' noted Neligan, 'by writing them on a piece of cartridge paper and placing them in an empty case, which was thrown from one to the other.' The wounded suffered particularly from heat and thirst, for neither stretcher-bearer nor doctor could reach them. Bradley dressed the wound of one man with a hole in his back the size of a half-crown piece: 'I wanted to try to carry him down but he would not risk it, and every time we fired a shot he used to groan as it gave him a shock, but we had to keep up the snapping or get rushed, and he lay there until about 8.30 p.m. when we got relieved.'

Sergeant Hackett was near Colonel MacCarthy O'Leary, concealed behind a low stone wall from where they could see the Boers watering their horses a mile and a half down the Tugela, when one of the men jumped up on the wall to take a better look at the distant enemy through a small telescope. Turning to the Colonel, who was seated on the ground looking severely at him, the soldier asked 'What are they doing, Sir?', to which his Commanding Officer replied 'They are saying, look at that damn fool soldier showing us where their position is. Get down!'[68]

The fighting on the 23rd had cost the South Lancashires an additional 24 wounded, including Major Reginald Hall, Captains Berkeley Goren and Stuart Upperton, and 2nd Lieutenant Cunliffe Marsh. 'Upperton and I were trying to locate where some very near firing was coming from,' wrote Major Hall, ... 'a bullet hit the top stone of our sangar and passed between our heads but the splinters of the rock hit us – Upperton got one in the eye and one in [the] cheek and I got two in [the] cheek. This was at 7 a.m. and we couldn't let Upperton leave till dusk as it would have been almost certain death to have left the trench. My splinters were nothing – only dust in the eye and slight trickle of blood down cheek – but it was a close thing.'[69]

The Battalion was relieved of its exposed position on the night of the 23rd/24th and moved back to Hill 244, remaining there in reserve throughout the 24th under a shrapnel fire which caused some casualties. Meanwhile, Hart's Irish Brigade made a costly assault on Buller's next objective – Terrace (or Hart's) Hill – and ended the day clinging precariously to its forward slopes.

Next day the South Lancashires re-crossed the pontoon bridge and retired to Hlangwane for a short, but very welcome, rest. They were particularly delighted to come across a canteen where such delicacies as cocoa and Quaker Oats were available. On the 26th the Battalion marched down to the Tugela where the men enjoyed a rare opportunity to bathe and rinse out their clothes.

The Battle of Pieters Hill

That evening orders were read out to the Battalion for a final grand attack on the Tugela Heights the following day. It was, in Lance-Corporal Bradley's words, to be 'neck or nothing,' and the South Lancashires were to assault the main Boer position. Buller had decided to launch an all-out offensive, using three infantry brigades supported by massed artillery to break through to Ladysmith along the railway corridor to Pieters Station. Three features dominating this route were to be attacked in succession from the right, where Barton's 6th Brigade was to take Pieters Hill. In the centre the 11th Lancashire Brigade was to capture Railway Hill (referred to in their orders as Green Hill), while on the left Norcott's 4th Brigade was to mount a renewed assault on Hart's Hill. The attacking infantry would cross the Tugela at a

68. Hackett, ibid.

69. Letter from Lieutenant Colonel Hall to Major Smythies dated Maritzburg, 19 March 1900.

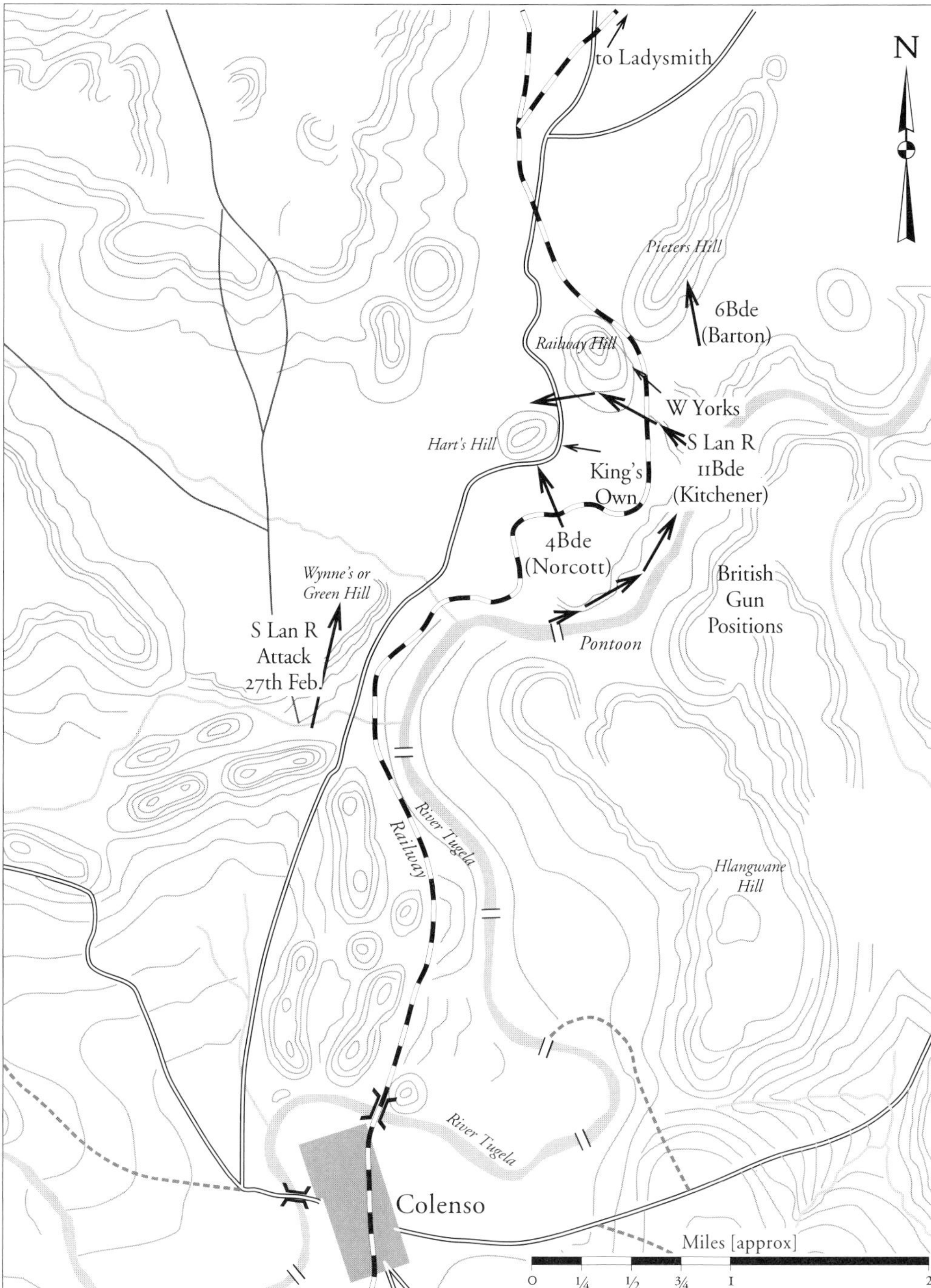

The Battle of Pieters Hill,
27 February 1900

new pontoon bridging site below Hart's Hill.[70] Morale in the South Lancashires was high, and William McCarthy O'Leary cabled home, to his wife at 10, Moor Park Avenue, Preston assuring her he was 'Never better in his life.'

The 11th Brigade was now commanded by Colonel Walter Kitchener, brother of the future Lord Kitchener (Wynne having been wounded on the 22nd), and now consisted of the King's Own, the South Lancashires, the York and Lancasters and the West Yorkshires.

Early on the morning of 27 February the assault brigades were on the march in extended order towards the pontoon bridge. Every soldier carried two hundred rounds of ammunition. They had been left in no doubt that Ladysmith must be relieved that day at all costs. They also knew that it was the anniversary of the British defeat by the Boers at Majuba in 1881. Now was their chance to expunge the stain of that reverse. The 11th Brigade halted short of the bridge to allow 6th Brigade to pass first. At about 7.30 a.m. the British artillery, including the heavy 4.7 inch naval guns, began pounding the enemy trenches. As the South Lancashires lay waiting for their turn to move, Sir Redvers Buller rode up to MacCarthy O'Leary, who came forward to greet him. 'Well Colonel,' said the General, 'how are the South Lancashires?' 'The South Lancashires are right,' was the gallant old Colonel's laconic reply. Buller later recalled how 'I rode round the battalion with him, and I thought they looked right, and a few hours after they proved they were right, for they did under his lead what up to then had been considered practically an impossibility.'[71] Lance-Corporal Mathew Kelly recorded in his diary: 'General Buller addresses our Regt. and says he has decided to assault Pieters Hill. He says he knows our Regt. well and has decided to let them attack the central position. He points the hill out to us. Looking from where we are it appears to be a long flat hill on the far side of the railway. On the right is a valley and a hill further on.'[72]

Then, as the men rested, a staff officer rode along the column with the timely and dramatic news of Lord Roberts' victory at Paardeburg and the surrender of Cronje's army. 'Majuba avenged already! Such shouting and cheering I never heard before,' wrote Private Neligan. 'Strong men wept for joy, chums shook hands with each other, the

70. The nomenclature of the various features of the Tugela Heights was, and remains, somewhat confusing, and contemporary diarists and newspaper correspondents quite frequently muddled them up. From the British left: Terrace Hill is also known as Inniskilling or Hart's Hill; Railway Hill is also known as Green or Kitchener's Hill; Pieters Hill (which gives its name to the entire action on the 27th) is also known as Barton's Hill.

71. Warrington Guardian, 23 February 1907 (Buller's speech in the Parr Hall at the unveiling of the South African War Memorial of The South Lancashire Regiment).

72. Diary of Lance Corporal M. Kelly, 'D' Company.

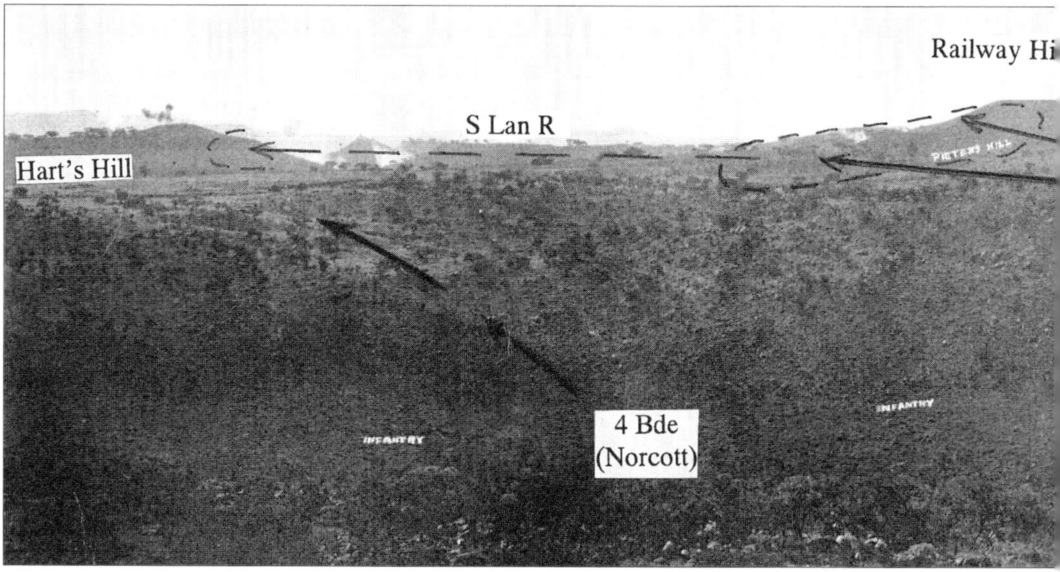

The Battle of Pieters Hill, 27 February 1900.

This panoramic photograph taken from across the Tugela, near the British gun lines, during the bombardment of the Boer trenches, has been marked to show the general lines of Buller's attack. Note that the South Lancashires assaulted Railway and Hart's Hills, and the nek between them, not Pieters (incorrectly annotated on the original photograph).

bluejackets ceased firing for the moment and commenced to dance the sailor's hornpipe around their guns. The Infantry stood up and cheered again and again; some threw, whilst others kicked, their helmets in the air, and everywhere could be seen manifestations of joy at the good news, which seemed to make all ranks, from the General downwards, only too eager to get at the foe. Shortly after this the order to move was given.'[73]

It was after mid-day when the 11th Brigade column reached the pontoon bridge, saluted by a Boer artillery shell which burst harmlessly some thirty yards from the South Lancashires. The Tugela ran swift between rocks at this narrow stretch. The hills rose steeply on the south bank to where the British batteries thundered, and on the enemy side a long tree-covered slope ran up to the railway line, beyond which reared the Boer-occupied heights. The Brigade moved slowly in single file along the very uneven riverside footpath, past a signpost on which someone had written 'The Road to Hell'. After an hour or so, they reached the mouth of a donga which separates Pieters and Railway Hills, climbed up the bank to their left and began to deploy. The West Yorkshires took the right flank and the King's Own the left, with the South Lancashires in second line as support and the York and Lancasters in reserve.

At 1.30 p.m. the West Yorkshires were ordered forward to seize fire positions from which they could support the main attack, occupying first the railway cutting due east of the Brigade objective, then a ridge of rocks above it, and finally the eastern slope of Railway Hill itself

73. Neligan, op. cit., pp. 41–2.

before being halted by a heavy enfilade fire. On their left, however, the majority of the King's Own, coming under fire from Hart's Hill, swung round and attacked that feature in error. This caused a critical gap in the centre of the Brigade advance, where the Boers were strongly entrenched on a small kopje between Railway and Hart's Hills.

The South Lancashires, meanwhile, had advanced up the slope in two lines ('A' to 'D' in first line, followed by 'E' to 'H') to the railway embankment. 'Here the enemy got sight of us,' wrote Lance-Corporal Bradley of 'H' Company in his diary, 'and put a very heavy rifle fire into us, and our comrades began dropping all around us, but the officers and men kept very cool and most of the men required no orders as they could see what was required of them and they moved quickly and formed up themselves ready to reinforce any part of the line.' There was an incessant fire, and it was a relief when the Battalion was ordered forward.[74] Colonel Kitchener ordered MacCarthy O'Leary to at once advance with his right half Battalion into the gap between the two leading units and stop the enfilade fire which was holding up the advance, while Major Hall, the Second-in-Command, was ordered to prolong the line to the right with the left half Battalion and support the attack.[75] Lance-Corporal Mathews of 'D' Company was with the right half Battalion: 'We reach the Railway, scramble through the barbed wire and cross the rails to have to cross another lot of barbed wire. All this time the Boers are pouring it in us hot as they can, and as we have 95 guns in action the uproar is deafening.

74. Bradley, ibid.
75. Letter from Lieutenant Colonel Hall to Major Smythies dated Maritzburg, 19 March 1900.

The Assault on Railway Hill.

A photograph taken as the South Lancashires advanced from the railway line (right, middle distance) towards the Boer entrenchments. Colonel MacCarthy O'Leary assaulted the Boer position in the nek (marked by smoke from the British artillery bombarment), while Major Hall moved up on his right to take the high ground of Railway Hill. At this point the South Lancashires are half-way across the open ground, having reached the points marked 'Infantry'.

But somehow we get through the wire and make for the valley between the hills.'[76]

Supported by the West Yorkshires, who kept a sharp fire up from their positions on the right, the South Lancashires worked their way up the steeply terraced hillside to the Boer trenches, across some five hundred yards of practically open ground, the only cover being a few rocks and bushes. Above the heads of the advancing troops, artillery continued to bombard the Boer entrenchments up to the last possible moment, their lyddite shells setting the grass ablaze and turning the ground yellow. From points of vantage on the far side of the Tugela, observers watched with mounting anxiety as the distant lines of khaki-clad figures approached the open ground before the Boer trenches. 'When about two hundred and fifty yards from the main position,'

76. Neligan, op. cit., pp. 42–3.

Col: McCarthy O'Leary. 1st South Lanc: Regt Killed S.A. 1900

Lieutenant-Colonel William MacCarthy O'Leary.
Commanding Officer, 1st Battalion The South Lancashire Regiment (PWV) 1896–1900. Killed in action at the Battle of Pieters Hill, 27 February 1900.

wrote Private Neligan, 'the firing was terrible, and the bullets came so thick that my regiment attempted to take cover behind a small rise in the ground, but this proved to be quite inadequate for the purpose.' It was recognisably the climax of the battle and all hopes depended on MacCarthy O'-Leary's men. Would their attack, like so many before them, falter and fail in the face of a withering fire from the Boer riflemen?

'And then came the most extraordinary revolution, sudden, astounding, brilliant, almost incomprehensible. Across the railway the South Lancashires suddenly rose up out of the ground, stones rose up too, and turned out to be infantrymen ... and all began to run, not in stiff lines, but with the graceful spreading of a bird's wings straight up the hill ... I watched, stricken with admiration and suspense.'[77]

This dramatic transformation of the battle was largely due to one man, Lieutenant Colonel MacCarthy O'Leary. Seeing that there was nothing to be gained by delay under fire, he ordered 'Fix bayonets – Prepare to charge!' and addressed his beloved 40th for the last time:

'Remember, men, the eyes of Lancashire are watching you today'.

Almost at once, the Colonel was wounded, but he stepped forward, a tall, imposing figure in front of the first line, and shouted 'Charge!' before being hit twice more and falling dead, close to the enemy trenches, in the act of waving on the leading companies.

'At his words,' wrote Neligan: 'the whole regiment rose like one man, and the black slope fairly twinkled with the glitter of the bayonets as they flashed in the sun. Like a wall of rock the gallant 40th closed upon their foe, and the best disciplined troops in the wide world could not have withstood that irresistible rush. Like demons let loose they charged upon the enemy, who quailed before the contact, and those who were able rushed precipitately away, falling in dozens under the bullets of our men. The Boers who were unable to escape sued piteously for quarter, and the Lancashire lads, now as merciful as they had been brave, gave it to them, though with bad grace, as they were burning to avenge the losses they had already sustained ... On they

77. J. B. Atkins, 'The Relief of Ladysmith' (1900), pp. 309–10. Atkins watched the charge from the heights opposite.

pushed until the last trench was taken, when they sat down among the rocks, happy in the thought that they had achieved their object and done credit to the best traditions of the old corps.'[78]

Lance-Corporal Mathews recorded his experience of the charge: 'Col. O'Leary is away on the right of C Coy. but we can see him plainly. We observe him throw his hands in the air and then we fix bayonets as we run. Mr. Jellibround [Lieutenant Gellibrand] says the order is "charge" and the next minute there is a great shout and the Col. goes down just as we reach the trenches.'[79]

Whilst MacCarthy O'Leary's men took the Boer trenches on the nek between Railway Hill and Hart's Hill, Major Hall's half battalion captured the left of the summit of Railway Hill itself. Not content with this, some seventy men of 'A' and 'B' Companies said, 'There's another bloody hill; let's take that.' So they did, charging off to their left front and driving the Boers with the bayonet from entrenchments to the rear of Hart's Hill. They were joined there by 'H' Company and by some of the King's Own. Major Hall, who assumed command when the Colonel fell, was only slightly exaggerating when he claimed that the South Lancashires had captured both hills and that Norcott's Brigade came up after Hart's had been taken. They were not, apparently, too pleased to find the South Lancashires on their objective, sheltering from artillery fire in the Boer trenches.[80] Sir Redvers Buller certainly had no doubt where the honours lay. In the words of his cabled despatch, 'the enemy's main position was magnificently carried by the South Lancashire Regiment about sunset.'

The Boer centre and left had been turned and the way to Ladysmith lay open. The watchers across the Tugela were jubilant. Buller himself later recalled that a sailor from one of the batteries had come up to him and said, 'Well, sir, I confess I am proud today. I have seen how Englishmen can fight, and I realize that they are quite as good, if not better, than the bluejackets.'[81] 'Surely nothing so beautiful was ever seen as the advance of Kitchener's Brigade at No. 2 kopje,' wrote another exultant witness: 'The bursting lyddite clothed the summit with a yellow veil; through this flashed the exploding shrapnel, and up and in through the smoke advanced a stately line of infantry, without a pause, until they had command of the kopje, and drove

78. Neligan, op. cit., p. 43.

79. Mathews, ibid.

80. Hall, ibid.; Oakeley, ibid.; Hackett, ibid. Lance-Corporal Mathews: 'While we halt at the trenches the Boers further on pour a heavy rifle fire into us as we make for a hill on the left but the Boers turn their pom-pom on us knocking a good many over. We hold this hill all night.'

81. Sir Redvers Buller's speech at the Parr Hall, Warrington on the occasion of unveiling the South African War Memorial of the South Lancashire Regiment, reported in *The Warrington Guardian*, 23 February 1907.

'Remember, men, the eyes of Lancashire are watching you today'.

Standing in Queen's Gardens in the centre of Warrington, the South African War Memorial of The South Lancashire Regiment takes the form of a bronze statue of Lieutenant-Colonel MacCarthy O'Leary, stepping forward, hunting rifle in hand, leading his men into the charge at the Battle of Pieters Hill. A memorial service is held at the monument each year, on the anniversary of the battle, by the Regimental Association of The Queen's Lancashire Regiment.

Boer Mass Grave.

Originally an entrenchment defending the nek between Railway and Hart's Hills, this was the position assaulted by MacCarthy O'Leary.

Major Thomas Lamb.

'I think I have lost an eye', he observed, 'but all that is troubling me is whether it will prevent me from taking part in the Bisley meetings again'. It did not.

Second-Lieutenant C. H. Marsh, DSO.

the enemy for ever from the banks of the Tugela. All the money, all the lives, all the misery caused by the war, are well repaid by this glorious battle. In Great Britain the new century has been baptised in the blood of her soldiers, and has opened in the flame of battle, but from the holocaust the courage of the British infantry comes pure and unsullied – a sure presage that the safety of the greatest country in the world is secure for ever in the arms of her soldiers.'

The action was not, in fact, quite over, for as the victorious South Lancashires consolidated their positions around Railway Hill and sent their prisoners to the rear, they were subjected to a very hot shrapnel, rifle and machine gun fire from the right, where the Boers still held the rear of Pieters Hill. Several men were hit before they could get under cover, including Major Thomas Lamb who took a fragment of shrapnel in his face. When asked if he was badly wounded, the gallant Major, who was a noted marksman, replied: 'I think I have lost an eye, but all that is troubling me is whether it will prevent me from taking part in the Bisley meetings again or not.' He had indeed lost an eye, but the following year he was back at Bisley, shooting as well as ever.[82] Second-Lieutenant Marsh took over the company and was awarded a DSO for his gallant conduct.[83] Private R. Brighouse was awarded a DCM for 'great coolness and resource under heavy fire … and when severely wounded in one side [he] insisted on removing his own accoutrements and attempted to dress his own wound while [the] remainder kept up rifle fire.'

This firing did not cease until darkness fell over the battlefield. Then trenches were dug, outposts were posted, and the light of lanterns flickered as parties searched for the wounded and carried them to a place of safety. Apart from the Colonel, the Regiment had lost a sergeant and four men killed and one officer and at least 34 NCOs and men wounded, of whom four died later.

82. Neligan, op. cit., p. 46.
83. The citation reads: 'The gallant conduct of this young officer on 27th Feb. was brought specially to my notice. After his company commander was wounded, he behaved in a most gallant manner, encouraging his men who were exposed to a heavy shrapnel, machine gun and rifle fire. A wound which he had received on Feb. 23rd had broken out and was bleeding.'

Graves of Lieutenant-Colonel MacCarthy O'Leary and four of his men.

This group of graves lies beside the railway embankment below Railway Hill, from where the South Lancashires' attack was launched.

Private James Humphries, who we last met on Spion Kop, had another narrow escape; his life was saved by Queen Victoria's presentation chocolate box when a bullet struck his haversack and lodged in the chocolate. At Humphries' request, the chocolate and bullet were sent to the Queen.[84]

Meanwhile some 50–60 Boer prisoners were escorted down the hill. Winston Churchill spoke to a private soldier: 'Only forty-eight, sir, and there wouldn't have been so many if the officers hadn't stopped us from giving them the bayonet. I never saw such cowards in my life; shoot at you till you come up to them, and then beg for mercy. I'd teach 'em.' Then, having vented his feelings, the soldier proceeded to feed his prisoners with bully beef and gave them water from his own bottle.[85] Neligan recounts the following dialogue between another of the escorts and a Boer officer:

'Boer Prisoner: "I say, my man, I will give you my parole if you will only walk along side of me; I wish to talk with you."

Lancashire Lad (thinking he was going to get something valuable) said: "Let me hev a look at it first to see how much it is worth."

The Boer prisoner explained that he meant to give him his word of honour not to escape.

84. *The Daily Mail*, 5 March 1900.

85. Churchill, *Ladysmith*, pp. 446–7. The reported number of prisoners varies from 69 (Mathews) and 66 (Hackett) to '50 or 60' (Bradley).

Lieutenant-Colonel R. H. Hall.

Second-in-Command to MacCarthy O'Leary, Reginald Hall took over the Battalion when the Colonel was killed at Pieters Hill and commanded it for the next two years.

Lancashire Lad: "Oh! Is that it; well, never mind; I'm reet enough as I am" – at the same time pushing the prisoner on.

The captive, not being accustomed to such treatment, exclaimed angrily: "You had better be careful, my man; remember I am a field cornet."

The Lancashire Lad scratched his head for a moment, and then remarked: "Si' thee, owd mon, I don't care if th'art a brass band tha'll hev to gooa in front!" And brandishing his bayonet, said: "Neaw goo on" – and he went.' [86]

As day broke on the 28th it was seen that the Boers had retired, and the South Lancashires were relieved in time for a welcome breakfast in bivouac near the railway line. Later that day British cavalry at last rode into Ladysmith, but the Regiment had a more immediate concern – the burial of their much-loved Colonel and his comrades. 'He was a gallant gentleman and a brave soldier,' mourned Private Neligan, who had served with the Colonel for some nine years. 'Like a father, almost, he behaved to his men during the campaign, never resting until his men had their rights and were made as comfortable as possible. I have seen him, when the regiment has been holding a position, going round the men, asking them if the cover they had was sufficient, while at the same time he would be exposed to the enemy's fire himself.'

'The men formed three sides of a square, which was filled up by our own officers and others from various regiments close by. Father

86. Neligan, op. cit., pp. 45–6.

Collins, the Brigade Chaplain, read the burial service, and one could hardly credit that these men, now with heads bent and arms reversed – and not a heart but was overflowing at the loss of our beloved Colonel and comrades – were the same men who only the previous day had wrought such awful disaster on the enemy. The service was read amid a profound silence, and many a silent prayer was offered up for the souls of those who had nobly laid down their lives for their Queen and country.' [87]

'Whilst digging the graves,' reported Major Hall, 'Sir C. Warren came to us and wished to address the Regt., but seeing the bodies laid out he wouldn't say anything before the funeral and hadn't time to wait, so he tore a leaf from his pocket book and wrote what I have enclosed for you to see.[88] He then shook hands with me and seemed extremely gratified at the conduct of the Regt. Sir Redvers Buller also rode by afterwards and called out, "Well done, South Lancashires". Everyone was talking of the South Lancashires, and Sir Redvers Buller, who witnessed it from the south bank of the Tugela, said it was the finest thing he had ever seen, and we heard the charge was the admiration of all who witnessed it.[89] The sad thing about it is that we have lost our dear Chief.' [90]

The Relief of Ladysmith

On 3 March 1900, Buller's Natal Field Force made its triumphant entry into Ladysmith. 'The Dublin Fusiliers had the place of honour marching through,' recalled Captain Edward Oakeley, 'the Lancashire

87. Neligan, op. cit., pp. 44, 46.
88. 'After the funeral of Colonel O'Leary and of the soldiers of the South Lancashire Regiment, I wish to express to Major Hall and Officers and soldiers of the South Lancashire Regiment the great pleasure I felt in bringing to the C in C your report of the gallant conduct of the Regiment in making the final charge and capturing the Boer trenches. Charles Warren.'
89. There was one notable exception. The bumptious young correspondent of *The Morning Post* conspicuously failed to acknowledge the South Lancashire's decisive role in the battle. Sergeant Hackett offers a persuasive explanation for Winston Churchill's strange oversight:

> Some 7 to 10 days earlier ... a horseman dressed as an officer rode up to the Battalion and enquired 'What sort of fellows are these Lancashire fellows', whereupon the C.O. waxed wrath and asked should not a junior officer salute before addressing his senior, ordered him to dismount and eventually ordered him to report, under arrest, to G.H.Q. I did not see this, having gone for water, but the Battalion was bivouacked in quarter column and it was on everyone's lips. I did see two staff officers come to the Battalion and the C.O. go with them. There was a great hubbub in the press and we all believed Churchill's report was pure spite against our C.O.

90. Hall, ibid.

The Relief of Ladysmith.
Buller's relieving army marches through the town, 3 March 1900.

Brigade with the XL heading them, being second. We were all fighting fit, swinging along with ragged uniforms, wood on our shoulders, carrying Boer trophies (a whole tent among them), most of us with beards and in fact looking like a lot of tramps – a contrast to the weak, pale-faced garrison in their best kit.' [91] Sergeant Hackett, too, was impressed by the pathos of the occasion: 'We marched through Ladysmith, General Buller at the head of the column, the Dublin Fusiliers leading (for their good work at Colenso) and the South Lancashires next (for Pieters Hill). Marching through two ranks, one each side of the road, it was sad to see these brave besieged men, clothes hanging on almost skeleton frames, leaning on their rifles as the order "Present Arms" was given; some stout hearts cried ... Next we passed the Cavalry, leaning on their lances and swords, and then the Town Hall where General Buller and General White stood mounted, so we had a good view at the order "Eyes Right". Through more infantry and out into the country and bivouac.' [92] Lieutenant Colonel Sir Henry Rawlinson saw them pass the Town Hall: 'I never heard the troops cheer like they did when they passed Sir George White today – they waved their helmets in the air and simply yelled, such magnificent men, too, full of reservists of course, making our poor garrison look mere boys – their clothes are tattered and torn of course, for it is now 18 days since they changed them – their khaki

91. Oakeley, ibid.
92. Hackett, ibid.

is split and torn to pieces, some of them hardly decent – many of them have got hold of Boer trousers of various shades of blue and brown to protect their nether ends – they carry no cooking pots but are all cooking in their mess tins ... most of the men carried a little bundle of dry sticks to cook their dinner with when they reach camp.'[93]

The news of the relief of Ladysmith was greeted with jubilation throughout the British Empire, but nowhere was enthusiasm greater than in Warrington. First to know, on 1 March, were the staff of *The Warrington Guardian* where 'in less time than it takes to write it the sound of heaving rolling machinery was drowned by an outburst of spontaneous applause in which the oldest and the youngest joined.' The glad news spread rapidly round the town. At Warrington Town Hall, the Town Clerk personally supervised the hoisting of a flag across which the word 'Ladysmith' was printed, while the Mayor despatched a telegram to General Buller, reading: 'Heartiest congratulations to you and your brave soldiers, especially to the men of the South Lancashire Regiment.'

It was a bright spring day, and, as the Church bells pealed out for victory, town and suburbs alike were hung with flags and bunting, and schoolboys rushed through the streets cheering and whistling 'Soldiers of the Queen'. 'The streets were crowded during the afternoon owing to the closing of some of the works,' recorded the *Guardian*: 'and the greatest enthusiasm prevailed everywhere. Rosettes were worn as a buttonhole, and even children in perambulators were seen carrying miniature flags, while many horses were decked with artificial flowers. At night a very unique sight was witnessed in Sankey-street. A large number of boys, headed by a couple of their number carrying lighted torches, marched in procession through the streets, singing "Soldiers of the Queen", and other patriotic airs. Each carried a flag, several of them were in mock military uniform, and one was got up as an old man with a flowing grey beard. The crowd laughed and cheered vociferously. The celebration was kept up until a late hour.'[94]

This spontaneous outpouring of jubilant relief was matched in towns and villages across Lancashire. The *Warrington Guardian* report of how the news came to Earlestown is typical:

'The anxiously-awaited information of the relief of Ladysmith was received in Earlestown about ten o'clock at the Post Office, and it instantly spread like wildfire. Everyone was delighted, and the tradesmen and householders began to decorate their places of business and

93. Rawlinson, diary, *c.* 10 March 1900.
94. *Warrington Guardian*, 3 March 1900.

General Sir Redvers Buller unveiling the South African War Memorial of The South Lancashire Regiment. Warrington, 21 February 1907.

houses with flags and bunting of all description, and in a short time the principal thoroughfares reminded one of some great fete day. Emblems were hoisted at the day schools and churches, including the Wesleyan, Cross-lane, and the Congregational, Crow-lane. The news was broken to the children in the schools by the respective masters, and invariably the children spontaneously gave vent to the patriotic spirit within them by lustily cheering Sir George White and General Buller. At most of the schools the children were given a holiday.

'The glad tidings at the works caused instant dislocation. Men threw down their tools and made their way into the streets. At the Viaduct works the employees, nearly 2,000 strong, were carried away by enthusiasm, and it is stated that not since the Crimean war has such a sight been seen at the place. As they left the premises the men heartily sang "Soldiers of the Queen", and many procured sticks and carried their coats shoulder high in processional order. At Vicars' Ironworks a similar scene was enacted. The men could not be restrained in their joyous exultation. At the Vulcan Ironworks 1,000 or more men also threw up their work for the day, and the same thing was experienced at the other works in the town.'

The mood in Lancashire on the morrow was more sombre, for late that afternoon news arrived of the death of MacCarthy O'Leary, as well-known and popular a figure in Warrington, where he had served for five years as Adjutant of the Volunteers, as he was in Preston. The flags which had floated in triumph over public buildings and business premises were lowered to half-mast, and an almost palpable gloom settled on both boroughs. In Preston, the garrison marched with muffled drums and black crepe armlets to attend a requiem mass at the English Martyrs Church, where the Colonel and his family had been accustomed to worship.

For 1st Battalion South Lancashire Regiment the triumphant entry into Ladysmith was followed by a return to more usual standards of military life. 'Next day,' recalled Sergeant Hackett, 'not having had a decent wash for seventeen days, orders for every man to shave and bathe were given. Nearly everybody had a beard about an inch long, and there was a rush to try and get a photo taken before it came off.'[95]

It was truly the end of the campaign, but not of the war.

95. Hackett, ibid.

PART III

The Great Advance

'General Officers, when issuing the orders for the attack of positions should confine themselves merely to explaining what they require to be done, leaving the details of how it is to be done to O.C. Battalions'.

(Lieutenant-Colonel Archibald Wright,
Commanding Officer, 1st Battalion The East Lancashire Regiment)

The East Lancashires Mobilise

On the outbreak of the South African War in October 1899 there seemed little prospect that 1st Battalion The East Lancashire Regiment, the old 30th Foot, would share in the impending campaign. The Battalion had but recently landed in Jersey for a tour of garrison duty in Fort Regent and were accordingly not included in the mobilisation of Sir Redvers Buller's Army Corps.[1] It was at first anticipated that this expeditionary force would suffice, with the troops already in South Africa, to deal with the Boer Republics, but as initial optimism faded the 5th and 6th Divisions were successively mobilised. Then, following the disasters of 'Black Week', orders were issued for the immediate mobilisation of the 7th Division under the command of Lieutenant General C Tucker CB. Its 15th Brigade consisted of 2nd Battalion Cheshire Regiment, 2nd Battalion South Wales Borderers, 1st Battalion East Lancashire Regiment and 2nd Battalion North Staffordshire Regiment.

The 1st East Lancashires had returned to England from Burma in December 1897 after seventeen years foreign service, having sailed to India in January 1880 under its ancient title, the 30th Regiment of Foot. The most notable incidents of their long eastern tour had been a terrible cholera epidemic at Lucknow in 1894, when 93 of the Regiment had died, and active service on the North West Frontier during the Malakand campaign of 1895. Lieutenant Colonel

1. The Battalion did, however, provide Buller with a 35-strong section of Mounted Infantry, commanded by Lieutenant G. E. M. (Gerald) Hill, which left Jersey on the 9 October. They remained detached from the Battalion throughout the war, serving with the Southern Company lst Battalion Mounted Infantry. (*The East Lancashire Regiment Bulletin*, May 1954, pp. 25–6, gives a nominal roll).

Lieutenant-Colonel A. J. A. Wright, CB, Commanding Officer, 1st Battalion The East Lancashire Regiment, 1899–1902.

St Helier, Jersey. Fort Regent, where 1st East Lancashires, the old 30th, were stationed in 1899, and the harbour from where the Battalion sailed for mobilisation on 19 December that year.

A. J. A. Wright,[2] an officer with 29 years' service in the Regiment, had commanded the Battalion since March 1899.

On 19 December 1899 the East Lancashires marched down to embark at St. Helier amidst scenes of whole-hearted public support. 'Long before the appointed hour of departure, available positions on the quay, promenade and parapet were occupied, the crowd massed being something like 12,000.'[3] At the quayside, where a guard of honour from the island's volunteer units presented arms, The Bailiff of Jersey made a patriotic farewell speech and presented each soldier with a briar pipe and a pound of best dark honey-dew tobacco, purchased by public subscription.[4] 'After cheers for Jersey, for the East Lancashires, and for the Queen, given amid a scene of unparalleled enthusiasm, the Regiment was called to attention and marched on board the S. S. *Vera* by companies, the Jersey Militia Band meanwhile playing the now popular "Soldiers of the Queen".' As the *Vera* cast off and steamed out, the band played 'Auld Lang Syne', flags dipped, and 'mightily ringing cheers from thousands of throats went up as

2. Archibald Wright was born 19 January 1851 at Portobello, near Edinburgh, and purchased an ensign's commission in the 30th Regiment 22 October 1870. He was promoted Lieutenant in 1871, was Adjutant of the 30th, 1879–80, Captain in 1880 and Major in 1890. During the Great War he commanded a brigade in England, and later an area in France, and was by then one of the very last serving officers to have purchased his commission.
3. *The Jersey Times and British Press*, 20 December 1899.
4. A further thousand briar pipes and a thousand pounds of tobacco were sent to the Battalion by the citizens of Burnley, while the few non-smokers were given £5 by an anonymous donor.

Officers of 1st Battalion The East Lancashire Regiment.

On mobilisation at Aldershot, December 1899. *Front row, left to right*: Lt P. C. W. Goodwyn, Lt & QM W. Holbourn, Lt F. J. O. Bonnyman and 2nd-Lt G. Clayhills. Seated: Capt L. Head, Maj C. R. M. O'Brien, Capt & Adjt L. St G. Le Marchant, Lt-Col A. J. A. Wright, Maj B. G. Lewis, Capt H. M. Browne and Capt L. l. Pile. *Third row*: Capt L. C. B. Hamber, Lt E. C. Da Costa, Capt F. H. Trent, RMO, Capt G. H. Lawrence, Lt R. A. Gosset, Lt R. Forrester, 2nd-Lt E. J. Wolseley and Capt G. E. Sharp. *Back row*: Capt E. A. Daubeny and Capt E. E. Coventry.

one', but, as the local newspaper also observed, 'the scene on the lower landing stage where the departing soldiers' wives were assembled in a group with their children, was pathetic and heart-stirring.'

The 1st East Lancashires completed its mobilisation at Aldershot. As Home Service battalion of the Regiment, it held many recruits and young soldiers not yet qualified for active service abroad, so 360 all ranks were formed into three depot companies, which were subsequently incorporated with the 7th Provisionaı Battalion, furnishing drafts as the men became available. The ranks of the 1st Battalion were replenished with some six hundred regular reservists, recalled to their old Regiment from civilian life. From towns and villages all over Lancashire they made their way to Fulwood Barracks, Preston. Local newspapers printed full accounts of the departure of many of these men, the following articles in the *Burnley Express*[5] being typical:

5. *Burnley Express and Advertiser*, 3 January 1900.

Sergeants of 1st Battalion The East Lancashire Regiment on Mobilisation, Aldershot, December 1899.
Front row, left to right: CSgt Blake, Master-Tailor Going, CSgt Connor, CSgt McKenzie, Bandmaster Blench, Sgt-Maj Mathewson, QM-Sgt Williamson, Mr Cawte, CSgt Longstaff Sgt Lawrence, CSgt Goodwin. *Second row*: Pro-Sgt Cox, Sgts Sullivan, Irwin and Griffin, Master-Cook Cates, Sgts Martin, Kainey and Pinder, CSgt Bull. *Third row*: Signals-Sgt Beeson, Sgt Woodbine, Armourer-Sgt Evans, Sgts Lewis, Burgess, Sisson, Devon, Fisher, Quinland and Harrison, Sgt-Drummer (Drum-Maj) Lydon. *Fourth row*: Sgts Millett, Hutton, Minnikin, Walton, Akhurst, Kennedy, Dunne and Doran.

'The departure of William South, of Burnley Lane, who has rejoined the East Lancashire Regiment, was accompanied by an outburst of enthusiasm that showed the feeling of the inhabitants of Burnley Lane. South, who wore a medal gained during previous service, was carried on a 'bus to Bank Top station about 3 o'clock on Saturday afternoon. He was a conspicuous figure on the very top of the vehicle, and attention was called to his departure by the Bank Hall Band, which went in front playing lively airs, and a large cheering crowd, which grew thicker as the procession got nearer the station.'

'Two other reservists, by name H. Livesey and John Thomas Wilkinson, left Padiham on Saturday to rejoin the East Lancashire Regiment. The men started from the drill hall, and hoisted shoulder-high were carried to the station, accompanied by the Volunteer Band, torchlights and a very dense crowd. The band played various selections and the crowd was very demonstrative, cheering and shouting ... At the station the platform was crowded, but the people were most orderly, and the send-off was therefore all the better. About 40 fog-signals were exploded as the train left, the band having previously played "Soldiers of The Queen", "Rule Britannia", "Auld Lang Syne", "Life's too Short to Quarrel", etc.'

The following week it was reported[6] that, 'Private O'Neil, of the

6. Ibid., 10 January 1900.

The East Lancashires embarking for the Cape, 13 December 1899.

1st Battalion The East Lancashire Regiment sailed from Southampton on the S. S. *Bavarian*, one of some two hundred British merchant ships chartered by the Admiralty. The eight thousand mile journey south took about three weeks.

1st East Lancashires, was given a hearty send-off from Clitheroe on Sunday evening. On the platform at the station the Borough Band played 'Auld Lang Syne' and "God Save The Queen", and cheers were given for the departing soldier as the train left. O'Neil has served eight years with the Colours and completed his term in the Reserve last year. He rejoined his old regiment last week on the understanding that he went to the front with the regiment.'

On the arrival of the reservists at Aldershot, the opportunity was taken to give them some refresher training in drill, manoeuvre, and musketry, and the time was otherwise fully occupied in issuing equipment and khaki serge clothing.

Meanwhile the Regimental Colours were taken to Burnley and were handed over with all due formality to the safe keeping of the Mayor and Corporation of the town, being deposited in the Parish Church of St. Peter's for the duration of the war. The scene was recorded in the *Burnley Express*: 'Never before have the streets of Burnley been so densely packed as was the case on Saturday, everybody being anxious to witness the imposing ceremony and demonstration in connection with handing over to the town, for safe-keeping, of the regimental colours of the 1st East Lancashire Regiment. The result was that many people, and especially children, got knocked about somewhat severely.'[7]

On 13 January the 1st East Lancashires left Aldershot by train for Southampton, and embarked on the S.S. *Bavarian*, which also had on board the South Wales Borderers. The *Bavarian* sailed at 3 o'clock the same afternoon. The strength of the Battalion on embarkation was 25 officers,[8] one warrant officer, 39 sergeants, 15 drummers, and 891 rank and file.

7. Ibid.
8. 7 Lieutenant-Colonel A. J. A. Wright (in command); Majors B. G. Lewis (second-in-command) and C. R. M. O'Brien; Captains H. M. Browne, L. l. Pile, E. A.

The Militia

Even before the 1st East Lancashires left Jersey, across Britain the Militia had been mobilised; amongst the first units to be embodied, on 13 December 1899, were the 3rd (Militia) Battalions of The South Lancashire Regiment and The Loyal North Lancashire Regiment. The South Lancashires moved into Fulwood Barracks, Preston, so recently vacated by their Regular battalion, while the North Lancashires, having embodied at Preston, went down to Shorncliffe and Lydd in Kent to complete their training. The 3rd East Lancashires were embodied a few weeks later, on 11 January, and on the 24th they assembled at Burnley and moved to the Curragh Camp, near Dublin.

Compared to the more strictly amateur Volunteer units, the old Militia might even be described as semi-professional. Its recruits were put through a basic training, at the Regimental Depot, almost comparable to that of a Regular soldier, and in 1899 their annual training liability included 27 days in camp (in 1882, in consequence of the war in Egypt, training had been extended to as much as 55 days). Many Militia officers and men subsequently served in the Regular Army for whom the old 'constitutional force' had provided, since the Napoleonic Wars, an important source of trained manpower. Historically, the prime purpose of the Militia was home defence, but during the Crimean War they had also volunteered for garrison duty overseas, relieving Regular battalions; so that in 1855–56 the 3rd Royal Lancashire Militia were stationed in Gibraltar, the 4th Battalion at Monaghan and Newry, and the 5th Battalion in Dublin.[9] This precedent was followed by even wider employment in the Boer War, for all three battalions volunteered for foreign service and eventually served as units in South Africa.

The 3rd Battalion Loyal North Lancashire Regiment was embodied at Fulwood Barracks on 13 December 1899. 'Large numbers of artisans and labourers,' reported the *Preston Herald*, 'might have been seen on Wednesday morning making their way along Deepdale-road to the Barracks. Those who arrived early in the morning were provided with

---

Daubeny, F. H. Trent, L. St. G. Le Marchant (Adjutant), L. C. B. Hamber, L. Head, G. H. Lawrence, G. E. Sharp ; Lieutenants E. C. Da Costa, E. R. Collins, E. E. Coventry; 2nd Lieutenants R. A. Gosset, G. Clayhills, P. C. W. Goodwyn, F. J. O. Bonnyman; and Quarter-Master W. Holbourn. There were also the following Militia officers attached, all of whom with the exception of the first named were subsequently gazetted to commissions in the Regiment: Captain C. J. Lloyd-Carson, Lieutenants G. D. Leake, S. H. Clement, E. J. Wolseley, and 2nd Lieutenant A. St. L. Goldie.

9. In 1881 these became, respectively, the 3rd Battalions of the Loyal North Lancashire, South Lancashire, and East Lancashire Regiments based in Preston, Warrington and Burnley.

Officers of 3rd Battalion The South Lancashire Regiment at Fulwood Barracks. The Battalion was mobilised at Preston on 28 December 1899 and left for South Africa on 16 January 1900. The Battalion was disembodied at Warrington in August 1901.

a good breakfast. All were taken before the doctor, examined, and, when passed, sent on to the storehouse. Here they received their equipment. Preston and East Lancashire are responsible for the majority of the men, but there were several from Manchester and Liverpool. The men were ordered to parade on the square at seven o'clock, and at that hour 940 militiamen in full marching order lined up.'[10] At half past seven the first detachment marched off amid loud cheering, headed by the Regimental Band; the remainder set off half an hour later, led out by the fifes and drums. The Battalion entrained for Kent that evening.

As the North Lancashire Militia marched out of Fulwood Barracks, the South Lancashires, 'a smart-looking and well-built body of men', marched in, having arrived at Preston from Warrington at five o'clock that same afternoon.

It was lunchtime on 28 December when mobilisation orders for the 3rd South Lancashires arrived by telegram; the news spread rapidly through the barrack rooms, where it was received with great enthusiasm. The Battalion's offer to serve in South Africa had been accepted and, together with seven other Militia battalions, it was to be ready to embark on or about 11 January 1900. The next fortnight was a very busy one as the battalion was clothed and equipped for active service. On Sunday 7th January the Colours were sent down to Warrington, with an escort of fifty men, and handed over to the Mayor's safe-keeping. 'The Colours and escort were met at the station by the band of the 1st Volunteer Battalion South Lancashire Regiment, which played them to the Town Hall, and thence in procession with the Mayor, Aldermen, and Councillors, and many of the inhabitants of Warrington to the Parish Church, the streets being almost impassable

10. *Preston Herald*, 16 December 1899.

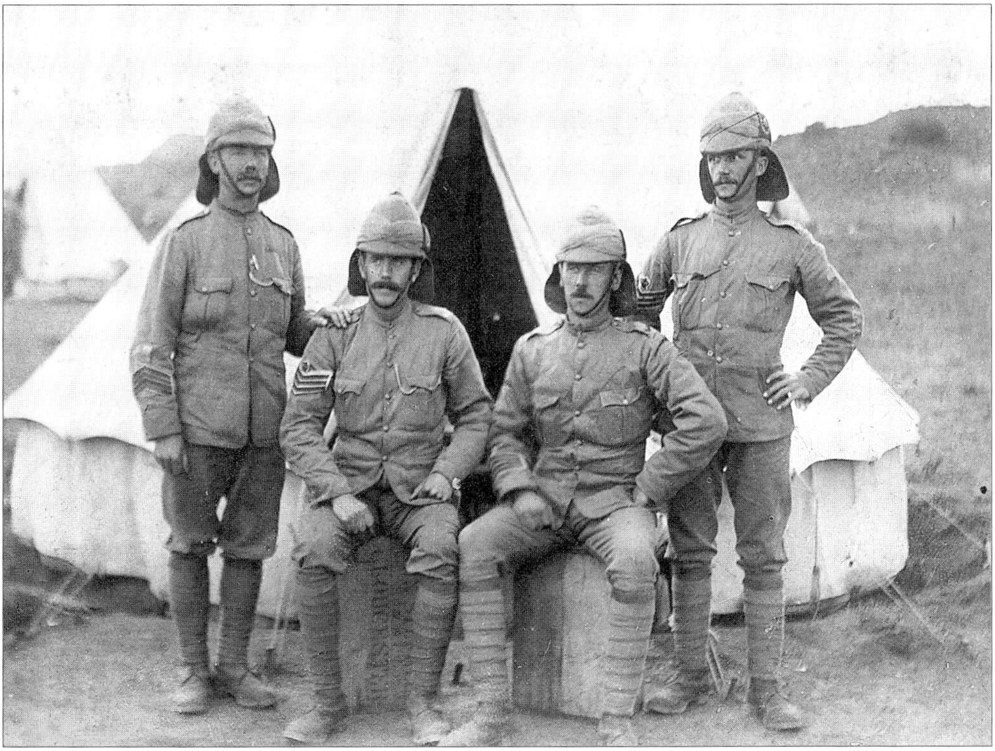

Staff Sergeants of the 3rd South Lancashires in camp at Colesberg, 1900.
Left to right: Sgt-Drummer Day, Sgt-Instructor Musketry Kirk, QM-Sgt Boast, CSgt Ingram.

owing to the number of spectators.'[11] On 16 January 1900 the Battalion left Preston by train for Liverpool and embarked, 787 strong, on the *City of Rome* to the deafening cheers of thousands of spectators on the Prince's Landing Stage.

Landing at Cape Town on 14 February, the 3rd South Lancashires were initially sent to secure the vital railway line from Naauwpoort to De Aar on the boundless veldt of northern Cape Colony, with headquarters at Hanover Road station. The area was still very much in the front line and lightly held, and for some days a Boer attempt to cut the railway was expected, but the crisis passed without an attack. As the Boers retired from Cape Colony the Battalion moved north, first to Rensburg and Arundel on 4 March, then to Colesberg, and finally to Norval's Pont on the Orange River, which was reached on 4 April. The Battalion was to remain there until August. The workload was heavy; strong outposts had to be provided for the defence of kopjes on both sides of the river, and large fatigue parties were required daily to assist the Railway Pioneer Regiment in the repair of the strategically critical railway bridge there, three spans of which had been destroyed by the Boers when they retreated across it in early March.

11. *Records of the 3rd Battalion South Lancashire Regiment*, Manchester, 1909, pp. 56–7.

3rd Loyal North Lancashire Regiment in Malta. Trooping the Colour in Palace Square, Valletta in front of the Main Guard, 1900. The Battalion formed part of the Malta garrison from 27 January 1900 until 2 March 1901, when they embarked for South Africa.

The 3rd Loyal North Lancashires had meanwhile embarked on 12 January for garrison duty in Malta, where from 27 January 1900 to 2 March 1901 they were quartered in Fort Manoel.

The 3rd East Lancashires assembled at Burnley Barracks on 24 January 1900 and, after being clothed and equipped, moved to the Curragh. Their stay in Ireland was short, for on 16 February the Battalion embarked on the *Servia* at Queenstown, with seven hundred all ranks, bound for the Cape. Disembarking at Cape Town on 14 March, the East Lancashire Militia were moved up to De Aar, where for nearly six weeks they camped on the west of the railway line.

Advance in the West

On the voyage to South Africa, 1st Battalion The East Lancashire Regiment suffered an influenza epidemic, which in many cases developed into pneumonia, largely caused, it was believed, by the cold and inclement weather to which the troops had been exposed on the rifle ranges at Aldershot. Two men died and were buried at sea.

The *Bavarian* docked at Cape Town on Sunday, 5 February. That afternoon Lord Roberts, the new Commander-in-Chief, visited the East Lancashires and, calling for Colonel Wright, expressed his welcome. 'I am very glad,' he said, 'your Battalion has arrived. I was afraid you were going to be too late to go with me.' The cheers which always greeted the appearance of the soldiers' much-loved 'Bobs' rang

Field-Marshal Lord Roberts of Kandahar, VC.

Hero of numerous imperial campaigns, ranging from the Indian Mutiny to Abyssinia, Afghanistan and Burma, 'Bobs' was 67 when appointed Commander-in-Chief in South Africa. This signed photograph was sent to the 3rd Loyal North Lancashires, of whom Lord Roberts was Honorary Colonel.

out the louder when his words were known and it was understood that the Battalion was to share in the success which all confidently anticipated for him. The arrival of the East Lancashires was indeed timely, for Roberts was at last ready to launch his counter invasion of the Boer republics.

The plan of campaign was remarkably simple in concept, involving a major offensive from the east into the Orange Free State to take Bloemfontein, then north-east to capture Pretoria and the Rand. Kimberley was to be relieved during the first phase of the operation, the advance on Bloemfontein, and Cronje's army was to be cut off and destroyed. Roberts also anticipated that his advance into their heartland would cause the Boers to reduce their force at Ladysmith, thereby enabling Buller to relieve that place by the end of February. In preparation for this great advance Roberts had assembled a corps of five divisions, some thirty-five thousand men and one hundred guns, along the strategic north–south railway line from Orange River Station to the Modder River. The plan involved considerable logistic risk, for once Roberts' army moved away from the umbilical railway, and until a rail link from Bloemfontein to the Cape was secured and reopened, it was dependent on lumbering and vulnerable wagon convoys for all its needs. It offered, however, an element of surprise, for Cronje had confidently assured his burghers that: 'the English do not make turning movements; they never leave the railway, because they cannot march.' His generalship was soon to be proven as defective as his knowledge of military history.

Next day, 6 February, Roberts left Cape Town in secrecy for the Modder River and the East Lancashires also left for the front in two troop trains. All heavy baggage remained behind, nothing being taken by officers or men except field kits. De Aar was reached on the early morning of 7 February, and orders were received for the troop trains to proceed north along the Kimberley line. At Orange River Station on the morning of the 7th, F Company[12] was ordered to detrain, and from this time until the end of the war this Company formed part of

12. Four officers and 136 men commanded by Captain Head, with Collins, Clayhill and Goodwyn as his subalterns.

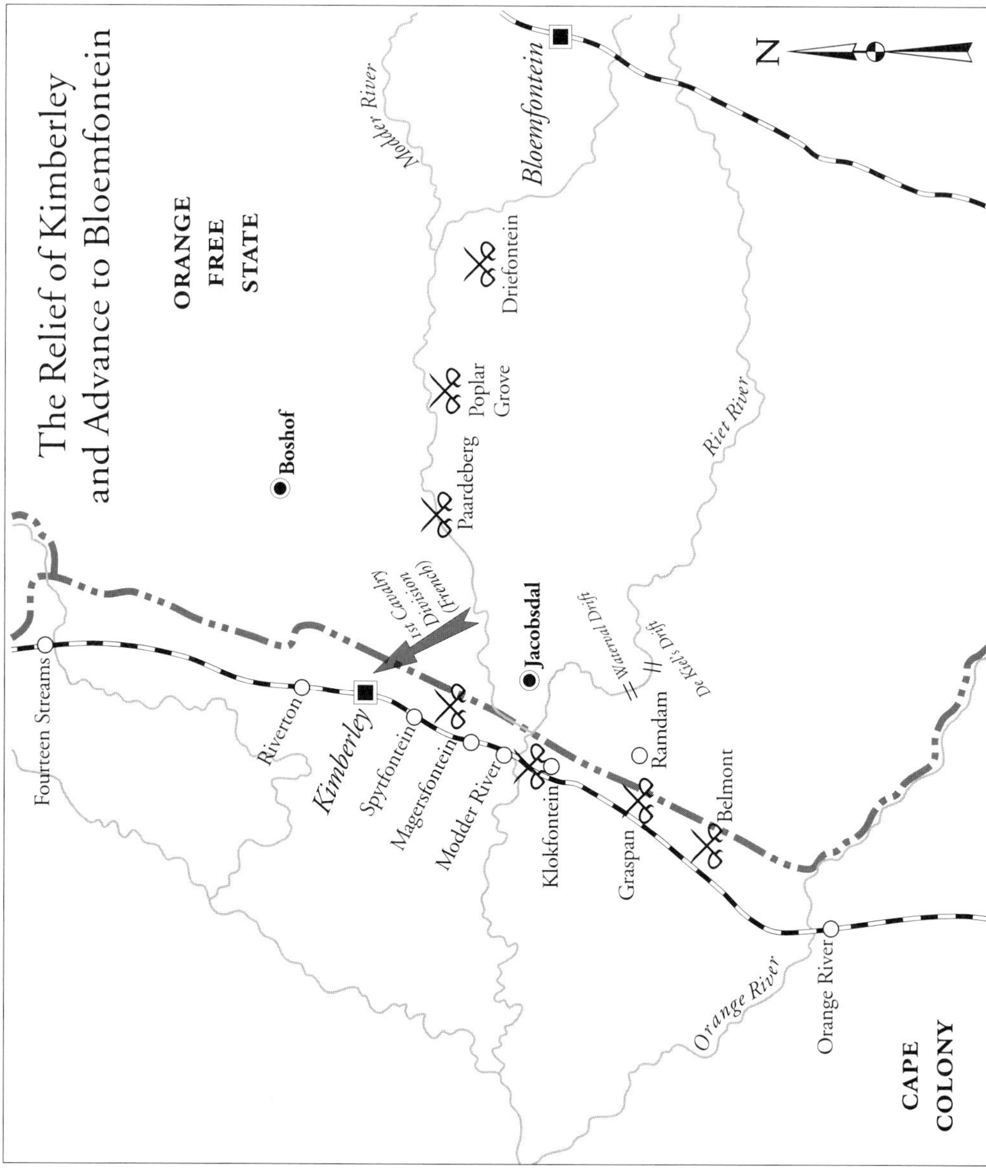

the 8th Battalion Mounted Infantry.[13] That same afternoon the Battalion detrained and encamped at Graspan, the 15th Brigade assembly area. The Cheshires had already arrived, and the formation of the Brigade was completed on the following day by the arrival of the South Wales Borderers and the North Staffordshires. Major-General A. G. Wavell[14] assumed command, and unit transport was issued.

13. On that same day the Mounted Infantry Company of 1st Loyal North Lancashires, commanded by Captain C. E. A. Jourdain, became a company of 3rd Battalion Mounted Infantry.

14. Father of Field-Marshall Lord Wavell.

The Great Thirst March

On the early morning of 11 February the first phase of the great advance began. Roberts planned to sweep north-eastwards to push between Cronje and his base at Bloemfontein with the intention of bringing about the relief of Kimberley by French's Cavalry Division, the defeat of the Boer general and occupation of the Free State capital. Tucker's 7th Division marched due east in a cloud of dust across the empty, almost featureless veldt to the farmstead of Ramdam in the Orange Free State, which was reached on the heels of the Cavalry Division. As in Natal, the troops marched with the lightest possible load; thirty pounds for officers and ten pounds for other ranks. Unit transport was restricted to two carts and two mules with reserve ammunition, a water cart, one buck wagon with tools and medical stores, and mules for the signals equipment. For the East Lancashires that first day's march was uneventful, the distance covered not over ten miles, and they were in bivouac at Ramdam soon after 10 a.m.

Captain G. H. Lawrence.
A keen historian, he donated many items to the Regimental archives.

Next day the advance was continued to the Riet River. This was a particularly difficult march for those Battalions that had only recently landed after three weeks at sea and whose ranks were filled with reservists, and was long remembered in the Regiment as 'The Great Thirst March'. Captain George Lawrence,[15] aged 31, was commanding 'E' Company:

'It had been decided that the Regiment should march at 4 a.m., but this was for some reason postponed and we were told to stand fast. At 7 a.m., just as breakfast was being prepared for us, we were ordered to fall in; consequently everyone started on empty stomachs, which was a fatal mistake and the troops paid heavily for this error on the part of their commander.

'It was the most trying march possible. We were fresh from board ship and unacclimatised, and we had 16 miles to cover to the Riet River under a burning, scorching sun which shone down pitilessly on

15. During the Great War he commanded the 1st East Lancashires in desperate fighting at Ploegsteert and Ypres in 1914–15.

us, causing the heat to radiate from the ground and strike up into our faces, parching us. Not a breath of air came to us, no shade and not a drop of water – it was a veritable fiery furnace.

'We covered half the distance all right, as our attention was rivetted on watching the shells bursting on the koppies and listening to the firing of the mounted troops, who were engaged in our front forcing a drift over the Riet River; but as soon as the Boers were driven back and there was nothing further to attract our attention, the sun seemed to gain in power, and our men felt the want of water. Most of them had already emptied their water-bottles, so the solitary water-cart was called up and half of its contents was doled out to the men, each man getting half-a-pint. As we marched on the sun became hotter and hotter, and soon the men were falling out in all directions from sunstroke (five of my own men went down), and we had to leave them where they fell, after opening their coats and dousing them with the precious contents of our water-bottles. Then we doled out the rest of the water and when that was exhausted it became Hell – men dropped out in all directions. We struggled on for another two miles, losing Major Lewis by the way, who, though riding, became unconscious and was laid between his horse's feet, the only shade available.

'At last we reached some wells where the Division halted and then every Regiment had to wait its turn; at last it came to ours and in time to my Company's; so I marched my men up and found the water to be some 15 feet down, so we let down our canteens tied to our putties and drank deep and long and soused our heads and shoulders with the water.

'After everyone had been watered, the Brigade formed up and marched off again, but, by this time I only had half of my Company left, and we also left behind us Captains Trent, Daubeny and Pile, who were utterly knocked up and could only lie under a tree and have water poured over their heads, and Lieut. Bonnyman who was delirious. We had another four miles to do before we reached the Riet River, and on the way my poor Col.-Sergt., Blake, was bowled over and fell as he was walking beside me, and we had to leave him behind for the ambulance; he died that evening of apoplexy.[16] His loss was a great blow to me and the Company – he was an excellent N.C.O. The Karroo at this point was thickly covered with men who had fallen out from the Division – the veldt being strewn with them.

'Finally, when we reached the river I only had my subaltern, Lieut. Wolseley, and 30 men left out of my Company of 100 men, and we were all fairly cooked. It was very lucky we had no fighting to do at

16. Colour Sergeant Blake, aged 32, 'a genial fellow, well-liked in Burnley', had managed to rejoin the 1st Battalion from the 3rd (Militia) Battalion on the outbreak of war.

the end of this very trying march, for I doubt if any of us would have been up to it. Every Company in the Division was in the same parlous state. So ended for us the most trying march of the campaign.'[17]

This gruelling trek very considerably thinned the ranks of the Battalion, no less than seven officers and three hundred men being temporarily incapacitated. Fortunately the Riet River was crossed without the infantry coming into action, and within a few hours after dark most of the sufferers had rejoined their companies on outposts. De Kiel's Drift, by which the Division crossed, had meanwhile been found impracticable for wagons, and it was not until the following afternoon that all the supplies and transport were across the river. The pangs of hunger (for no rations could be issued) were thus added to the trials of the day; but fortunately next morning a troop of the 16th Lancers drove through the outpost line a herd of captured goats, which were quickly bayonetted by the men and cooked in their canteens; the first substantial meal for over 36 hours.

The Capture of Jacobsdal

On the night of the 14th the advance was continued in a northerly direction to Wegdraai, where on the following morning the 15th Brigade was detached to occupy the small town of Jacobsdal. General Wavell advanced with the North Staffordshires as advance guard, followed by the South Wales Borderers and the Cheshires on the right and left flanks respectively, with 75th Battery Royal Field Artillery in the centre supported by half of the East Lancashire Regiment. The baggage was guarded by the remaining four East Lancashire companies, which also furnished the rear guard. The town was found to be occupied by some three hundred burghers, who offered only a short resistance to the infantry attack, which was carried out, as the Brigadier afterwards said, 'with less confusion than on an Aldershot field day'. Officers and men had in fact completely recovered from the fatigues of the 'Great Thirst March' and were now fit for anything.

A 'senior officer' of the East Lancashires sent the following account of this action to the *Burnley Express*: 'When the scouts got in range of the village the Boers opened fire and wounded two of them. Our guns then came into action at 1,900 yards and shelled some kopjes close by the town, on which we could see the Boers. After a time the North Staffordshires advanced to the attack, supported by the South Wales Borderers. As the guns had ceased firing the Cheshires were closed up. They were formed up for attack, and supported by the South Wales Borderers. A few bullets went pretty close, but the Boers

17. *XXX Journal*, August 1910.

soon bolted out of the town, and we walked in. We had no casualties ... So ended our first fight.'[18]

Waterval Drift

That same day, as has already been related, Kimberley was dramatically relieved by French's cavalry. Further south, though, where Roberts' main supply column, some two hundred wagons pulled by three thousand oxen, was still on the north bank of the Riet at Waterval Drift, disaster threatened. A raiding party of some 1,400 Boers, two guns and one pom-pom under Commandant Christian De Wet, who was to prove the outstanding guerrilla commander of the war, had been watching the convoy for two days, and, as the 7th Division moved on, saw the opportunity to strike. The story is taken up by Second Lieutenant George Clayhills, aged 22, of the East Lancashire Regiment Mounted Infantry:

Second-Lieutenant G. Clayhills.

Awarded a DSO and twice Mentioned in Despatches for gallantry with the Mounted Infantry in South Africa, George Clayhills fought with the 30th in the opening battles of the Great War and died, with many Regimental contemporaries, at Ploegsteert in 1914.

'The 8th Mounted Infantry, under Colonel Ross, arrived at Waterval Drift just before dark on the 14th, after a long march, and bivouacked on the near side of the Drift; part of the 7th Division being on the far side. On the 15th the M.I. were to act as escort[19] to the large ox convoy then in laager at the Drift. Owing however to some misunderstanding the Boers occupied the kopje overlooking the Drift, and when the section (Staffords) of the 8th went up expecting to relieve the Infantry, they were met with a heavy fire and lost heavily. During the whole of the 15th the Boers kept up a heavy fire from guns, pom-poms and rifles, and succeeded in stampeding a number of the oxen, making it impossible for the convoy to move. During the 15th, part of the 14th Brigade and some mounted troops[20] came back from Jacobsdal to relieve the convoy, but the Boers, now about 1,000 strong, could not

18. *Burnley Express and Advertiser*, 12 May 1900 (the correspondent may have been Lieutenant Colonel Wright, the Commanding Officer).
19. The convoy had been escorted from Belmont, via Ramdam, as far as the Riet by the 1st Loyal North Lancashire Mounted Infantry Company, under Captain Jourdain, but on the 14th they were ordered north to Wegdraai. 8th M.I. were only some 250 strong, the balance of the battalion having been left at Orange River for lack of horses.
20. Including half the Loyal North Lancashire Mounted Infantry.

be driven off, and after darkness an order was received from Lord Roberts to abandon the convoy and move on Jacobsdal. During the action Cr.-Sgt. Connor, who was acting Sgt.-Major, showed great gallantry in carrying messages under fire and in helping to get up ammunition from the river bank, for which he was recommended and gained the Distinguished Conduct Medal.'[21] In the course of this eleven-hour fight the East Lancashire M.I. Company suffered five casualties. Lord Roberts' rash decision to abandon his main supply convoy was almost certainly unnecessary, and his troops were to suffer severely for his mistake.

The Battle of Paardeberg

The halt of General Wavell's Brigade at Jacobsdal from February 15th until March 5th, to protect Lord Roberts' communications during his operations against Cronje at Paardeberg caused the keenest disappointment to the East Lancashires, but gave ample opportunity for the Battalion to become more acclimatised and accustomed to the local conditions of warfare. These included daily fluctuations of temperature which appeared extreme to those more used to the equable climate of Lancashire: 'Men were lying about in pools of water, soaked to the skin, and shivering with the cold night air,' wrote Sergeant Frankland, 'while during the day the sun would be sweltering.'[22] The capture of Roberts' supply convoy at Waterval Drift had an immediate impact on rations. In his diary entry for 16 February, Private F. G. Weaver recorded: 'Served out with ration of flour and having no fat had to use the dubbin for boots. Made passable pancakes.'

Private Bill Williamson later recalled how the Battalion had a rough time between convoy work and outpost duty on short rations and in extreme weather: 'We were living in the open, and were saturated with rain very often, but on one occasion it was terrible during the night. We were drenched to the skin, and there was nothing for it only to get up and move about to keep the life in and let the water simply run out of our clothing. During that awful cold, dark night and early morning we were very miserable, but sometimes through the night I heard the very familiar voice of a man named Murphy, whose other name (by chance) was 'Spud'. He seemed to be quite cheerful. I asked him what he thought of the situation, and he said it was just a matter of history repeating itself. No one was in a way of talking, but I just forced myself to ask him to explain himself, so my friend 'Spud', in a rather loud voice, said: 'The foxes have holes and the birds of the

21. *XXX Journal*, April 1911.
22. *Burnley Express and Advertiser*, 2 June 1900 – Sergeant Frankland, 1st East Lancashires, writing from Karee, 29 April 1900, but speaking of Jacobsdal.

air have nests, but the East Lancs hath not where to lay their heads.' I *may* have smiled – I doubt it – but many a time since I have laughed outright, as 'Spud' was anything but a Bible student.'[23]

Both the East Lancashire and Loyal North Lancashire M.I. Companies took part in the subsequent operations against General Cronje, who was cut off, trapped and eventually forced to capitulate with 5,291 men at Paardeberg on 27 February. The North Lancashires were involved in the encirclement and capture of an outlying Boer position on a kopje. Lieutenant Clifford and 23 North Lancashire Mounted Infantry of the Kimberley garrison also earned the medal clasp for Paardeberg, having escorted an urgent convoy of bread, baked in the De Beers Mine ovens, from Kimberley to the battlefield. After the surrender, 1st Loyal North Lancashires were ordered down from Kimberley to the Modder River to conduct the Boer prisoners to Cape Town.

Colour-Sergeant C. Connor, DCM. Charles Connor joined the East Lancashires at Burnley in 1884, serving first with the 2nd Battalion, in Ireland and at Gibraltar, and then with the 1st Battalion in India and Burma, including the Chitral campaign of 1895. On mobilisation for South Africa he was Colour-Sergeant of 'F' Company, which was converted to Mounted Infantry.

The Advance to Bloemfontein

The mounted infantry of both Regiments were in action again on 7 March at Poplar Grove, where the East Lancashires escorted the naval guns, while the North Lancashires, now part of a reorganised 1st M.I. Brigade, were under a heavy fire most of the day about Middelpunt Farm, and in the action at Driefontein on 10 March following which the Boers fled to Bloemfontein.[24]

After Cronje's defeat the 15th Brigade was ordered to rejoin General Tucker. Leaving Jacobsdal at mid-day on 6 March, the Brigade accordingly met Divisional Headquarters at Poplar Grove on the early morning of the 9th. On the following day the general advance under

23. Reminiscences of an Old Lilywhite, by WT Williamson, *East Lancashire Regiment Journal*, March 1932.

24. Medal clasps for Paardeberg were awarded to three officers (Head, Clayhills and Goodwyn) and 45 N.C.O.s and men of the East Lancashire Regiment M.I., while five officers (Head, Collins, Clayhills, Goodwyn and Hill) and 85 other ranks of that Regiment earned the bar for *Dreifontein*. Apart from the section from Kimberley, the North Lancashire M.I. had two officers (Jourdain and Macaulay) and 56 other ranks at *Paardeberg*, while Jourdain and 54 men were present at *Dreifontein*.

Lord Roberts was continued towards Bloemfontein, which surrendered on 13 March. The 7th Division, on the extreme right, advanced by Petrusberg, Driekop, and Panfontein to Poundersford Farm, five miles outside the Orange Free State capital. 'In three days we marched 63 miles! We paraded at noon one day and arrived at our destination at 6 a.m. next morning, a distance of 20 miles, and a good many hours to be under arms. Our longest march was 25 miles in one day. Our men were now perfectly fit, and most marches were accomplished at night, or early morning. We arrived without incident of note at Bloemfontein on the 16th March, after having carried out a flank march on half-rations in about as good time as any recorded.'[25] Later in the war the East Lancashires became so well known for their rapid marching prowess that they earned the nickname 'Lord Roberts' Greyhounds'.

No opposition was encountered on this march, but the hardships of the troops were considerable, compounded by the loss of Roberts' supply convoy at Waterval Drift. 'The men were on half biscuit rations, with their groceries cut down to an almost irreducible minimum. Of fresh meat there was plenty, for cattle were driven in rear of the columns, but the proverbial toughness of the 'trek-ox' vied with the hardness of the ration biscuit in its tax on the digestive and masculatory powers of the troops. The horses, without hay or oats, had to subsist on what they could pick up on the veldt; the heat by day was intense for those on foot; and the scarcity of water was such that it was a problem of the greatest difficulty even to meet the barest demands of necessity. Washing, as far as the Regimental Officers and men were concerned, was an impossible luxury.'[26]

Although the East Lancashires escaped, in its severest form, the devastating epidemic of enteric and dysentry which afflicted the troops who had been operating on the banks of the Modder River,[27] the effective strength of the Battalion on entering Bloemfontein was reduced to 19 officers and 695 other ranks – a wastage, allowing for detachments, of over one hundred men.

The Battle of Karee Siding

The East Lancashires had only a short halt at Bloemfontein, where they had expected to have remained longer to rest the men and recover

25. *XXX Journal*, June 1912 – This narrative, in effect a Battalion War Diary, was compiled some years before that date, at the request of the then Commanding Officer, by an officer who served throughout the campaign.
26. Ibid. 12 May 1900.
27. The wing of 1st Loyal North Lancashires at the polluted Modder River had eighteen deaths from disease in the first three months of 1900; the 1st East Lancashires, by contrast, lost no men from sickness over that period.

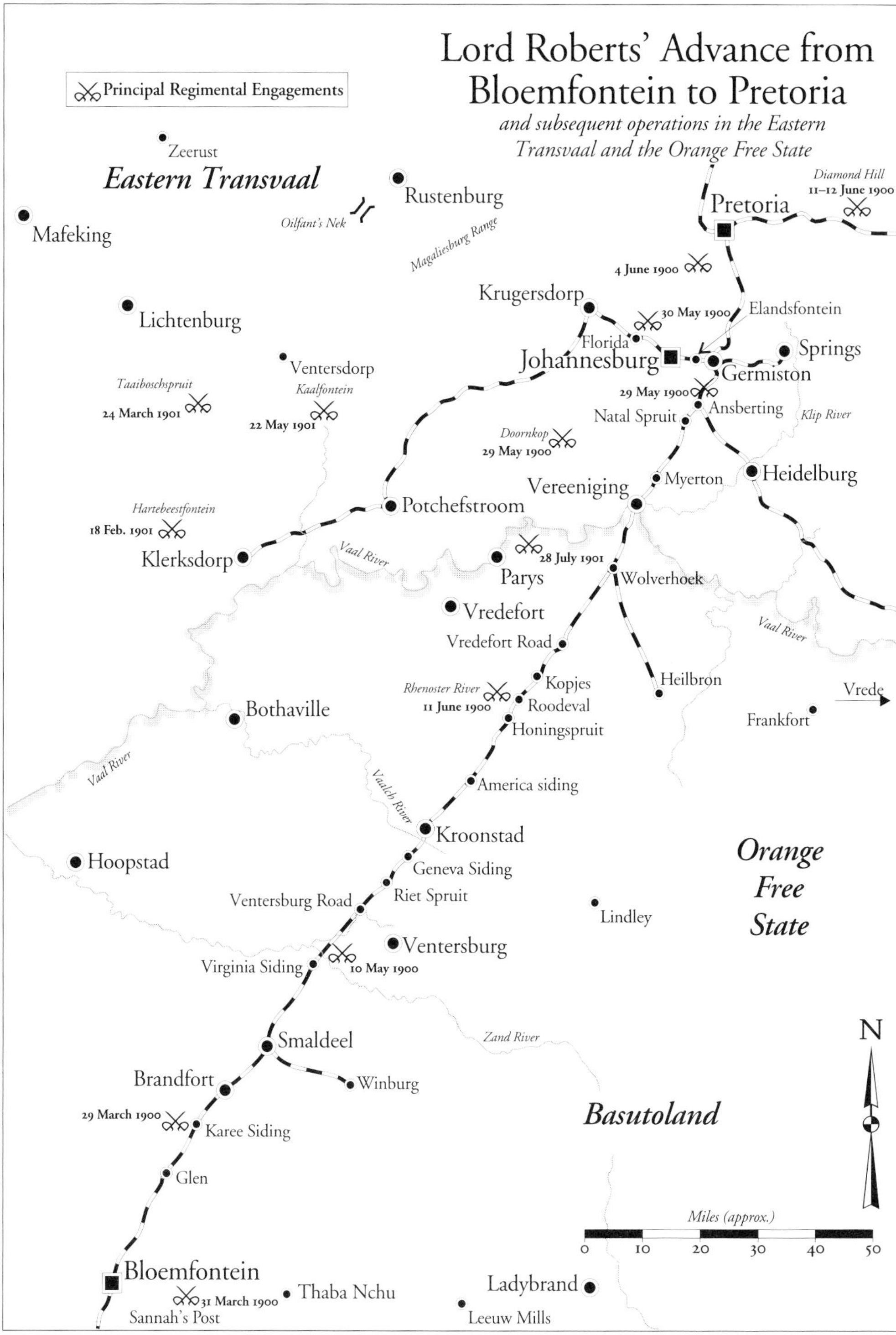
Lord Roberts' Advance from Bloemfontein to Pretoria
and subsequent operations in the Eastern Transvaal and the Orange Free State
Principal Regimental Engagements
Eastern Transvaal
Zeerust
Mafeking
Rustenburg
Oilfant's Nek
Magaliesburg Range
Pretoria
Diamond Hill
11–12 June 1900
4 June 1900
Krugersdorp
30 May 1900
Elandsfontein
Lichtenburg
Florida
Johannesburg
Springs
Germiston
Ventersdorp
Taaiboschspruit
24 March 1901
Kaalfontein
22 May 1901
29 May 1900
Ansberting
Natal Spruit
Klip River
Doornkop
29 May 1900
Myerton
Heidelburg
Vereeniging
Potchefstroom
Hartebeestfontein
18 Feb. 1901
Klerksdorp
Vaal River
28 July 1901
Parys
Wolverhoek
Vredefort
Vaal River
Vredefort Road
Kopjes
Heilbron
Rhenoster River
11 June 1900
Roodeval
Vrede
Bothaville
Honingspruit
Frankfort
Vaal River
America siding
Vaalch River
Kroonstad
Hoopstad
Geneva Siding
Orange Free State
Riet Spruit
Ventersburg Road
Lindley
Ventersburg
Virginia Siding
10 May 1900
Zand River
Smaldeel
N
Brandfort
Winburg
29 March 1900
Karee Siding
Basutoland
Glen
Miles (approx.)
0
10
20
30
40
50
Bloemfontein
31 March 1900
Thaba Nchu
Ladybrand
Sannah's Post
Leeuw Mills

1st East Lancashires in action at the Battle of Karee, 29 March 1900.

the baggage, including tents, left at Graspan. But on 26 March the 7th Division was inspected by Lord Roberts, who expressed himself pleased with the appearance of the men, and two days later it was on the move to the Glen, some 18 miles north of the capital. 'We acted as rear guard, and had to cross the Modder at an awkward drift. Our men worked like Trojans, and got the guns and waggons over in splendid style. We got into camp about 4 o'clock. Just as we had sat down and had had dinner we were informed we were to march next morning at 6.30 and fight the Boers, who held a strong position to the north-east.'[28] Roberts had ordered the 7th Division to attack the Boers at a small railway station called Karee Siding, where they had established a defensive position some three miles long on a series of kopjes dominating further progress north along the railway. The enemy numbered some 5,000 men under Commandant Smuts, including the famous 'Zarps', the Johannesburg Police, reputed to be the best fighters in the Boer army.

On the morning of the 29 March the East Lancashires paraded at about 7.30 a.m., each man having been issued with 150 rounds of ammunition and a ration of biscuits and tinned meat. At 10 a.m. the 7th Division advanced north along the railway line, with 14th Brigade on the right and 15th Brigade left. The Battalion was on the extreme left of the infantry attack. The left wing of the advance was extended by French's cavalry, while on the right Colonel Le Gallais' Mounted Infantry Brigade, including the East Lancashire M.I. Company, worked round the Boers' flank. The East Lancashire Company was

28. *Burnley Express and Advertiser*, 12 May 1900

in action from 11 a.m. until dark, escorting a section of 'pom-poms'. There were three lines of kopjes, and the flanking movement of the mounted troops manoeuvred the Boers out of the first two of these, but then the advance of the encircling horsemen was checked in close country. It would be up to Tucker's infantry to clear the main Boer position.

'The first line of koppies was reached at 11.30 a.m.,' wrote Captain George Lawrence[29] of the 1st East Lancashires, 'and the guns unlimbered for action, but no Boers were to be seen, so we advanced carefully to the second line of koppies, where we could look down into a fine valley with trees, a farmhouse and two dams of water, and beyond them was another line of koppies. Everything looked very peaceful; our Brigade, the XV, under Brigadier-General Wavell, was ordered to descend into the valley, so with the Cheshires leading, and ourselves next, we crossed the crest line and began to descend into the valley, when a few shots were heard from the other side of the valley and our scouts came galloping back, and shortly after a tall koppie, some 200 feet high and covered with trees, about one and a half miles away, woke up and saluted us with bullets, so we retired gracefully behind the crest line, having had two men of the Cheshires wounded; here we waited for two hours while the guns searched every nook and tree on that koppie.' Most of the men took the opportunity for a nap.

The Commanding Officer, Lieutenant Colonel Archibald Wright, takes up the tale: 'About 1.30 p.m. a heavy musketry fire commenced on the right of the 15th Brigade. This was the 14th Brigade heavily engaged with the Boers on our right front. The 15th Brigade remained lying behind the crest till about 2 o'clock, when the order was again given for the South Wales Borderers, Cheshires, and East Lancashires to advance, the North Staffords remaining as a support. These Battalions accordingly advanced in line (loose order) for about 500 yards and then lay down.[30] Heavy artillery and musketry fire continued on our right, but, although the 15th Brigade was under a desultory musket fire lying in the open, no orders were received for further action until 3.10 p.m., when Major Carlton, the Brigade Major, came to me with orders to attack a line of heights running east of Houtenbeck Hill.'

The main feature was some mile and a quarter long and two

29. Article by Captain G. H. Lawrence in the *XXX Journal*, 1910.

30. 'The formation employed in the attack at Karee and on all subsequent occasions,' wrote Colonel Wright, 'was as follows: Companies detailed for the 'firing line' extended one or more sections at 10 paces, with the remaining sections (also extended) following in support. The leading sections were preceded by two scouts. The Companies in reserve moved generally in fours, in line, or in lines of Company columns, until they came within effective musketry range.'

Lieutenant-Colonel Archibald Wright.

He commanded 1st East Lancashires throughout the war in South Africa.

hundred foot high, but the orders were restricted to the assault of a detached kopje which formed its eastern spur: 'The East Lancashires will attack that kopje', said the Brigade Major, pointing to the detached hill. 'Two companies in the firing line, two companies in support, remainder second line.' Colonel Wright was not impressed. 'I pointed out that if this plan was adopted the Battalion would be enfiladed by the commanding kopje on the west, and suggested that I should first capture this hill. His reply was, 'Those are your orders, Sir'. I therefore issued instructions in accordance with these orders, but realising at once the danger such an advance would entail upon the Battalion by its being enfiladed from the more commanding kopje, I countermanded these orders and issued [new ones], but too late to arrest the forward movement of E Company.'[31]

The Commanding Officer's new orders were as follows: Captain Sharp was to take his company up a wooded ravine on the west side of an adjacent spur of the main kopje. Major O'Brien, with the companies of Captains Daubeny and Trent, was to demonstrate opposite the south side of that kopje and, when he saw Captain Sharp had gained the summit of the ravine, he was to advance and attack the hill from its southern face. Captain Hamber's and Lieutenant Da Costa's companies were to act as a reserve and to occupy a deep donga [dried-up water course] some 800 yards from the base of the hill.

Meanwhile Captain George Lawrence with 'E' Company had already moved off to attack the small detached kopje in accordance with the original orders received from the Brigade Major. This is his account[32] of what followed:

'The advance for about 400 yards was through trees, and then a nullah was encountered, some 20 feet deep, into which we dropped and scrambled up the other side, from here to the foot of the koppie was 500 yards of bare veldt, without any cover at all. As soon as the right half Company of E, under Lieutenant Wolseley, appeared out of the nullah they came under fire, to which they laid down and replied, and were reinforced by the left half Company under Sergt.

31. Article '1st Bn The East Lancashire Regiment in The South African War', *XXX Journal*, June–August 1912, quoting Lieutenant Colonel Wright.

32. *XXX Journal*, 1910.

Left Lieutenant E. J. Wolseley.

Edward Wolseley, aged 19 and commissioned the previous year, was Mentioned in Despatches for gallantry at Karee when 15 out of the 22 men in his section were killed or wounded. He later served with the Mounted Infantry Company and was wounded in April 1901.

Right Sergeant H. Clowes, DCM.

Hutton. And from here the advance was carried on by rushes of half Companies until they got to 150 yards from the base of the koppie, where the fire got very hot, bullets coming from the front and right flank and dashing the dust up into our faces. Over our heads our guns were bursting shrapnel and searching the crest line splendidly, quartering every bit of the ground, but not a Boer was to be seen, We lay here for some 15 minutes returning the fire, when Lieutenant Wolseley, with No. 1 section, attempted a further rush, but as soon as he rose and rushed forward towards a kraal in front, he got on to slightly higher ground which had been protecting us all, and came into full view of the Boers on the right who enfiladed him well – most of his killed and wounded being shot from the right – and he lost 5 killed and 7 wounded in a few minutes out of 20 men, and the survivors retreated to the nullah. It was here that Pte. Clowes won his D.C.M. for carrying Pte. Birtwistle, who was mortally wounded in six places, under cover in spite of a very heavy fire, during which

The East Lancashires attacking at Karee.

From a sketch inside the Regimental Christmas Card for 1900.

he was shot through both forearms and had a bullet through his water-bottle.[33] Corporal Bamber, of No. 1 section, was also given the D.C.M. for his gallantry on this occasion, and Corporal Wallace was mentioned in despatches.

'The remainder of E Company had only three men wounded. Lieutenant Wolseley rejoined the firing line with the remnants of his section, and soon after we were reinforced by B Coy. under Capt. Trent, and Major O'Brien, acting second in command, ordered us to fix bayonets and charge; so in conjunction with A and G Companies., who were further on our left, we charged with cheers to the foot of the koppie, and began climbing up; it was very steep, and fortunately the Zarps bolted, or else they might easily have shot us all down as we panted and scrambled up the 200 feet of boulders and bushes. A Company, under Capt. Daubeny, had two men wounded. On arrival

33. Private Henry 'Chuckles' Clowes had joined the XXX at Lucknow in November 1892 and served in India and Burma, including the Chitral Campaign of 1895. At Karee Siding he was sent ahead as one of the scouts of 'E' Company and had nearly reached the foot of the kopje when the Boers opened fire on him. Remarkably, he was not hit as he ran back to report to his Company, then in the donga. He rejoined his section and advanced with it. When Private Birtwistle, a Burnley man and another veteran of India, was mortally wounded, he went to his assistance and stood up while hauling him under cover. One bullet went through Clowes' water-bottle, then another through both his forearms. He was eventually induced to go for promotion and was Machine Gun Sergeant when invalided out in 1911 as a result of his old wounds.

at the top of the koppie there was not a Boer to be seen; they had. bolted all along the line as our koppie was the key of the position. We re-formed our companies on the top and advanced to the further edge, where we had a wonderful view of Brandfort Plain, and could see the Boers galloping away in the distance to the right, under shelter of the koppies the 14th Brigade were attacking; while on our left front, General French and his Cavalry were being held up in the open plain, and heavily shelled by the Boers, who were holding a donga that traverses the plain midway between Karee and Brandfort.'[34]

The gallant charge of the East Lancashires had taken the Boers' main position by about 6.15 p.m., effectively ending the action and opening the way for Lord Roberts' eventual advance on Pretoria.

'Thus ended the fight of the Karee Siding', wrote Colonel Wright. 'Our total casualties were 5 killed[35] and 12 wounded, and of these 5 killed and 10 wounded were all in the section of E Company under 2nd Lieut. Wolseley. The strength of this section was 22, of whom 15 were killed or wounded, whilst every man in the section, with the exception of Lieut. Wolseley and a Corporal, had a bullet through some part of his clothing or equipment. One man with the machine gun was also wounded.

'The advance of the section over the open and under a perfect hail of bullets was a splendid performance, and it was led in a most gallant manner by its Officer. At the same time the loss of life was unnecessary, as but for the orders issued by the G.O.C. through his Staff Officer this advance would not have taken place till the hill commanding the

34. Details supplied by other eye-witnesses of the action understandably vary. The following account was published in the *Burnley Express and Advertiser*, 2 June 1900: 'As the infantry got within rifle range they were subjected to a very heavy Mauser fire, but our men, taking advantage of every inch of cover, crept closer and closer, extended in a long line with plenty of interval. It was difficult for the Boers to shoot effectively ... As the Lancashires advanced towards the ridge, a pom-pom was turned upon them and a party of Zarps, stationed in the kraal, fired into their rear, compelling them to retire to the cover of the donga. Supports were not available but the Lancashires were not to be beaten. Two companies crept along the donga until opposite the farm and kraal, then rushed up the steep bank and stormed the place in gallant style, driving out the Zarps with loss. The ridge was soon afterwards taken by the rest of the battalion, the pom-pom retiring before our men could capture it.'

35. Corporal Carey and Privates Birtwistle, Banberry, Day and Dooley. They were buried the next day in separate graves on the side of a small koppie, opposite to the one they had so gallantly helped to take. Writing home to Darwen, Private J. J. McGlone recalled how two other Darwen lads, Day and Dooley, were killed: 'Poor Dooley! I shall never forget him as long as I live. He was pulling a bullet out of Private Day when he got one in the stomach. It made a gash you could get your fist in. The poor fellow kept saying to me 'Oh dear, Mac! Please finish me for I am done for.' The bullets were flying in all directions.' (Letter to *The Preston Herald*, 23 May 1900).

East Lancashire Regiment graves at Karee.

detached kopje had first been captured. General Officers, when issuing the orders for the attack of positions should confine themselves merely to explaining what they require to be done, leaving the details of how it is to be done to O.C. Battalions.

'Four Companies, under Major O'Brien, bivouacked that night on the hill they had captured (known afterwards as East Lancashire Hill), whilst the three remaining Companies returned to the farm by Karee Siding where they bivouacked. At 2 a.m. next morning the transport, which had been left behind at Glen, arrived, when Officers and men were able to get their blankets and make themselves fairly comfortable for the remainder of the night.

'Next morning General Tucker rode through the camp, and addressed the following remarks to a group of men: 'I have just received a congratulatory telegram from Lord Roberts. On these occasions, men, I get the praise, but it is thanks to you that I earn it. You had a damned hard nut to crack, and you did it damned pluckily.' General Wavell, on our return from the fight, said to me, "Colonel Wright, I was very pleased with the way the East Lancashires took the kopje." ... I may add that in a conversation between General Wavell and myself a few days after the fight, General Wavell informed me that General Tucker was on the point of retiring to Glen when the whole situation was changed by the capture of the heights by the East Lancashire Regiment.'

Sannah's Post

The successful attack at Karee Siding was not followed up for over a month, for Roberts had decided to consolidate around Bloemfontein before resuming his advance north to Pretoria. His priorities were to reopen the railway line from the Cape (on which 3rd South Lancashires were now labouring hard at Norval's Pont) and to build up his army and its supplies, ready for what was to be the final offensive into the Transvaal. Meanwhile he was persuaded that the Free Staters could be pacified by clemency, proclaiming an amnesty and sending small parties of troops into the surrounding country to receive the submission of the Boers and collect surrendered arms.

On 15 March, however, intelligence was received that the Boer Commandant Olivier with six to seven thousand men was retreating north from Colesberg and Stormberg and would pass some forty miles east of Bloemfontein. Roberts made a half-hearted attempt to block this move by sending Broadwood's 2nd Cavalry Brigade and Alderson's 1st M.I. Brigade (with both 1st and 3rd M.I.) to Thaba N'chu, near the Basuto frontier and astride Olivier's route. The 3rd M.I. under Lieutenant Colonel Pilcher, including the Loyal North Lancashires Mounted Infantry Company, reached Thaba N'chu on 20 March. The following morning they pushed on to Leeuw River Mills to secure a valuable store of flour. The small force was now very isolated in enemy territory. Pilcher entrenched himself, sent out patrols in all directions, and awaited reinforcement; but none came. On the 22nd the mounted infantry exchanged shots with the enemy, of whom a large number with wagons were seen trekking in a north-east direction. Olivier had escaped, and the whole situation east of Bloemfontein was becoming precarious. As so often during the Boer War, the hunters were about to become the hunted.

Nevertheless, Pilcher remained around Leeuw Mills until the 26th, when with great daring he rode further east to the Boer settlement at Ladybrand[36] with one hundred horsemen, including 25 of the North Lancashires under Captain Jourdain, and seized the local landrost and a field cornet. It was a dashing piece of bluff, but the arrival of some four hundred Boers adversely altered the situation. Covered by his Maxim gun, and taking his prisoners with him, Pilcher beat a hasty retreat to his camp at Leeuw Mills. 3rd M.I. did not remain there long, for on the 28th patrols saw large bodies of the enemy moving

36. Eighteen miles from the Mills and about forty from Thaba N'chu.

towards the camp. That night the mounted infantry slipped away, reaching Thaba N'chu the following morning. They were now with Colonel Broadwood's main force, some 1,700 strong all told, encumbered with civilian refugees and a convoy of over one hundred lumbering wagons.

Towards midday on the 30th Broadwood learned that some three to four thousand Boers were on the march from Ladybrand, while a further enemy force threatened his northern flank. The exposed force retired towards Bloemfontein, along a track which forded the Modder River near the water pumping station at Sannah's Post[37] and then crossed Koorn Spruit, two and a half miles further on. It was about 3.30 a.m. on the 31st when Broadwood's column crossed the Modder and bivouacked. 3rd M.I., having protected the right flank from Olivier's pursuing commandos during the march, now formed the rear guard. Even as Broadwood's men threw themselves down to rest an audacious trap was being prepared for them by De Wet, who had ridden south under cover of darkness with 1,500 burghers and four guns. De Wet himself, with 350 men, set an ambush where the track to Bloemfontein disappeared into the steep-banked Koorn Spruit, while the remainder of his force, with the guns, occupied positions to the north and east of Sannah's Post, overlooking the British camp. Their role was to be that of beaters, driving their quarry into the ambush.

The trap was sprung shortly after dawn when the astonished camp was shelled and came under rifle fire. Broadwood decided to withdraw his force across the Koorn Spruit and sent off the vulnerable convoy first, followed by his two batteries of horse artillery, while his mounted men remained to cover the move. No scouts were sent ahead. Encouraged by the firing to their rear, wagons and guns hastened to the drift where, quite oblivious of impending disaster, one after another they descended to the river bed and found themselves covered at close range by hundreds of Boer rifles. Resistance was out of the question, and within minutes the wagons and a battery were surrounded and captured. The alarm was raised just in time to save 'Q' Battery Royal Horse Artillery and Roberts' Horse from the same fate. The battery wheeled about and, under an intense fire, came into action at a range of less than one thousand yards, firing steadily until most of the gunners were shot down. After six hours the survivors[38] of 'Q' Battery were ordered to retire, but by then their prompt and gallant action had prevented the Boers from cutting off Broadwood's entire force,

37. These water works, some 23 miles east of Bloemfontein, were the source of all drinking water for the capital and were accordingly held by a small British garrison.
38. Four members of 'Q' Battery were awarded the Victoria Cross for this famous action.

which was inspired by their example. 'As the mutilated remnant of two batteries of Horse Artillery tottered through the line of prone mounted infantry covering its withdrawal,' wrote *The Times* correspondent, 'the men could not restrain their admiration. Though it was to court death to show a hand, men leapt to their feet and cheered the gunners as they passed.'

The Mounted Infantry had initially remained in position as rear guard, engaging the Boer gunners and riflemen to the north-east. Then, with the Boers encircling their left, they were ordered to join the general retirement south, to where the cavalry had found an alternative crossing of Koorn Spruit. 'By successive companies, Rimington's Guides and the 1st and 3rd M.I. Battalions gradually fell back towards the positions further south, which were being held by Alderson's second line ... As each company retired behind the next, the Boers advanced in rushes up to within a hundred yards, only to be stopped by the fire of the company that remained to face them. There was no confusion and no undue haste, where all seemed to have a noble emulation to save a comrade or to retrieve the day from utter disaster ... The Boers pursued right up to the drift; then, after a final skirmish with the 3rd M.I. left to hold it, they returned to gather up their spoils.'[39] The British force then retired on Bloemfontein by way of Bosman's Kop.

Broadwood had lost 138 men killed and wounded and 430 taken prisoner, the latter including a sergeant and nine privates of the Loyal North Lancashires, and seven guns.[40] His defeat had been redeemed only by the heroism of 'Q' Battery and the steadiness of the mounted infantry. Speaking at Bosman's Kop to Colonel Alderson, he said: 'Will you please let all under your command know how much I appreciate the work done by your brigade today. It was splendid. If any unit should be mentioned it would be the 3rd M.I.'

Shortly afterwards the mounted infantry units were regrouped. 3rd M.I. were brigaded on 10 April with the New Zealanders and the Queensland M.I. to form 3rd Corps, while 8th M.I., now commanded by Captain Head of the East Lancashires, was grouped on the 19th with Lumsden's Horse, Loch's Horse, and M.I. units from the West Riding and Oxfordshire as 8th Corps.

At the conclusion of the sieges of Ladysmith and Kimberley, the 1st Battalions of the South Lancashire Regiment and the Loyal North Lancashire Regiment respectively had remained for some time in the vicinity of those places to rest and re-equip. The South Lancashires were for a time pulled back to Pietermaritzburg to refit, but Sergeant

39. *Times History*, Vol. IV, p. 43.
40. Mounted infantry, when unhorsed in a mobile action, were particularly vulnerable to capture.

Hackett did not take to the place: 'Troops were not liked in the one main street town and there was not much to do except keep firm from being jostled off the pavement by laughing, truculent negroes. There had been some fights, and troops were warned to go out in numbers, not less than three. There was a small billiard saloon which we frequented for snooker and skittles, but the attitude of the negroes was not pleasant and we walked on guard. Later this exhibitionism developed into a war between two impis and troops had to be diverted to keep the peace. Hotels were out of bounds.'[41]

The Volunteer Service Companies

Both Battalions received reinforcements, which notably included a Service Company made up from the Volunteer Battalions of each Regiment, making up for the companies converted to mounted infantry. The call for the Volunteers to offer themselves for active service had met with a remarkable response throughout the British Isles, and nowhere was the response more hearty or public support greater than in Lancashire.

Even before the outbreak of war, in September 1899, Lieutenant-Colonel J. C. Ridgeway, Commanding 1st Volunteer Battalion The South Lancashire Regiment, called a special parade at the Drill Hall, Warrington, at the urgent request of the officers and men, to consider the question of volunteering for service in South Africa. The result of this parade was an unanimous offer by the whole Battalion to serve overseas. It is worthy of note that this spirited offer was the second in the whole of Britain to be received by the War Office, being beaten only by a similar offer on the previous day by a London unit. The offer was accepted, but it was not until early January 1900 that the Battalion was called upon to make good its pledge by raising a half-company for service with the 40th in South Africa. The other half of this Volunteer Service Company was to be found from the 2nd Volunteer Battalion, at St Helens and Widnes. There was much competition for places, but the required three officers and 113 N.C.O.s and men, commanded by Captain F. M. Appleton, were eventually chosen. On Saturday 13 January the Warrington men took the oath of allegiance to the Queen at the Town Hall, before the Mayor, Alderman Henry Roberts, and marched into Orford Barracks for training.

That same evening the St Helens and Widnes volunteers were entertained to a farewell dinner at the Fleece Hotel, St Helens by their Commanding Officer, Lieutenant-Colonel W. W. Pilkington,

41. Hackett, op. cit.

Volunteers of the South Lancashire Regiment at the Town Hall, Warrington.
This is the Third Contingent of part-time soldiers from 1st Volunteer Battalion South Lancashire Regiment, commanded by Lieutenant B. Fairclough (right), photographed in their Home Service uniform after taking the oath before the Mayor.

and on Monday 15 January the detachment left for Warrington. 'Never before in the history of the borough had there been such a demonstration as was made in connection with this departure. Earlier in the day there had been a storm, and further trouble in the same direction was threatened, but this did not prevent the streets from being crowded with thousands upon thousands of the most enthusiastic sightseers. The works were temporarily stopped; places of business closed; the school children were given a holiday; flags and other decorative devices were used to effect upon the Volunteer Hall, the Town Hall, the Gamble Institute and other lofty buildings. A parade at the Volunteer Hall was attended by 500 men of the Battalion who, after a brief address from the Colonel, accompanied by their own band and that of the Volunteer Engineers, escorted the detachment to the Town hall and then to the railway station. At the Town Hall the men were met by the Mayor of St Helens (Councillor J. Beecham), the Mayor of Widnes (Alderman George Ingram Neil), and a representative gathering of townspeople, who wished them "God speed". Then followed the ever-to-be-remembered march to the station, and the "send-off", which was as cordial as it was demonstrative.'[42]

'The Warrington men attended divine service at the Parish Church on Monday, 19th February. The church was crowded, and it was estimated that nearly 1,000 persons were unable to gain admission. The service was, naturally, of a most impressive character, the Rector (the Rev. Canon Willis) preaching, and subsequently handing to each man a specially printed prayer, given by Mr Birtles, photographer, for their use while away on active service.

42. The Volunteer Service Company (1st South Lancashire Regiment) in South Africa During The Boer War, compiled by Captain F. M. Appleton, Warrington, 1901, p. 33.

Captain Francis Appleton, 1st Volunteer Battalion South Lancashire Regiment, of Grappenhall, Warrington.

Commanding First Active Service Company, The South Lancashire Regiment.

'The service was followed by a patriotic demonstration in Parr Hall, where the men were entertained to dinner. The march from the church to the hall was quite a triumphal procession, headed by many torch and flag bearers, and the town was suitably decorated. The large building was crowded, the body of the hall being filled with those who were joining the Volunteers at dinner, and the platform and galleries with spectators; a charge made in aid of the Volunteer Fund having only the effect of sharpening competition for places at what was rightly felt to be an historic gathering. Speeches bubbling over with patriotism and containing unreserved expressions of confidence in the ability of the men going to the front to maintain the honour of this portion of Lancashire were made. So good had been the response to an appeal made to the town on behalf of the men, that the Mayor was able to hand over to each man a field glass and a life policy for £100 in favour of his nearest relative.'[43]

On the evening of 19 December 1899 the right wing of 1st Volunteer Battalion of The Loyal North Lancashire Regiment met at their headquarters drill hall in St Wilfred's Street, Preston. 'The men were in plain clothes, fresh from the loom, the counter, and the desk, but there was an unmistakably patriotic air about every one of them. The muster was a record one and has never before been exceeded in the annals of local volunteering,' reported *The Preston Herald*. 'The men all seemed in the highest spirits, absolutely bubbling over with enthusiasm,' when their Commanding Officer addressed them, calling for volunteers from the detachments in Preston, Longridge, Chorley and Horwich to form a composite company for the line Battalion in South Africa. 'The men were then asked individually as to whether they were in favour of going out on active service, and declared to a man that they were.'[44] The left wing of the Battalion paraded at Chorley to offer their services, as did the Volunteers of the East Lancashire Regiment at Blackburn and Burnley.

The Loyal North Lancashire Volunteer Company left Fulwood Barracks, Preston at 10.30 on the evening of 23 February. 'Previous to their departure,' reported *The Preston Herald*, 'the men were drawn up on the square of the barracks and addressed by Colonels Carter

43. The Volunteer Service Company, p. 32.
44. *The Preston Herald*, 20 December 1899.

Volunteers of the Loyal North Lancashire Regiment leaving Preston.

The First Contingent of men from the Volunteer Battalions of the Loyal North Lancashires marching down to Preston railway station on 23 February 1900. They joined the 1st Battalion at Dronsfield, north of Kimberley, four weeks later.

and Widdows. General enthusiasm prevailed; the air was frequently rent by the cheering of the rest of the garrison, and the speeches could only be imperfectly heard. The general tenor of the remarks, however, was thoroughly patriotic ... The strains of "Auld Lang Syne" and "Soldiers of the Queen" and other airs were heard as the men moved down Deepdale Road. As the town was neared the crowd became greater, until it reached enormous proportions in Fishergate. The members of the Conservative Working Men's Club had taken advantage of the occasion to develop a fireworks display, and a series of rockets were sent up as the men passed, while Councillor Barton's band, which was posted close by, played patriotic airs. The scene at the station was a remarkable one. A huge crowd stormed the barricades, vainly striving to secure admittance ... The bands meanwhile made the rafters ring as they played "Rule Britannia" and "Cock of the North". The train steamed out about twenty minutes past twelve, and as the wheels moved a perfect fusillade of fog signals was fired. The men, it may be stated, are all insured for £100 as a result of a special subscription paid, and will receive £2 each when aboard ship. One hundred and sixteen pounds of tobacco are also to be distributed among them when they reach Southampton.'[45] They set sail the following day on the transports *Mexican* and *Assaye.*

The First Volunteer Service Company of the South Lancashire Regiment left Warrington in the early hours of 23 February. Before they left Orford Barracks, Major Adam, Officer Commanding 40th Depot, had the 1st Battalion Colours marched from the Officers' Mess

45. *The Preston Herald*, 24 February 1900.

A Private of 1st Volunteer Battalion The South Lancashire Regiment.
Front and rear views of full marching order for service in South Africa.

to the Company lines, where they were unfurled and shown to the soldiers. 'Major Adam, after describing them and pointing out large numbers of Battle Honours, spoke a few inspiriting words to the Company, trusting that its members in the Service Company would do nothing to disgrace what were now their Colours too. After supper, the Company fell in at twelve midnight in perfect silence and good discipline, upon which they were complimented by Major Adam, and faced the fiery ordeal awaiting them outside the barracks gates, and eventually reached Bank Quay Station in very much extended order.' [46] 'Our last impression of Warrington,' wrote Lieutenant Lewis, from Widnes, 'was 70,000 or 80,000 people trying vainly to reach the platform at Bank Quay Station.'

Later that day the company embarked at Southampton on the *Avondale Castle* for Table Bay. Lance-Corporal Moss, from Earlestown, recorded his impressions of life on a troopship. The novelty of sleeping in hammocks occasioned much innocent amusement: 'When everyone has retired for the night, the hammocks, being light in colour, look

46. Captain F. M. Appleton's diary, in *The Volunteer Service Company South Lancashire Regiment in South Africa*, p. 130.

like nothing more than rows of pigs hung up, back downwards. The sight tempts a fellow to perform with a stick underneath.' He describes how the long winter evenings were spent: 'We seek out our usual happy hunting ground, near the stern of the vessel. The men sit, lie or lounge in various and innumerable attitudes. Pipes, cigars, cigarettes are in plenty, and are at once lit. Songs are sung – and murdered; yarns are told, and general conversation indulged in. The men are in a peaceful mood. The night may be as black as pitch. It is impossible to see anything over the rail except the white foam made by the ship cutting through the water.

'In course of time the orderly brings in the rations for supper – biscuits and cheese. These biscuits, or wooden platters, are very good so far as digestion is concerned. The teeth must be firmly set in them, and then, with both hands, the eater must press heavily up and down. Everything comes to him who waits. So in the present case. In process of time the biscuit gives way, the bits fall all over the shop from the sudden breaking of tension, and a resounding snap is heard for miles.' [47]

The South Lancashires trans-shipped at the Cape for Durban, which they reached on 28 March, while the Loyal North Lancashire Company disembarked at Cape Town on the 15th and marched into Main Barracks. 'We were there two days,' wrote Sergeant Lindsay, 'when we got a sudden order to go to the front. Then there was such a packing up of kit bags and stores, getting them on the wagons, and drawing 150 rounds of ball ammunition each. We were a little over an hour in packing up and getting down to the station. There the people of Cape Town, gave us grapes, biscuits, matches, and lime juice. Then our railway journey of 654 miles commenced. The train stopped at different stations for meals, and it was at the first stop that we got our first ration of bully beef and biscuits ...' After spending a night in the train at Kimberley Station, where the roof still had Boer shell-holes, on 20 March the Volunteer Company joined 1st Battalion The Loyal North Lancashire Regiment in camp at Dronfield. 'We got a very hearty reception from the men who cheered like mad, and did everything they could for us, pitching our tents, etc.' [48] The South Lancashire Volunteer Company received an equally warm welcome when, on 29 March 29, they marched into the camp of the 'Fighting Fortieth' at Surprise Hill, outside Ladysmith.

The East Lancashire Volunteer Company did not immediately join its 1st Battalion, being employed at Laingsburg on the Cape to Kimberley railway line, from where Private G. H. Birnie wrote in April to his friends in No. 1 Total Abstinence Club at Darwen: 'We have got

47. Lieutenant H. H. Lewis, article in *The Volunteer Service Company*, pp. 35–7.

48. Sergeant C. C. Lindsay, letter written at Boshof, 26 April 1900, published *The Preston Herald*, 23 May 1900.

The first camp in South Africa of the East Lancashires' Active Service Company.

The Volunteers were initially based at Laingsburg, tasked with security duties on the Cape to Kimberley railway, but later joined their 1st Battalion at Johannesburg.

the Easter holidays over and it has been very quiet out here. On the Thursday night before Good Friday the "assemble" went about twelve o'clock, and we had to turn out and set off over the hills and mountains after the Boers. We were sorry we did not get any prisoners, and we returned at six o'clock in the morning about seven miles to camp. We had a very good service on Good Friday. We have a grand choir, consisting of about twelve of us, and service is held every Sunday ... We got orders to be in readiness to proceed to the front any day, but I don't think we shall get there.'

Boshof

On 28 March Lord Roberts ordered Lord Methuen's 1st Division forward to Boshof in the Orange Free State, and the Loyal North Lancashires arrived there on 4 April 4 after a three-day march. The section of mounted infantry, under Lieutenant Clifford, which had been in Kimberley during the siege was still with the Battalion[49] and formed Lord Methuen's personal escort. On 5 April this section, with the Imperial Yeomanry in their first action, surprised, surrounded and completely destroyed a marauding international force of French, Dutch, Germans and Russians led by the Count de Villebois-Mareuil,

49. On the 19 April this section left for Bloemfontein to join the Loyals M.I. Company with 3rd M.I.

a renowned French soldier of fortune, who had intended a raid on Boshof. The Count was killed, and the following day the Loyals provided the escort and firing party at his military funeral.

On 7 April Lord Methuen pushed on again to the north-east with a column, including the Loyals, for ten miles and camped on a kopje at Zwartzkoppiesfontein, where he was ordered to halt until his further advance could be supported. On the 20th the column returned to Boshof, fighting a reaguard action all the way against a Boer force of some two thousand men and two guns. One private soldier of the Battalion was wounded. Sergeant Lindsay of the Active Service Company, 1st Volunteer Battalion, wrote the following account of this withdrawal to his Sergeant-Major in Preston:

'At dinner time of the 20th we had orders to strike the camp and retire into Boshof. We had not moved above a mile away before the Boers opened fire on the convoy. Our Regiment brought up the rear, so we were told off as rear guard, the Volunteer Company being extended and covering the rear, We could see the shells bursting over the wagons, though some of them struck. The Boers had two guns and a Pom-Pom. The enemy soon got in our rear. Then the rifle bullets came humming among us. It was vexing, for we were not allowed to reply, the convoy being too big to leave – it was six miles long – and we had to put up with it till dark. But our artillery silenced their guns. Then we had a trying march to Boshof. We kept stumbling in the dark over rocks, etc. We were weary, I can tell you, and some of our chaps were drinking out of the muddy pools on the road that the artillery horses had splashed through. When we got in camp we had coffee and biscuit, so that "bucked us up". We had to bivouac that night, and it was cold after sweating, but in the morning we were all right.'[50] The Volunteers, in their first action, were said to have 'behaved very well.'

The Malta Mounted Infantry

That same month a detachment of 2nd Loyal North Lancashires, part of the Malta Mounted Infantry Company, saw their first action. This company, raised from the regular infantry battalions of the Malta garrison and commanded by Captain J. E. Pine-Coffin of the 2nd Loyal North Lancashires, arrived at Cape Town on 20 March 1900 and travelled by rail to Aliwal North, there to join Major-General Brabant's Colonial Division. The name of this ad hoc company appears to have given rise to the erroneous impression that it was composed of Maltese; indeed, when they joined his division, General Brabant expressed his

50. Sergeant Lindsay, ibid.

regret that the only languages he could speak with any fluency were English and Dutch!

On 14 April the Colonial Division marched north to the relief of Wepener on the Basuto border, where a British force was besieged by De Wet. The Boers attempted to block this advance at Bushman's Kop, where there was considerable fighting on 21–22 April. In a letter to his mother, Lieutenant Francis Braithwaite of the North Lancashires gave an account of his company's part in this action:[51]

'We ... reached Bushman's Kop last Saturday about 3 p.m., when we for the first time came in contact with a large number of the enemy. Attfield, with No. 3 Section of the Company, scouted the position and [was] fired upon, losing two horses killed. They were then assisted by some of the Border Horse, but as they could not extricate themselves without loss I was sent to a ridge behind them to cover their retirement, where some of the Border Horse assisted me. We succeeded, and they retired without loss, having caused the Boers to shew us their dispositions. I had no casualties in my section. We returned to camp about 7 p.m. and bivouacked on a nearly empty stomach.

'Started at 7 a.m. on Sunday morning with the whole force to attack the position, moving round by the right. After the scouts had ascertained that the Boers were in the same position as they were the previous night, the Artillery shelled the position and the Infantry attacked [it] whilst the Colonial Division made a wide turning movement of about 6 miles. We attacked the enemy almost in rear, but as they threatened a flank attack on us we retired on our horses and made another turning movement which succeeded admirably. During the retirement one of my men was unfortunately wounded by a rifle bullet, although he was quite 2000 yards from the enemy. He was not got into an ambulance until close on midnight and had to ride some 12 miles with a hole in his thigh; we move too fast for an ambulance to keep up during a fight.

'We were ordered to remain on our position till the next morning, so set about killing sheep and getting stores from farms close at hand, when 'boom boom' came some shells and then came the Boers, and we had to ride like blazes for cover. After about an hour's rifle fire we repulsed [them] just before dusk, so there we were on a hill, without water or forage and only about half a pound of tinned beef and a piece of biscuit per man, to wait till morning, with a probable attack during the night. I had another man hit, but fortunately not wounded. However, morning came at last and showed that the Boers

51. Lieutenant F. J. Braithwaite letter dated Wepener, 26 April 1900 (manuscript family transcript).

had vanished, so you may imagine that there was not much time wasted in catching [a] sheep and killing it, or in the parties going off to collect bread, forage, tea, flour, etc at the different farms, and we finally had the best breakfast I have ever had in my life.' Wepener was relieved on 25 April 25, but De Wet, avoiding converging British columns, had slipped off northwards.

From Bloemfontein to Brandfort

We now turn again to follow the fortunes of the East Lancashires who, after their action of March 29th, remained in occupation of the position at Karee Siding until May 3rd. The wide extent of ground to be covered entailed constant outpost duty on the troops. The Mounted Infantry Company was similarly employed, for the first week, 30 March to 6 April, at Karee Kloof, and then at Spytfontein Farm, where on 14 April the 8th M.I. outposts were attacked by some three hundred Boers, supported by a similar number. Captain Leonard Head of the East Lancashire Company commanded the defence, and repulsed the attack after two hours fighting. The Mounted Infantry had some respite from their defensive duties when, on 23 April, they took part in a two-day operation to the south-east, including the seizure of the bridge over the Modder River at Krantz Kraal.

The 3rd East Lancashires also appeared north of Bloemfontein at this time, for on 28 April, having left De Aar two days earlier, they detrained at Glen to take on security duties in that forward area. Next day two companies, proudly escorting guns to the scene of a skirmish, met some of their 1st Battalion who were, according to the Regimental Record, 'surprised to find us so far up country and so soon after landing'.

The 1st East Lancashires had by this time a somewhat scarecrow appearance. Their clothing was worn to barely decent rags, and their boots were in holes. Eventually an officer was sent back to Bloemfontein, and he returned with a complete change of clothing and boots for every man just in time for an issue to be made before Lord Roberts resumed his advance north.

The great advance may truly be said to have started on 30 April, when the mounted troops on Roberts' right flank advanced north. The East Lancashire Mounted Infantry Company took part in a reconnaissance in force of the enemy positions to the east of Brandfort. Having driven in the enemy outposts, the mounted troops were attacked by some two thousand Boers with two guns and some pom-poms. Heavy fighting ensued, and the East Lancashire Company, escorting a section of British pom-poms, was nearly cut off covering their withdrawal. The East Lancashires suffered only one casualty,

Private Howard, and a few days later he wrote of his experiences in a letter home to Burnley:[52]

'On the 30th of last month we left Spytfontein to find out the strength of the Boers before Brandfort. We left about three in the morning, and, after about a four hour's ride, we fell in with the Boers in a strongly entrenched position. My company was escort to the guns, and we had no sooner got in sight than they commenced to shell us. The enemy found the range with their first shot, and I tell you they came pretty thick. They fired about fifty rounds at us, and if all their shells had burst there would have been some casualties. We fell back about a thousand yards out of range, and then the guns opened on the Boers with shrapnel shell, and very soon silenced their guns. The Boers came round a large kopje on our right, trying to flank us, but we were waiting for them, and as soon as they came over the kopje we let them have it. It was a near shave with Lumsden's Horse. They were near being caught in a trap. They crossed over the Boer line of fire, and about twenty men were kicked over. They galloped behind us, and then we had our turn. We fairly peppered them when we got the chance. As we were crossing over, I got shot by a stray bullet. It caught me in the fleshy part of the arm, below the elbow, then passed out though my haversack, and then across my stomach, tearing the skin and flesh for about four inches. It was all right again after I got it dressed. After driving the enemy back we returned to camp.'

Lord Roberts resumed his advance north on 3 May. Two infantry divisions, the 7th and 11th, marched up the line of the railway, the most direct route to Johannesburg and Pretoria, while the mounted troops pressed forward in front and on the flanks, forever manoeuvring to outflank their elusive enemies. The Boers based their defence, or rather their fighting withdrawal, on a succession of river lines – the Vet, Zand, Vaalsch, Rhenoster, Vaal and Klip. These formed formidable natural obstacles even if undefended, but the Boers had entrenched themselves to cover the main crossings. From each of these redoubtable positions, though, bombarded by Roberts' artillery and with the British cavalry and mounted infantry threatening their flanks and rear, the Boers retreated with little more than token resistance. As they retreated, the railway bridges and culverts were enthusiastically dynamited by a party of 'Irish-Americans', including a number of future Sinn Feiners.

The 15th Brigade left Karee Siding on the early morning of the 3rd, the East Lancashires forming the advance guard. As the Battalion

52. Private W. Howard, letter dated Kroonstad, 15 May 1900, published in the *Burnley Express and Advertiser*, 20 June. Before recall to the Colours he had been a conductor with the Burnley Tramway Company.

The East Lancashires under artillery fire during the advance on Brandfort, 3 May 1900.

approached the enemy's position on the hills east of Brandfort, it came under artillery fire at about 3,000 yards range, a few shells bursting over the leading sections as they lay in a mealie field. An artillery duel ensued, until the Boers limbered up and retired northwards. To avoid unnecessary casualties the infantry attack was held back by orders from Lord Roberts. In a letter home,[53] Private T Cullen of the 1st East Lancashires related his experience of this action:

'About midday the Boer shells commenced to fall amongst us like hailstones, but fortunately for our regiment three shells failed to burst, or I should not have been able to tell you about this. The position they held was a very important one as it took them from March 19th until May 3rd to prepare it against our advance, but when the artillery came into action and commenced to shell them it only took about one hour and a half to shift them from their position and put them to flight. The artillery did splendid execution amongst the Boers. It was an artillery duel from start to finish, for the infantry brigade never came into action, as the enemy fled before our guns. We then commenced to advance, the East Lancashires leading in skirmishing order, and followed them until sunset, but they never came up with them. They had made good their escape.'

53. Published in the *Burnley Express and Advertiser*, 20 June 1900. Private Cullen, a Reservist and Burnley postman, wrote on 23 May from Bloemfontein, where he was recovering from a fever.

Battle of Zand River

The Vet River was crossed on the 6th without serious resistance, but on May the 10th the 15th Brigade made contact with the enemy at the passage of the Zand River, some ten miles to the east of the railway line. The East Lancashires again formed the advance guard on this occasion and, the Battalion earned considerable praise at the time for the manner in which it carried out the attack. Lieutenant Colonel Wright wrote down the following account of the fight:

'On arrival at Junction Drift, Zand River, I heard an altercation taking place between Generals Tucker and Wavell. General Tucker, very excited, was asking Wavell if it were safe for him to take his artillery across the drift as it was being shelled by the Boers from a hill to the north, and his artillery was unable to reply effectively owing to the greatness of the range. As I had come up to report to General Wavell that a company, under Captain Sharp, had crossed the river and occupied the opposite bank, I said I would be pleased to bring up the rest of my Battalion and take the artillery across. This evidently was good news to Tucker, for he told me to go and fetch the Battalion at once. This I did, and the 18th Battery and ourselves crossed and took up a position on the north side of the river, where the Battery opened fire on the Boer position. The Battery was heavily shelled, and some of the shells fell among our men, but the only casualties were one man killed and two wounded in the Battery.

'Two Boer guns on a hill about 4,000 yards to the west also opened fire on the Battery. General Tucker, who with his staff was close to me, said, 'I wish I could take that hill. It is the key to the position.' I replied that if he would let me attempt it with my Battalion I thought it could be done. His answer was, 'By God, Wright, do you think so? Go and do it.' I turned to General Wavell and said, 'Shall I go, Sir?' He nodded his head, and so I gave the order for the five companies to advance. Captain Daubeny's Company had been detached as an escort to guns, and Captain Sharp's Company was some 500 yards to the left. Captain Le Marchant was sent to tell Captain Sharp to advance and form the left attack. We advanced in line across perfectly open ground, being harmlessly shelled all the time by the Boer guns. After proceeding some 1,500 yards we came to some rising ground where the men lay down sheltered from view and fire.

'Having reconnoitred the ground in front, three companies, under Captains Sharp and Hamber, and Lieutenant Wilson, advanced through some mimosa jungle till they reached a spruit having almost precipitous banks some 20 foot high. The men dropped into the bed of the stream and lined the opposite bank. Here they lay for a short time to rest, and Captain Le Marchant went back to bring up the remainder of the Battalion. The Boer guns were now about 2,500 yards distant. I ordered Lieutenant Wilson's Company to advance by sections in extended order across an open space, about 600 yards to the foot of a kopje. As these sections advanced they were severely shelled by two 'pom-poms' on a hill to the left and also by the Boer guns from the further hill to the north. Although the pom-pom shells burst on the left flank of each of the sections, no one was hit, and the shells from the big guns burst harmlessly at a considerable height above us. The moment the sections reached the foot of the kopje, they were sheltered from both the gun and pom-pom fire.

'A section under Lieutenant Wilson and 2nd Lieutenant Leake advanced up the kopje, but the moment they arrived at the top they came under fire from a farmhouse some 500 yards to the right. The men were at once ordered to lie down behind rocks, A perfect hail of bullets swept over the ground, wounding, however, only one man. Luckily at this juncture, the Maxim gun, under Lieutenant Da Costa at the spruit, saw these Boers and opened fire on them; this at once caused a cessation of fire so far as those on the kopje were concerned. The men were ordered to rise and to open fire on the Boers at the farm, who at once ran to their horses and retired rapidly.

'Meanwhile the Boers in the vicinity of the guns discovered the section on the kopje, and they advanced in skirmishing order, approximately about 400. As there were only three sections of G Company on the kopje at this time, I went to the edge and tried to signal to the companies in the spruit to advance. No one, however, appeared to see me, and when I turned to a bugler and ordered him to sound the advance, he replied that he had no bugle![54] Things looked somewhat critical. The sections on the kopje were ordered to fire with 1,600 yards elevation. The Boers continued advancing, but when they arrived some 1,200 yards distant, the fire was too hot for them, and they retired on their guns, limbered up, and all made a precipitate retreat north. Captains Hamber and Sharp, with the other companies, had meanwhile advanced to support the company on the kopje, and in crossing the 600 yards from the spruit to the kopje, also came under a sharp pom-pom fire from the hill on the left.

'I ordered Lieutenant Wilson with his Company to advance and seize the hill just evacuated by the Boers. This he did, and found that the Boers in their hasty retreat had left their camp kettles with their dinners behind. The men of G Company were accordingly able to enjoy a good meal washed down by excellent coffee.

54. There was a General Order at that time that no bugle calls were to be sounded. Hence the bugles had been discarded. The order appears to have been at once rescinded, for Colour Sergeant Pegum of the 1st South Lancashires recorded in his diary for 20 May: 'Our bugle calls started again today.'

'General Wavell having now come up, I was ordered to advance with the Battalion on to some hills about a mile further north. From these heights we could see the Boers in the distance galloping off. Here we remained for about an hour and were then ordered to retire to some ground a mile in rear, and there bivouack for the night.

'Thus ended the fight of the Zand River. The Battalion had captured what General Tucker considered the key of the position with the loss of one killed[55] and five wounded. We also captured 11 prisoners and several ponies. Had this attack been supported by mounted troops we should undoubtedly have captured the Boer guns on the hill, if not all three, certainly 'Long Tom'; but when the Boers retired it was impossible for our men to move quickly enough to prevent them limbering up and galloping off.

'When I first saw the Boers advance to attack the three sections of G Company on the kopje, I estimated their numbers at about 1,000 men, but later at Johannesburg I met General Louis Botha's Orderly Officer, who was present and remembered being attacked by the East Lancashires. He said that we were opposed by 480 Boers, 80 of whom were at the farm and holding the spruit. He had never been under such a hot musketry fire and they had had some 80 killed and wounded. One of the prisoners, a German correspondent, said he had never seen such a splendid advance as that of the East Lancashires from the spruit to the kopje; it was irresistible and it was quite impossible to stand against it.' The action at Zand River commenced at 5.45 a.m. and the hill was captured by 1.15 p.m.

Writing four days later to a friend in Burnley, Private W Walker of 'H' Company recalled his own impressions of this engagement:

'We kept marching daily until we came to the Zand River. Here we came across a force of Boers, about 15,000, with big guns and pom-poms on the other side. They thought to prevent us crossing, or, at least, to delay us a long time, as they said that if we did cross at all it would take us fourteen days at least. As a matter of fact, it did not take us many hours, although at first we thought it impossible to get the guns across, as the river runs between banks 20 yards high, and the water is bordered on each side by quick-sands. You will understand the difficulties our artillery had to contend with when I say we had to cross the river three times in about 200 yards in front of the Boer position, with their guns playing on us. This was on account of the river winding in and out. Then the regiment was ordered to take a hill on which the Boers had a pom-pom and a lot

55. Private William Crane, a Reservist from Burnley who had previously served seven years with the Regiment in India, was killed by a pom-pom whilst eating a biscuit. A married man with three young children, he was in civilian life a sawyer at Bank Hall Colliery and played in the Bank Hall Band.

of riflemen. This we did in fine style, and it does not speak much for Boer marksmanship when you consider our small list of casualties, viz., two killed and four wounded, although they were firing into us at about 300 yards before they turned and ran away, and we won the hill, without being supported by a single regiment until the very last, when the 24th came up after we had shifted the Boers.[56] I must give great credit to our artillery, as they are splendid shots, and as far above the Boers in shooting as the moon is above the earth.'[57]

The East Lancashire M.I. Company, still in 8th M.I. and acting as escort to a section of pom-poms, also took part in the general advance to Brandfort. On 3 May, together with 4th M.I., they formed the right of the attack and engaged the enemy from 9.30 a.m. until night fell, taking successive positions during the day. The 1st Loyal North Lancashire M.I. were also in action on that day, when the Company came under fire east of Brandfort and held their position until the enemy's flank was turned. The North Lancashire Company was in action on the 4th at Constantia, where the enemy was posted with two guns. The Lancashire lads dismounted and, being on the extreme left of the firing line, made a containing attack while the New Zealanders and Queenslanders put in a dashing right flanking attack. On the 5th both the East Lancashire and North Lancashire companies advanced again, overtaking and engaging the Boer rear guard on the banks of the Vet River. A passage was forced late in the afternoon, but fighting continued until dark.

Over the next few days the mounted infantry closed up to the Zand River, the East Lancashires camping on its south bank near Virginia Siding on the night of the 9th. On the following day, while the 1st East Lancashires were seizing the key to the Boer centre, their comrades in 8th M.I. threatened to turn the enemy's right flank, fighting a running battle all day under a heavy shell fire, advancing on foot in extended order across a plain seamed with dongas. Writing from Kroonstad on 15 May, Private Howard of the 1st East Lancashires Mounted Infantry, recovered from his wounds, gave the following account of the Company's activities:

'We advanced on Brandfort on the 3rd, and had a good day's fighting there. We drove them out and encamped for the night. We advanced the following morning, and caught up with the Boers at a place called Virginia. They were strongly entrenched there, and it took some time to drive them out. We afterwards passed over their entrenchments, and to look at them you would fancy it was impossible

56. The 24th were of course officially titled The South Wales Borderers, but it remained very usual for infantry battalions to be known by their pre-1881 numbers.

57. Private Walker, letter fom Kroonstadt, dated 14 May, published in the *Burnley Express and Advertiser*, 27 June 1900.

Captain L. Head, Commanding 1st East Lancashire Mounted Infantry Company.

to drive them out of their earthworks. I am sorry to say we lost our captain in that engagement. He was shot through the lungs, and died the same night. He was the only one hit belonging to the company. His name was Captain Head.[58] We are resting here for the day, and make a general move on to-morrow morning. I don't suppose we shall have another rest until we get to Pretoria.'

From Kroonstad to the Rand

With the capture of crossings over the Zand River, the road north lay open. The East Lancashires advanced with Tucker's 7th Division on the morning of 11 May and reached the town of Kroonstad without opposition on the 12th. Here they remained ten days. 'The weather was very cold at nights,' wrote one of their officers, 'although by day the thermometer registered 86 degrees. The men had only one blanket, but we were all issued a warm khaki sort of pea-jacket which was a great comfort to us. The first few days' rest at Kroonstad was by no means unacceptable, with its opportunities for relaxation and exchange of experiences with friends in other columns. Supplies too had been running short, and it was possible here to buy bread at 2/6 a loaf. An almost prohibitive price indeed, but how gladly paid after a prolonged spell of hard ration biscuit! But what was perhaps more appreciated was the luxury of a daily bath.'[59]

During the halt at Kroonstad, Captain Jourdain of the Loyal North Lancashire M.I. went on a raiding expedition with 34 of his own men and some Canadians, and after an all-night ride of 35 miles captured 24 armed Boers, returning with them to camp.

The advance north from Kroonstad was continued on 21 May. The 7th Division, marching to the west of the railway behind a Mounted

58. Captain Leonard Head, in command of 8th M.I. at the time of his death, was the only East Lancashire officer killed in action during the South African War. Born 24 June 1867 at Tunbridge Wells and commissioned on 11 February 1888, his entire service was with the 30th, of which he had been Adjutant 1894–98 in India, Burma and at home. He married at Thayetmyo, Burma in 1896 and had a daughter. Head was succeeded in command of the East Lancashire Company by Lieutenant Collins.

59. Article '1st Bn The East Lancashire Regiment in The South African War', *XXX Journal*, June–August 1912.

Infantry screen, met with no opposition; but the daily marches were long and tedious and the various river crossings were attended with considerable difficulties. On 23 May, for instance, having completed a thirteen-mile march, and gone into bivouac, as everybody hoped for the night, the East Lancashires were suddenly ordered, whilst dinner were still cooking, to advance to the Rhenoster River, five miles further on, and assist the sappers in preparing the drift for the passage of the Division on the morrow. The Rhenoster, a clear, sandy little stream, had very steep banks, and the approaches to the drift on both sides had a gradient of some 30 degrees. Work continued by torchlight throughout the night, and by morning the passage was practicable for the artillery, which was all across by 9 o'clock. It was 3 p.m., however, before the whole of the baggage had crossed, wagon after wagon having to be hauled up the sandy slope by long lines of soldiers, heaving on drag ropes in the fierce mid-day sun.

Watching Roberts' army advance over the wide, dusty expanses of the veldt, Winston Churchill saw an almost biblical migration: 'Long brown columns of infantry, black squares of batteries, sprays of cavalry

Hauling Artillery across the Rhenoster River, 24 May 1900.

Having worked all night to improve wheeled access to the drift, the East Lancashires hauled on drag ropes in the fierce sun to pull guns and baggage wagons up the slope.

flung out far to the front and flanks, 30,00 fighting men together, behind them interminable streams of waggons, and in their midst, like the pillar of cloud that led the hosts of Israel, the war balloon, full-blown, on its travelling car.'

On 25 May the 4th and 8th Corps M.I., together with 'J' Battery Royal Horse Artillery, were sent ahead to force the Viljoen's Drift crossing of the River Vaal at Vereeniging. The Vaal was reached at 10 a.m., and, while the artillery shelled the enemy from their positions on the south bank, the mounted infantry swung west and, with the East Lancashire Company well to the fore, crossed into the Transvaal by an unguarded drift lower down the river, outflanking the Boers, securing the north bank and capturing the settlement. This well-executed coup de main was in time to prevent more demolitions by the 'Irish Brigade', who retired in haste, and to capture a large quantity of most welcome supplies. They were now in a country of collieries and slag heaps, an area which must have appeared incongruously familiar to many of the Lancashire lads. The actual crossing of the Vaal caused relatively few difficulties, but the small Klip River was a more serious obstacle on the 29th, for whilst the infantry, crossing early in the morning, pressed on towards Elandsfontein, the wheeled transport was delayed all day on the south bank by the total collapse of the sappers' temporary bridge under the weight of a heavy gun.

At dawn that same day Colonel Henry rode out with the 4th and 8th M.I. with orders to seize the strategically vital railway junctions at Ansberting and Elandsfontein, east of Johannesburg, at all costs. At Natal Spruit, some ten miles south-east of Johannesburg, they caught up with the Boer rear guard and had an exciting pursuit after a train full of the enemy, which was nearly captured after a chase up a steep incline. On reaching Ansberting Junction they were strongly opposed by a Boer force supported by artillery and pom-poms, who retired after a three-hour engagement. Brushing aside all resistance, they rode on through the industrial Rand. At 3 p.m. 8th M.I. reached Elandsfontein, where confusion reigned as parties of enemy attempted to flee north to Pretoria and to evacuate locomotives, while civilians came out to watch the fight. After some opposition, the mounted infantry occupied positions north of the town and railway station. It had once more been a highly successful coup. Of this exploit, Arthur Conan Doyle wrote: 'Colonel Henry's advance was an extremely daring one, for the infantry were some distance behind; but after an irregular scrambling skirmish, in which the Boer snipers had to be driven off the mine heaps and from among the houses, the 8th Mounted Infantry got their grip of the railway and held it. The exploit was a very fine one, and stands out the more brilliantly as the conduct of the campaign cannot be said to afford many examples of that well-considered audacity which deliberately runs the risk of the minor loss for the sake of the greater gain.'[60]

Some fifteen miles to the west, on the other side of Johannesburg, the Loyal North Lancashire M.I. Company (in 3rd M.I.) and Lieutenant Hill's East Lancashire Section (in 1st M.I.) had also reached the Rand. Operating as part of Hutton's 1st M.I. Brigade with General French's Cavalry Division on the left flank of Roberts' main advance, they had been involved in a sharp engagement against some four thousand enemy at Doornkop on the 29th, and the following day they were again in action north of Florida, where French secured the railway line from Johannesburg to the west. Boer artillery opened up in front, and the mounted infantry extended while the British guns replied. The Loyals Company was sent with the Queenslanders to work round the enemy's left flank while the remainder of 3rd M.I. advanced straight onto the position. A Boer gun was captured and Captain Wigram Clifford of the Loyals took two prisoners, of whom one was a German officer. The following day he also captured four armed cyclists.

That night Tucker's Division bivouacked in intense cold outside the mining town of Germiston, the troops being without blankets, food, or firewood. They had marched 126 miles in seven days, a remarkable average rate of eighteen miles a day. On the 30th, two companies of the 1st East Lancashires were detached under Major Lewis to occupy Germiston, which was garrisoned by a detachment of the Regiment until April 1901. The remainder of the Battalion moved with the 7th Division on the same afternoon to within a short distance of Johannesburg, the Golden City, bivouacking for the night near the Jumpers Mine. The 8th M.I. were sent to seize Waterworks Hill, Johannesburg, and engaged small parties of the enemy throughout the day.

On 31 May the East Lancashires marched into Johannesburg with the 7th Division and defiled past Lord Roberts, who had taken up his position in front of the Government Buildings. The men were in exuberant spirits, and as the dusty khaki columns of the 7th Division streamed past the saluting base, the ragged but jubilant men broke into spontaneous cheers for 'Bobs'. The Battalion halted for the night on the Orange Grove Road to the north of the town. Next day orders were received for the 15th Brigade to garrison Johannesburg. The East Lancashires accordingly went into quarters at the Agricultural Show grounds, where the men were accommodated in sheds normally used for cattle and poultry shows, but sheer luxury to the troops after their four months' bivouacking on the veldt.

60. A Conan Doyle, *The Great Boer War*, 1901, p. 438.

The advance from Bloemfontain had entailed hard marching but little serious fighting. However, its very rapidity, an essential factor of its success, had involved privations which were accentuated by a harsh climate and country. 'During the recent operations,' said Lord Roberts in his congratulatory orders to the Army, 'the sudden variations in temperature between the warm sun in the daytime and the bitter cold at nights have been peculiarly trying to the troops; and owing to the necessity for rapid movement the soldiers have frequently had to bivouac, after long and trying marches without firewood and with scanty rations.' Four months' arduous campaigning had thinned the ranks considerably, and in the 1st East Lancashires there were now only 585 N.C.O.s and men of those who had originally embarked with the Battalion. The War Diary provides an interesting statistical comparison of the wastage in the ranks of the Reservists and 'time serving' men (i.e. those soldiers who were serving with the Colours on the date of mobilisation), concluding that the stamina of a man was at its best between the ages of 25 and 30.[61]

Shortly after their arrival at Johannesburg the East Lancashires were reinforced by a strong draft from home, mainly composed of young soldiers, and by the Volunteer Company from Laingsburg. Regimental officers considered that: 'Their lack of previous experience and of requisite training placed these Volunteers, more especially at first, at some disadvantage when considered in comparison with Regular troops. But, acting as the Eighth Company of the Battalion, their Officers and men showed the keenest spirit of emulation, and their excellent discipline and loyal endeavours to remedy their deficiencies in training rendered them a valuable reinforcement after a few weeks' association with their comrades of the line.'[62] The terms of enlistment for the Volunteers being for one year only, the first company, under Lieutenant Howard, returned to England in April 1901, and were replaced by a second contingent under Captain Carus and Lieutenant Munn.

From Johannesburg to Pretoria and Diamond Hill

On 3 June Lord Roberts resumed his advance to Pretoria, thirty miles to the north, and ahead of his main body rode the Mounted Infantry.[63]

61. The ordinary Regular Reservists, aged 25–30, had least wastage (23%), followed by the younger 'time serving' men (28%), and then the Section 'D' Reservists, aged over 30 (36%). Least fit, or effective, were the 70 Militia Reservists who had joined in April, 11 of whom had been lost in 6 weeks.
62. War Diary.
63. 4th and 8th Corps M.I., the latter including the 1st East Lancashire M.I. Company, the whole force commanded by Colonel Henry.

The capital of Kruger's Transvaal was protected on its southern side by a series of ridges, crowned with forts, and although the latter were undefended there was some resistance further south at Six Mile Spruit, where the Boers held both sides of the stream. The Mounted Infantry, moving between the Johannesburg and Potchefstroom roads, began the action at 7 a.m. on the 4th and soon dislodged the Boers from the south bank, driving them back about two miles to a high ridge south of Pretoria. There the burghers held for a while and even attempted to outflank the left of the British advance, but the Mounted Infantry moved a further mile west along the ridge to check them. For a while they exchanged fire with Boer riflemen on the next ridge, some six to eight hundred yards away, but then these in turn were outflanked from the west by Hamilton's and De Lisle's columns, and by mid-afternoon a general British advance caused them to flee. The East Lancashire M.I. Company had been in the firing line for nine hours and had suffered two casualties, both wounded. Pretoria capitulated the following morning, 5 June 1900.

The 1st Loyal North Lancashire M.I. Company and Lieutenant Hill's East Lancashire Section also took part in the advance on Pretoria. Moving on the left of the army with French's cavalry, they were involved in the encirclement of the Transvaal capital, which they approached from the north-west. They saw no action during this operation. The following week, however, they were engaged at the battle of Diamond Hill, some fifteen miles east of Pretoria, where Botha with some six thousand men and 22 guns had taken up a strong position on hills astride the Delagoa Bay Railway. Roberts determined to drive off this threat to the capital, and attacked on 11 June. His plan was to force a Boer withdrawal by enveloping both flanks, though the greater part of his force was deployed on the right and right centre, where Diamond Hill itself was finally taken in a two-day battle.

Hutton's M.I. Brigade, including the East Lancashire Section of 1st M.I. and the Loyal North Lancashire Company of 3rd M.I., advanced with General French on the left flank to work round the enemy right and prevent his redeployment.[64] The country was very thick, and on the second day the Loyals Company fought dismounted, climbing up the high Kameelfontein Ridge to reinforce 1st M.I. This position was under fire from two long-range guns from the front, one field gun from the left, and a pom-pom from the left rear, in addition to rifle and machine gun fire, but the cover among the rocks was good and,

64. Lieutenant Hill, two sergeants and twelve J.N.C.O.s and men of the East Lancashire Regiment were awarded the medal clasp for Diamond Hill. They had one man (Lance-Corporal G. Dwyer) wounded on the 11th. The Loyal North Lancashires had Captains Jourdain and Clifford present, with Lieutenant Macauley and 38 men. Private Drew was wounded on the 11th and taken prisoner.

A short rest on trek for 1st Loyal North Lancashires. The main body of the Battalion marched some 1,290 miles in the course of the war, and individual companies and detachments trekked more than twice that distance.

although the Boers kept up a heavy fire until dark, the Company suffered no casualties. At dusk the remainder of 3rd M.I. came up the hill, which was entrenched in expectation of a night attack, but in the morning it was found that the enemy had withdrawn. Roberts had achieved his limited aim, but, as the Transvaal army was still in being, so had Botha.

Battle of Rhenoster River

Meanwhile, across the whole front of some 350 miles, from Bechuanaland in the west, through what was now the Orange River Colony, and across the Drakensberg mountains to Natal, other British divisions were on the move.

On 14 May Lord Methuen's 1st Division set out from Boshof with the 1st Loyal North Lancashires in its main body, marching north-east for eleven days by way of Hoopstad and Bothaville towards Parys and the Rand. Again there were difficulties in crossing rivers with the inevitable ox convoy. On 24 May near Bothaville the passage of a steep-sided drift over the Vaalch took all night, with the infantry hauling on drag ropes. On the 25th, however, the division was diverted to Kroonstad, where the Battalion arrived three days later, having marched almost two hundred miles in fifteen days.

The Loyal North Lancashires did not remain long at Kroonstad, for on the 29th Lord Roberts received information that the Highland Brigade was in difficulties at Heilbron and ordered Methuen with the 9th Brigade to march to their assistance. The column left early on the 30th, but at 2 p.m. news was received that the Heilbron garrison was not in immediate danger, followed at once by an urgent summons to the relief of a regiment of Irish Yeomanry, surrounded and hard pressed by Piet De Wet near Lindley. Methuen's force made a forced march to the rescue, but were too late; the Yeomanry, outnumbered, outgunned and out of supplies, had been obliged to surrender. Methuen then continued on his original mission to Heilbron, arriving there on 7 June.

Roberts had taken a deliberate risk when he pressed on to Pretoria in early June, for behind him, despite all his well-meaning attempts at conciliation and pacification, the irreconcilable remnants of the Free State army were still at large and might strike at any point along his extended line of communications. Most prominent among their commanders was the redoubtable Christian De Wet, already an experienced guerilla leader. On 7 June De Wet attacked the railway north of Kroonstad with some fifteen hundred men and six guns, defeating a militia battalion at Roodeval, capturing supplies and cutting both rail line and telegraph links to Roberts. Methuen was called on to restore the situation and on 9 June he marched west from Heilbron with his 9th Brigade, including the Loyal North Lancashires. On 11 June the column came in sight of the railway, in time to see several explosions but too late to prevent them. Turning south down the line from the Heilbron-Vredefort road, he came up with De Wet at the Rhenoster River and at once attacked.

After a vigorous artillery bombardment, the Infantry advanced on the right, to the west of the railway, while mounted troops swung round the left flank to reach the rear of the Boer position. The Loyal North Lancashires were on the left of the infantry attack, with four companies in the firing line and four in support, and the Black Watch were to their right. De Wet had determined to fight a short action and then withdraw, so deployed his burghers on kopjes north and south of the river with their horses conveniently tethered to the rear. 'D' Company, under Captain Francis Logan, led the attack. The enemy could not at first be seen, but after a while, as the spirited advance pushed on, they were spotted making for their horses to avoid being outflanked. Nevertheless, 'D' Company stormed a kopje and took seven prisoners, burghers of the Heilbron Commando who left it too late to join their fleeing comrades. De Wet, however, had escaped. The Battalion had no casualties in this engagement, which, though dignified with the title 'Battle of Rhenoster River', was in reality little more than a skirmish. The whole episode was, however, indicative of the future course of the war.

Two days later Captain John Pine-Coffin rode up the line from Kroonstad with his Maltese Mounted Infantry (M.M.I.). His diary entry for that day, 13 June, betrays the confusion and frustration left in the wake of De Wet's Raid:

'We marched at 4.30 a.m. Beastly cold & dark. Long march in the same direction we went on patrol. The M.M.I. is distributed in every direction, no-one quite certain where anyone else is, entirely owing to the many different orders & changes of orders. The whole thing thoroughly mismanaged by General Knox & others. No enemy was seen, which was lucky for us. I had to go on as a scout to Hony-Spruit [Honning Spruit] Siding, about 18 miles, and met Methuen's force there. They had let the enemy slip away. Returned after this to Kronstat [Kroonstad]. Must have ridden about 50 miles. Heard that we were to march at once to Geneva Siding. Refused to do it, as horses completely done up.'

The Biggarsberg

East of the Drakensbergs, Sir Redvers Buller's force at Ladysmith, three divisions of infantry and one of cavalry, was also included in Roberts' great advance. Some seven to eight thousand Boers were strongly posted in the passes of the rugged Biggarsberg range to his north, commanding the routes to northern Natal and the Transvaal. Buller planned to manoeuvre them out of this position by moving his left up to Elandslaagte to fix, divert and deceive the enemy while his right swung decisively round by way of Helpmakaar to outflank them.

On 4th April the 1st South Lancashires, still in the 11th Brigade of 5th Division, left their camp at Surprise Hill, north-west of Ladysmith, for Modder Spruit, and reached Elandslaagte the next day. They remained in that area, digging trenches, manning outposts, and training, for some six weeks. The Boer lines were only some four thousand yards away so great vigilance was required, particularly when the Battalion held the dominating Jonono's Kop feature.

'This must have been a very important position to hold', wrote Sergeant Hackett, 'for an attack was expected by day and by night the two or three weeks we were there. Discipline was very strict, movement limited and everybody kept on the alert and practised by false alarms. One never knew the minute, by day or by night, and

Operations in Northern Natal
Katbosch Spruit
Standerton
Zand Spruit
Volksrust
Wakkerstroom
Laing's Nek
Majuba
Vrede
TRANSVAAL
Alleman's Nek
Botha's Pass
De Wet Farm
Wools Drift
Utrecht
Vryheid
DRAKENSBERG
Newcastle
Blood River Poort
ORANGE FREE STATE
Ingagane
Buffalo River
Blood River
NATAL
Hatting Spruit
Mount Impati
Talana Hill
De Jager's Drift
ZULULAND
BIGGARSBERG
Glencoe
Dundee
Sunday's River
Wachbank
Wessels Nek
Harrismith
Jonono's Kop
Buffalo River
Elandslaagte
Surprise Hill
Modder Spruit
Ladysmith
Spion Kop
Pieters
Tugela River
Potgieters' Drift
N
Colenso
Chieveley
Blaauw Krantz River
Frere
Bushman's River
Miles
0 5 10 15 20
Estcourt
Durban

on the whole it was a very uncomfortable time. Day outposts were relieved just before dark and they slept in their tents that night. Inlying picquets slept fully dressed, rifles loaded and bayonets fixed. They were turned out (by whistle) at least twice during the night and the whole company were expected to be ready to move in two to three minutes at most. They were inspected (by hurricane lamp) and any N.C.O. or man having a buckle or even a button undone were charged before the C.O. next day. More than one N.C.O. lost his stripes there.'

There was also some patrol activity on both sides. In his diary for 7 May Private Wain of 'B' Company recalled an attempted Boer incursion: 'On outpost duty during the night one of our sentries challenged someone approaching and, in receiving for an answer 'Hands up', let fly a shot. The outpost fired several volleys, wounding one man through the stomach. He died shortly afterwards. They turned out to be a party of about 20 Boers who had tried to blow up the shaft of a coal mine but bolted on our opening fire.'[65]

Buller's move against the enemy's eastern flank worked as planned, and the Boers were obliged to abandon their entrenchments on the Biggarsberg, together with the towns of Dundee and Newcastle, and fall back towards the formidable Laing's Nek position. Lieutenant Geoffrey Mott recalled the first few days of the South Lancashires' advance into Northern Natal:

'On 14 May, we received sudden orders to move, marched 10 miles under trying conditions, dust storms and veldt fires. Next morning, minus breakfast, we made a forced march of 12 miles to Wessels Nek. My Company went on out-post and no rations arrived for 24 hours. 17 May found us at Waschbank Farm under the Biggarsberg. Rather a pleasant spot with rose bushes on the walls. Refreshing ourselves with water from an apparently clear stream, we found it to be strongly perfumed. Imagine our disgust when, continuing the march, we found Kaffir scouts further up performing their ablutions with Pears soap!! The rum ration that night, however, put things right. 18 May reveille was at 1.30 a.m. and we went by moonlight about 12 miles to camp beyond Glencoe. The Burghers here had left hurriedly and had burnt up farms and a blacksmith's shop. Later that day a further 6 miles to Hattings Junction, to find the station and bridges wrecked. Collected fresh vegetables from a Trappist monastery.'

Private Ashton of 'H' Company also described that early morning march through the Biggarsberg to Glencoe: 'In the pale moonlight it was difficult to see very far, but as daylight advanced we obtained a splendid view of the surrounding country. Mount Hlaticulu and the

65. Private G. Wain manuscript diary (copy).

'The Last Supper'. Officers of the 1st South Lancashires have a last meal together before leaving Jonono's Kop on an eventful six-week trek. Colonel Hall is central, with beard.

Impati Range, with their snow-capped peaks, looked very stern and forbidding in the cold morning air, whilst on every side huge towering crags and precipitous mountain slopes were passed without opposition, which, had they been held by a handful of resolute men, would probably have resulted in another Colenso. After a stiffish climb we arrived on top of the berg, the temperature, owing no doubt to the altitude being over 5,000 feet, was very cold, though dry and bracing. Hoar frost covered the veldt, giving it the appearance of an English winter. An hour's marching brought us to Glencoe, where, after a short rest, we continued our advance to Hatting Spruit. The following morning, whilst crossing the spruit, one of our men (J. Lowndes) slipped whilst jumping from one stone to another, and fell headlong into the water. We pulled him out, wet to the skin, amidst roars of laughter. We always refer to that place now as Lowndes's Spruit.' [66]

Sergeant Hackett too was in his usual buoyant spirits: 'The weather was on the whole fine and sunny as we trekked across the open veldt, but occasionally a large cloud would appear ahead on the horizon and ... would move towards us. 'Halt' would be ordered, and 'Get overcoats off the wagons', but before the first bundles were unpacked we got it, and, after a ten to fifteen minutes soaking, a column of steam would move on as our clothes were dried on us by the sun.

66. Article by Lance-Corporal W. Ashton in *The Volunteer Service Company in South Africa*, p. 58.

The 1st South Lancashires' bivouac in Wessels Nek, 16 May 1900.

When wet, mud, boot-top deep, was a nuisance. We could not sit or rest; just stand and lean on the 'Soldier's Best Friend'. The troops had a midday halt for a meal, supposed to be an hour; some would raise a little fire and hope to make some hot tea, but the annoying part was the invariable interruption to fall in quickly and march, and mess tins of warm or nearly boiled water would be kicked flying, only for the mess tin to have to be retrieved. Surprisingly, there was little or no grumbling; the men took everything 'all in a day's work' spirit, singing and laughing until tired, then quiet and dogged. Our section was lucky to have the happiest man I have ever met in 'Doggy' Hoare. 'Doggy' was a miner, about 5′ 6″ tall and as deep chested as he was broad, all bone and muscle. Rarely without a grin, he didn't care if it snowed, and his jokes and chuckles, his choruses and chaffing, kept the whole company in good spirits on the march or in camp or bivouac. Such a good humoured man, 'Doggy' was never tired and his care-free laugh was infectious.

'Sometimes [the march was] just hard going all day long, and sometimes broken periods whilst the advance guard felt their way, for the Boers harassed the front and were not far away on the flanks and rear. Occasionally we heard a few rounds fired by the advanced guard battery to clear rising ground. Only on a few occasions did the main body have to extend, and on three occasions we fixed bayonets and charged up the hill in front, only to see the Boers riding hard away a couple of miles ahead. A few times we hastily extended to the flank and after marching outwards for half a mile to a mile we would reform and join the column.'[67]

Lieutenant M. C. A. Green on the railway line between Glencoe and Dundee, Northern Natal, May 1900. Green had been posted in from the 2nd Battalion in India. He was killed in command of that Battalion at Ypres in November 1914. Behind him, reading a letter, is Lieutenant Harold Kane.

Personal hygiene on trek was difficult, but according to Sergeant Hackett there was an original way of dealing with lice: 'When halted early in bivouac, men were advised to clean their underclothing, and we had sport in turning them inside out and putting them on a big ant heap. The grey backs hadn't a chance with the ants, and it was interesting watching the fights and the ants stocking their larder. A pity they did not take the eggs as well.'

After ten days of marching and counter-marching the South Lancashires found themselves, on 23 May, on the banks of the Ingagane River, just short of Newcastle, where the retiring Boers had demolished a three-span iron bridge carrying the vital Natal railway line. The repair of this line was Buller's immediate priority, for along it would come the supplies to support his advance into the Transvaal. Over the next four days, working in two 4-hour shifts, the Battalion built a temporary wooden bridge across the river, relaid the track on a diversion loop, and repaired a blown culvert further up the line. Buller came himself to check progress and on 24 May he sent a message to the 40th urging them to celebrate the Queen's Birthday in the best possible way by repairing the railway with all speed. The work was hard, digging and levelling the loop, and carrying twelve inch square, twenty foot long logs for the trestle bridge, and at times the air was purple with oaths, so much so that an Engineer officer complained to Colonel Hall about the men's swearing. 'That's just our Lancashire men's way,' replied the Commanding Officer. 'The harder they swear the harder they work, the deeper the pick the swifter the spade. Just leave them to it and your job will be finished before dark.' It was, and within the week Buller was able to bring up by rail a reserve of 21 days' supply for his further advance. The Battalion then joined the main body of Buller's army, massed north of Newcastle.

67. Hackett, pp. 1–3. Paragraph order changed.

Ingagane Railway Bridge.

Work in progress (*above*) constructing a temporary deviation (*below*) around the demolished bridge.

South Lancashire Regiment bivouac, De Wet Farm.

The Battalion had a few days rest here in early June 1900 before the Battle of Botha's Pass.

Botha's Pass

Ahead the Boers held Laing's Nek, dominated by Majuba Hill of fateful memory, with a force of some four to five thousand men. Such was the natural strength of this position that, as with the Biggarsberg, they would have to be manoeuvred out. Buller determined to turn the Boers' right flank by seizing Botha's Pass, one of two possible routes over the Drakensberg range. He could then march north to Volkrust, behind Laing's Nek. But first he had to divert the Boers' attention from that flank, and accordingly on 29 May the 5th Division was sent east from Wools Drift on the Transvaal border to capture the town of Utrecht. The 1st South Lancashires were advance guard to the column. On the 31st Utrecht surrendered and, having disarmed the remaining Boers and run up the Union Flag, the 5th Division returned to Wools Drift on 1 June.

Buller was now preparing his assault on Botha's Pass, and on 2 June the South Lancashires marched north to De Wet Farm at the foot of the Drakensberg mountains, where they had a few days rest. Fresh bread and meat were issued, the first for three weeks and a welcome change to bully beef and hard tack biscuits. There was time also to take a much-needed bathe in the river and to wash clothes. As Sergeant Hackett relates, 'the grapevine became mysterious with many rumours. I remember we were relaxing very nicely in the afternoon sun when an hour later we were off again and climbing to a plateau where we bivouacked, made tea and had an issue of rum. Later there was another issue of rum, so we knew there would be

South Lancashire Officers ready for an early start.

something doing next day ... Orderlies came round saying there would be a Religious Service on the flank opposite where we were sitting around a big cowflap fire, radiating heat for some fifteen yards around. Apparently [the men] didn't like leaving that fire, for instead they suggested a sing-song and urged a Corporal, with much laughter, to sing a ribald song known to them. After some hesitation he was persuaded and the men, quietly but heartily, joined in, and as there were numerous verses they were a happy lot that soon after got under the blanket.'

Before dawn the following morning, 6 June, the South Lancashires moved off towards Botha's Pass escorting two 5-inch guns and two 4.7-inch naval guns. On the 7th Lieutenant-Colonel Hall took four companies forward to support the occupation of the Van Wyk feature, facing Botha's Pass, by the 10th Brigade. That night the South Lancashires bivouacked at Yellowboom Farm, just behind Van Wyk hill, with the main body of the assault force.

At first light on the 8th Lieutenant-General Hildyard of the 5th Division, to whom Buller had entrusted the critical attack, gave his orders from the vantage point of Van Wyk hill. To his left front, five miles to the north-west the stony track wound steeply up to where an Orange Free State frontier post stood at the summit of Botha's Pass itself, while from that point the Drakensberg escarpment ran north-east and south, forming a bare and precipitous amphitheatre above a green valley. Below these frowning heights the Ingogo River, and the road, ran through a gorge some five miles from the pass before emerging onto more level ground between Van Wyk hill and the foot of the escarpment. Hildyard ordered the South African Light Horse[68] to secure the gorge and cover the advance of the 2nd and 11th Infantry Brigades, who on debouching from the defile would deploy to their right and assault the hights on a five mile front north-east of Botha's Pass. The 11th Brigade, with three battalions up, would be on the left, and the 2nd Brigade on the right, while two mounted brigades were poised ready for pursuit. As at the Tugela Heights, success would largely depend on suppression of the enemy defences by the British artillery, hauled laboriously into position on Van Wyk hill and other heights.

Back at Yellowboom Farm, the South Lancashires had breakfast before sunrise that morning, and by eight o'clock they paraded with the rest of the Brigade, ready to move. General Hildyard rode along the lines, greeting the South Lancashire officers with a grim smile, 'Good morning, Gentlemen; a nice fine day to enter the Orange Free State.' Reassuringly, the hills reverberated with British gunfire as the artillery bombardment scoured the Drakensberg crest-line. At 10.30 a.m. the Infantry of 11th Brigade marched off in column of fours, following the narrow road through the gorge which was by now held by the South Africans.

It was about noon when the South Lancashires, last unit in the brigade order of march, emerged from the Ingogo ravine and crossed a bridge over the river. Before them on the open grassland, the rest of 11th Brigade was already drawn up for battle in two lines a quarter of a mile apart, facing the rugged escarpment to their right. Objectives for the leading battalions were pointed out, three spurs; the York and Lancasters had the left, the King's Own the centre, and the South Lancashires the right spur to attack. The Lancashire Fusiliers were in support. Away to the right, about a mile away, the 2nd Brigade was also preparing to assault. Captain Francis Appleton noted the battalion attack formation: 'Our firing line was in two lines, and the first line extended to ten paces, and we ('H' Company, the Volunteers) came as third line, or reserves, four companies under Major Adam, and extended to one pace.'[69]

There was the inevitable wait, with nervous alarms, while final dispositions were made. Private Ashton, also a Warrington Volunteer in his first action, had time to take in the scene: 'It was a picturesque sight, and one calculated to make you feel a trifle excited, and your

68. Captain Arthur Solly-Flood DSO of the South Lancashires was Adjutant of the SALH. As Major-General A Solly-Flood CB CMG DSO, he was Colonel of The South Lancashire Regiment 1921–40. Several North Lancashire soldiers were also serving with this highly effective unit.

69. Captain F. M. Appleton, diary in *The Volunteer Service Company in South Africa*, p. 138.

11th (Lancashire) Brigade extending to attack Botha's Pass, 8 June 1900.
The view north from Van Wyk hill towards the Drakensberg escarpment. 'Emerging through a cleft in the hill', wrote Sergeant Hackett, 'we had a wonderful view. Formed up on level green grass ground, in two lines a quarter of a mile apart and facing to our right, was the whole Division, and as we were the last Battalion up we were on the extreme right.'

heart to beat a little faster, to see thousands of khaki-clad figures, their bayonets glistening in the sun. The mad gallop of the Field Artillery, clearing everything as they dash past into action; the mounted orderlies and staff officers galloping hither and thither; and the effects of the shells, which go screaming overhead, put vigour into your frame, and you feel possessed of superhuman strength.'

At last the order to advance was given and the long lines surged forward to the foot of the mountain, expecting at any moment to be met with a storm of fire from above, but not a single shot was fired. Then the whole brigade mounted the slope, vying with each other to get to the top first. Private Wain of 'B' Company thought it the hardest climb he had ever made. 'The sides of the hill were almost perpendicular, and not a bit of shrub and very little grass to help us.' In some places, according to Ashton, the ascent was so steep that soldiers had to dig their bayonets in the ground to help them up. Still, to everyone's relief, the enemy did not open fire. Colour-Sergeant Pegum could not understand why the Boers had not entrenched themselves at the top of the hill, but Buller, in his despatch, attributed this to their previous experience of well-directed artillery fire and consequent reluctance to occupy so exposed a position. In the event, having paused several times to recover their breath, the brigade reached the top without opposition. On the crest Captain Appleton spotted a Boer trench and gun epaulment, and was thankful that they were unoccupied.

1st South Lancashires formed up ready for the attack, Botha's Pass.

The South Lancashires' firing line had barely reached the top, and were getting their breath back when, in Private Wain's words, 'We was met with a perfect hail of bullets, and our friend 'pom-pom' – and I must say they was very bad marksmen, or else they would have mowed half of us down.' 'What's them, Jem, ar'na they brids?' enquired one rather deaf ex-miner as the bullets whistled overhead. Sergeant Hackett, who was well up with the early arrivals, ran forward some two hundred yards and lay down as he came under rifle fire from some Boers occupying rising ground half a mile ahead. Lieutenant Geoffrey Mott, a noted shot, estimated the range at 300 yards, but perhaps he was on the right of the South Lancashires, where there was greater resistance in front of the 2nd Brigade. The Battalion was well balanced to meet this threat, for on nearing the crest Major Adam had closed the reserves up to about one hundred yards behind the firing line. Now, while the firing line advanced in short rushes, he hurried them forward until they were within twenty yards of the supports, then wheeled them to the right to deal with the enemy on that flank. This movement was most fortunate for 'H' Company, who would otherwise have been caught by a pom-pom burst ten yards to their front. The South Lancashires' Maxim, under Lieutenant Robert Trousdale, now came into action and, according to Lieutenant Mott, 'did great execution.'

'We soon got to work and returned their fire,' wrote Private Wain, 'and advanced very slowly towards their position, passing several newly made trenches, and it was proof they had left in a hurry, for they had not time to take their picks and shovels with them. During this

Lieutenant Robert Trousdale with the South Lancashires' Maxim.

Trousdale was later awarded a DSO for gallantry at Itala, to which he earned a bar, in addition to an MC, in the Great War.

the 2nd (Brigade) had climbed a ridge of hills about a mile to our right and had made a flank attack which was so successful that between their fire and ours we soon had the Boers on the run.' The Battalion advanced about one thousand yards, to a low grassy ridge, where they were obliged to halt. The Boers had previously burnt off the grass in front of their position to give a clear field of fire, and now they fired it again to cover their retreat and prevent pursuit.

In any event, Buller's bold plan and the resolute and audacious attack of Hildyard's men had been outstandingly successful. By 3 p.m. the assaulting troops had routed two thousand Boers, captured the head of the pass and were established in strength on the crest-line of the mighty Drakensberg for the loss of but two killed and thirteen wounded. The South Lancashires had one man killed, Private Duffy, a well-known 'A' Company 'character', and several slightly wounded. Sergeant Hackett remembered Duffy well: 'On leaving Ladysmith he had his own bucket and wangled water, sometimes from the water cart, and with a tin of sherbet and a glass and a teaspoon he went around the bivouacs crying 'Who wants a Fizzer, tickey a Fizzer' and did a good trade every time.'

Hackett, his uniform blackened from the burned grass, had good reason to recall the sequel to that day's events: 'Towards evening we moved a couple of miles north-east and, digging a knee trench, we awaited the arrival of the transport. There being one road up for the whole Division, it was daylight before ours arrived. Seven thousand seven hundred feet above sea level on the top of the Drakensberg Mountains in the "Land of the Mist" was no joke, and that 8th June night was the worst in my life. Down came the mist, and with it a driving sleet and thin cutting rain which soon went through our

The South Lancashires' bivouac at Botha's Pass the morning after the fight.

All accounts agree that the night 8/9 June was far more unpleasant than the fight. 'From early afternoon there was a cold wind blowing', recalled Lieutenant Lewis. 'Towards evening a thick mist came on, and our wagons were miles away with the hill to climb. From about six to one a.m. was about the most wretched seven hours I ever spent.'

Indian khaki, and all we could do was to sit in the trench or just walk its length up and down. Some strong hefty men cried, and everyone welcomed daybreak and the lifting of the mist, and, an hour after, the transport. Great coats and blankets were issued, and a tot of rum, and the gradely sight was the long fire the cooks had got going, with dixies of water heating for tea.'

For Private Wain, as for many others, that night was 'the worst I ever had in my life', but in the morning after rum, coffee and half an hour's exercise he had managed to thaw out a bit and was pleased to share the glory of the day with his victorious commander. 'General Buller rode up to us while we was having breakfast and told us that we had done excellent yesterday, for he said it was a tough job and he looked very pleased over it, and he had a good word and a cheery smile for everyone.' That much-maligned general must have felt considerable satisfaction at the further vindication of his tactics and of the men of the Natal Field Force.

Two days later there was another brilliant victory for Hildyard's 5th Division when they most gallantly assaulted a formidable Boer position at Allemann's Nek. This time the 10th Brigade had the honours of the day, somewhat to the chagrin of the South Lancashires, whose role was limited to occupying a spur to cover the advance. 'Our Regiment had a large hill to take about 3 miles away, and we took the position without meeting any opposition,' recalled Hackett. 'We were then ordered to take another hill 3 miles away, but just as we were setting off the order was cancelled and we was to remain and hold the position we had captured. About 1 p.m. fighting commenced on our flank and kept on till dark. We did not come under fire that

The end of a long march.

Lieutenant Ewart, 1st South Lancashires, in bivouac near Standerton, June 1900.

day. I afterwards heard that the 10th Brigade had captured Almonds Nek and the enemy were in full retreat, and the reason our order was cancelled was that General Talbot-Coke, in command of the 10th Brigade, asked permission for his boys to take the position as they had not had many chances of doing much during the campaign. His request was granted, and it did not wash with the 11th Brigade for they was eager for the fray and it was the first time in the war that they had acted in support to the fighting line. But it was a rather lucky thing for us that it was altered for the 10th lost heavily.'

Captain Appleton watched the battle from in front of his company position: 'Artillery opened fire from high ground three miles in front of us, about 2 p.m., while the Infantry advanced. We had a splendid view at a safe distance, and saw the Infantry gain the heights and take the position just as the sun went down. Boer position very strong; pass here went between two high ranges and at right angles to them, and with a conical hill in the centre, upon which Boers had a big gun, shelling our Artillery. Our guns made splendid practice, and raked the whole Boer position with shrapnel and lyddite, setting fire to the left range of hills. Boers lost over 120 killed and our casualties were about 85 killed and wounded.'

The battles of Botha's Pass and Allemann's Nek effectively turned Laing's Nek, the much-vaunted 'Gibraltar of Natal', and the Boers now beat a hasty retreat. Two days later the South Lancashires marched into the Transvaal town of Volkrust, then on up the railway line to Standerton, which they reached on 24 June. White flags fluttered from every farm, burghers came in to surrender their arms, and it seemed to many on both sides that the war was practically over.

East Lancashire sentry on guard at a Rand gold mine.

Outside the Orderly Room of 1st East Lancashire Regiment, Johannesburg, 1900.

PART IV

Boots and Saddles

'We were soldiers, fit successors of the men who, in the Peninsula, at Waterloo, and in the Crimea, had helped to make, and uphold, the proud record of the old XXXth.'

(Colour-Sergeant James Ferguson,
1st Battalion The East Lancashire Regiment)

By mid-summer 1900 most participants in the South African war, both Boer and Briton, were persuaded that peace was only a matter of weeks away. The armies of the Boer republics had been beaten in the field, their capitals were occupied, the greater part of their territory had been over-run, and the majority of the Afrikaner population were apparently, if resentfully, resigned to defeat. Lord Roberts' velvet-gloved policy of bringing the war to a speedy and humane conclusion by offering lenient terms to surrendered Boers appeared to be working. On every hand farmhouses flew the white flag and Boers came in to surrender their weapons and pledge neutrality. The prevailing optimism, shared by most British soldiers from Roberts downwards, was reasonable enough at the time, for by the relatively civilised standards of nineteenth century warfare the Boer republics should have opened negotiations for peace. Tragically for South Africa, a relatively small number of hard-line Afrikaners refused to accept defeat and branded their surrendered brethren as traitors. Adopting guerrilla tactics, these 'bitter-enders' prolonged the war for almost two dismal years.

Johannesburg Garrison

With the surrender of Johannesburg on 31 May 1900 the first phase of the campaign may be said to have closed as far as the 1st Battalion East Lancashire Regiment was concerned. Lord Roberts entrusted the security and administration of the Transvaal capital and surrounding areas of the Rand to the 15th Brigade, and the Battalion was occupied in such exacting duties until the end of April 1901. Companies were scattered in garrison of various posts along the Rand, from Johannesburg to Springs, and on the main railway line between Pretoria and Vereeniging.

During this period several Regimental officers held appointments in the military administration. Major O'Brien was appointed President of the Military Tribunal established for the trial of criminal and military offences amongst the civilian inhabitants, and Lieutenant Da Costa became a member of the court. Captains Daubeny and Hamber were appointed Railway Staff Officers, whilst at Germiston Major Lewis filled the office of Magistrate. The policing of Johannesburg was also at first entrusted to companies of the battalions in garrison; two companies of the East Lancashire, under Captains Lawrence and Sharp, were detailed for the district of Fordsburg, while Captain Trent's Company went to Dournfontein. This arrangement, however, was superseded early in July by the formation of a special force, the 'Johannesburg Military Police', under the immediate command of the Military Commissioner of Police. The East Lancashires detailed two subalterns (Lieutenants Gosset and Pirouet), twelve sergeants, and 140 privates for this force, and in recognition of their responsible duties they received extra duty pay, ranging from five shillings a day for a private upwards.

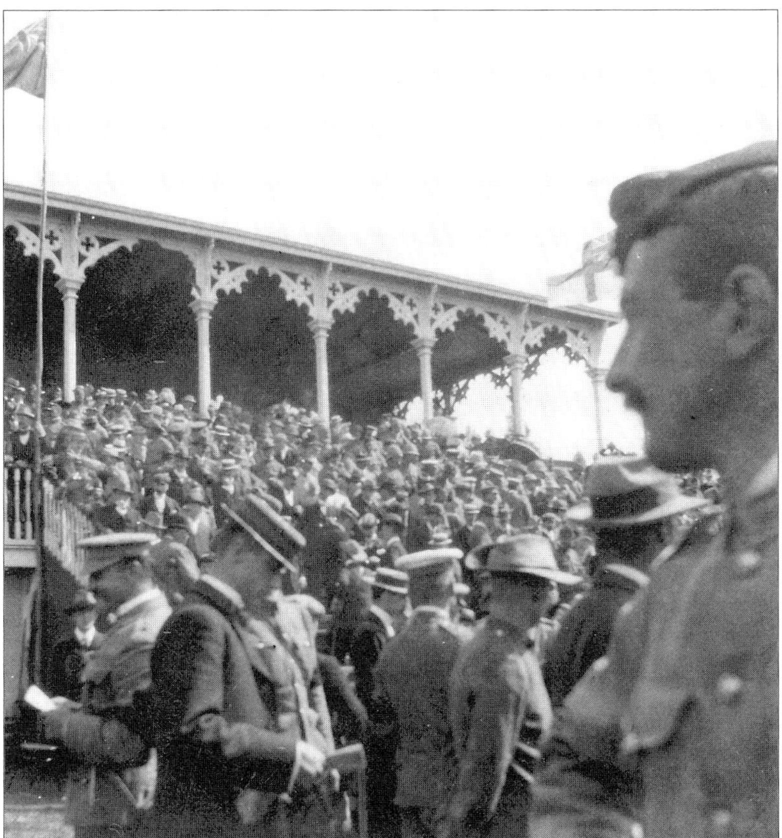

A race meeting at Johannesburg, 1900.

Lieutenant Coventry, East Lancashire Regiment, on the right.

The cosmopolitan society of the Rand welcomed the 'Khakis' of all ranks with an open-handed hospitality, which, even if not always disinterested, lacked nothing in spontaneity and warmth. The comparative immunity from serious disturbance, which characterised the administration of the Rand under Martial Law, was in no small degree attributable to the excellent relations established between the inhabitants and the military. The few isolated attempts at conspiracy against the garrison were detected in their early stages, and were frustrated with little difficulty. The most dangerous plot was for an uprising on 14 July 1900. There was to be a military steeplechase at the racecourse on that day which would be attended by most of the British officers in Johannesburg. The plan was to shoot down the officers and then to overwhelm the small garrison. Fortunately the plot was given away. The chief conspirators were surrounded and arrested on the night of the 13th, and by daybreak nearly five hundred of their followers were in custody.

It would be tedious to follow in detail the distribution of the companies during these months. The constant risk of attack and the complete isolation of many of the smaller posts required untiring vigilance and ceaseless attention to mundane routine, a striking contrast to the exciting activity of the previous months. The tedium was relieved, it is true, at the larger stations like Johannesburg and Elandsfontein by the comings, goings and bustle of those important centres. From time to time the sporadic activity of neighbouring commandos called for more active measures, and small mixed columns were formed from such troops as were available to act against the offenders. On one of these occasions, at the end of August 1900, two East Lancashire companies, under Captains Lawrence and Sharp, were attached to a column, under command of Lieutenant Colonel Bradley, which came into contact with a Boer commando near Modderfontein during a thick fog. A sharp engagement ensued at close quarters, and resulted in several casualties, including two men severely wounded in Captain Sharp's Company. During November, and again in the following January, Lieutenant-Colonel Wright commanded a similar column operating to the south east of Johannesburg. In September two Companies, under Major Twynam,[1] went further afield, joining a force under General Broadwood who was operating to the west of Pretoria.

1. As a 22-year-old subaltern of the 59th, Humphrey Twynam had been Mentioned in Despatches for gallantry at the battle of Ahmed Khel in Afghanistan, 19 April 1880, the last occasion on which the Regiment formed square around its Colours in the old style. Captain William Holbourn, Quartermaster of the 1st Battalion in South Africa, had also fought in the battle as a young soldier.

Escorting Boer prisoners up to Pretoria.

Members of the Volunteer Service Company, East Lancashire Regiment engaged in one of their many routine duties during their time on the Rand.

Mounted Infantry

The superior mobility of the mounted Boers, however, outpaced the 'foot' Infantry. Not so the ubiquitous Mounted Infantry, who consequently assumed even greater importance in the British war effort. On 8 June the East Lancashire Company of 8th M.I. was ordered to defend the vital, and vulnerable, railway line from the Cape, with posts at Meyerton and Vereeniging, where they remained until 9 February 1901. During this period the Company was continually in contact with local Boer commandos, and in fifteen different engagements lost five N.C.O.s and men killed, three wounded, and eight taken prisoner. Captain Ernest Collins DSO, who commanded the Company at that time, later wrote the following account of one such incident:

'On 28th August, 1900, a patrol, under Lieut. [Percy] Goodwyn, of an N.C.O. and six men left Meyerton, where a section of the East Lancashire Company, 8th M. I., was stationed and proceeded westwards to try and locate Theron's laager, which was supposed to be some 11 miles out near a farm called Hartebeestfontein. Sergt. Dawber was the N.C.O. with this patrol. On reaching Hartebeestfontein the presence of the enemy was very apparent as numbers of waggons and

Signalling to a column.
Captain Sharp, East Lancashire Regiment (centre, arms folded) has been observing Boer movement – note telescope – and in this photograph his signaller is transmitting the information by heliograph to a nearby column.

horses were visible some way from the farm. Posting some men to keep watch, Lieut. Goodwyn, with Sergt. Dawber and the rest of the patrol advanced towards the farm and there surprised two Boers, who had foolishly left their horses and rifles outside. These were immediately made prisoners and ordered to mount, and under Sergt. Dawber, and the men of the patrol, were just being led off to Meyerton, when the owner of the farm dashed out and started firing at them with a revolver. Lieut. Goodwyn immediately engaged him with his Mauser, and was lucky enough to hit him with his fifth shot, the Boer having emptied his revolver without effect. This firing, unfortunately, roused all the Boers in the district, who were, as a matter of fact, Theron's Commando, so the patrol had nothing left but to gallop for it. Sergt. Dawber and the two men who were in charge of the prisoners led, the rest under Lieut. Goodwyn, kept slightly in rear.

'The country was very difficult, there being several ridges of kopjes between Hartebeesfontein and Meyerton. The Boers, whom Lieut. Goodwyn estimated at about 60 in number, soon began to gain on them, being better mounted, and divided into several parties, scattering for points so as to cut them of from Meyerton, while some in rear were always firing at them. This race continued for six miles to a farm

East Lancashire Mounted Infantry. British soldiers soon became as adept as the Boers at living off the land, and this soldier has returned from a foraging expedition with a plump goose across his saddle bow.

called Vlakfontein, owned by a foreigner, who called himself Jackson. Here the country closes into a narrow pass with kopjes on either side about 600 feet apart. Some of the pursuing Boers had reached this before the patrol and opened a cross fire on them as they passed through. Sergt. Dawber's horse was hit in the head and, turning a somersault, threw its rider, luckily without stunning him. He immediately sprang up and, rushing up to one of the prisoners, unhorsed him and, mounting his horse, galloped on with the other prisoner towards Meyerton; all this was done in a moment under a heavy cross fire. Lieut. Goodwyn's horse having given out, he shouted to the patrol to scatter, while he, by great luck, got a horse from an Englishman called Page, who worked on Jackson's farm, and galloped on, bare-backed, after Sergt. Dawber. The scattering of the patrol had the desired effect as it confused the pursuing Boers, who scattered themselves chasing single men. Meyerton was still four miles ahead, but when once through the neck the country was open, and although more than one horse was hit by the fire, only one man, Pte Brooks, was taken. The dismounted prisoner, of course, was left to his own devices. Sergt. Dawber galloped on with his prisoner and reached Meyerton safely, being soon followed by other members of the patrol, as the Boers hesitated to come too close to the line. The prisoner turned out to be a man of some importance in the Commando, but refused to give his name. Both the Boers' horses and rifles were brought in.' For their share in this daring escapade, Lieutenant Percy

Lieutenant P. C. W. Goodwyn, DSO.

Goodwyn was awarded a DSO and Sergeant John Dawber received the DCM.[2]

Further south down the same line, the Loyal North Lancashire portion of the Malta Mounted Infantry had since June been stationed at Ventersburg Road Station and Riet Spruit, near Ventersburg. Captain John Pine-Coffin, their OC, soon acquired a reputation for energetic and successful patrolling. Such maps as were available were often sketchy and inaccurate, giving a marked advantage to those who knew the country, but before long the North Lancashires too were familiar with their surroundings and were able to navigate with growing confidence. 'One picks up the way to get about fairly easily,' wrote Lieutenant Francis Braithwaite, who found the best available map for most purposes to be 'Briton or Boer', a commercial publication which, at 20 miles to the inch and without contours, offers only the most general impression of the terrain. 'The men have improved wonderfully. At Bloemfontein I had to send a party to a farm 9 miles away, and the other side of the town, but was able to show them a bit of the road where it crossed a nek. They found their way straight there. Before starting for this country they would not have done it on such meagre information.'[3]

Small, helter-skelter mounted actions were commonplace, with local tactical advantage of numbers or ground swinging from one side to the other. Captain Pine-Coffin cryptically noted a typical incident in his diary for 2 August: 'Was woke up during the night by report that train had been blown up. Got an engine & sent it with armed party to the place. Took out all the M.I. & escorted the engine. Found the whole train on fire, 3 men killed & general confusion. The American

2. Lieutenant P. C. W. Goodwyn, whose father, an old XXXth officer, had recently commanded the 59th, was himself to command the 7th East Lancashires in heavy fighting on the Somme during the Great War. John Dawber, who enlisted in 1890, retired from the Regiment as a Colour-Sergeant in 1911, leaving behind him, in the words of the Regimental journal, 'a record that might be envied by any man and a good example for the young soldier to follow.' Both served with the M.I. Company throughout the war and distinguished themselves on several other occasions.

3. Letter from Lieutenant F. J. Braithwaite, 2nd Loyal North Lancashire Regiment, dated Riet Spruit, 27 June 1900.

Sergeant J. Dawber, DCM.

Consul & Lord Lennox in train. Had them sent back to V[entersburg] Road, also the dead and wounded. At once pursued the Boers & followed them up for 10 miles, found them, had a great fight, killed 3, wounded 10 others, took some prisoners, & covered ourselves with glory. Generals & all kinds of people came down to see me & congratulate me. The American Consul was very funny about it, altogether everything turned out well.'[4]

His diary entry for 10 September 1900, when De Wet was in the area, recounted another such chase: 'Got information Boer commando had crossed the line going west. Followed them up with all mounted men, found them & fought them at Cyphergat. Had a very hard fight & took a koppy, driving enemy off in disorder. Captured two prisoners-of-war. Did this myself. Got useful information from them. Enemy lost 7 killed, 3 wounded. Our losses 2 killed, 2 wounded. Returned home, horses and ourselves done up. There were 3 commandants with this commando joining De Wet.' Next day he wrote: 'Buried our dead ... Had telegrams from Lord Roberts, Generals Kelly-Kenny and Allen. They all seem very pleased about it. We are beginning to get rather well known. The M.M.I. very pleased with themselves.'[5]

Skirmishing continued on an almost daily basis as the ever-present but elusive Boer commandos tried, with some success, to disrupt rail and telegraph lines. Mounted Infantry patrols often found themselves outnumbered by the enemy, and on Sunday 14 October the Company had a serious engagement. 'Got news that there were about 60 Boers near Cyphergat. Arranged with neighbouring stations to combine with me for an attack on position [Pine-Coffin had some one hundred and fifty men with a 'pom-pom' and a Maxim]. We carried the kopje & drove the Boers off. Shortly after we were surrounded by nearly 1500 of the enemy & had to fight our way back for nearly 10 miles, being

4. Diary of Captain J. E. Pine-Coffin DSO, p. 107, printed in *One Man's Boer War* (ed. Susan Pine-Coffin), Bideford, 1999. Private A. Daw of 2nd Loyal North Lancashires, who was wounded in this action, was awarded the DCM.
5. Pine-Coffin, p. 131. Private T. Maher of 2nd Loyal North Lancashires was killed in this action and Corporal F. Peacock, who was awarded the DCM, was severely wounded.

Major J. E. Pine-Coffin, DSO, 2nd Loyal North Lancashires.
Described as a 'beau-ideal column commander'. (*Photograph courtesy of Mrs Susan Pine-Coffin*)

hard pressed by the enemy the whole way. By twice altering my line of retreat, we got thro' & took up a position on a hill & drove the Boers back. We fought them for 1 hour & gradually made good our retreat. Poor Attfield was killed, also Pte[s] Argyle & Kenyon, & 4 wounded. We had a very difficult retreat, and several times thought we should have been caught. On Monday we buried our dead & sent the wounded to Kroonstad. All thro' Monday the Boer patrols were quite close to the station, & some cavalry scouts were driven in. Hope now that steps will be taken to clear the country.' [6]

In December 1900 Pine-Coffin was promoted local Major and given command of 9th M.I., a new unit including the Malta Mounted Infantry. By the end of March he was operating as a column commander in the Ventersburg area.

6. Pine-Coffin, p. 151. Privates W. Argyle and G. Kenyon of 2nd Loyal North Lancashires was killed in this action and Privates C. Bell and H. Healey were wounded, while Lance-Sergeant Gowan was awarded the DCM.

Militia on the Line

Some sixty miles further south, the 3rd East Lancashires had marched up on 17 May to Karee Siding, and on to Brandfort, which was to be their headquarters for over a year, until 9 June 1901 when they moved a few miles north, to Virginia. Detachments were posted along a fifty-mile stretch of the railway, from Glen and Karee Siding in the south to Eensgevonden and Vet River in the north, from where they patrolled the line and garrisoned the stations. There was little large-scale enemy activity in this area, but occasional Boer snipers took their toll and the Battalion suffered six casualties from enemy action, a small number considering the vulnerability of sentries and patrols. Robust counter-measures were taken: 'No. 3874 Pte E. Williams ('B' Coy) died on 17th Sept, he having been shot whilst patrolling the line at night,' records the Regimental Digest. 'The shot was fired from an occupied farm, and in consequence the farm was burnt down.' Water-borne diseases were a far more lethal enemy, and the Battalion had 46 deaths from typhoid and dysentery.

Another hundred miles or so further south, the 3rd South Lancashires moved up the line in August 1900 from Norval's Pont to the important Springfontein junction, from where they also garrisoned the stations at Van Zyl Spruit and Jagersfontein Road. Having completed work on the vital bridge, the latter weeks of their stay at Norval's Pont had been relatively quiet, with time for field firing and to train a mounted infantry company of two officers and fifty men, and indeed the first two months at Springfontein were also peaceful. This changed markedly in early October, when Boer commandos moved south into the district.

On 13 October two mounted infantry patrols of the 3rd South Lancashires were ambushed by Commandant Pretorius' commando. Lieutenant E. M. Hanbury and Private T. Cantello were shot dead and Private J. Morrison was wounded. Pretorius then sent a message to Lieutenant A. H. Spooner at Jagersfontein Road, informing him what had happened and threatening to shell and attack the post unless he surrendered. The station was reinforced and the threatened attack was not made, but numbers of enemy remained in the surrounding country, frequently skirmishing with the Mounted Infantry, while for the next three weeks the railway lines north and south of Springfontein were blown nightly. The flashes of the exploding dynamite could be distinctly seen from the Battalion's trenches, but little could be done for at that time there were no block-houses on the line. Traffic on the railway was hardly delayed, for the damage was repaired within an hour or two each morning; nevertheless, the Battalion was required to remain in its trenches every night from 12 October to 6 November.

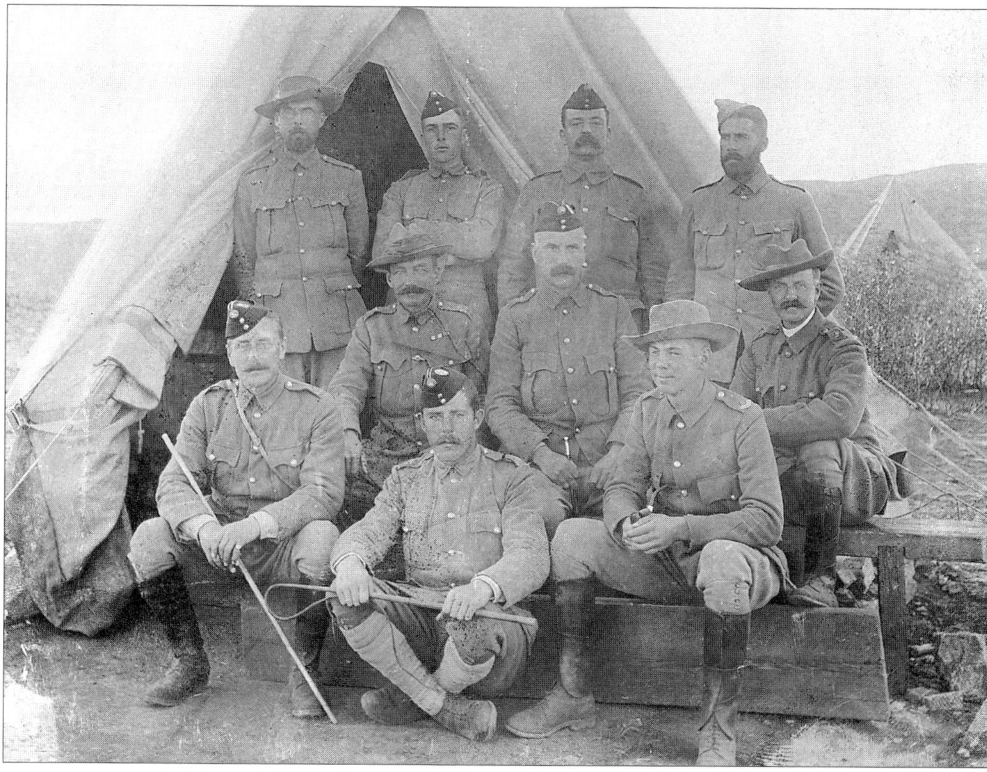

Officers of 3rd Battalion South Lancashire Regiment, South Africa 1901.

There were a number of unsuccessful night attacks on the South Lancashires' positions, in one of which Sergeant Chapman of the 1st Battalion was mortally wounded, and it appears that a full-scale attempt on Springfield by Fouché's commando, some twelve to fifteen hundred strong, was only averted by the timely arrival of 3rd Grenadier Guards at the end of the month.

On 11 November Lieutenant Clarkson, with 'D' Company, was sent up to Kruger's Siding, which was threatened by the enemy, and on the evening of the 13th he received a letter from Commandant Scheepers informing him that the line was destroyed on both sides of him and calling upon him to surrender. He declined, whereupon, in the words of the Regimental Record, 'things were made rather hot for him' for 24 hours, when the Boers were driven off with the assistance of two companies of the 3rd Grenadiers and an armoured train.

The railway lines and surrounding areas were frequently traversed by Boers moving in and out of Cape Colony. During the first three months of 1901, Kruger's Siding was a favoured crossing point, and the line was constantly blown up and the camp almost nightly alarmed, so much so that an armoured train nearly always patrolled that section of line. Line-crossers were not always successful. On 5 February some

Major E. K. Heath (*8th from left*) and his crew with No. 6 Armoured Train, wrecked by a contact mine at America Siding, 17 May 1901.

The armoured trains were an integral part of the defence scheme for the lines of communication, providing a mobile reserve of firepower.

of De Wet's men came unawares on a post of the 3rd South Lancashires, and Barend Enslin, one of his most trusted scouts, was wounded and taken prisoner, while on the night of the 9th the Mounted Infantry Company, supported by an armoured train, had a brisk action with Fourie's commando, who were crossing the line north of Kuilfontein, killing three of them.

On 17 May the Battalion lost one of its longest-serving members when Major E. K. Heath was killed. He was commanding No. 6 Armoured Train, for which he had volunteered, when it ran into a contact mine at night near America Siding.

It was not until June 1901 that the block-house system was introduced on the South Lancashires' section of the line, and on the 28th of that month the Battalion entrained for Cape Town on its way home, reaching Warrington on 3 August.

On 30 March 1901 the 3rd Loyal North Lancashires arrived in South Africa from Malta. They too were destined for the long lines of communication, albeit further down country than their sister Militia battalions. Headquarters were at Port Elizabeth, with companies detached on the line to Norval's Pont, at Arundel, Cradock and Barkley Bridge. On 8 February 1902 the Battalion was ordered to concentrate at Port Elizabeth for embarkation, reaching Southampton on 14 March. It was disembodied at Preston the following day.

Maxim machine gun detachments of 3rd Loyal North Lancashire Regiment.
The Battalion served on the lines of communication in Natal, with headquarters at Port Elizabeth, from March 1901 until February 1902.

The 3rd Loyal North Lancashires had only one significant brush with the enemy, near Stormberg on 27 November 1901, when a patrol, including Major Cowper, Lieutenant Mackie and seventeen Mounted Infantry of the Battalion was caught in a pass by a strong body of Boers who first cut off their only line of retreat and then seized a hill commanding the British party's position. The patrol behaved with great coolness, and, riding by one at a time, most of them escaped the trap, but Private Fisher was killed and two others were seriously wounded, while the two officers and three men were taken prisoners. Lieutenant Mackie won especial praise for the way he handled his men and for his efforts to bring away one of the wounded.

South Lancashires in the South-East Transvaal

It will be recalled that the 1st South Lancashires, having taken part in Buller's advance through northern Natal into the eastern Transvaal, had reached Standerton on 24 June. From that date they were employed in securing the Army's lines of communication between Standerton and Volkrust. From 26 June to 2 August Battalion Headquarters was at Katbosch Spruit, with detachments at Leeuw Spruit and Kromdraai; then from 3 August to 3 September at Zand Spruit,

South Lancashire entrenchments at Katbosch Spruit.
Guarding the vital railway lines of communication, July 1900.

with a detachment at Gras Kop,. Having marched some three hundred miles in six weeks, enduring hot days and frosty nights on a staple diet of bully beef and biscuits, the South Lancashires welcomed this change, particularly when, once the railway line was open, their tents arrived. Trenches were dug to protect the camps, outposts posted and the line was patrolled, while occasionally there were convoys to be escorted.

'While in these camps,' wrote Lieutenant Lewis of the Volunteer Company, 'we obtained our first insight of the personal character of the Boer farmer. There were several farms scattered about, some with their owners resident – surrendered or too infirm to fight – others still on commando. These farms were all well searched for arms, &c., and well watched. As to their tenants, the inclination was to trust them less the more we saw or knew of them. Their sympathies were either openly anti-British or too much the other way to believe, a feature, I am sorry to say, more marked in the Boer women than the men. In several cases in the neighbourhood, farmers, after taking the oath of neutrality, were found with rifles and ammunition hidden on their premises, or in some way aiding the fighting Boers. Their stock was confiscated and the farms burned – strong measures, no doubt, but as just as they were strong. There would be less talk of 'inhumanity' in such cases had the talkers' own bodies been in the neighbourhood of those particular farms.'[7]

7. Lieutenant H. H. Lewis, article in *The Volunteer Service Company South Lancashire Regiment in South Africa*, pp. 43–4.

A ration train for the South Lancashires, Katbosch Spruit.

Rail was the principal means of re-supply in South Africa.

Captain Appleton outlined the 'farm' policy at that time: 'All farms invariably fly a white flag upon the arrival of British troops in their vicinity. If owner surrenders and gives up his arms and takes oath of neutrality, the farm and property are respected, and if necessary protected. If firing takes place at us from farm, or other hostile acts, such as visits from Boers, or information given to them, farm stock is removed and farmer taken prisoner. If telegraph or railway is damaged within a certain radius, farm is burned. This seems severe, but it has been found that more lenient treatment was not appreciated or respected. To give one instance. While one such farm was being burned near Paardekop, the lady of the house was weeping and gnashing her teeth and loudly protesting her innocence; but the missing telegraph insulators from damaged veldt wire were found in her loft. The Boers were nearly all unreliable and lie like the devil.'[8]

The enemy was ever close at hand, sniping, cutting telegraph wires, and looking for opportunities to attack the railway, and in response the South Lancashires were involved in several raids. One such expedition was mounted on 2 July by 'B' Company, who had the previous day been ordered to hold themselves in readiness to turn out at a moment's notice, and was recorded in his diary by Private Wain:

8. Captain F. M. Appleton's diary, in *The Volunteer Service Company South Lancashire Regiment in South Africa*, p. 143.

South Lancashires digging trenches, Leeuw Spruit.

The South Lancashires receive their first issue of presents from home, July 1900.

'My company fell in at 4.30 am and marched off in the dark with orders to make no noise nor strike any matches. We arrived at a farm at daylight and halted. Shortly afterwards a number of Boers came out and we opened fire. They were taken by surprise, but mounted their horses and made a dash for a donga, firing as they went. Several got away. We got three of them, also a large stock of cattle, sheep and 50 horses.'

Sergeant Pegum was in action a week later: 'On 8th July we went out, 'H' and 'F' Companies with three companies of Y&L Regt, also four guns, as a reconnaissance in force. I saw about 30 Boers. They retired. We fired our guns. Having found out the strength of the Boers, we retired. After a delay of two hours, while we were retiring, the Boers advanced and fired several shots amongst us. Two squadrons of Bethune's Mounted Infantry were behind us. They galloped through our ranks. We were ordered to halt and fire by alternate sections whilst the guns got into position again. Then the guns fired and we carried out the retirement successfully. I was glad to learn that there were no casualties although we had a heavy fire poured on us. We returned to camp having completed about 20 miles march.'

On 27 July Major Adam set out from Kromdraai with about 46 men of the Volunteer Company to bring in some stock, which a farmer had sold to the Army before the Boers could take it. 'Some half-dozen transport wagons accompanied us,' recalled Corporal Howard, 'and after we had walked for a mile or so the Officer Commanding gave us the privilege of riding in the wagons. This order was a most welcome one, as it was about the only chance we had given to us since our arrival in the country, and it naturally raised our spirits. We commenced to sing, but making such a noise was hardly suitable to Major Adam, who rode up and politely informed us that we were not having a picnic to Blackpool. We had been on our way about an hour when we were joined by a squadron of Bethune's Mounted Infantry and some gunners of the 86th Battery with two guns.

'On reaching our destination, which was a Dutch farm, I was told off with three other men for observation duty alongside the Vaal River, and about 900 or 1,000 yards in front of the rest of the party. The three other men's names were Boardman, Lowcock and Almond. Captain Appleton came with us to show us our post. Just across the other side of the river there was a kopje, and our orders were to particularly watch this, and a farm on our right, as the enemy had been reported there in force early that morning.

'Our Captain had left us, and had got about half way back to the farm, where our men were loading the wagons with farm stock, when our attention was drawn by Lowcock, who was on sentry, to the fact that there was a mounted party riding up the kopje in front of us. They had got up on the other side. We looked round to see if those at the farm had noticed it, and saw quite a commotion there, everybody running for cover. The Boers had spotted us, and, before one could say Jack Robinson, they started firing.'

Private Pendlebury was on sentry at the farm: 'We saw about 50 galloping over a hill in front of the farm called Blue Kop. I at once ran and gave information to the first officer I could find, which happened to be the B.M.I. officer. He at once gave the alarm. Just then the Boers opened up a heavy rifle fire into the camp and bullets were flying all around the place. We at once returned the fire. Then the guns we had with us opened fire into them, and scattered them in confusion, and they galloped away faster than they came, leaving one or two behind killed or wounded.'[9]

Meanwhile, Corporal Howard and his comrades had to extricate themselves from their exposed position. 'Down we dropped, and for a minute (which seemed like a week) we were under the impression that we should have to throw our checks in, but we were very agreeably disappointed, for the enemy were firing too high. Bang went one of the guns, and we knew the gunners had begun to work. There was a lull in the Boers' fire when the shell came over, and our only chance lay in taking advantage of the slackening of their fire, for they were getting a little nearer the range. We made our minds up when the next shell came over to put ourselves as far away as possible. Another shell, and we tried our best to break the record for about 80 or 100 yards, when we had to again owing to our friends on the hill trying to make us carry some pieces of their lead in our bodies. Our Captain was in a worse position than we were, for, being further away, he ran the risk of all their bullets. We never expected to see him safe and sound even if we managed to get through all right. Under cover of the artillery fire and our men at the farm keeping up a heavy rifle fire, and dropping and running alternately, we managed to get cover in a cattle kraal belonging to the farm. On going to report, the first man I saw was Captain Appleton, and I was very glad to see that he was unhurt, as we were.'[10]

'We started back for camp with 150 head of cattle, 100 turkeys and 8 wagon loads of produce. We could not fetch all the stock because we were afraid that the darkness might lead us into a trap. We all returned to camp safe and sound and well pleased with our outing.'

In August Sergeant Hackett had a long day out from Zand Spruit, where his company was entrenched on a high hill about two miles east of the railway station. 'One afternoon, on day outpost, we looked down on a hurried troop movement below and heard shots which, we believed, was a minor ambush of a mounted column. They looked so tiny from our height we could not distinguish what was really happening, but one felt weird looking down on a battle. Soon after, about three o'clock, there was a stir; rifles and ammunition were inspected, a haversack ration issued, and orders to parade at two

9. Diary of Private W. H. Pendlebury, Volunteer Company South Lancashire Regiment. Pendlebury, of 17 Kirkland Street, St Helens, was the company cook.

10. Sergeant J. Howard (promoted from Corporal in South Africa), article in *The Volunteer Service Company South Lancashire Regiment in South Africa*, pp. 67–8. Sergeant Howard lived at 3 Whittle Street, Warrington.

Preparing breakfast on outpost – soldiers of the South Lancashire Regiment.

o'clock the following morning. We moved, in pitch dark, down the track to a small plateau where, when daylight arrived, we found a battery of artillery and some more companies of the Battalion.

'The gunners were short of range finders so Cpl. Attwood and I were ordered to join them. "Can you ride a horse?" said the C.O. "Yes," said Attwood, and got one. "No," said I, and the C.O. said, "Oh, well jump up on one of the limbers." An N.C.O. guided me to the first limber and I climbed up and sat between the two gunners on bare boards whilst they sat on strapped-down blankets. When the column moved off, the infantry marched down the track, but did the gunners? Heaven help me, I thought my last day had come. They galloped across country, down hill at first, over boulders, rocks, ant-hills, ditches, nothing was an obstacle to them as they steeple-chased gaily along, the limbers often at an acute angle and me, with a range-finder in my left hand and rifle in my right, and only a foot-board to bear against, bouncing up and down like a jack-in-the-box and trying to stick on for dear life. Those two gunners were like statues. They never smiled or looked right or left, let alone spoke, all the while; they just left me to it. When the halt was signalled the limbers swung round at a canter and I had to jump off on the turn

Reveille on the veldt.
South Lancashire officers breakfast in their 'bivouac', a stretcher windbreak, on trek near Wakkerstroom, September 1900. At night the temperature plunged and, with only a waterproof sheet and a blanket, considerable ingenuity was required to keep warm.

and land on two feet without being run over. My luck was certainly in that day.

'Actually we were pursuing a number of Boers who seemed to enjoy playing cat and mouse, for as soon as the battery halted they galloped, until the third halt [when], having hidden behind a fold in the ground, they met us with a fusillade. No one was hit. For about three minutes everyone stood stock still, except for the limbers moving to the rear, then, as some cavalry on the right front flank moved in, the Boers fled to a farm one and a half miles ahead and the gunners firing a few rounds [four] sent them galloping away. A short halt and the battery returned and, halting at the first farm, went on, leaving me to make my way home, five miles away ...

'Arriving at camp in the dark about eight o'clock, tired and hungry, I found no tea, fires out, and, to complete the happiness, I was suddenly asked why I wasn't on outpost; so without undressing I trekked off to the trench. I remember posting the sentry, and watching dawn rise, and 'all clear', and the next was about midday when I awoke in the trench in a layer of water; it had been raining.'[11]

The harshly variable climate, rather than the Boers, was the main enemy to men living in the open, often on a restricted diet. 'Autumn brought heavy showers with thunder and lightning,' wrote Sergeant Hackett, 'the latter at times awesome. One night [31 October] on

11. Sergeant E. Hackett, *Taken For A Ride*, article in *The Regimental Chronicle of The South Lancashire Regiment*, Vol. XXII, No. 1 (1954).

A halt on trek.

The 1st South Lancashires enjoy a short break at Clutterbuck Hill, near Zand Spruit, September 1900. The group of officers in the foreground comprises:
Front, left to right: Lt-Col Hall, Capt Goren, Lts Robson and Lewis.
Rear: Lt Wynn, Capt James, Lt Woods, Capt Appleton, Lts Green, Skinner, Milman and Travis-Cook.

outpost we watched a storm approach. It was very loud and violent as, from a dense black cloud, four streaks of forked lightning, peculiarly like the legs of a table in form, descended to earth. For over an hour we watched it coming from the horizon, over the camp towards us. As it drew near and the air very heavy I went and sat with the sentry, for I felt we would get it and guessed he would be as nervous as I felt. Feeling it passing over, and expecting anything to happen, we were relieved to watch it passing on and wondered (I do to this day) how it was those four streaks descended so close around us and we were unscathed. Next morning we heard the cavalry part of the camp was struck and ten men killed, others injured, and casualties among the horses.

'As winter fell, so the nights were hard frost on this high ground. One removed one's boots and placed them under the haversack for a pillow at the head of the ground sheet, wrapped the puttees around one's feet, put on the overcoat and, throwing the blanket over all, tried to make it air-proof by tucking it in all around and burying one's head underneath. Soon the blankets crackled, and at reveille were like a sheet of ice …

'This cold weather brought about much stomach upset in the

Lieutenant Clarke-Jervoise, South Lancashire Regiment, on trek.

Battalion and a number of men were sent down, mostly with dysentry, and we were saddened to hear of the death of many of our pals after only four or five days in hospital.[12] I had colic and couldn't eat anything, but smoked many pipes. I tried chewing, per advice, but that was awful … Three days before reaching Standerton my colic became chronic and I had to report sick, receiving that cure of all ills – a No. 9 pill. On parade I was ordered to the ambulance and had to ride amidst a dozen others, which, bumping over cart ruts and tracks, was anything but relieving, so at the midday halt I rejoined the Company as it marched off again – marching was better than riding.' Hackett was ordered back to hospital. 'A medical orderly put me in an empty marquee, one of a dozen, and left me until a man arrived with my dinner and told me the Battalion was moving off at 2 p.m. Well, I thought, nobody has been near me, I'm not staying here. So I picked up my kit and back to camp to find them gone. Following on, I caught up and was told all the sorts of fool I was. It

12. Sergeant Hackett does not mention that his own brother, Drummer F. Hackett, died at Pietermaritzburg of 'enteric' (typhoid) on 8 August 1900.

His servant, Private Ford, returning from a foraging expedition with mealies and a chicken.

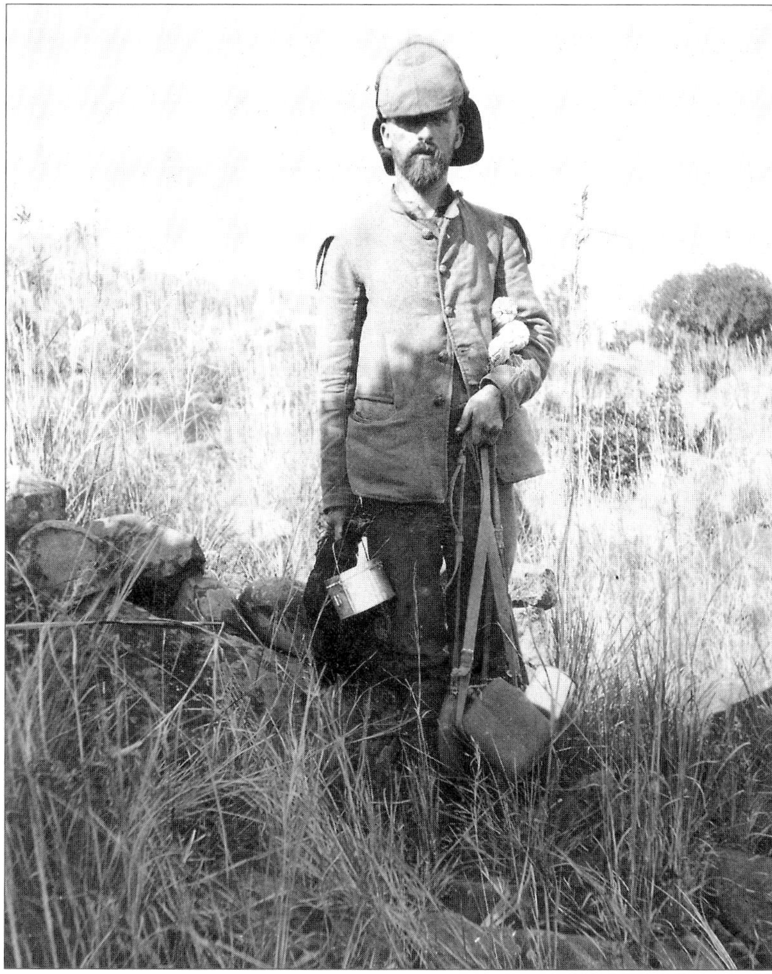

was a couple of days after [that] the Captain stared at me and said "What are you doing here? I thought I left you in hospital," and was only mollified when I pleaded not to leave the Battalion. It was he in his kindness that had sent me to hospital, and his was the mildest remark, "Damned fool". But esprit de corps apart, Africa was a land of adventure, of romance and mystery. Had I not devoured the books of Rider Haggard, the big game hunters and others ...?'

On 4 September the 11th Brigade was on the move again, marching south-east. It had been decided to clear the border country of south-east Transvaal and northern Natal, leaving permanent garrisons at Wakkerstroom, Utrecht, Vryheid, De Jager's Drift and Dundee. The Brigade occupied each of these in turn, and on 10 November the 1st South Lancashires garrisoned De Jager's Drift, remaining there for two months.

'This march, about ninety miles long, was an experience very

Grave of Drummer James Hackett.

Died at Estcourt of 'enteric' (typhoid) on 8 June 1900, aged 19. He was a younger brother of Sergeant Hackett the diarist, who had this memorial erected.

different from our previous long trek,' wrote Lieutenant Lewis. 'In the first place the force was composed differently, the proportion of mounted troops being much greater. The work of the Infantry consisted almost entirely of escorting guns and baggage while on the move, and outposts when encamped. The escorting was a painfully tedious business, with a baggage train three or four miles long, the most difficult of roads, and the oxen worn out. The poor beasts dropped in hundreds, and were left on the veldt to die. The marching, at times, was hard work as, while the wagons moved along such road as there was, we were out on the flanks, going up hill and down dale all day long.'

'Our journey was now south-east towards Swaziland,' recalled Sergeant Hackett, for whom this trek was something of a literary pilgrimage. 'We would not see the fabulous town of Johannesburg, nor Pretoria. We had turned back and were driving some commandos of Boers before us ... After a few days we arrived at Wakkerstroom and bivouacked. Yes, there we were, right in the heart of Rider Haggard's "She". I was thrilled, and more so that evening when our Section was paraded and marched to the top of the mountain mentioned in the book. I think I half-expected "She" to appear in the mist, somewhat like a vision.'

Transport parked near Utrecht.

'The escorting was a painfully tedious business, with a baggage train three or four miles long, the most difficult of roads, and the oxen worn out.' This photograph gives some idea of the slow-moving baggage trains that the Infantry had to protect on trek.

The harsh realities of war could not, however, be denied for long. 'During the few days we spent here we had the distasteful job of searching every house for rifles and ammunition, and, owing to feminine opposition, had to be politely ruthless. My party found several, old fashioned and new, even to an Elephant Gun. At the last house the resistance was stubborn. We found nothing downstairs and, though the men were reluctant to press further, I insisted on going upstairs. In one bedroom the young woman tried hard to keep us out – "Mother sick in bed" – but I was suspicious and, entering, searched a large box, under blankets, etc., and found four brand new shining .450 Winchester Express rifles and 150 packets of ammunition. Two more, used, were in the cupboard, and I'll bet that if we had had the temerity to turn the old lady out of bed, for she was not sick, we would have found more. The Boers had not been disturbed in these parts before and the place was an arsenal and storehouse.'[13]

Leaving a battalion at Wakkerstroom, the column marched on to Utrecht, Vryheid and De Jager's Drift. There were no major incidents, but it was gruelling work for man and beast, often on reduced rations, and, as Hackett relates, the enforcement of march discipline was no easy matter: 'It was on one of those very hot days marching. We crossed a river and halted midday. An order came, "Fall out and fill all water bottles". No sooner started than the whistle sounded "Fall in", and soon we were on the march. Being rear company, it was our

13. Hackett, *On The Road To Pretoria*, pp. 8–9.

Officers and NCOs of 1st Volunteer Battalion South Lancashire Regiment, South Africa, 1901.

On leaving the 1st Battalion, the Volunteer Service Company served in northern Natal for a further six months before returning to Warrington.

job to collect stragglers, and so we hurried the men to rejoin the Battalion. The Adjutant [Lieutenant Arthur Bailey] rode back on the same errand, and all were got away except one Volunteer. Unhurried, he continued to fill his bottle. "Fall in at once," said the Adjutant. "Aw reet, when I've fill't water bottle," said the man. "Fall in, do you hear," said the Adjutant. "Aw reet, I will when water bottle's fill't." "Do you know who you are talking to?" said the Adjutant. "Aye, aw knows thee reet enough, but I'se too b——y tired to talk to thee," replied the man, not even looking up. Expecting the earth to open up, I was relieved to see the Adjutant smile as he rode away, saying "See he catches up".'[14]

On 13 October the first Volunteer Service Company left the 1st South Lancashires, bound, as they imagined, for home. The Volunteers, having been thanked for their services by Colonel Hall, presented arms to the Colonel and marched off in the early dawn, whistling 'Auld Lang Syne' and the Regimental March, 'God Bless The Prince of Wales' as they swung over the Blood River bridge. In fact the following day, when they reached Dundee and enquired about their train home, the Volunteers were detained until further notice, and indeed served a further six months in South Africa, at Dundee, Ladysmith and Albertina.

14. Ibid., p. 8.

Cooking Christmas Dinner, 1900.

1st Battalion South Lancashire Regiment at Dornberg. The original caption to this photograph adds that 'the man second from the right has since died through dysentery'.

At De Jager's Drift, where the South Lancashires arrived on 9 November, the Battalion camped on a hill overlooking the Blood River crossing. It was, according to Sergeant Hackett, an easy time: 'Only one section on outpost by night meant three in bed. The outpost consisted of one sentry post and patrols right and left, to meet the others every alternate half hour ... From the hill one could see for miles and a signalling record was made by [Private] Jack Cannon [actually Canning] when he read a lamp message one night from one hundred and eighty miles away.' Boer commandos were, however, never far away and there were frequent alarms. 'All hands to sleep in the trenches tonight,' wrote Private Wain in his diary for 28 November, 'as a commando of young Vryheid Boers & a German commando of 50 men have been seen coming this way from Scheepers Nek.'

Four companies were detached on Dornberg for a week, where they concentrated on strengthening the defences. 'During this period', wrote Lieutenant Geoffrey Mott, 'I started a Company team on gun drill (15 pounder) and in my spare time managed to enjoy a little shooting. I attended a kaffir service in a kraal on 9 December and found it most interesting. Next morning I commenced a short musketry course with my Company. On 13th we escorted a convoy to De Jagers Drift and then on to Scheepers Nek, after dislodging a party of Boers there. Gough's M.I. from Nqutu pursued the enemy.'

On 18 November Captain 'Mickey' Lynch, sole survivor of the South Lancashire officers who fought on Spion Kop, died in hospital of enteric fever.

The First De Wet Chase

We last saw the 1st Loyal North Lancashires with Lord Methuen at the Rhenoster River action when, on 11 June 1900, they chased De Wet off the Cape to Pretoria railway. Throughout June and the first half of July the Battalion remained in the Kroonstad-Heilbron area, providing garrisons along the beleaguered railway line and escorting convoys. Then on 12 July Lord Methuen was ordered to proceed with his 1st Division to reinforce the British presence in the western Transvaal, where Boer activity was increasing, and specifically to clear the road from Krugersdorp to Rustenburg, where Baden-Powell had a small garrison. The Battalion entrained at Kroonstad on the 15th, in very crowded open coal trucks, and, travelling by way of Johannesburg, arrived at Krugersdorp on the morning of the 17th.

Next day the Division moved off in two columns, the North Lancashires being in No. 2 Column under Major-General Douglas. The marching was hard, the route lying among rocky and precipitous kopjes which the Infantry was obliged to crown, but, though the Battalion deployed for attack at Doornkop, Boer resistance proved feeble and on 21 July Methuen pushed them across the Magaliesberg Range at Olifant's Nek with little loss. Two companies of the Loyal North Lancashires were dropped off to hold this vital pass, and when on the 23rd Methuen moved south again, Kekewich was left to garrison Olifant's Nek with his own Battalion, two mountain guns and a few mounted men.

Kekewich's men worked hard to entrench the nek, which was a strong position. Three and a half companies then held the defensive posts, the remainder being kept in reserve. Rations were short, but foraging parties were sent out, gathering oranges and sweet potatoes, and the Battalion baked its own bread and butchered its own meat. Heliograph communications were maintained between Olifant's Nek and Rustenburg, seven miles to the north. On the 25 two companies were called for to reinforce the garrison of Rustenburg, and on 1st August another two companies were sent there under Major Jackson, leaving five companies under Kekewich at the Nek.

There then began one of those extraordinarily inept sequences of bungled staff work which all too frequently bedevilled British generalship in South Africa. On 30 July 1900 the Free State General Prinsloo surrendered and well over four thousand burghers laid down their arms. This encouraged Lord Roberts in his conviction that victory was in sight; but by no means all the Free Staters had surrendered. In particular, Christian De Wet had escaped with two thousand five hundred men and several guns. Riding for some two hundred miles in a generally north-west direction from the Brandwater Valley, and somehow, despite frequent rearguard skirmishes, eluding repeated British attempts at pursuit and interception, the guerrilla leader had slipped across the Vaal. Ahead lay a natural barrier, the wild Magaliesberg Range and behind him British columns, directed by Lord Kitchener, snapped at his heels. On 6 August Methuen joined in the chase, confident in the knowledge that the vital pass at Olifant's Nek was securely barred to De Wet by the Loyal North Lancashires. The capture of the most dangerous, slippery and obdurately defiant, of all the Boer commanders seemed assured.

On that same day, however, Kekewich had received, by heliograph, a message which originated in Roberts' headquarters at Pretoria, ordering him to abandon Olifant's Nek and join Lieutenant-General Sir Ian Hamilton's column [15] that night. Another inept message ordered Baden-Powell to evacuate Rustenburg. Withdrawal from the Nek at night was no easy matter, but the defences were dismantled as far as possible and the position was abandoned at 10 p.m. Five miles from the Nek the wagons became hopelessly bogged, and the Battalion halted for the night in a cordon around them. The terse diary notes of Private Hart, Volunteer Company 1st Loyal North Lancashire Regiment, give some idea of what this involved for Kekewich's men:

'Aug 6th. Examining guard on Rustenburg road at 6 a.m., came off 6 p.m. Got to bed at 7 p.m. Ordered to move off at 9 p.m. Silent march until 12 midnight when we arrived at a very bad morass or swamp. Had to unload wagons and carry goods across until 3.30 a.m. We were up to our waists in sludge and water, it was blowing cold all the time. We were for outpost in extended order. Got to bed at 3.30 a.m. and tried to sleep, the sleep of the just.

'Aug 7th. Up at 5.55 a.m. Got 3 spoonful of rum and got the rest of the convoy over the swamp. Had breakfast at 10 a.m., full rations. Gen. Ian Hamilton took command over us here. Went 15 miles on Pretoria road. Halted at 5 p.m.

'Aug 8th. Up at 6, off at 6.40 a.m. Went 13 miles. Halted for the day. Gen. Hamilton ordered us extra rations, as he said we all looked starved.' [16]

De Wet's line of retreat now lay wide open, and on 10 August the

15. Hamilton's force included the Loyal North Lancashire Mounted Infantry Company of 3rd M.I.
16. Diary of Private O. Hart, Volunteer Service Company, 1st Loyal North Lancashire Regiment.

Boers reoccupied Olifant's Nek. Meanwhile Ian Hamilton's force, which was supposed to be blocking the Boer's progress, was unaccountably crossing the Magaliesberg by Commando Nek (a pass further to the east), heading south. Methuen's pursuing troops approached Olifant's Nek on 14 August, having marched 154 miles in six days, were understandably frustrated to see their prey vanishing over the pass. 'The rage and vexation of officers and men,' reported a correspondent to *The Diamond Fields Advertiser*, 'was unrestrained, loud and long.'

The Loyal North Lancashires were now south of the Magaliesberg and on the 17th, having been marched round in a circle, supported a brigade attack on Olifant's Nek from the opposite direction to their withdrawal of ten days before. Several days hard marching though the bush veldt followed, often on half or even quarter rations. The Mounted Infantry skirmished with the Boer rearguard, and some prisoners weretaken, but on 24 August the 'De Wet Chase' was called off and the Battalion was ordered to Pretoria. It had been a thoroughly unsatisfactory episode.

After two days in the Transvaal capital, during which the Loyal North Lancashires were reinforced by a draft of three officers and 150 reservists, who had been guarding Lord Roberts' quarters, the Battalion was ordered to Mafeking. They left on the 27th, in open trucks and under heavy rain, on a five-day roundabout journey stopping at Ladybrand, Bloemfontein, Naauwpoort, De Aar, Kimberley and Vryburg. At Kimberley, which was reached at daybreak on the 31st, the Battalion was met by the Mayor and would have been entertained by the townspeople that afternoon had time permitted; but the Battalion left again almost at once, leaving Major Coleridge and the transport to enjoy the reception.

At Mafeking, which was reached on 1 September, the Loyal North Lancashires rejoined the 1st Division. The Battalion spent the first week refitting, very necessary as most of the men were in rags after trekking through the bush veldt. The Division, tasked with clearing the South-Western Transvaal, formed two flying columns, one commanded by Lord Methuen and the other under Brigadier-General Douglas. The Loyal North Lancashires were initially with Methuen's column which, on 9 September, marched off in an easterly direction towards Lichtenburg. The Division was then diverted south to relieve the supposedly beleaguered garrison of Schweizer Reneke, returning north again through Olifant's Nek to concentrate at Rustenburg on October 8th. The mounted element of the columns, supported by the artillery, fought several small actions during this march, but the Battalion was not actively engaged, being chiefly involved in the tiresome but necessary work of convoy escorts and outposts.

Loyal North Lancashires digging a defensive position.

Next day Methuen's columns set off again, moving west towards Zeerust in pursuit of De la Rey, who had some seven hundred men and several guns. The country was difficult, favouring hit and run tactics, and the columns were frequently sniped, but although companies were several times extended, the enemy avoided contact. On 17 October Methuen reached Nooitgedacht, on the Little Marico River. He had just pitched camp when it was shelled by a Boer Creusot gun, which at once found the range. Unluckily, the first round landed in the Battalion lines, killing one soldier and mortally wounding another. Six more men were hit by shell splinters. The Battalion took shelter in a dry spruit, where it formed up, then deployed to hold the kopjes.

Zeerust was reached on the 18th. Here the Battalion was split, and it was indeed destined to operate in detachments for the remainder of the war. The Volunteer Company left for home (or so they thought) and the remainder of the Loyal North Lancashires were divided between Methuen's and Douglas's columns, which continued to scour the western Transvaal, and provided garrisons. Companies of the Battalion were stationed at Klerksdorp, 26 November–25 December, and Ventersdorp, from 28 December.

The Siege of Zeerust

On 1 November 1900 Major Paul Churchward was appointed Commandant of Zeerust, which was to be garrisoned by 'B', 'C', 'D' and

Zeerust Detachment Band, 1st Loyal North Lancashire Regiment.

'G' Companies of the Loyal North Lancashires, together with some Imperial Yeomanry and two New Zealand guns. Defence sectors were allocated on the 2nd and the companies set to work entrenching their posts – South, West and Signal Kopjes, and the gaol. On 9 November the garrison paraded for the Prince of Wales' birthday, hoisting a Union Flag made by the ladies of Zeerust, and a detachment band was formed using town instruments.

Towards the end of November rumours of an attack on the town led to a temporary augmentation of the garrison, but the threat failed to materialise and the reinforcements soon departed. However, there were at this time some 1,500 Boers active in Zeerust District and pressure on the isolated town was mounting. On 26 December there was a smart skirmish when 'G' Company went out towards Botha's Farm as escort to a convoy, and a sharp rifle fire was opened on them by some forty Boers occupying a position at Maricopoort. Some Yeomanry were at once sent out in support, but retired under a heavy fire and took up a covering position while twelve men of 'C' Company went up the heights and cleared them. The Boers were reported to have lost two killed and two severely wounded.

Next day a few shots were heard, the alarm gun was fired at 9 p.m. and the garrison stood to arms, but nothing occurred. Neverthless, over the following days further measures were taken to strengthen the defences, including the formation of a Town Guard and a Mounted Infantry section, some dozen of the North Lancashires on spare horses. On 30 December telegraph communications were cut of and Zeerust was practically besieged.

The New Year, 1901, found the little garrison of Zeerust awaiting attack in their waterlogged trenches. On 6 January word reached Zeerust that the enemy were advancing in strength on the town, and at 5 o'clock the following morning the Boers made a determined attack, pushing in the garrison's mounted patrols and opening a heavy fire on 'G' Company at West Kopje, where two men were hit in getting to their trenches. Firing then became general on all sides, and especially heavy at West Kopje and the gaol.

At 9.30 a.m. the fire slackened, and at 10 a.m. a flag of truce was sent in with an unsigned note in Dutch:

'From General Beyer to the Commander-in-Chief of the British Troops at Zeerust. I hereby call upon you to surrender unconditionally before 3 o'clock in the afternoon. If not, it will be my duty to bombard you from all sides. If you do not surrender I shall hold you responsible for all the women and children in the village.'

Churchward refused to recognise this peremptory demand, but as a precaution moved the women and children into the Dutch church in town for safety. No bombardment followed, but at 11 a.m. firing increased in intensity against South Kopje, and then, after the usual Boer lunch break, against the south-east examining guard. The New Zealand guns silenced a party of Boer riflemen who were firing from ridges above the gaol, but heavy musketry continued till dusk, when the enemy withdrew. Except at West Kopje, they had never come within a thousand yards of the British entrenchments, and the defenders conserved their ammunition by not replying much to the ineffective Boer fire. Of the Loyal North Lancashire detachment three men were slightly wounded.

Success was subsequently marred by two unfortunate accidents. Early on the 8th, while visiting the sentries, Lieutenant Charles Bingham was fired on in error by one of his own men and shot though the left arm, which had to be amputated. Then on the 13th another veteran of the siege of Kimberley, Lieutenant Augustus Wallace, blew himself up whilst attempting to lay a lyddite shell mine, a device of his own invention, above the gaol. A gunner corporal was also killed, and several others who were looking on were scratched by stones from the explosion. The garrison did not, however, give up with its experiment, and on the 18th several new mines were successfully laid around the defences.

Although the immediate threat to Zeerust now receded, the town was still cut off and as the weeks passed re-supply was clearly not imminent; nevertheless, as at Kimberley, the garrison took the offensive when opportunity offered, and raids were mounted to harass the Boers and seize their stock. An example of such activity must suffice. On 21 April Major Churchward took out a reconnaissance in force to search some farms known to be frequented by the enemy. At daybreak, as the infantry took up positions, the farms were shelled and a party of Boers was seen to be clearing out of them. Corporal Lewis and six North Lancashires pushed on to the farms and fired on the retreating Boers, accounting for three of them. One of the North Lancashires was slightly wounded.

Usually when armed parties left the town on patrol there were few Boers to be seen, but unarmed parties invariably attracted their attention; and so when on 18 March the garrison chaplain left Zeerust for Mafeking with the mail he was soon intercepted and the mail captured. Next day the Yeomanry, supported by a half company of North Lancashires, went out to see if they could ascertain his fate, but found only an empty mail bag and some field service prayer books. As the Yeomanry retired, about thirty Boers tried to cut them off, and a race ensued for a ridge which the enemy gained first; but the North Lancashires opening fire on them caused the Boers to withdraw, and the force returned safely to Zeerust.

It had for some time been anticipated that Lord Methuen's column would return to Zeerust before long and raise what amounted to the investment of the little town, but on 27 April a message was received that he must not be expected for some time and that provisions in the town (originally six months supply) must be made to last as long as possible. By this time there were no luxuries available and the men were smoking tea leaves instead of tobacco. The arrival of a convoy on 22 May was therefore most welcome and effectively ended the state of siege.

Battle of Hartebeestfontein

As already mentioned, the remainder of 1st Loyal North Lancashires were at this time split up in detachments around the western Transvaal, the details of whose frequent comings and goings in column, garrison and convoy it would be as tediously repetitive to follow as they often were for the participants at the time. However, there were several incidents of particular note, and these will now be described.

By 18 February 1901 'A' and 'H' Companies of the North Lancashires had been with Lord Methuen's column for some six weeks, marching nearly four hundred dusty miles in the usual game of cat and mouse. The column had been reasonably successful, and only the previous day had captured a laager with some forty prisoners, forty wagons and carts, fifteen hundred cattle and six thousand sheep and goats. But on the 18th, a little in front of Hartebeestfontein, its route wound through a narrow, rocky ravine, flanked by fifteen hundred invisible Boer riflemen, supported by a 7-pounder Creusot gun, who outnumbered the effective British strength by two to one and held what a Regimental account describes as 'a practically impregnable position' on the hillsides. Methuen's men had to clear the heights on either side, which were contested every yard of the way. Early in the morning the 5th Imperial Yeomanry assaulted and captured the Boer positions on the right of the road, but according to the contemporary divisional history the stronghold on the left proved far more difficult to take:

'A series of ridges and kopjes ran at right angles to the road, the front facing the direction the column was going being a high krantz or cliff, steep enough to be difficult of ascent. The Boers occupied the ridges and kopjes and effectually commanded the road, so that it was absolutely necessary to dislodge them before the column could proceed on its way. The 10th Imperial Yeomanry and [Australian] Victorians were advanced against the position, extending to the left and advancing up the steep rock-strewn slopes of the hill. A deadly fire was poured into them, but they pressed on and, after a severe struggle, drove out the enemy and occupied the ridges and kopjes; but the Boers fell back to the edge of the krantz or cliff, a short distance off, where they had splendid cover and from whence they kept up a hot fire on our men, and for a time it seemed that it would be impossible to move them. The two sides were separated by a very short distance, some of the firing being at twenty yards range. Our fellows showed remarkable bravery, and stuck to their work, regardless of losses, determined to win the day or die in the attempt.

'The action commenced at dawn, and at 10 o'clock, very little progress having been made, Lord Methuen ordered up two companies of the Loyal North Lancashires who formed part of the convoy guard, under Major Murray. They had to advance over an open space, during which time several were hit, but they moved forward grandly as if on parade and got to their position, which was an extension of the Yeomanry and Australian line to the left. They settled down to their work and the increased weight of metal hurled at the Boers soon told, and their fire slackened perceptibly until, about midday, they broke and cleared in all directions.'

During this action the Loyal North Lancashires suffered more fatalities than on any other occasion in the war, with particularly heavy losses among their leaders. Lieutenant Arthur Hewett and Colour-Sergeant Dorey were killed whilst directing 'A' Company, Lieutenant William Creak was shot dead one hundred yards from the Boer position, and Corporal Meade, Lance-Corporal Ousley and Private Jenks also died, while eight N.C.O.s and men were wounded. The total British loss was 15 killed and 34 wounded. That of the Boers was, as usual, not disclosed, but 18 dead were seen.

The gorge was then held while the convoy moved through, the North Lancashires remaining out on picquet until 5 a.m. next day.

Lord Methuen highly complimented the two companies and presented them with a Boer flag.

'The Boers reckoned that it would be impossible for our force to drive them out and they had counted on an easy victory. A Boer stated that he could scarcely believe that such a small force of British, or indeed any force, could have driven them out, the position having been strongly entrenched.'[17]

Attack on the Ventersdorp Convoy

Meanwhile, 'E' and 'F' Companies of the Loyal North Lancashires, together with Battalion Headquarters, were operating out of Ventersdorp and Potchefstroom, heavily involved in garrison security and convoy escorts. Major Philip Palmes was now in command, as Colonel Kekewich was commanding the district.

On 22 May 1901 a full convoy set out from Potchefstroom for Ventersdorp, commanded by Major Palmes and with Lieutenant Robert Flint's 'E' Company as part of the escort. They were to meet half-way with an empty convoy coming down from Ventersdorp, commanded by Captain Purchas (South Wales Borderers), with which was Lieutenant John Wells with 'F' Company. The arrangement was that the Ventersdorp escort would take over the full convoy while the Potchefstroom escort returned there with the empty wagons. The two convoys duly completed their exchange and parted at 5.30 a.m. on the 23rd. The mounted men with the Ventersdorp escort were rather raw Imperial Yeomanry, fresh from home, and so Lieutenant Wells went with the advance screen to guide them. Thirty men of 'F' Company moved in support, with another twenty escorting the convoy's single gun, and fifty Royal Welsh Fusiliers supported the rear screen.

Approaching Kaalfontein at 6.30 a.m., the left front and flank of the screen suddenly came under a heavy fire at short range. The Yeomanry screen fell back through the supporting North Lancashires and retired to a position in rear. Lieutenant Wells and his thirty men charged forward and took up a position on a wooded ridge. On the same ridge, some two hundred yards away, they were faced by forty Boers, and a close quarter fire-fight ensued. The convoy, massed on the road below, was soon surrounded by the enemy and under a heavy fire from all sides. Sergeant Barrowman, with the 'F' Company artillery escort, occupied a position between Lieutenant Wells' position and the convoy, while the gun fired case shot. The Royal Welsh Fusiliers held a small kopje to the rear of the convoy.

17. *With Lord Methuen from Belmont to Hartebeetfontein*, Klerksdorp, 1901, pp. 65–6.

After two hours fighting the escort heard the welcome sound of a distant gun; the Potchefstroom party, having heard the firing, were returning to the assistance of their Ventersdorp comrades. By now Wells' advance party was under fire from all sides, but on the tree-covered ridge it was difficult to locate the enemy. Boer voices were heard close to the North Lancashires' position, and Corporal Waterhouse and two men were sent to reconnoitre. Unfortunately the patrol's presence was revealed when a rifle was discharged, and the concealed Boers opened fire at a hundred yards range, hitting the Corporal twice and mortally wounding Private Gallagher. Lieutenant Wells sent a request to Captain Purchas for more men, so that he could turn the Boers' flank, but none could be sent.

The enemy now lit the grass to windward of the British position, and under cover of the smoke mounted men were seen bearing down on the convoy. The escort near the wagons engaged the approaching Boers and, as an obstacle, fired the grass near the convoy.

Suddenly, the situation changed; the firing to the rear weakened and mounted men appeared from that direction, followed hot-foot by the infantry of the Potchefstroom convoy escort, including 'E' Company, under Major Palmes. At 11.30 a.m. the enemy, estimated at three hundred, drew off from all sides.

Two hours later the Ventersdorp convoy, having suffered some twenty casualties, continued its march, but at 2 p.m. the Boers returned to the attack in even greater strength and tried to rush the rearguard. A running fight continued until the convoy came within artillery range of Ventersdorp. The convoy was halted near a drift, heavily engaged to the front and rear, and Lieutenant Wells and his men were moving up to clear some kraals held by the enemy, when a gun was heard from the direction of the town and a shell burst on the enemy position. At this, the Boer attack perceptibly weakened, the enemy gradually withdrew, and the convoy, battered but intact, reached Ventersdorp that evening.

The total casualties of the escort were forty killed and wounded, but the Loyal North Lancashires came off relatively lightly, one killed and three wounded. Corporal Waterhouse and Privates Brown, Gallagher, Gaskell and Wyatt were brought to notice for gallant conduct in this action.

Attacks on convoys, slow-moving and attractive targets, were commonplace, but one more instance must suffice. On 1 August 1901 'B' and 'G' Companies were escorting an ox convoy near Schietfontein. The convoy was marching at night, and in the dark the advance screen ran into a party of Boers, mistaken for Yeomanry. 'G' Company, being the advance guard, was caught in the ensuing hot fire. Lance-Corporal J. Entwistle was killed and Corporal C. Street and Privates

East Lancashire Regiment bivouac at Olifant's Nek.

Four companies of the 1st East Lancashires, under Lieutenant-Colonel Wright, operated in the Magaliesberg Mountains in August 1901 as part of Brigadier-General Hamilton's column. (*Photograph by Private P. H. Mitchell, Volunteer Service Company*)

J. Allinson and E. Ascott were wounded. The mules began stampeding, but steady fire from 'G' Company cleared the enemy, and order being restored in the convoy, it proceeded.

On Trek with the East Lancashires

The connection of 1st Battalion The East Lancashire Regiment with the Rand ended in May, 1901, when, for the first time since their arrival at Elandsfontein eleven months earlier, all the companies were concentrated at Springs, in accordance with instructions from the Commander-in-Chief, in readiness to join mobile columns. The re-union was, however, of brief duration. Four companies, under Major Bridges Lewis, proceeded on 18 May to Standerton, there joining Colonel Raleigh Grey's column; whilst a week later the remaining four companies and Battalion Headquarters, under Lieutenant-Colonel Wright, also moved to Standerton for Brigadier-General Gilbert Hamilton's column. The period of three and a half months during which the half-battalions were associated with these two columns may be considered as the third phrase of the 1st East Lancashires' war. 'The nature of the operations, directed as they were against a highly mobile enemy with no definite plan of campaign, necessitated rapid

East Lancashires escorting a baggage train, Hamilton's column, 1901.

movement, frequently at night, and incessant marching and counter-marching, but gave little occasion for distinction to the Infantry, whose unpretentious task it was generally to protect the baggage whilst the mounted troops operated actively, and to perform the necessary outpost duties, which were indeed very onerous.' [18]

Brigadier-General Hamilton's column consisted, in addition to the East Lancashire companies, of the 5th Dragoon Guards, 13th Hussars, four guns and two 'pom-poms'. Throughout the period the Boers took no serious offensive measures against General Hamilton, but, contenting themselves with sniping at extreme ranges, displayed their usual evasive tactics. It will be sufficient, therefore, to record that after operating for some days west of Standerton, the column was transferred by rail to the Krugersdorp District, and during June operated against De la Rey and Kemp to the west of that town and north of the railway line. In July operations were carried out further to the west as far as Wolmaranstad, where, on 26 July, Potgeiter's laager was captured together with 20 prisoners. Towards the end of August the scene was changed again, to the Magaliesberg Valley, where successful movements resulted in the capture of about one hundred Boers.

During the three and a half months spent with Hamilton's Column, a total of 1,100 miles was covered. Continued movement is however no guarantee against monotony, and the exacting nature of the work, accentuated by the absence of exciting incident, made heavy demands on the endurance of the men, who, nevertheless, carried out their arduous duties with commendable zeal, earning the Brigadier's highest praise. 'On parting with the East Lancashire', he wrote, 'the Brigadier-

18. XXX Regiment War Diary.

East Lancashires bathing.

A rare but welcome respite from heat, dust and dirt.

General wishes to express his high appreciation of the manner in which all ranks have invariably performed their duty. They have proved themselves indefatigable on the march, no matter how long or how incessant. On outpost duty they have been most reliable. Their conduct has been admirable'.

Meanwhile the half Battalion under Major Lewis had been employed in similar operations with the column commanded by Colonel Raleigh Grey, who was succeeded in July by Colonel Garratt of the Carbineers. This column also included mounted troops, the 6th Queensland Imperial Bushmen and the 7th New Zealanderers, four guns and one 'pom-pom'. It was engaged in operations in the Eastern Transvaal between Standerton and Ermelo, in the north of the Orange River Colony, and in the Gatsrand, and was constantly in contact with small parties of the enemy, accounting during the period for 165 Boers killed or taken prisoners, and capturing nearly 200 wagons and thousands of cattle and horses, besides arms and ammunition.

Colour Sergeant James Ferguson[19] of the 1st East Lancashires was

19. James Ferguson enlisted in the East Lancashire Regiment at Blackburn in 1888, aged 16, and served for 28 years, being discharged on pension in 1916. Rejoining within months, he ended his service as a Captain. Ferguson took part in many campaigns, and was Mentioned in Lord Kitchener's South African Despatches, 1902, and by GOC 42nd East Lancashire Division for gallantry at Gallipoli in 1915. Under the pen-name 'Sphinx' he was a frequent contributor to the Regimental journal. His three brothers, five nephews and his son all served in the Regiment.

with Garratt's column, and later wrote of an adventure which occurred to him on 9 August 1901. He prefaced his story with a vivid description of the column on the march and in bivouac:

'We were the advance guard of our small column, moving along in the vicinity of the Vet and Zand rivers, near Bultfontein, Orange River Colony. Our advanced screen of mounted troops were some distance in front of us, quite out of sight, in the folds of the veldt, and moving, perhaps, amongst and beyond the belt of trees skirting the river. Our little column, under Colonel Garratt, shared with other columns in a combined movement to clear bands of Boers from the district in which we were then operating … It was looked upon as a break in the monotony of our everyday life to find, sometimes, that the enemy had been forced to make a stand, check our advance, cause us to seek cover for our baggage, food, and forage waggon; and to require the united efforts of our little column to dislodge him, and get him to move again.

'We had seen the veldt, when we first set out, like a great brown

The British Officer, cartoon.

AS HE IS SUPPOSED TO BE AT HOME.

DRAWN FROM LIFE AT THE FRONT.

BY CAPTAIN SKINNER, 1ST SOUTH LANCASHIRE REGIMENT.

(Lent by Mr. Gilbert Dalziel, London.)

sea of waving, withered grass. We had seen it fired by the Boers, on many occasions, in the hope that it would interrupt our march, and envelop us in its flames. Indeed, so common did this practice become, in the hope of entrapping us, and also destroying good grazing for our cattle and that of other columns, that often, for days together, we have marched over blackened ashes which, when stirred up by our feet in marching, would be blown into our faces, smarting our eyes, almost blinding us, and giving each the appearance of a chimney sweep after a good morning's work. On these days, the undulating veldt, looked upon from rising ground, resembled nothing so much as a great black sea with a heavy swell on.

'But, on the day of which I now write, all this was changed. Rain had fallen in plenty since the burning; and the veldt was, once more, showing green and fresh. The day was bright and cheerful and the particular part where we found ourselves, was pleasant to look upon. Then, too, we were moving towards the railway, where we were looking forward to a fresh supply of food, as we were on short rations, owing to our having some prisoners; each prisoner meaning a reduction in our limited food supply. The thought of perhaps getting two – or even one – day's bread ration, amongst maybe fourteen days' rations of service biscuits, was something to look forward to. Also, we might touch the railway at a place where a pint of beer per man, and a fresh supply of tobacco, might be obtainable.

'Our march this day had been very pleasant; it was one of those days one likes to recall; a day to make one feel that life on the veldt is worth living. All around we see the great expanse of veldt in its most alluring aspect. Here and there, where it dips down to where a small stream that, hidden from our view in the distance, supplies water for a dam, one catches sight of a picturesque farmstead, showing up white in the bright sunlight against the green background of the trees and shrubbery; their appearance taking something from the loneliness of the veldt. A nearer view shows us these farmsteads are roofless and deserted. The charred and blackened beams, the remains of the roof that has fallen in, lying in a heap between whitewashed walls, together with twisted iron bedsteads and other lumber, bear silent witness of the stern reality and ravages of war. But we have long grown accustomed to this, and our eyes see only the picturesque beauty of the whole, as it appears to us.

'Swinging along – with the freedom and ease that has come to us with long hard practice since the war began – we represent the fittest, the tender-footed, soft-hearted having gradually dropped from among us. We are not pretty to look upon. What of our face can be seen behind the dust of the march, is tanned and blistered with the sun, and exposure to the weather. Patches of dry skin hang loosely from our noses, and from the sides of the face of each of those who are still fastidious enough to shave daily when opportunity offers. Generally, each has a growth of whiskers; from the stubby one day growth to, in some cases, a full beard of five or six inches long, of which the possessors seem inordinately proud.

'Our uniform – bleached with rain and sun – is many coloured. The elbows are out of our coats, the seat out of our trousers, or they are both roughly patched. Our boots are down at heel, and gaping at the toes. Our equipment matches our general appearance, which is very different to our smart appearance of a few months previous, when we helped to police and garrison Johannesburg.

'The only articles about us which, still, under all circumstances, seem to keep their 'spick and span' appearance, are our rifles and bayonets. But every man is fit. And to see us swinging along, making our hardships the subject of a laugh and joke; forgetting, in the bright sunshine, the misery of the previous night, when, after a long weary day's march, we took our turn on outpost duty; remaining unsheltered throughout a night of fierce storm, of thunder, lightning and rain of which South Africa can boast – you realise that our bearing and spirits are the outward sign of a splendid confidence in ourselves, and in each other, together with a worthy pride in our corps and calling. Seeing us thus must often have made the hearts of our commanders swell with pride – pride in us, and in the old corps we represent; for our unkempt appearance was due only to the exigencies of active service. We were soldiers, fit successors of the men who, in the Peninsula, at Waterloo, and in the Crimea, had helped to make, and uphold, the proud record of the old XXXth.

'This afternoon of the 9th of August, 1901 found us as described; rough, ragged and unkempt, but full of life and health; in a condition to fully appreciate and enjoy, the wild beauty of the vast veldt, and our gipsy sort of life upon it. Orders were given for the column to bivouac on a small hill. Soon we were drawn up in order, our mules and oxen outspanned and free to roam, a certain distance, under a cattle-guard; and to enjoy, to the full, the sweet herbage here afforded. It was a splendid spot for a bivouac; and the news that came to us later in the evening, when it was published in our orders that the column would halt here the following day, was most welcome. The object of the halt was to rest our cattle and the horses of our mounted troops, and to let them have the advantage of the excellent grazing afforded. But for us, also, it meant an opportunity for a clean up and – for those who were lucky enough to possess it – a change of underclothing.

'By this time in the evening, when "Orders" were published, our bivouacs were arranged for the night; the men had broken their day's fast on some coffee and biscuits, and the cooks were busy round their fires cutting up meat and cooking dinner – our most substantial meal of the day. We observed the aristocratic custom of late dinners in those days! Looking down the slope on which the column rests, the scene is most picturesque; lines of bivouacs, formed of blankets supported on rifles, rows of carts and wagons; and here and there a tent, marking the dining places of the officers of the various units. Rows of saddlery indicate the horse-lines of the mounted men, many of whom can be seen busying themselves in preparing a meal; every two or three seeming to have a little fire to themselves. Some are attending to their saddlery, whilst others are sitting, or lying about, smoking. A mounted troop, which had formed the rear guard, are just filing into their places in the lines. Some are still mounted, and others are leading their horses, carrying over their shoulder a fence post, or the branch of a tree, for their fire. Here and there, among them, one catches sight of a fowl, or leg of a pig – picked up during the day – dangling from their saddle. These men, from Australia and New Zealand, have been quick to learn the art of foraging. To look upon them now, one would scarcely realise that only four months ago most of them were raw troops, new to the game. Now they are seasoned veterans.

'Beyond them, at the rear of the column, are some hooded ox-wagons; and, moving about between them, one catches a glimpse of a sun-bonnet, and a woman's form. With these wagons are a few Dutch women and children, who have fallen into our hands, together with the wagons and some male prisoners that may be seen lying about near the head of the column, under a guard with fixed bayonets.

'Down below them, again, on the sweep of the green veldt, are what appear to be a multitude of horses, mules and oxen with mounted Kaffir 'boys' moving about among them, and a guard of troopers, mostly without coats, holding the bridle of their saddled horse with their leg or arm, over which it is drawn, while they, themselves, lie about smoking or snoozing. Beyond them, again, the eye rests upon a thick belt of trees, which encircle the rear and the right flank of our camp, but some distance from it, and which marks the curve of the river, the direction of which we had followed during most of the day's march.

'There is a movement now among the infantry at the head of the column. A company is falling in for outpost duty. With their rifles slung across their shoulders, each one is carrying his bundle of bedding, consisting of two blankets, and his great coat, rolled up in a waterproof sheet, and secured with coat straps. Soon the horses and cattle will be withdrawn to their lines, and the column will settle itself down to its well-earned rest. Then, a couple of hours or so after darkness has

Colour-Sergeants James Ferguson (*right*) and Pat Lydon, DCM (*left*).
Photographed at Meiktila, Burma in 1897 when Ferguson was a Sergeant and Lydon was Drum-Major.

fallen upon them, there will not be a spark of fire, or light, visible among them, to mark their position.'

James Ferguson, who had noted a herd of springbok, determined to take the opportunity of the day's halt to go hunting with a comrade, Colour-Sergeant Pat Lydon.[20] 'Accordingly, the following morning, as soon as possible after "Orderly Hour", which was held at 9 a.m., we each provided ourselves with a bandolier, filled with ammunition; he taking his rifle, and I a pretty little sporting magazine Lee-Metford, which belonged to the Captain of my Company, and which his servant, who volunteered to lend it me, assured me that the Captain – a keen

20. Colour-Sergeant Pat Lydon (see photograph, above), who later became Regimental Sergeant Major, was, like Ferguson, from a Regimental family. His grandfather, Private Luke Lydon, was with the 30th at the storming of Badajoz in 1812, and subsequently, as a Sergeant, became Regimental Schoolmaster. His father, Sergeant Dominick Lydon, was wounded with the Regiment at the Battle of the Alma in the Crimea, 1854.

sportsman himself – would not have the least objection to my taking; remarking, 'that a round or two fired out of it would help to clear it.' Well, to tell the truth, I had my doubts about what the Captain might have said, had I asked him. Not that I think he would have refused me, in ordinary circumstances. Boers were known to be hanging around, and I doubt if the Captain would have approved of two men going any distance, certainly not for mere pleasure. Being very bent upon going – "just a little way", as we told ourselves – we thought it prudent to say nothing.

'So about 9.30 a.m. we sauntered forth towards the river lying on the right flank of our Column, and about a mile distant. On reaching this we found it to be a small stream, running over a wide sandy bed, between steep, broken, sandy banks. Up till no we had not seen a sign of game of any sort, and we were feeling a bit disappointed. We thought of returning, but the morning was so pleasant, and it was so early, that we agreed to get across to the other side of the river, where there were no trees, and we could see the beyond. So over we did get, and scrambling up the steep sandy bank, found ourselves upon ground broken by dry water courses, sloping down to the river from which we had just climbed. From here, owing to the tress on the further side of the river, we could not see any sign of our bivouac, which lay beyond them. Looking towards it, the river seemed to wind round to our right. We turned our backs upon it and set out for the crest of the rising ground, which appeared to be about a mile and a half away. By this time we realised we were far enough away from camp to be in danger of coming across straggling Boers, who might be spying around; but a spirit of adventure seemed to have taken possession of us, and we went on.

'We had, soon after camp, taken the precaution of carefully examining our rifles and ammunition, and charging our magazines; and as we advanced up the hill, we took all the precautions of scouts reconnoitring. We moved about fifty yards apart; and, as we halted occasionally; to look and listen, the great silence of the veldt seemed oppressive. We felt entirely alone. We could scarce realise that our friends were almost, if not quite, within sound of rifle-shot; but we continued our way until reaching the top of the rising ground, where we halted, lay down and looked around.

'Down below us, to our front, the ground sloped away for about three hundred yards; and then gradually rose again for about the same distance; to the top of a long, low ridge, which stood out like a great wall upon the veldt. Behind that, the ground appeared to fall away, and then to gradually rise again in a long continuous slope, to the distant skyline. To our right the skyline, from our point of view, did not appear more than a mile or so away – the ground rose so steeply in that direction. The ridge we were on, and the rising ground in front of us formed a sort of trough, about six hundred yards wide and about a thousand yards long. At the head of this, where the ground sloped upwards to our right, stood a farmhouse, with a sheep-kraal in the near distance. We had, in ascending the hill, taken the precaution of making for the lower end of the ridge, where it sloped away abruptly towards the river, so that we were distant about one thousand yards from the farmhouse.

'From here, as far as the eye could see, excepting ourselves, not a sign of life was visible; yet before another hour had passed this quiet spot, over which we now looked, was destined to be the scene of a little adventure, which nigh cost my comrade and I our lives.

'On nearing the top of the ridge on which we now lay, we had gradually closed inwards towards each other, so that we were now close together; and in possession of cover which would afford us good protection from rifle fire, from any direction. This was our object in making for this spot; our only anxiety had been that it might be occupied by an enemy, lying in wait for us; so that we had approached it very gingerly. Here we rested, looked around, and made our plans. We decided to move up to and investigate the farmhouse. Curiosity, as much as anything else, drew us to that. So advancing carefully into the trough, we again separated, and turning to our right, moved upwards towards the farmhouse. As we advanced we ... charged our rifles, and carried them ready for instant use; and keeping the sheep-kraal as much as possible between ourselves and the house, we moved cautiously forward.'

The kraal proved to be packed with dead and wounded sheep and goats, giving off a terrible stench, but otherwise the only sign of life at the farm was a ferocious looking black bulldog, lying on the verandah.

'On our finding the house was not occupied, as we feared it might have been, by an enemy, we seemed to cast all serious thoughts of them off altogether. On leaving the house we decided to give the sheep-kraal a wide berth, and kept about three hundred yards from it, on the windward side. When we came opposite it, we found that one of the lambs had wandered round to our side; it was very small, and looked – from where we were – no bigger than an ordinary good sized rabbit. I had been longing for something to try my rifle on, and this, I thought, a good opportunity; so, judging the distance to be two hundred yards, I put up the flap of the backsight giving the elevation for that distance, and fired. I went short. My comrade tried a shot and did likewise – we had misjudged the distance. I put the three hundred yards flap up, got upon my knee, fired again; and the lamb rolled over dead. Had it not been for the report of those shots, ringing out through the stillness of the veldt, we might, in all probability, have returned to camp without the experience I shall here relate.

'As we continued our way, after firing, my comrade drew a 'pull-through' out of his pocket, and we cleared our rifles. I remember making the remark that 'It would be a surprise to us if, instead of buck, which we came out for, we dropped across a few buck Boers.'

'We had scarcely gone one hundred yards after I made this joking remark, and would be only about eight hundred yards from the farmhouse, and now in the bottom of the trough between the two ridges, when we heard shouting behind us. Looking back, we saw – about six hundred yards away – charging down upon us, three horsemen. My comrade exclaimed 'Look out, they're Boers!' I said 'I don't think so!' and, somehow, don't think I did – at first. I had some vague idea that they might be a patrol of our Australian troopers up to a 'lark'. 'Anyway', I said, 'I will be prepared'. So, turning my back towards them, that they might not notice me – we were halted then – I slipped two more rounds into my magazine, to replace the two expended. As we stood there waiting, the old black bulldog would leap up to lick the hand of first one and then the other of us. I had just stooped to pat him – still keeping an eye on the horsemen – when my comrade exclaimed, "They're Boers!".

'Just before this, one of the three, for some reason I could never understand, wheeled to his left, and rode up towards the sheep-kraal, near the house, where he remained inactive – as far as we could tell – throughout all that happened. The two remaining horsemen rode up to less than two hundred yards of us, and we could distinctly hear the shout "Hands Hoep!" Then, almost immediately, without appearing to draw rein, they slid off the side of their horses, and – as if their rifles had been previously loaded – fired upon us. As their bullets whistled past us, we immediately threw ourselves down upon our stomach, some few yards apart.

'Then commenced between us and the Boers a duel. I think they fired quicker than we did, although our magazines were charged. In throwing myself down my helmet had rolled off my head, and lay about a yard to the right of me, in line with my shoulder. One of the Boer's shots struck the ground between the helmet and me, throwing some sand up into my face; another shot struck near my left knee, and I could feel the earth dashed up over that also; but I remained unscratched. My comrade shared the same good luck, and remained untouched throughout.

'After the first few rounds the Boers appeared to "lose their heads", and fired too rapidly to be accurate, whereas we fired more deliberately. I remember that for each shot I selected the man who appeared to be aiming or about to aim. On talking it over afterwards, I found my comrade had done the same; consequently our fire unnerved them, and, where they missed, we struck home with every shot. We were so close to them that we could distinctly hear the striking of our shots on horse or man.

'My comrade fired first, and struck one of the men on the leg, near the foot, causing him to hop round for a second and then attempt to mount his horse; this my comrade shot, and wounded; whilst I attended to the other man. Then both Boers, for a second or two, attempted to mount, when we again shot both horses. Then the Boer, whom my comrade had wounded in the leg, lay down and prepared to fire, when a shot struck him and he lay still; so that only one was left to deal with. This one, whilst firing wildly, would turn occasionally and call "Help!" Presently, although wounded, as we knew, in at least two places, and still refusing to give up, he managed to get upon his horse, which, in his efforts to get mounted he caused to plunge and then turn broadside on, when it received a shot through its body, which made it plunge again, throwing its hind legs high in the air, and its rider clean over its head. The Boer, picking himself up, commenced to run towards the farmhouse, still calling "Help! help!" Putting another flap of my little backsight up, and aiming low, I brought him down about fifty yards further on.

'Then my comrade and I, jumping to our feet, made for the horses, which, although hit so often, were still standing. On our getting up and going forward towards the animals, we caught sight of the cowardly comrade of the two unfortunate men who now lay on the veldt. He must have been looking on during the fight, and now, seeing us advance in his direction, he rode away up, and over the hill, as though himself and horse were possessed. His riding away, together with the other Boer calling for "Help!" made us all the more anxious to get away, as soon as possible from a spot where we would be so exposed in case of a further attack. Therefore, we selected a horse each. They stood some little distance apart, one near each of the, as we believed them to be, dead Boers. My comrade took the nearer one, and was hurriedly examining it, when it fell at his feet – dead.

'The other horse had strayed to within about ten or a dozen yards of the body of the Boer who had attempted to run away. I caught this horse and, after looking it over, had put the reins back over its head and was just about to lead it off when, suddenly, the sharp report of a rifle – "Flup" – a bullet struck the horse beside me, passing through its head, and grazing my left shoulder, dropping the unfortunate animal at my very feet. There, not a dozen yards from me, with his rifle still held in his hand, staring at me as though his eyes would start from his head, sat the Boer whom I had believed dead. My comrade, as he told me afterwards, had just turned round in time to catch sight of the Boer as he was in the act of firing, and the sight for the moment, had made him spellbound; he was quite unable to shout or move until after the report. The wounded Boer, I suppose, seeing an opportunity to avenge himself and his comrade, had fired at me point-blank as I faced him, a few paces distant but unable to see him on account of the horse's head and neck, which was between us.

'For a moment we stared at each other, then "You Sewar!" – the contemptuous exclamation, picked up in India, rose unconsciously to my lips – "I've a mind to brain you!", and I raised the butt-end of my rifle. "Throw your rifle away!", I ordered, and he did so. He took his bandolier off his shoulder and threw that from him also, then, with a moan, he rolled over on his back. We – my comrade and I – saw how badly he was wounded, but we knew not how soon the Boer who had galloped away, might return with the help that this wounded man had called for and appeared to expect. So, promising him that we would send our ambulance waggon to him on our reaching camp, and taking his rifle and bandolier, also that of his comrade, whom we found to be dead – shot through the heart, whilst leaning over his rifle in the act of loading, one hand still grasping the rifle, while a round lay in the unclosed breech – we paused only to decide whether we should make straight for camp in the way we had come, which was the nearer, or return to it by a circuitous route.'

The two Colour-Sergeants chose the second option, but had further adventures before eventually reaching camp. By the time a party reached the two Boers, James Ferguson's former adversary was dead. 'Looking at him as he lay still in death, one hand still clutching his hat, which lay on his head, partially covering his face, as though shading his eyes from the sun's rays, I thought of the bitter revengeful spirit. [With] his last dying effort, he had striven – and so nearly succeeded – to lay me, as he and his comrade now lay, a stark corpse upon the veldt. This, his last and dying impulse, I had thought, in the heat of the moment, to be cowardly. But who may judge his motive? He saw in me, no doubt, one of his country's foes, whom to kill was, to him, a sacred duty to the cause he fought for. Patriot! Fanatic! – Call him what you will – he proved himself a brave soldier. He met a brave, if reckless, soldier's death. He and his comrade, in their last fight, died nobly like true men for the cause in which they believed. They scorned to surrender where they failed to win – they died as a soldier should; and they merit a soldier's praise. We took their bodies back to camp, together with the saddlery of the dead horses, in the cape cart which we brought out with us. There were no marks whatever about the clothing of the dead men by which they could be identified, but on reaching camp there were, among the Boer women and men prisoners with our column, those who recognised them. They were given a respectful burial on the high veldt, in front of our column and in the presence of a few of their own countrymen and women.

'By this time it was near "sun-down". It was my Company's turn for out-post duty, and they were already turning out for that purpose. After remaining behind to satisfy the natural cravings of the 'inner man' with some food – the first since early breakfast – and to get equipped for duty, I joined them after they had taken up their position, and just as darkness was settling o'er the veldt. The men of my post were just putting the finishing touches to their defences – they always prepared in case of attack – when I arrived among them. I found that the position of our post was within half-a-dozen paces of the newly made graves of the two Boers.

'Spreading out my waterproof sheet, and rolling myself in two blankets, I laid down. I was so stiff and exhausted with my day's unusual exertion, that I did not ruminate for long on the curious freak of fate, or fortune of war, that had that morning drawn myself and comrade away from our camp, led these two men – now dead – against us to their doom, and brought me, one of the instruments of their fate, to sleep beside their graves on this, the first night of their burial.'[21] As the 'Battalion War Diary' tersely comments, 'This is one of the many instances which might be quoted against the prevalent belief in the superior marksmanship of the Boers'.

Vryheid

On New Year's Eve 1900, Private Wain of the 1st South Lancashires heard that a move from De Jager's Drift was imminent: 'We expect to move to Vryheid to relieve the [King's Own] Lancasters. They was attacked by the Boers the other day [10/11 December] & after 15 hours hard fighting drove them off. Colonel Gawne & 11 others of the Lancasters killed & a number being wounded & taken prisoners.' Rumour was for once correct, but it was nearly another fortnight before the Battalion marched for Vryheid. Meanwhile Geoffrey Mott had, as usual, found time for some sport:

'We held a race meeting on 2 January across the Buffalo River, but the jumping was very poor, and 2 bookies who attended had a pretty thin time. A detachment of Gough's M.I. took us on at cricket on a very bumpy wicket, the Regiment winning easily. During the first 10

21. Article by 'Sphinx' (Colour-Sergeant J. Ferguson) serialised in the *XXX Journal*, 1910.

South Lancashire soldiers building the 'Great Wall', Vryheid.

(*Photograph by Captain E. F. Oakeley*)

Maxim machine gun on the 'Great Wall', Vryheid.

Pioneers of 1st Battalion South Lancashire Regiment, Vryheid.
Pioneer Sergeant Cartwright is seated left, and next to him is Private Wilson, a Regimental footballer.

days of January I fished the Buffalo River on 3 occasions, catching 10 barbel weighing 39 lbs; averaging nearly 4 lbs.'

The South Lancashires left De Jager's Drift on 11 January 1901, and Private Wain made notes on the move in his diary:

'Jan 12th. Marched off at 6.30 am for Scheepers Nek. The scouts reported enemy on the Nek. Our artillery opened fire but after a few shells they cleared off & we halted on the Nek for the night.

Jan 13th. Left Scheepers Nek for Vryheid at 6 am. A very hot day. We had a bit of excitement, having a brush with the enemy. The Mounted Infantry had a bit of bad luck for they had almost got about 200 of the Swaziland Border Police when they had to retire owing to our own gunners mistaking them for the enemy.

Jan 14th. Went on to Lancaster Hill, which is a very high one overlooking the town. We relieved the Lancasters, who marched off at 1 pm. The Boers did a little sniping during the night but no one hit.

Jan 15th. My Birthday. Start the usual trench & sangar making. The fortifications that the Lancasters had would not do our Colonel, for he has started to make a large wall with loop holes in which when complete will take in the whole top of the hill.'

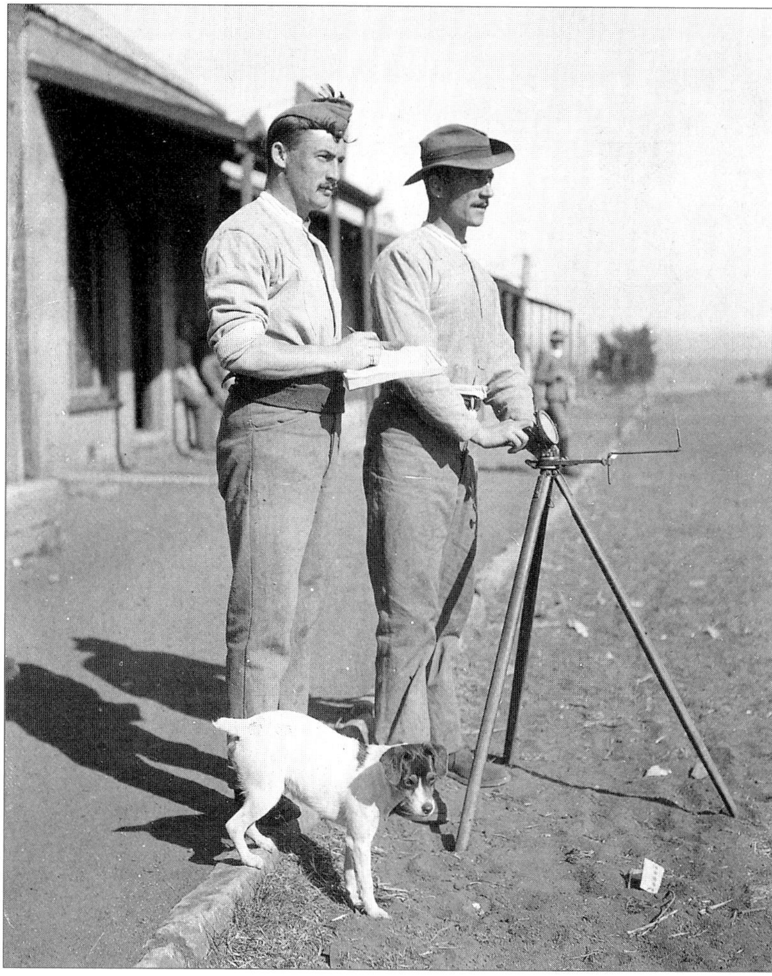

Regimental signallers, South Lancashire Regiment, Vryheid.

Our friend Sergeant Hackett described Vryheid, capital town of the former Vryheid Republic, where 1st Battalion The South Lancashire Regiment would be based until the end of the war:

'Small, neat and compact, it was built around the Green, on which stood the Dutch Reformed Church. An ideal place, nicely sheltered at the foot of the hill. The population, about three hundred, were mostly women and some elderly men. Any contact with the civilians or house visiting was [at first] forbidden, penalty D.C.M. Later we were allowed leave to go down into the town for the day.

'On the hill, life was a bit hectic for a couple of months until defences were strengthened and another threatened attack died away. North, east and south, the hill sloped steeply down, but on the west a valley, about three miles long and level with the top of the hill, swept away between hills. At our end was a three inch gun and at the other end a 4.7 gun. The C.O. decided to build a wall a mile

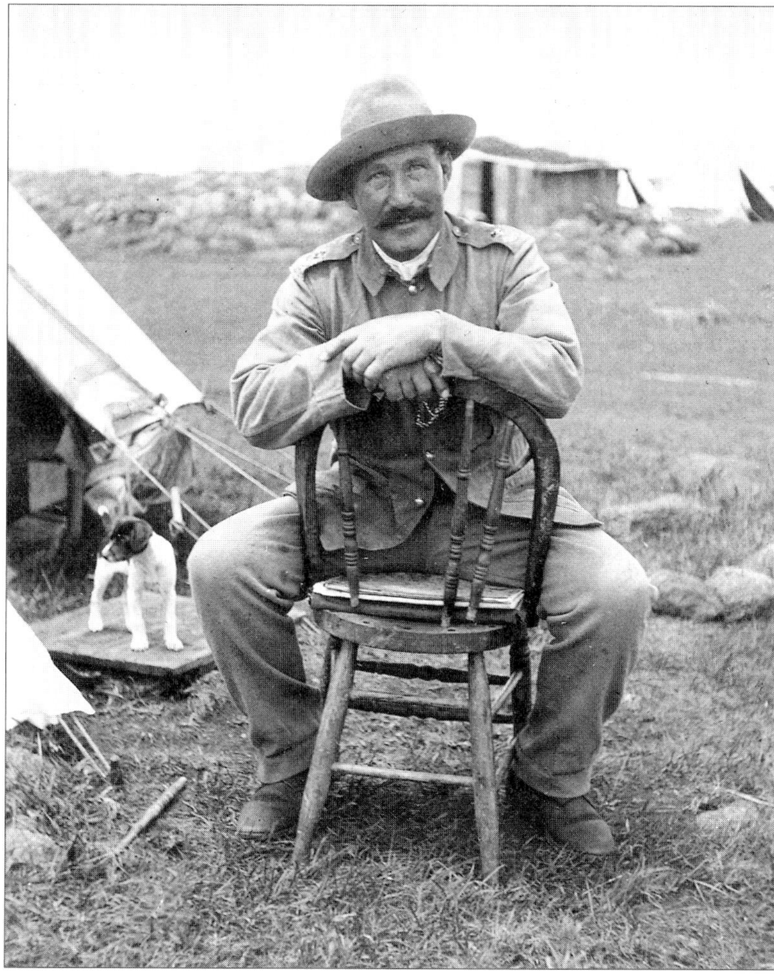

The Quartermaster.
Lieutenant & Quartermaster A. H. Huxford, 1st South Lancashires, Vryheid 1901.

long between the two, ten feet wide at base, ten feet high, and two feet wide at the top, loopholed for kneeling and standing. Parading at 8.30 a.m., all marched to the wall to be built and worked until noon, and again from 2 p.m. till 4 p.m. (more to keep men occupied, I believed).

'The barbed wire entanglements in front [were] to be widened to eighty yards, with empty jam tins fastened on every strand. Nervy sentries were, for a little time, a nuisance, the jam tins on the wire, blown about by the wind, helped them to see movement, and a shot brought everybody standing to.

'Outposts at night were [at first] three on and one off, and for a long while the 'one off' meant sleeping in a stone sangar immediately behind the defence line. Soon matters became normal. And night outposts were one in four. Those coming off did not parade in the morning, those going on did not parade afternoons.

The Ration Stand, Vryheid.

'The hill was covered with large boulders of iron stone, through which ran two or three thin seams of gold. When it rained the rivulets ran black with coal dust. Outside the wire, in front of our Company position, a few of us dug a hole four yards square and 5 feet deep. When the hole filled with rain we took it in turns to bathe and keep clean, having bought underclothing in town.

'Living on the hill was healthy and attractive, the air so rarified we could hear the natives miles away, talking to one another in their chanting sing-song as they worked amongst their crops some distance from one another. A pleasant interlude was woodcutting fatigue. Fully armed, we marched some two miles along into the country, chopping down trees in a wood and loading them on wagons.' Always in the background, though, was a watchful enemy: 'We could see the Boers walking openly on the south spur of the hill. Occasionally the 4.7 spoke to them.' Ceaseless vigilance was required, but so well did the South Lancashires carry out their duties that the Boers nicknamed them 'the Regiment that never sleeps.'

At times the elements seemed a greater threat than the enemy. 'Storms were frequent and violent,' wrote Sergeant Hackett, 'thunder crashed and the lightning so vivid it lit up the countryside for half a minute at a time. The Signallers lived in an Indian pattern tent near H.Q. One night the occupants watched a small ball of light travel the length of the pole across the top and back again, and then there was a flash as it travelled down a pole against which popular Jack

Sergeant-Major Simon and the Staff Sergeants, 1st South Lancashires.

Cannon [Canning] was leaning, writing a letter to his wife, and killed him, rendering the remainder helpless until one got out and gave the alarm. It took stretcher parties and helpers all night to carry the thirteen down to the hospital in town throughout the storm and pitch dark. The telephone operator had a narrow escape, for on returning to his hut after helping the Signallers he found it had been struck, his instrument damaged and his pipe twisted out of shape.'

Despite this, both Mott and Hackett enjoyed their time at Vryheid. Race meetings, polo and cricket matches, boxing and tennis tournaments, sports days, band concerts and game shooting punctuated the operational routine, and even a garrison tennis gymkhana. For Christmas 1901, much to the delight of the South Lancashire lads, eight barrels of beer arrived from a Warrington brewery.

There was a curiously cordial relationship with the local Boers. 'The Townsfolk were very friendly,' recalled Geoffrey Mott, 'especially the Emmett and Botha families. It seems strange looking back, that we received hospitality and played tennis with the nieces of the Boer Commandant whilst the war was still in progress!' The Commanding Officer was friendly with the Pastor of the Dutch Reformed Church and, according to Hackett, frequently played the organ in the Church.

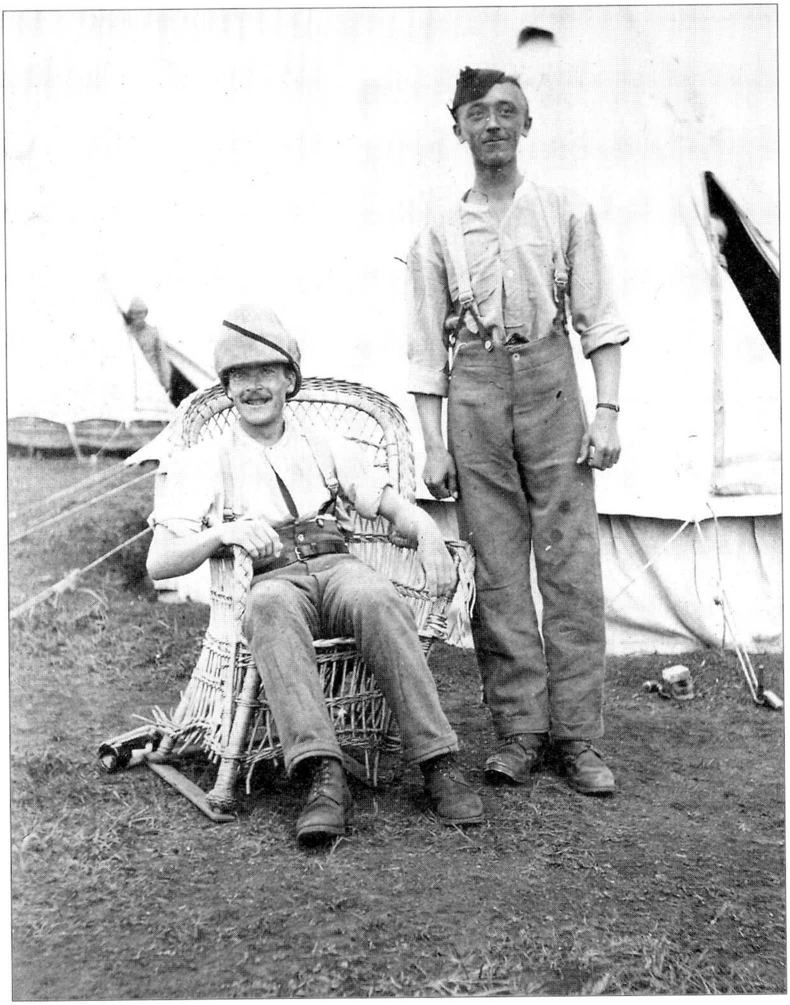

Orderly Room Staff, 1st South Lancashires.

Sergeant Ward (*left*) and Corporal Heppenstall. The latter died of dysentery at Vryheid.

In August 1901, Mott recorded, 'Kitchener issued a Proclamation that all Commandants, Field Cornets etc. not surrendering would be transported for life and all Burghers would have to pay for maintenance of their families in our hands. Next morning Captain Goren rode out with this Proclamation for Commandants Henderson, Emmett, Sholz [22] etc. The latter opened his document and burst out laughing! Healths were drunk by both sides in Goren's whisky! White flags came in during the day and a great number of Pom-Pom shells and an old Indian Frontier musket were found under our mess floor when trying to eject cats. Another party under Major Upperton were captured at Scheepers Nek, delivering a Proclamation to General Potgeiter, but later released by Cheere (pronounced 'Cherry') Emmett.'

22. Probably Captain P. J. Scholz, Vryheid Commando scout corps, killed in the attack on Fort Itala, 25/26 September 1901.

Quarter Guard, 1st South Lancashires, Vryheid.

Sergeant Hackett was intrigued and impressed by the local people: 'The Zulus were the most moral race in the world. I remember the Battalion marching over Blood River ... on a reconnaissance towards Utrecht. Walking about one hundred yards to the side of the track towards Vryheid, with a large bible in her hand, was a Zulu girl, over six feet tall and dressed in the usual bead skirt, waist to knee only. Skin glistening in the sun and hair in small curls, she was a picture for an artist as, unselfconscious, she gazed at the column as she walked. I did not hear one ribald remark from the men, let alone a wolf whistle. The picture commanded respect.

'The Zulus were very friendly, and there was a little difficulty in keeping them neutral, so Chief Khama was invited to bring his Impi on to the hill for a demonstration. A small platform was rigged up and [there], seated on chairs, were Khama and our C.O. Khama's staff, dressed in the weirdest martial costumes you could imagine,[23] stood around. Marching up and facing them in line, the Impis chanted their war songs as they advanced, dancing slowly and waving spears and shields, and it was amusing to see them, smilingly, threaten us

23. Hackett describes the dress of one young Zulu as a helmet, Highlander's serge coat, shiny leather waistbelt with a sword, another over his shoulder, grass skirt and bare legs and feet. The author is reminded of similar apparitions at a Regimental Waterloo Parade in Swaziland in 1965.

South Lancashire 'Zulus' (a studio photograph in Ladysmith).

The Lancashire soldiers were in fact very aware of the part played by the thousands of native auxiliaries who supported the British Army and had a particular admiration for the Zulu stockmen and drivers: 'What our army owes to these men and beasts nobody will ever know', wrote Lance-Sergeant J. Hunt, a South Lancashire Transport Sergeant from Warrington, 'but they have done their duty well. The great difficulties they have overcome, the almost impassable drifts they have crossed, the heights they have attained, are now matters of ancient history, but will never be forgotten by the members of the South African Field Force.'

as they came (we were unarmed), hoping, no doubt, to see us get alarmed. When ten yards away, Khama halted them, though they continued the chanting and teasing, to which some of ours pulled a face or put up their fists, which set the Zulus talking and laughing most amusedly. They then moved to the left flank in column, youngest men in front and grouped by precedence, single men, married men and elder men. From there they charged across our front all together, and could those young men leap, in bounds of four or five feet at a time! Gallantly, the aged, grey-haired men kept up, though running was an effort. Back again and, reforming in line, they gave a final chant and salute, and, marching away, continued their singing, a delighted body of men, leaving us a bit awe-struck.'

Although the 1st Battalion was destined to remain in garrison at Vryheid until the end of hostilities, large drafts of South Lancashires

Mounted Infantry of The South Lancashire Regiment.

served with the 24th, or Gough's, Mounted Infantry and the 5th Division Mounted Infantry. When suitably qualified volunteers were called upon for the latter, almost the whole Battalion claimed familiarity with horses. One hundred and fifty men were selected and, after a month's riding school on the hill, they moved off under their own officers to join the newly formed mounted unit.

North Lancashire Mounted Infantry

In the latter stages of the war the various mounted units – Regular Cavalry and Mounted Infantry, Colonials and Yeomanry – provided the main British strike force; indeed they were the only element of Lord Kitchener's Army capable of keeping up with the Boer commandos and beating them at their own game. They were organised in columns, usually of some fifteen hundred to three thousand men, with guns and Infantry in support. The success of a column depended very largely on the capabilities of its commander, but also on the professionalism of his troops, which was variable. The Yeomanry, with their thin veneer of military experience and relatively short service, were in general the least capable or reliable. The best of the Colonials were excellent, but others shared the disabilities of the Yeomanry and

(*Top*) North Lancashire Mounted Infantry, Eastern Transvaal.

(*Bottom*) Boer prisoners under 3rd Mounted Infantry guard, Eastern Transvaal.

added an indisciplined addiction to loot. The long-service Regular Mounted Infantry, riding with more courage than style, and with knife, fork and spoon stowed away in the puttee, vied with the best of the Colonials for campaigning expertise, dash and dependability.

After the unsuccessful 'De Wet Chase' of August 1900 the Loyal North Lancashire Mounted Infantry, still part of 3rd M.I., were transferred to the Eastern Transvaal, joining General French at Carolina, and were with him when, on 13 September, he 'dropped through the clouds' to capture Barberton. In January 1901 they took part in the

3rd Mounted Infantry crossing a drift, Eastern Transvaal.

defence of Belfast, and then rode with Colonel Henry's column. On the afternoon of 27 January, at Twyfelaar, between Carolina and Wonderfontein, the Company was called upon to assist the Imperial Light Horse rearguard, which had been attacked by the enemy in thick mist and rain. As the Imperial Light Horse retired and the Boers brought up artillery, the Company had a hot time until infantry reinforcements arrived. One officer and three men were hit. Lance-Corporals Fletcher and Woodhouse were brought to notice for coolness under fire that day, while Lieutenant Kenneth Macaulay carried on his duties even though mortally wounded. Fighting was renewed the following day. Two sections of the Company flanked the advance guard, which was soon engaged. Lieutenant Smyly's section raced the enemy for some high ground and reached it first, hitting three Boers, but Private Hickey was killed and two others were wounded.

The Company continued to operate with columns in the Eastern Transvaal and on the Swaziland border, under Smith-Dorrien and Allenby. There was constant marching and skirmishing, and frequent raids, ambushes and sniping, with a slow but steady trickle of casualties. On 13 June, for instance, No. 1 Section was ambushed at Mooiband when acting as advanced guard to the column and Privates Perry and Moss were killed, the former described as 'the best and most intelligent scout in the Company.' This continued until 2 July when detachments were based at Belfast, Wonderfontein, Machadadorp, Pan and elsewhere, engaged mainly on convoy duties.

East Lancashire Mounted Infantry

We last saw the East Lancashire Regiment Mounted Infantry at Vereeniging and Meyerton, defending the railway. On 7 February 1901 the Company was ordered to Elandsfontein, where 8th M.I. was mobilising prior to joining a mobile column consisting of 800 men and six guns. The column moved initially to the western Transvaal where, under command Lieutenant-Colonel H. P. Shekleton of the South Lancashire Regiment, it operated against De la Rey, Kemp and Smuts.

The Company was engaged in several skirmishes but no major actions until 24 March when, between Taaiboschspruit and Wildfontein (west of Ventersdorp), Shekleton combined with Major-General Babington in a surprise attack on De la Rey. Having deceived the Boer leaders into believing that they were retiring, the British mounted troops charged into De la Rey's convoy and, riding with loose rein and firing at the gallop, scattered one thousand burghers across the veldt. Part of the East Lancashire Company formed Shekleton's advance guard and, together with the Bushmen and New Zealanders, was one of the first units to ride into the convoy. The other part of the Company was rearguard to the British convoy and was engaged from dawn till dark in its successful defence against some five hundred men commanded by Smuts. De la Rey's own despatch made clear the extent of his defeat: 'The enemy attacked us and as far as we could see there was nothing but mounted men in full gallop. The enemy charged us so actively and in such wide formation that we all ran the danger of being surrounded or captured. We were thus compelled to retire again with the loss of nearly the whole of our laager.' Two guns, a 'pom-pom', six Maxims and 77 wagons were captured, while some two hundred Boers were killed, wounded or captured.

On 31 March, at Ventersdorp, Colonel Shekelton handed over his column to Colonel Sir Henry Rawlinson, another energetic officer with a good eye for ground, who soon established a reputation as one of the most effective column commanders.

Rawlinson continued to co-operate with Babington in pursuit of De la Rey, and the 8th M.I. took part in several engagements including, on 2 April, a rearguard action against Smuts near Rietpan. On the 13th Rawlinson left Ventersdorp in search of Smuts' laager, which was known to lie to the south-west, and attacked it at Kaffir Kraal at dawn on the 14th. The burghers fled, abandoning their guns and wagons. The Boer commandos, however, had remarkable recuperative powers and De la Rey reappeared at Hartebeestfontein with two thousand men. He was attacked there on the 18th by the combined British columns, but without success, and Second-Lieutenant Edward Wolseley of the East Lancashires was severely wounded.

On 22 April 22 two hundred men of the 8th M.I. were escorting a supply convoy from Syferkuil to Klerksdorp when it was attacked on Reebokfontein Farm by seven hundred of De la Rey's burghers. During the fight Lieutenant Percy Goodwyn, who was in command of the left flank guard, saw sixty Boers making for a kopje which commanded the position from which the British guns were firing. Gathering ten of his men, he raced the enemy for the top of the hill. As the East Lancashires galloped for the kopje, Corporal Connery received five wounds, and his horse was hit twice, but still he rode on. Both sides arrived simultaneously, and, although overwhelmed by numbers, Goodwyn and his men maintained their position long enough for the guns to withdraw. The Boers massed 180 men against the little band, who were eventually rushed with the loss of two killed, three wounded and the remainder taken prisoners,[24] but not before Private Burrows had collected rifle bolts from the casualties and thrown them away to prevent the enemy getting them. For gallantry on this occasion, Lieutenant Goodwyn was awarded the DSO and Corporal Connery and Private Burrows were Mentioned in Despatches and received Special Promotion from Lord Kitchener for Distinguished Conduct in the Field.

Rawlinson's column remained in the Western Transvaal for another three months, operating with some success against De la Rey and Kemp. During this time the East Lancashire Company met their 1st Battalion, with Hamilton's and Garratt's columns, for the first time in nearly eighteen months. Then, on 27 July 1901 Rawlinson crossed the Vaal, at Lindique Drift, and entered the Orange River Colony. The following day the column was in action:

'1st East Lancashire Company, acting [as] advance guard to the column, came upon a local commando, 180 strong, in a strong position at Bloemfontein farm. On coming under fire, the Company galloped the position under a heavy fire and seized the key [to the position], enfilading the enemy on both sides. On [the East Lancashires] being reinforced by the Oxford Company, the enemy retired to a second ridge, some 800 yards behind, and were again chased out of it. The column coming up, a general pursuit ensued through Parys, and to within four miles of Vredefort. The whole of the enemy's convoy and

24. Privates J. Gannon and A. Levine were killed, Private R. Wardley mortally wounded, and Corporal (promoted Sergeant) S. Connolly and Private M. Brennan severely wounded. Other members of the party were Lieutenant P. C. W. Goodwyn, Corporal C. Clarke and Privates J. Burrows (promoted Corporal), B. Howson, R. Coleman and E. Hitchen, all taken prisoner but later released.

stock fell into our hands, besides 25 prisoners. Our casualties, nil. Colonel Rawlinson thanked the 1st East Lancashire Company on returning to camp, stating that the success of the day was entirely due to the gallant way they rushed the enemy from two strong positions. Strength of the Company on this day was about 65 all told.'[25]

Rawlinson's column now moved south to take part in a co-ordinated drive to clear an area bounded by the Vaal and Modder rivers and by the two north–south strategic railways. The column's line of advance lay some miles to the west of the Bloemfontein to Pretoria railway, with Major John Pine-Coffin's column on its left. We have an account of the Malta Mounted Infantry (2nd Loyal North Lancashire) part in this drive from Lieutenant Francis Braithwaite, writing to his mother on 8 August, 'On trek 8 miles north of Brandfort':

'We left Honning Spruit on Sunday 26th July, marching to America [Siding] that day, and, leaving at 10.30 that night, moved out to surround a farm about 8 miles east of Kroonstadt by day break. We found no Boers there. Then back to Kroonstadt by midday, had 3 hours halt and then on to Boschrand 8 miles south. Stopped the night, and next day by a circuitous movement to Ventersburg Road. The next day I rode to Virginia through Riet Spruit [his base] and got the guides back to Ventersburg Road. Polo in the afternoon as fast as the ponies could be changed, dinner, 2½ hours sleep, [then] at 10.30 that night a long night march. No Boers. Resting that day and night at Kaal Vallis Diamond Mines. Next day spent on top of Kopje Alleen rounding up stock. Very few Boers.

'Next day movement south – plenty of stock, few Boers – and orders to join in a big sweep to south. Back to camp, early move following next day, crossing Zand River 5 miles west of railway. Next day across Doorn River. Next day Smaldeel. Next day 5 miles S.E. of Vet River Station. Today here. We have got as a result of all this moving 3 prisoners, a few wagons and carts and refugees, about 200 stock and 40,000 sheep. Tomorrow through Brandfort, I expect, towards Bloemfontein. I don't know what the other columns have done – there are 10 others in line with us.

'I collected your box of shirts etc for the men at Smaldeel and dished them out today; the men appeared very pleased. I hope they will write and thank the women for them; please thank them very much for me.'

Rawlinson's column reached the Modder river on 10 August and then, after a few days rest at Glen, he was given a roving commission to follow up Smuts' commando, which was at large in the hills of

25. *Records of 1st East Lancashire Company 8th Mounted Infantry*, pp. 11–12 (typescript account in QLR Archives).

the south-east corner of the Orange River Colony. The column caught up with Smuts at Sterkfontein on 25 August, taking 19 prisoners, but the commando then prudently dispersed. A few fugitives were subsequently picked up, and the East Lancashire Company captured Daniel De Wet after a three mile chase near Dewetsdorp. Moving south, the column had a brush with Kritzinger's commando, at Elandsberg on 7 September, then continued to the Orange River at Aliwal North.

Blood River Poort

Kitchener often expressed impatience at the ponderously 'safe' tactics of many column commanders, but bold offensive action was only effective if based on reliable intelligence. Otherwise it could lead to disaster. In September 1901 Louis Botha, with some fifteen hundred men, attempted an invasion of Natal. British mobile columns were hastily mustered to intercept him, and on the 17th Lieutenant-Colonel Hubert Gough, one of the most dashing and successful cavalry commanders of the war, came up with two to three hundred burghers near a gorge known as Blood River Poort, some fifteen miles west of Vryheid. Gough had three companies of the 24th Mounted Infantry, including a South Lancashire section of about thirty men under Sergeant Nolan, and two guns. He watched as the Boers, apparently unaware of his presence, unsaddled at a farm near the mouth of the gorge, and decided to seize this rare opportunity of coming to close quarters with the elusive enemy. Sending word for reinforcements to support him, and believing that he had achieved surprise, Gough set out at once to take the enemy in the rear.

As his mounted infantry deployed for the attack, they suddenly saw, with a confused horror, that they had ridden into a trap. Seven hundred mounted Boers charged into their right flank, yelling and shooting, while the bush erupted with a terrific fire from burghers lying in ambush. The right-hand company was at once ridden down, the guns were overrun and captured after a brief struggle, and within minutes the fight was over. Outnumbered by over five to one, with 44 men killed and wounded, Gough and 240 survivors were compelled to surrender. Some of the South Lancashires fought to the last round, for Private H. Gavin (promoted Corporal) was Mentioned in Despatches by Lord Kitchener for 'Conspicuous gallantry in holding position in face of heavy fire and overwhelming numbers till ammunition was all expended'; but the outcome was inevitable and Sergeant Nolan was taken prisoner with 25 of his men, of whom three were wounded.

The Boers were unable to hold prisoners, so their usual practice was to strip them of anything useful and then let them go. This occasion was no different, as Sergeant Hackett relates: 'After relieving them of everything down to their socks, they were released and some walked naked, and others almost so, to Vryheid, where a collection of clothing and comforts of all kinds was made for them. I had to give my spare shirt and socks, balaclava, scarf, etc.'

Itala

Botha was too weak to cross directly into Natal over the Buffalo River, so rode on south into Zululand, seeking a less well-defended route. The frontier of Zululand was guarded by two British camps – 'Forts' Itala and Prospect – and having been informed that they were weakly held, Botha decided to attack.

The British garrison at Itala consisted of three hundred men of the 5th Divisional Mounted Infantry, including a strong detachment of the South Lancashire Regiment under Lieutenant Robert Trousdale, and two guns, the whole commanded by Major Chapman. The lightly entrenched camp was rather vulnerable to attack, being dominated by Itala mountain, and so when, on the afternoon of 25 September, Major Chapman received information from his Zulu allies that an attack was imminent, he occupied the bare, unfortified summit with a detachment of eighty mounted infantry under Lieutenants Kane and Lefroy. After dark that evening Botha surrounded Itala and prepared to attack with some two thousand burghers, and at midnight they assaulted the isolated outpost. We have an account of what followed from Colour-Sergeant Duffy of the South Lancashires:

'We had a large perimeter camp to defend. The key was the top of the hill from which there was a slope terminating in a ridge overlooking a level piece of ground on which we had our camp and horse lines. The key position was held by the M.I. detachment of the South Lancashires, Dublins and Dorsets. Five impis of Zulus were embodied, but having only their stabbing assegais and shields they were not much use.

'The Boers, elated by their recent victory over Gough's M.I. at Scheeper's Nek [actually Blood River Poort], and confident in their superior numbers, crept right up the hill crest to within reach of the bayonet. This was he first occasion that they had been so close since Pieters Hill, and under the light of the brilliant moon, fierce hand-to-hand fighting followed. Lieut. H.R. Kane [South Lancashire Regiment], the gallant commander of an isolated position, was killed while shouting 'No surrender', and every man of his post was either killed or wounded.

'The bayonet, which the Boers feared more than the bullet, was freely used, but despite this, the attackers displayed such courage and

'No Surrender!'. The Defence of Fort Itala by 5th Mounted Infantry, 26 September 1901. (*Drawing by R. Caton Woodville*)

determination that eventually they got almost on top of two field guns which were firing case shot over open sights.

'At dawn the Boers were in possession of the top of the hill and cleverly concealed in the spruits and dongas. We, however, held the ridge overlooking the camp and had a good field of fire; any advance on their part would be costly. On the other hand, they had the advantage of the commanding position and freedom of movement. Movement was, denied us owing to the unerring and merciless rifle fire, which we duly respected and kept well under whatever cover our position afforded. When their sharpshooters couldn't get a human target they concentrated their fire on our horses in the lines. Those not so devilishly engaged 'dammed' our water supply, which ran from the top of the hill. As the parched wounded lying about were crying for water, this was our greatest catastrophe. Several times during the day the Boers endeavoured to raise the attack, but on each occasion they were driven back with heavy losses. About 9 p.m. there was a fierce fusillade of rifle fire which lasted about quarter of an hour. A complete cessation of the hostilities followed. Scouts were sent out to reconnoitre the cause for this unexpected blessing and it was found that the 'burghers' were retiring.' The defenders were down to less than one hundred rounds per man when Botha, having lost at least one hundred men, called off the attack and fell back to the north.

The commander of the Regiment's detachment, Lieutenant

R. C. Trousdale, was awarded the DSO 'for the plucky way he worked the Maxim gun, after both the men with him had been killed', while Colour-Sergeant Duffy was Mentioned in Despatches – 'Though wounded early in the action, [he] continued to fight and exercised great control and influence over his men.' The Regiment's losses, particularly among those who fought to the last man on Itala mountain, were heavy – nine killed and eight wounded. Colour-Sergent Duffy has written an interesting account of the aftermath of the Itala engagement:

Lieutenant Harold Kane, 1st South Lancashires.

Killed in action at Itala, shouting 'No surrender!' when his detached post was overwhelmed.

'We collected our wounded, a number of which we had to leave at Jim London's farm, and retired on N'Kandhla. There were very few British residents at N'Kandhla, but all gave over their houses and beds to the wounded and rendered every assistance possible. The small jail, in which there were some Zulus under life sentence, was also evacuated and turned into a hospital, the Natal Frontier Police in charge peremptorily ordering the prisoners to 'return when the war is over!' The wounded were in a terrible plight. There was scarcely any food and no medical appliances. Our Medical Officer, who had courageously gone to the top of the hill to attend the wounded there, had been commandeered by the Boers to deal with their casualties. Finally, the Veterinary Officer undertook the treatment of our cases. He carried out his self-imposed task very efficiently, as many have occasion to remember.

'Of the few horses remaining scarcely any were fit, and after everything was more or less ship-shape we commenced patrolling the country in mule-wagons (most humiliating). On returning from one of these jaunts, three days after the Itala fight, we were astonished to see two figures on top of the ridge, near N'Kandhla, our base. One was a Zulu and the other a white man. We advanced to collect them and found the latter to be Private Fallon, who had been struck off as dead. He had been on top of the hill with Lieut. Kane and was so badly wounded that the Boers, thinking he was dead, had stripped off all his clothing. On recovering consciousness, and with wounds still unattended to, Fallon had wandered about naked until he was met by the humane Zulu, who gave him all the clothing he possessed – an Army jersey, and that had seen better days. Fallon's appearance was indescribable. He was severely wounded and had been lying naked and without food during three cold nights and scorching hot days. Undoubtedly he would have died from exposure and privation but for the friendly Zulu, who guided and assisted the emaciated derelict to N'Kandhla, sixteen miles distant from the Zulu's kraal.

'Shortly afterwards I also collected a Boer memento in the form of a bullet, and in company with Fallon and other casualties we were evacuated by ox-wagons to Etshowe [Eshowe]. The journey will live long in the memory of any who shared it. It was a night-mare. At Etshowe there was a civilian doctor but no hospital, beds, dressings or medical comforts and, regardless of our wounded condition, we were bedded down on wooden 'bedboards' infected with 'jiggers'. Next morning the journey was continued in the cumbersome old ox-wagons. The roadway, if such it may be called, was narrow and precipitous and we were forced off the beaten track by a column of advancing troops. The G.O.C. caught sight of us and on seeing our plight he halted his column and gave us the right of way. We travelled all day until we reached an hospital train and here we were accommodated comfortably, even though medical treatment was primitive and many essentials were lacking. We had two days and nights on the train until eventually we reached Pinetown, about seven miles from Durban. Here a hutted hospital had been established and we received the best of attention, the doctors and nurses being unsparing in their efforts to make us comfortable. Fallon, who had severed an artery in his shoulder, had a nasty time and finally had to have his arm amputated. On recovery, he was sent to England and I, then being marked fit, rejoined the battalion in Zululand.'

Fort Prospect was more strongly entrenched than Itala. It was held by 35 of the 5th Divisional Mounted Infantry, again including some South Lancashires, and 51 of the Durham Artillery Militia. Early on the 26th it was attacked by five hundred Boers under Grobelaar. A thick morning mist and covered approaches assisted the attackers, but despite repeated and resolute efforts they were unable to break into the post's defences, and towards evening they drew off with some sixty casualties. The defenders had lost one man killed, Private G. Duckworth of the South Lancashires, and eight wounded.

Battle of Bakenlaagte

Following these demoralising defeats, Botha retreated to the north, marching through Swaziland to avoid British columns. As so often, the commandos very rapidly recovered from their losses and resumed their predatory activities in the Eastern Transvaal.

The Loyal North Lancashire Company 3rd Mounted Infantry entrenched after the Battle of Bakenlaagte.

'If it had not been for the 3rd M.I.', stated Brigadier-General Alderson, 'the whole camp would have been taken, from what I can make out.'

On 20 October 1901, the 3rd Mounted Infantry came under command of Lieutenant-Colonel G. E. Benson,[26] one of the most successful and highly-regarded of all Kitchener's column commanders. Seeing that Benson's column was unsupported, Botha concentrated his forces, and from the 25th parties of Boers harassed the rear and flanks of the British force. On the 30th, in torrential rain and an obscuring mist, the Boers saw their opportunity. Delayed at a drift by some bogged wagons, Benson's rearguard of some 280 mounted men, mostly 3rd Mounted Infantry, had become isolated from the main body. At the start of this action, the Loyal North Lancashire Company formed the rear screen and was heavily engaged for some twelve hours, steadily repelling enemy rushes which grew in strength and boldness throughout the day. The British guns, stationed on a ridge to the rear of the mounted infantry, could do little to help due to the poor visibility. Eventually the mounted troops were ordered to abandon the last of the wagons and fall back to Bakenlaagte, where the main body of the column had encamped. As they withdrew, at about 4.30 p.m., a determined charge was made by the enemy, a large body of whom galloped into the rear guard, overthrowing the artillery escort. A furious struggle ensued on the ridge, where the guns were served until the last gunner dropped and the Yorkshire Mounted Infantry and Scottish

26. Some twenty volunteers of the Loyal North Lancashire Company had already served with his column 22 July–30 August in the oddly-named 'Gorgonzola Scouts'.

3rd Mounted Infantry watering their horses.

Captain Jourdain, O. C. Loyal North Lancashire Company, on left.

Horse lay dead or wounded around them. The rest of the 3rd Mounted Infantry retired on the main body's camp, which was hurriedly entrenched and successfully held.

The action at Bakenlaagte had been a serious reverse, redeemed only by the heroism of the rearguard and the preservation of the main body. Colonel Benson and 65 of his men were killed, and another 165 wounded, while two guns were captured. The losses of the North Lancashire Company were, however, remarkably light; Private Rigby was killed and Private Howcroft wounded.

The rest of the year was spent by 3rd M.I. in the Carolina district, attached to Colonel Mackenzie's column and chiefly engaged in convoy work.

A Night March and a Dawn Gallop

Benson had been one of Kitchener's favourites, but other British column commanders were consistently successful, and none more so than Colonel Sir Henry Rawlinson, under whom the 1st East Lancashire Mounted Infantry Company was still serving in 8th M.I. We have already noted his operations in the Western Transvaal and Orange River Colony. On 26 September his column was redeployed by rail from Burghersdorp in Cape Colony to Heidelberg, south-east of Johannesburg. From there the column moved by stages into the Eastern Transvaal.

The Loyal North Lancashire Company 3rd Mounted Infantry 1902.

Rawlinson's favourite tactic had long been the night approach march followed by a gallop at dawn into the enemy laager, but this required reliable intelligence and sound guides, which was now provided for him by the eccentric Colonel Woolls-Sampson and his private army of African scouts. Operating in the Bethel – Ermelo area under command of Major-General Bruce-Hamilton, Rawlinsons' column had a remarkable run of success in December 1901.

'At Oshoek the 1st East Lancashire Company was the leading company of the 8th M.I. when the charge was made on the enemy's laager.[27] At Friehartsfontein, the 1st East Lancashire Company again distinguished itself in the pursuit of the enemy, which lasted over 11 miles of country. At the third of General Bruce-Hamilton's successes, the 8th M.I. had no share owing to the Yeomanry who were in front of them during the night march losing touch with the column in front ... Bruce-Hamilton's columns [then] moved out from Ermelo [to the] east, crossing the Vaal, and attempted to surprise the enemy at Baukop, which failed owing to heavy thunderstorms. December 21st: Another attempt was made to surprise Commandant Grobler at Maryvale, but just as the columns galloped for the enemy's laager at dawn a thick fog came down and the enemy escaped, leaving their stock, carts, &c., and a few killed and prisoners in our hands.'[28]

27. Lieutenant G. Clayhills was Mentioned in Despatches 'for good leading in capture of laager on December 3rd 1901'. 93 prisoners were taken at Oshoek, twenty miles south-west of Ermelo, and in his report to Kitchener General Hamilton 'ascribes great credit to the 8th Battalion Mounted Infantry, who displayed both dash and enterprise in closing with the enemy and preventing their escape.'

28. *Records of 1st East Lancashire Company 8th Mounted Infantry*, p. 16.

Officers of the East Lancashire Company 8th Mounted Infantry.
Seated, left to right: Lt G. Clayhills, DSO; Capt E. R. Collins, DSO; Lt P. C. W. Goodwyn, DSO.
Standing: Lts E. J. Wolseley and A. C. Aubin. (Photograph probably 1902)

Rawlinson's has left his own account of one of these dawn raids:

'It was just light enough to see as we began to trot on, and then just at 3.45 a.m., as we came over the rise, the whole of the Boer laager lay at our feet only some 800 yards off. The Mounted Infantry let go a cheer and a whoo-hoop which must have been a rude awakening to the laager – a few odd shots, the whiz of one or two bullets and the whole of our line of over 2,000 mounted men set off at a gallop, yelling with delight – we never waited to shoot – the more the Boers shot the more we yelled. My orders were that none of the men were on any account to stop at the laager. There was to be no looting of wagons or waiting to shoot, our objective was to be the mounted Boers and the gun we heard was with them.

'I don't think I have ever seen a prettier or more exhilarating sight than that was in the grey of dawn – The M.I. all streaming away just like a pack of hounds and giving tongue like Red Indians. We had a pretty long gallop of nearly 7 miles. The horses did well and we were rewarded by collecting 53 prisoners ... only 6 got away. We killed 4 and had one officer, 8 M.I., slightly wounded in the leg ... Having stopped the hunt and collected the 'game' we went back to the laager ... There we found some 67 more prisoners, about 3000 cattle and some 30 carts and wagons.'[29]

The weather now closed in, with heavy and continuous rain and fog, and the columns moved into Ermelo on Christmas Day; but by the New Yaer they were on the move again, riding east towards Swaziland. There on the banks of the Ingwempisi (an area well known to the East Lancashires' successors in 1964–65) Commandant Erasmus and his small commando of 42 men were surprised in a dawn raid on 3 January, the Commandant surrendering personally to the East Lancashire Company, which was leading the column at the time. Returning to Ermelo, they were involved in another raid in the Bethel area, 11–13 January. After a rapid night march, the column came upon the enemy at dawn and, after a short skirmish and pursuit, some 32 prisoners were captured, together with stock and wagons, while five enemy dead were picked up.

Botha's commandos in the Eastern Transvaal were so crippled by this series of dawn raids that Kitchener decided to transfer Rawlinson and his column to the north-eastern corner of the Orange River Colony, where De Wet and his cohorts were still at large, and so on 18 January the East Lancashire Company rode into Standerton, escorting prisoners who had been taken during recent operations.

Blockhouses and Drives

We left 1st Battalion East Lancashire Regiment on trek in the Western Transvaal. That phase of their war came to an end in August 1901, to be succeeded by a spell of 'block-houses' and 'drives'. This methodical system, developed by Lord Kitchener, is explained by Lieutenant Gerald Hill, who commanded the East Lancashire Section of 1st Mounted Infantry throughout the war:

'The strategy which underlay the evolution of the blockhouse system in South Africa was both defensive and offensive. Having secured the railways by blockhouses, the next step was to secure the roads in a similar manner. This done, 'drives' became not only possible but effective. As the blockhouses multiplied, the area of manoeuvre for the enemy contracted. Without the 'drives' the blockhouses would have been purely defensive, and of little use. Without the Blockhouses the 'drives' would have beaten the air.

'The blockhouses were at first erected at intervals of about one and a half miles. At this interval they largely prevented the destruction of the

29. Letter of Colonel Sir Henry Rawlinson dated Bethel, Tuesday 10 December 1901 (National Army Museum).

railway lines and trains, but with so wide a separation it was not possible to stop parties of the enemy from crossing the line at night. The interval was therefore decreased to a half to three-quarters of a mile.

'It is beyond dispute that the blockhouse system shortened very considerably the resistance of the Boers, who relied in carrying out their guerrilla warfare on freedom of manoeuvre and mobility. I saw

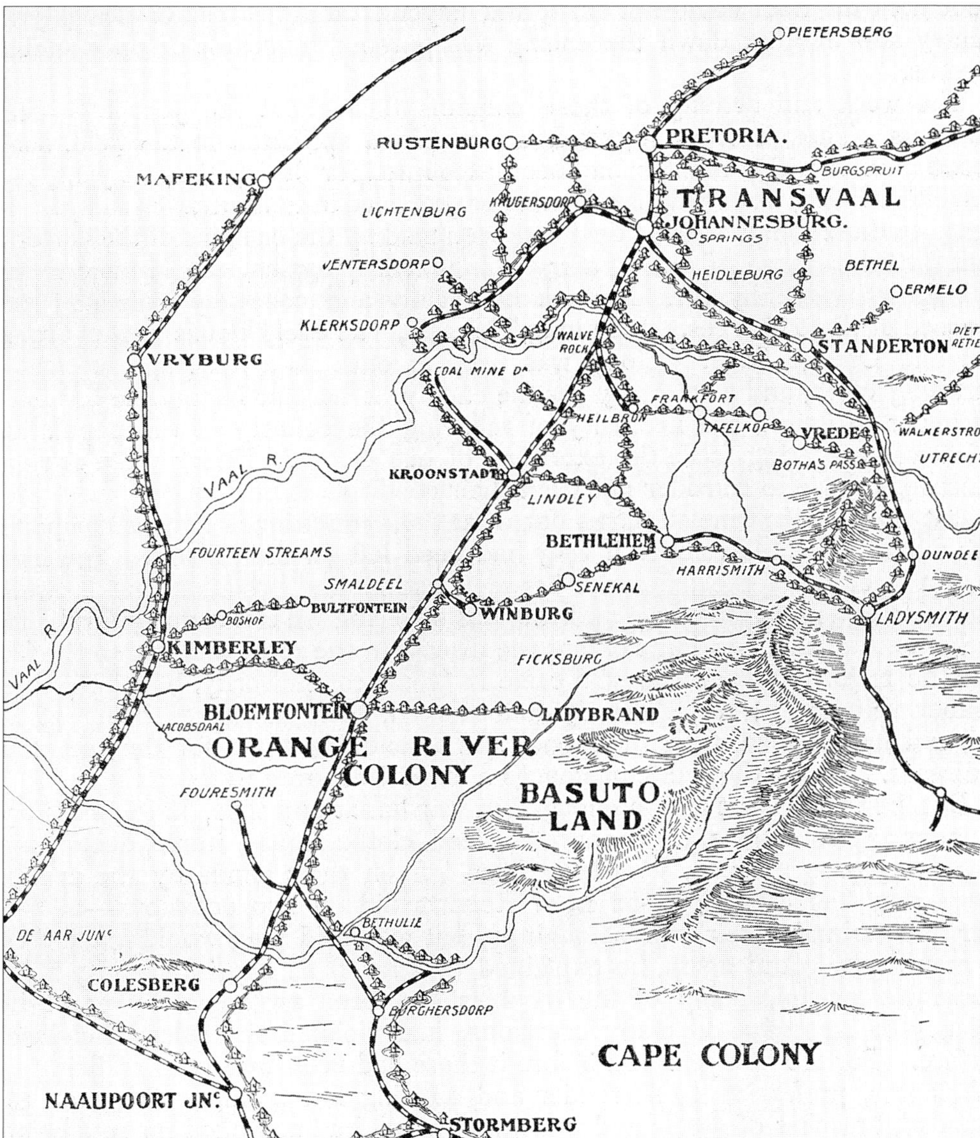

The Blockhouse System.

First the railway lines were secured, then further blockhouse lines were erected along strategic roads and natural features, denying freedom of movement to the enemy and providing a network of defended lines within which mobile columns could methodically clear the country of Boer commandos.

it in operation, and know that after its introduction we were convinced of a speedy and certain end to the war.'[30]

The near-contemporary Battalion account[31] of this last phrase of the war is a good low-level exposition of how this strategy translated into practice:

'For two months after leaving the columns the Battalion was disseminated along the railway line between Vereeniging and Wolverhoek, and on the branch line to Heilbron; whilst at the end of October four companies were pushed on to Frankfort, O.R.C., which town was connected with the railway terminals at Heilbron by a line of block-houses. A month later the whole Battalion was concentrated at Frankfort with a view to the extension of the line eastwards along the Vrede road. The work of erecting the block-houses was at once commenced by a party of Royal Engineers, with the assistance of Kaffir labour, two or three block-houses being completed daily and immediately garrisoned by parties from the Battalion.

'The progress made was slow, but there were few idle hands. Whilst the sappers gave their expert attention to the fixture of the corrugated iron sections, and the Kaffirs dug, some of the East Lancashire companies were employed in erecting a barbed-wire fence from blockhouse to blockhouse, and the others were spread out in front, watchful against any attempt to molest the workers. Ten days' labour saw the head of the line near Dundas Farm, some ten miles east of Frankfort, and it was at this point that the Boers made their first effort to check further progress. Previous information had been received of a considerable concentration of the enemy in the district, and Colonel Wright had asked for assistance. A few Yeomanry were dispatched from Heilbron, but their inexperience rendered their presence a source of anxiety rather than of strength. On the early morning of 9 December, a Boer Commando, about 450 strong, under Commandant Ross, made a demonstration against the camp. Shelter trenches had been dug round the lines on the previous evening, and when the first shot was fired at break of day the companies on outposts were already standing to arms. This readiness apparently disconcerted the Boers, for they did not press the attack, but contented themselves with keeping up a continuous fire on the camp for four hours, during which time they took the greatest care not to expose themselves except at extreme

30. Article, The Blockhouse System in the Late South African War, *The Lilywhites' Gazette.*

31. *XXX Journal*, June 1912. This narrative, in effect a Battalion War Diary, was compiled some years before that date, at the request of the then Commanding Officer, by an officer who served throughout the campaign. The original draft, in the Regimental Archives, is marginally annotated by Colonel Wright and other participants. I have usually preferred the original, unsanitised, version of events.

ranges. The want of guns and of mounted men rendered counter measures impossible. This futile attempt resulted in three casualties amongst the East Lancashire men, whilst two natives and several transport animals were placed hors de combat. The Boers suffered in equal proportions. In the afternoon a reinforcement of one gun, R.F.A., and 100 men of the Imperial Yeomanry arrived.

'A few days later, the head of the block-house line being then three miles beyond Dundas Farm, the value of these Yeomanry was unpleasantly demonstrated. They were sent out by Colonel Wright to cover the working parties, and had taken up a position along a naturally defended ridge. A half company of the East Lancashire was in support on a hill about a mile behind, and Colonel Wright with the Adjutant had ridden out to the ground in front of this support to reconnoitre positions for additional block-houses. Whilst thus engaged, he saw a party of some 200 men galloping towards him from the ridge where he had posted the Yeomanry. There had been no firing in front, and the first and natural impression was that the Yeomanry for some reason or another were coming in. But why this haste; and why so many men? A second glance revealed the sombre garb of the Boer interspersed with khaki uniforms, and the Colonel and Captain Le Marchant, being at the time dismounted, ran, leading their horses, up the hill towards the support, whose attention had also been directed to these mysterious horsemen. The doubt of their identity was soon dispelled by the brisk fusillade which they opened as they rode; but the steady fire of the half company quickly brought them to a standstill, and after a brief interchange of shots, the party galloped off. The Yeomanry, it appeared, had been surprised and swept up in detail by this commando, with scarcely a shot fired! Many of them were carried backward in the charge of the Boers across the plain, and the appearance of the khaki uniforms in the van had misled the support until the last moment. The total want of training, and consequent lack of steady discipline, which characterized the later contingents of Yeomanry, are sufficient to account for this incident, which does not necessarily reflect on the personal courage of the individual.[32]

'This episode was not the only indication of active hostility. The outposts were kept continually on the alert. Individual men straying even a short distance from their block-house were occasionally ambushed; and more than once the seductive bait of poultry in a deserted farm led a foraging party to its doom. But no determined attack was made on the Battalion. The Boers however were apparently only waiting for a favourable opportunity, which the constant vigilance

32. This was 33rd Imperial Yeomanry. In the margin of the draft Regimental account, a contemporary editorial hand has written: 'Is this too strong? I think not. The Yeomanry were disgraceful on this occasion – nearly lost us the Colonel.'

On Tafel Kop. Colonel Rimington and Major Damant in conference with Lieutenant-Colonel Wright on top of Tafel Kop, February 1902, while Captain da Costa sends a heliograph message.

imposed on the Battalion by Colonel Wright had hitherto denied them. Their chance soon came.

'Two Columns under Colonel Rimington and Major Damant had been ordered to co-operate with the Battalion in order that the block-house line might be completed. At dawn on December 20th, as Major Damant's Column, after a difficult night march in a severe thunderstorm, was advancing in a widely extended formation against scattered parties of the Boers within a few miles of the East Lancashire camp, a portion of it, including the guns, under the Commander himself was entrapped by a superior force by means of a cleverly devised ruse, in which the unjustifiable use of khaki uniform played an important part. Damant and his men fought with great gallantry, but his small party of some 90 men was almost annihilated, and the guns were only saved by the arrival of the scattered portions of the column.[33]

'With the assistance of Rimington's and Damant's columns a further advance was now possible; and under the direction of General Edward Hamilton, who, recently placed in command of the block-house line, had hastened up from Heilbron, the headquarters of the Battalion were installed on Tafel Kop on December 22nd. Tafel Kop, which, as its name implies, has the flat top peculiar to the hills of South Africa, rises some 500 feet above the level of the plain, and forms a landmark conspicuous for miles around. It became a most valuable

33. In the margin of the Regimental account Colonel Wright has noted that while 90 was the official figure, he believed Damant to have about 300 men: 'They had 36 killed and I think about 80 wounded. I know we buried 36 but do not remember the exact number of wounded. Damant's guns were captured but retaken by Rimington's column.'

Road making up the side of Tafel Kop.

Dundas Farm Post with Tafel Kop in the distance.

signalling station, and the Battalion signallers under Lieutenant Wethered did most useful work during the closing months of the war, when the lamp and the heliograph had no small share in the success of Lord Kitchener's 'drives'; and the place was of equal importance as a supply depot, on which the 'driving' columns could draw.

'The construction of that section of the block-house line which had been entrusted to the East Lancashire, from Frankfort to Tafel Kop, was now complete; its extension towards Vrede, where it was met by the line from Newcastle, was carried out in January by the 2nd Battalion Essex Regiment; and subsequently, between January and March, the Battalion took over from that Corps an additional three miles of block-houses east of Tafel Kop, being relieved in the block-houses at the Frankfort end by the West Kent Regiment.[34]

'The garrison of each blockhouse consisted at first of one N.C.O. and eight privates, but later the number of privates was reduced to six. The garrisons had no sinecure. Day and night a vigilant watch was maintained. The least alarm during the hours of darkness rendered continuous sleep impossible. The daylight was employed in the never-ending task of erecting a chain of obstacles with which it was hoped to make the line impassable. Many methods were devised with that object. The barbed wire fence, running from block-house to block-house in the form of an obtuse angle, was elaborated into a formidable and bristling barrier. A so-called 'uncuttable' ¼ inch steel wire was added to the treble twisted strands of barbed wire, which formed the constituent parts of the fence. The stays had to be anchored to big stones buried deep in the ground. An alarm wire, consisting of a single strand of barbed wire, was stretched through loops on the standards, and kept taut by means of weights hanging at each end, so contrived that if the wire was cut the noise of the weights falling on tins placed underneath would alarm the sentries. Rifle rests were provided at every block-house in order to secure accurate fire in the dark along the line of fence; and alarm guns were placed at intervals.[35] Finally the excavation of a deep trench, parallel and close to the wire fences was commenced. The execution of this elaborate system of obstacles fully occupied the days until the end of the war; nor was the ditch completed, even then, to its proposed dimensions (6 feet deep by 6 feet wide) owing to the extreme difficulty of the soil.

'The summit of Tafel Kop, on which a strong detachment was permanently posted, was also fortified with kraals and sangars, whilst its base was ringed with block-houses and wire entanglements, and along the almost precipitous sides of the hill a zig-zag road was cut, with infinite labour, from top to bottom. A smaller entrenched post, half way between Tafel Kop and Frankfort, was also formed at Dundas Farm, where the headquarters of the companies for the western section of the line were stationed under Major Trent.

'The dreary drudgery of these undertakings was relieved by occasional

34. According to Hill, 'the whole line, 87 miles in length, consisted of 187 block-houses, garrisoned by 2,558 men, or by 30 men to a mile.'
35. Hill states that: 'Along the fences automatic alarms and flares were placed, and also fixed rifle batteries of four to six rifles which could be fired by one man. Each block-house was connected to its neighbour by telephone, and contained its own water supply and reserves of food and ammunition.'

adventures. Several vain attempts were made against individual block-houses, in every case at night. These were frustrated, but the garrisons did not always escape scot-free. In one instance, perhaps the only really determined effort to capture a block-house on the East Lancashire line, five men of the garrison were wounded, chiefly by the splinters flying from the corrugated iron as the bullets pierced the roof.[36] After this experience the immunity of the garrisons was secured by a traversed trench round the exterior of the block-house. The trench gave good protection, and had the additional merit of having loopholes on the ground level. The disadvantage was that the garrison, in case of attack, was less concentrated than within the interior.

'The enemy were more successful in their attempts at crossing the line than in their efforts to effect the capture of a block-house. It has been suggested that in this respect some blame attaches to the men on guard for want of vigilance. The admiration due to the splendid qualities of the Infantry soldier compels an emphatic denial of any general accusation of this nature. The truth is that the efficacy of the obstacles was not proof against the desperation of driven masses, nor against the courage and ingenuity of individual men. After peace had been proclaimed, a Boer boasted that he had often crossed and re-crossed the barrier without being fired at. He had taught his horse, he said, to jump the wire fence even in the dark, and he offered to give an exhibition of the animal's powers. Such an occurrence must however have been rare. Still it was certainly feasible for a small party to creep down under cover of darkness to the fence without being observed; and it is obvious that the time required to cut the wire and dash through the gap, gave little opportunity for the garrison, even with their rifles ready loaded on the rests, to prevent the passage. It was seldom that a wire was cut without the garrison taking alarm. That small parties succeeded in breaking through is not therefore necessarily to the discredit of the garrisons, who for the most part were ever zealous in taking every possible precaution.

'With larger bodies the physical difficulties of the barrier were even less, nor was the risk proportionately much greater. Only on one occasion, however, was an attempt by a large body made to force a passage on the line held by the Battalion. This was on March 24th during the progress of a 'drive'. The system of 'driving' had been inaugurated in February, and the north-eastern area of the Free State had been thrice beaten. Whilst these 'drives' were in progress the block-house line was further strengthened by the establishment of intermediate entrenched posts of six men. On the night in question

36. This incident occurred on 24 January 1902 near Dundas Farm. The wounded were Corporal S. Bailey and Privates J. Hannaway, R. Hanson, T. King and F. Morris.

these picquets were in position between nearly every two blockhouses, but whether by accident or design the Boers selected, for the point of passage, two block-houses, the close proximity of which had appeared to render an intermediate post unnecessary. With this in their favour, their proceedure was direct and rapid. A large herd of cattle was driven straight through the fence, uprooting the standards, and tearing down the wire like paper in its progress. The fence was levelled to the ground, and the gap thus created gave easy passage to the wagons and Cape carts, which dashed through close behind. Meanwhile parties had been detailed to attract the attention of the garrisons of the two blockhouses away from the point where the passage was being forced, and every available rifle was turned against them. The contest was unequal, but the crossing was not effected without loss to the Boers. The commando consisted of some 150 men under Commandant Alexander Ross, and it was afterwards ascertained that Ross himself had been severely wounded, whilst two others were killed and six wounded. In addition, over 100 horses, 18 mules, and 20 head of cattle were abandoned. There were no casualties amongst the garrison of the block-house, the outer walls of which were however absolutely riddled with bullets. It had been a warm quarter of an hour for the occupants.'

On 22 January 1902 the East Lancashire Mounted Infantry Company arrived at Tafel Kop, with Rawlinson's column, to take part in drives in that north eastern part of the Orange River Colony. But first there was a night excursion north-east, 23rd–24th, to surprise a local commando at Leeuwspruit and take 32 prisoners.

Over the next two months the Company was involved in successive drives in an area between Heilbron and Harrismith bounded on three sides by block-house lines and on the fourth by the Drakensberg range. As the columns drove shoulder to shoulder across the country, like beaters at a shoot, the enemy became increasingly desperate. On the night of 7 February, near Heilbron, there was a determined effort to break back through the driving troops and the Boers charged right up to Lieutenant Goodwyn's picquet. Nine dead and four wounded were picked up opposite the East Lancashire line the following morning.

Towards the end of February the column was involved in a north – south drive, taking the eastern flank. This involved a remarkably difficult march on the tops of the Drakensberg, during which, on one occasion, 8th M.I. spent nine hours hacking a path for their horses down the mountain side, one of the most extraordinary feats achieved by mounted troops during the war. The result of this operation was the surrender to Rawlinson's column of Meyer's commando, 778 prisoners, together with 4,000 horses, 25,000 cattle, 250,000 sheep

Blockhouse manned by the Volunteer Company Loyal North Lancashires near the Modder River on the Cape to Kimberley Railway Line.

and 200 wagons. A final drive took Rawlinson's men west again, to Kopjes station on the railway line, sweeping up another 56 prisoners on route, but De Wet had once more escaped, to join De la Rey in the Western Transvaal.

Pitsani Blockhouse

By 1 September 1901 the whole of 1st Loyal North Lancashires, albeit still fragmented in detachments, was quartered on the western border of the Western Transvaal, with Battalion Headquarters at Mafeking, acting as a depot, with companies in garrison there, at Christiana, Lobatsi and Zeerust when not with columns.

Block-houses were also manned on the railway line north of Mafeking, and on 28 November one of these, at Pitsani, was attacked at dawn by 150 Boers. The garrison, nine men of 'B' Company commanded by Sergeant Waring, were called on to surrender but refused, fighting back with steady gallantry. The enemy occupied a ganger's hut close to the block-house, but as there were known to be women and children in the hut the blockhouse garrison would not fire at it. The Boers were beaten off with the loss of four of their number, while the Sergeant and Privates Rigby and Watson were wounded and the remainder of the garrison were all more or less scratched by splinters.

Inside a Blockhouse.

Manned by the Volunteer Company Loyal North Lancashires.

Sergeant Waring was strongly commended by Lord Methuen, who sent the following message: 'Please compliment the sergeant and garrison of the blockhouse on its excellent defence. I expect nothing but what is of the best from the 1st Loyal North Lancashire Regiment.'

The Tweebosch Disaster

The opening months of 1902 were, however, little less than disastrous for British arms in the Western Transvaal. Here, apart from the Mafeking railway line to the west, there were few block-house lines and it was accordingly that much more difficult to carry out effective drives. Indeed, on more than one occasion in that wild country the hunters had become the hunted. First came a regrettable reverse on the Klip River, south-east of Johannesburg, when a detachment of 28th Mounted Infantry, newly arrived from Malta, was led into an ambush and lost sixty killed and wounded, the latter including Major Dowell, Lieutenants Bridges and Colley, and Drummer Louis of 2nd Loyal North Lancashires. On 24 February Lieutenant-Colonel Von Donop's column was cut up by De la Rey, and then on 7 March at Tweebosch (also known as Klipdrift) Methuen suffered an even more humiliating defeat.

On 2 March he had marched out of Vryburg with a column commanded by Major Paris which comprised three hundred Regular infantry (200 Northumberland Fusiliers and 100 Loyal North Lancashires, four guns, two Maxims and a very heterogeneous collection of 891 mounted men from eight different units, Yeomanry, Cape Police

Lord Methuen rallying his men at Tweebosch, 6 March 1902.
Abandoned by the mounted irregulars, the artillery and Infantry fought on until their ammunition was expended and the General had fallen. (*Drawing by C. M. Sheldon*)

and South African irregulars. The North Lancashires were a composite group, mostly of 'B' and 'G' Companies, commanded by Second-Lieutenant William Paul. Lieutenant Earnest Fitzpatrick accompanied Methuen as his Aide de Camp. The Regimental Digest of Services has the following account of what followed:

'On the 6th [March] the column, nearing Leuwspruit, came in touch with Van Zyl's commando, which was driven off by artillery fire, and the column laagered at Tweebosch.

'At 3 a.m. on the 7th the ox convoy with the infantry left, followed by the mule transport and mounted troops at 4.30 a.m. The enemy were all round in numbers, specially in rear. The ox convoy was halted to allow the mule transport to close up to it, and the rearguard was reinforced with mounted men and two guns. An attack on the right flank was also developing, which was held off by the infantry and two guns 4th Battery Royal Field Artillery. The North Lancashire detachment was extended alongside of the two guns, the whole being next to the ox convoy.

'The Boers, riding in five lines, rushed through the rear screens, firing from their saddles. The mounted troops got a panic and bolted, and the mule convoy, which was closing up, stampeded, together with the ammunition carts. Many of the horsemen never drew rein until Kraaipan was reached. Officers, including the General, tried to rally them, but it was of no avail. The two guns in rear were at once captured. The infantry kept up a steady fire and kept the enemy off the guns near the convoy. The Boers used the guns captured from Von Donop's convoy with effect. Some mounted troops, under Major Paris, held out in a kraal, but the shell fire made them surrender. The detachment kept up a steady fire until their ammunition (the 150 rounds carried on the man) was expended and the troops around the convoy surrendered, Lord Methuen being wounded and nearly all the gunners *hors de combat*.' This accords closely with Lord Methuen's own report, in which he quite rightly blames the undisciplined conduct of the mounted troops for this debacle and praises the stand made by the Regular gunners and infantry who, outnumbered by some five to one and with no reserves of ammunition, 'held out in a most splendid manner until about 9.30 a.m. … until further resistance was impossible' (i.e. about three hours after the collapse and rout of the mounted troops). The casualties were 68 killed and 121 wounded. Lieutenant Fitzpatrick was among the wounded, and the detachment had nine other casualties, of whom two were killed and one died later. The detachment were taken prisoners and were sent into Kraaipan, reaching Mafeking next evening.

Following this disaster, troops were poured into the Western Transvaal, which was now the most significant remaining area of organised Boer military activity, and among these reinforcements were Sir Henry Rawlinson's column with the veteran 8th Mounted Infantry. The 1st East Lancashire Mounted Infantry rode into Klerksdorp on 23 March and were in action at dawn the following day when co-ordinated drives were launched in the Western Transvaal. The Company covered eighty miles in the next 24 hours, a record for the campaign, for the loss of one man killed.

The North Lancashires, meanwhile, were much involved at this time in convoying materials for the construction of additional block-house lines, which were pressed ahead with as rapidly as possible, and in thickening up the block-house line on the railway between Pitsani and Maribogo by manning trenches and an armoured train.

Thirteen British columns were in motion, scouring the wilderness for De la Rey's 'bitter-enders', and two of them were under command of Colonel Robert Kekewich. On 11 April, at Rooiwal, Kemp and Potgeiter launched some seventeen hundred horsemen in a desperate charge against Kekewich's columns, and were bloodily defeated. It was the last pitched battle of the Boer War, and by a remarkable coincidence was won by the officer whose North Lancashires had been on the receiving end of the opening shots.

Prisoners and Friends

Away to the east, where the South Lancashires still kept vigil on

'Ordered Home'. The Volunteer Service Company Loyal North Lancashires, Vryburg, 10 July 1902. (*Photograph by Lieutenant C. K. Potter, 2nd V.B.*)

Lancaster Hill, columns were constantly moving in and out of Vryheid, which served as supply base for the area, and from time to time Boer prisoners were brought in or surrendered themselves. 'The most important capture', wrote Mott, 'was General Cheere Emmett[37] and I had the honour and the pleasure of looking after him for 24 hours. It was indeed a pleasure, for though his captors told me he had notified them of his intentions to escape, I found him extremely interesting. He was a great sportsman and had been a collector of big game for the Cape Town museum. He slept in a bed alongside mine and we talked of our experiences – hunting and shooting in particular – until midnight. I had my revolver under my pillow and a lighted candle close at hand; Cheere begging me to put out the latter, but I declined, considering him altogether too great a risk. Although I enjoyed his company, it was with some relief that I handed him over for his journey down country.'

By now it was clear to most of the Boer commanders that there was nothing to be gained by prolonging a war they could not win. Peace was in the air, and the Boer delegates made their way to Pretoria for a peace conference. On 6 April Louis Botha was escorted into Dundee by Lieutenant Woods and the South Lancashire Mounted Infantry. Hugh Woods has left his own account of an historic mission: 'Shortly before the end of the South African War, when peace negotiations were opened between Lord Kitchener and General Louis Botha, the Mounted Infantry Company of the 1st Battalion, which I

37. Vecht-General J. J. C. Emmett was captured at Broederust in the Ngotsi Hills on 15 March 1902.

On the road to peace – near Vryheid, 6 April 1902.

Lieutenant Hugh Woods (*left*), Commanding the South Lancashire Regiment Mounted Infantry, meeting General Louis Botha (*centre*), his staff and son, near Scheeper's Nek to escort them into the British lines to attend the peace conference at Pretoria. (*Photograph by Lieutenant Travis-Cook, South Lancashire Regiment*)

commanded, was stationed at Vryheid. Arrangements had been made for General Botha and other Boer delegates, then at Waterval, to attend a peace conference, and under a white flag I was sent with letters to General Botha. About five miles from Vryheid we met the delegates, with whom were the General, and his son, and staff, and escorted them to the railhead at Dundee, where the party were received by an officer of Lord Kitchener's staff. General Botha was very amiable, and as I rode alongside him for most of the way we conversed freely. Among other matters we discussed were polo, in which he was keenly interested, and horse-breeding in South Africa.' Geoffrey Mott met them en route and made his own peace offering, a box of chocolates for Botha's young son.

On the 20th of that month, Mott met the Boer General again: 'Hearing that Louis Botha was returning from a Peace Conference at Vereeniging, I rode out to a drift on the Umfolozi river and waited for him and his escort. Saluting him, I asked if I might take his photograph. He said (gruffly), 'How long will it take?' I replied, 'About 1/800th of a second'. He couldn't help smiling as he gave his consent, and I took two very excellent snapshots.'

Peace negotiations resumed on 15 May, and meanwhile a new and disturbing threat to the Boers had arisen on the borders of Zululand, near Vryheid; the Zulus, eager to avenge past defeats at the hands of the Boers, and more recent cattle raids, had become increasingly restless as their enemies grew weaker. Sergeant Hackett witnessed the build-up: 'On outpost I reported to 'rounds' a gathering of natives, dancing around a fire in the railway station yard, some half mile distant, and was told to keep a watch on them. They had been there two nights and it looked like a war dance. Three nights later they were still dancing and chanting, and we could see them, with others sitting around. The dancing grew more furious until, about 10 p.m., I reported the dancing ended and the fire out. Next day news came [that] a Boer Commando had been attacked by Zulus with heavy casualties.' This was the Zulu attack on Holkrantz, on 6 May, when 56 Boers were killed and three wounded.

'About mid-day the Native wounded arrived, some on horseback, with gaping wounds, and others walking and pointing to their unbound wounds, shouting happily 'Hey Jonnie, me fight.' Now the

General Louis Botha and his staff on return from the peace conference, 20 April 1900.

A photograph taken at the Umfolozi Bridge, near Vryheid with the General's permission by Lieutenant Geoffrey Mott, 1st South Lancashires.

question of neutrality occurred, but a separate hospital was wired off for them. They would not lay on the beds or cots, only on a blanket on the floor. Next they would not stay in marquees, only on the floor outside, their relatives visiting and cooking for them. Within a week they had torn off their bandages – were they not warriors, and was it compatible with the dignity of a warrior [that] his wounds should be hidden, and not braved and chanted to? – and gone to their kraals, where, we learned, many died.'

The prospect of African uprisings similar in nature to Holkrantz was one of the factors which eventually decided the Boer leaders, gathered at Vereeniging on 31 May 1902, to accept surrender terms, and early the following morning the welcome news came over the wire from Kitchener at Pretoria, 'Peace was declared last night.'

On 16 June Lieutenant Geoffrey Mott, as Intelligence Officer of 1st South Lancashires, was the junior of a party of British officers who rode out with General Bruce Hamilton to take the surrender of the Vryheid Commando. 'That evening,' he wrote, 'we prepared dinners for 600 Boers in the town. Generals Myburgh, Cheere Emmett and Jordaan dined with us, the latter singing two most amusing comic songs.' Perhaps it was, after all, the last of the 'Gentlemen's Wars'.

APPENDIX I

Honours and Awards

Awarded for Service during the South African War, 1899–1902

The East Lancashire Regiment

Companion of The Bath
Lieutenant Colonel A. J. A. Wright

Distinguished Service Order
Major B. G. Lewis
Major H. M. Twynam
Major T. Capper
Captain and Adjutant L. St G. Le Marchant
Captain E. R. Collins
Lieutenant G. Clayhills
Lieutenant P. C. W. Goodwyn
Captain and Adjutant C. W. T. T. Goff

Distinguished Conduct Medal
Sergeant Major J. T. Mathewson
Sergeant Major J. P. Lydon
Colour Sergeant H. Willis
Sergeant Major (QMS) S. H. Williamson
Colour Sergeant C. Connor
Colour Sergeant W. Oxford
Colour Sergeant F. Sisson
Sergeant J. Dawber
Sergeant J. McLoughlin
Sergeant H. Miller
Corporal H. Bamber
Lance Corporal J. T. Finch
Private H. Clowes

The South Lancashire Regiment (Prince of Wales's Volunteers)

Companion of The Bath
Lieutenant Colonel R. I. Blackburne

Distinguished Service Order
Lieutenant Colonel R. H. Hall
Major M. H. Hall
Major A. F. Tarbet
Captain A. Solly-Flood
Lieutenant and Adjutant A. H. Bailey
Lieutenant C. H. Marsh
Lieutenant R. C. Trousdale

Distinguished Conduct Medal
Sergeant Major J. A. Altman
Sergeant Major G. Devlin
QMS S. T. Boast
QMS T. Foster
Colour Sergeant E. O'Brien
Colour Sergeant T. A. Simon
Sergeant W. Price
Private H. Bracken
Private P. Coulter
Private J. Brighouse
Private H. Gavin
Drmr G. Handley

The Loyal North Lancashire Regiment

Companion of the Bath
Colonel R. G. Kekewich

Distinguished Service Order
Major H. F. Coleridge
Captain C. J. Daniel
Captain C. E. A. Jourdan
Captain J. E. Pine-Coffin
Captain R. W. Thompson
Lieutenant J. B. Wells
Lieutenant C. Wigram
Lieutenant F. W. Woodward

Distinguished Conduct Medal
Sergeant Major E. C. Mudge
Sergeant Major R. Rowley
CQMS A. Hills
Colour Sergeant I. Mossop
Colour Sergeant E. Wilkinson
Sergeant F. Davis
Sergeant C. Hodgson
Sergeant T. J. Hodgson
Lance Sergeant G. Walker
Corporal H. Dandy
Corporal F. Peacock
Private A. Daw
Private A. Hands
Private H. T. Johnson
Private A. McDermott
Private M. Moran
Private J. Taylor

APPENDIX II

Regimental Casualty Lists

Compiled from casualty returns, medal rolls and Regimental records.
Battle casualties are shaded.

The East Lancashire Regiment

No.	*Rank*	*Name*	*Casualty*	*Place*	*Date*	*Remarks*
4828	LCpl	Potter, R.	Wounded & captured	Stormberg	10 Dec. 1899	E Lan R Sect 1st M.I.
914	CSgt	Blake, C. E.	Died of sunstroke	De Kiel's Drift	12 Feb. 1900	
3798	Pte	Parkinson, T.	Died of disease	Cape Town	13 Feb. 1900	
1856	Pte	Connery, S.	Wounded	Waterval Drift	14 Feb. 1900	1st E Lan R M.I. Coy
3056	Pte	Whelan, J.	Wounded	Poplar Grove	8 March1900	E Lan R Sect 1st M.I.
5875	Pte	Banberry, J. W.	Killed	Karee	29 March 1900	
649	Pte	Birtwistle, W.	Killed	Karee	29 March 1900	
3216	Pte	Day, J.	Killed	Karee	29 March 1900	
2526	Pte	Dooley, T.	Died of wounds	Karee	29 March 1900	
5433	Cpl	Bamber, H.	Slightly wounded	Karee	29 March 1900	
2882	Pte	Blendle, W.	Severely wounded	Karee	29 March 1900	
3461	Cpl	Carey, E.	Dangerously wounded	Karee	29 March 1900	Died 30 March
3184	Pte	Carroll, E.	Slightly wounded	Karee	29 March 1900	
3018	Pte	Clowes, H.	Severely wounded	Karee	29 March 1900	Awarded DCM
3155	Pte	Coulson, J.	Slightly wounded	Karee	29 March 1900	
5430	Pte	Davis, W.	Slightly wounded	Karee	29 March 1900	
5782	Pte	Dorrington, P.	Dangerously wounded	Karee	29 March 1900	
3341	Pte	Gibney, J.	Slightly wounded	Karee	29 March 1900	
5416	Pte	King, J.	Slightly wounded	Karee	29 March 1900	
5008	Pte	Preston, G.	Severely wounded	Karee	29 March 1900	
3284	Pte	Ryan, A.	Died of disease	Bloemfontein	2 April 1900	
3724	Cpl	Price, J.	Died of disease	Karee	4 April 1900	
9845	Pte	Bannon, J.	Died of disease	De Aar	6 April 1900	3rd Bn
7461	Pte	Quigley, M.	Died of disease	De Aar	13 April 1900	3rd Bn
4798	Cpl	Mainwaring, J.	Died of disease	Glen	21 April 1900	M.I.
8274	Pte	Westall, H.	Died of disease	De Aar	27 April 1900	3rd Bn
6642	Pte	Hargreaves, W.	Died of disease	De Aar	28 April 1900	3rd Bn
1559	Pte	Howard, W.	Wounded	Houtnek	30 April 1900	M.I.
268	Sgt	Lishman, J.	Died of disease	De Aar	4 May 1900	3rd Bn
4458	Pte	Watts, J.	Died of disease	Bloemfontein	6 May 1900	M.I.
5787	Pte	Hindle, T.	Killed	Schippans Farm	6 May 1900	
1608	Pte	Crane, W.	Killed	Zand River	10 May 1900	

No.	*Rank*	*Name*	*Casualty*	*Place*	*Date*	*Remarks*
4665	Pte	Finch, J.	Wounded	Zand River	10 May 1900	
2369	Pte	Foster, J.	Wounded	Zand River	10 May 1900	
6518	Pte	Hilditch, G.	Wounded	Zand River	10 May 1900	
3465	Cpl	Lord, J.	Wounded	Zand River	10 May 1900	
2499	Pte	Waring, J. W.	Wounded	Zand River	10 May 1900	
	Capt	Head, L.	Mortally wounded	Zand River	10 May 1900	OC E Lan R Coy, 8th M.I. Died Bloem-fontain 11 May.
	Maj	Browne, H. M.	Died of disease	Bloemfontein	23 May 1900	
8952	Pte	Clarkson, J. R.	Died of disease	Green Point	Cape Town	26 May 1900
5137	Pte	Wood, R.	Died of disease	Kroonstad	27 May 1900	
9047	Pte	Sisson, J.	Died of disease	Brandfort	28 May 1900	3rd Bn
6840	Pte	Smith, A.	Died of disease	Bloemfontein	30 May 1900	3rd Bn
541	Pte	Burns, N.	Died of disease	Brandfort	2 June 1900	3rd Bn
9752	Pte	Smith, G.	Died of disease	Springfontein	2 June 1900	3rd Bn
5172	Pte	Coleman, C.	Died of disease	Wynberg	3 June 1900	E Lan R Sect 1st M.I.
5677	LCpl	Morton, R.	Wounded	Vredefort	4 June 1900	
3175	LCpl	Foster, B.	Wounded	Near Pretoria	4 June 1900	E Lan R Coy
2651	Pte	Leeming, A.	Wounded	Near Pretoria	4 June 1900	E Lan R Coy
	2Lt	Forrester, R.	Died of disease	Kroonstad	6 June 1900	
8053	Pte	Davies, J. H.	Died of disease	Bloemfontein	7 June 1900	3rd Bn
8671	Pte	Clough, J.	Died of disease	Smaldeel	8 June 1900	3rd Bn
7205	Pte	Gaskell, J.	Died of disease	Bloemfontein	8 June 1900	3rd Bn
7789	Pte	Eccles, J.	Died of disease	Brandfort	9 June 1900	3rd Bn
4971	LCpl	Dwyer, J.	Wounded	Diamond Hill	11 June 1900	E Lan R Sect 1st M.I.
9017	Pte	Warburton, T.	Died of disease	Bloemfontein	12 June 1900	3rd Bn
364	Pte	Lee, A.	Wounded	Klipdrift	13 June 1900	3rd Bn. Accident
7159	Pte	Harrison, W.	Died of disease	Brandfort	14 June 1900	3rd Bn
9150	Pte	Newsome, J.	Died of disease	Bloemfontein	15 June 1900	3rd Bn
6304	Pte	Mock, S.	Died of disease	Bloemfontein	20 June 1900	3rd Bn
9235	LCpl	Greenwood, T.	Died of disease	Pretoria	21 June 1900	3rd Bn
487	Pte	Openshaw, W.	Died of wounds	Virginia Siding	21 June 1900	3rd Bn. Accident
4266	Pte	Carney, T.	Died of disease	Bloemfontein	23 June 1900	3rd Bn
9042	Pte	Harris, W.	Wounded	Brandfort	23 June 1900	3rd Bn. Sniped, right shoulder
9960	Pte	Kenyon, J.	Died of disease	Bloemfontein	24 June 1900	3rd Bn
9421	Pte	Stones, R.	Died of disease	Bloemfontein	24 June 1900	3rd Bn
4809	Pte	Dixon, J.	Died of disease	Brandfort	28 June 1900	3rd Bn
7357	Pte	Davis, W.	Wounded	Brandfort	4 July 1900	3rd Bn. Sniped, right arm
7549	Pte	Oldfield, J.	Died of disease	Bloemfontein	5 July 1900	3rd Bn
5715	Pte	Dickinson, J.	Died of disease	Johannesburg	10 July 1900	
2446	Pte	Fowler, J.	Died of disease	Springfontein	10 July 1900	3rd Bn
7287	Pte	Kershaw, Died of disease	Johannesburg	11 July 1900	1st Volunteer Coy	
8778	Pte	Prior, B.	Died of disease	Springfontein	15 July 1900	3rd Bn
5567	Pte	Tracey, W.	Died of disease	Johannesburg	15 July 1900	
9685	Pte	Payne, F.	Died of disease	Wynberg	16 July 1900	3rd Bn
5074	Cpl	Hampton, H.	Died of disease	Johannesburg	7 Aug. 1900	
4755	Pte	Anderson, J. A.	Wounded	Bankfontein	22 Aug. 1900	E Lan R Sect 1st M.I.
769	CSgt	Oxford, W.	Severely wounded	Modderfontein	28 Aug. 1900	Awarded DCM

No.	Rank	Name	Casualty	Place	Date	Remarks
6369	Pte	Robinson, J.	Severely wounded	Modderfontein	28 Aug. 1900	
4378	Cpl	Blake, D.	Prisoner	Meyerton	30 Aug. 1900	E Lan R Sect 1st M.I.. Found dead I Oct.
367	Sgt	Beeson, W.	Died of disease	Johannesburg	9 Aug. 1900	
6032	Pte	Thompson, J.	Died of disease	Bloemfontein	4 Sept. 1900	3rd Bn
6358	Pte	Brown, J.	Died of disease	Brandfort	9 Sept. 1900	3rd Bn
9704	Pte	Leeming, M.	Killed	Smaldeel	17 Sept. 1900	3rd Bn
3874	Pte	Williams, E.	Died of wounds	Brandfort	17 Sept. 1900	3rd Bn
2945	Pte	Coupe, S.	Killed	Near Schweizer Reineke	21 Sept. 1900	E Lan R Coy, 8th M.I. (detached)
9944	Pte	Wilson, W.	Died of wounds	Virginia Siding	15 Oct. 1900	3rd Bn
6256	Pte	Rogers, J.	Died of disease	Bloemfontein	1 Nov. 1900	
1541	Pte	Robinson, W.	Died of disease	Johannesburg	2 Nov. 1900	
3209	Cpl	Fitzgerald, R. J.	Dangerously wounded	Vereeniging	9 Nov. 1900	E Lan R Coy, 8th M.I. Died 10 Nov.
5836	Pte	Crook, R.	Died of disease	Springfontein	13 Nov. 1900	3rd Bn
221	Pte	Thompson, R.	Died of disease	Bloemfontein	17 Nov. 1900	3rd Bn
574	Pte	Marsh, T.	Died of disease	Brandfort	25 Nov. 1900	3rd Bn
6151	Pte	Southworth, R.	Died of disease	Bloemfontein	1 Dec. 1900	
9339	Pte	Hargreaves, T.	Died of disease	Bloemfontein	4 Dec. 1900	3rd Bn
444	Pte	Beattie, H.	Died of disease	Bloemfontein	6 Dec. 1900	3rd Bn
150	Pte	Boyle, M.	Died of disease	Brandfort	6 Dec. 1900	3rd Bn
9434	Pte	McGorty, J.	Severely wounded	Smaldeel	12 Dec. 1900	3rd Bn
4592	Cpl	Donnelly, J.	Died of disease	Elandsfontein	17 Dec. 1900	
9807	LCpl	Loard, J.	Died of disease	Vet River	18 Dec. 1900	3rd Bn
9230	Pte	McLoughlin, J.	Died of disease	Bloemfontein	18 Dec. 1900	3rd Bn
9818	Pte	Fowler, J.	Died of disease	Vet River	27 Dec. 1900	3rd Bn
6010	Pte	Greenwood, R.	Died of disease	Vet River	1 Jan. 1901	
7663	Pte	Kelly, J.	Died of disease	Vet River	1 Jan. 1901	3rd Bn
4786	Pte	Kiteley, T	Severely wounded	Seacowpoolnek	1 Jan. 1901	E Lan R Sect, 1st M.I.
3359	Pte	Brunton, J.	Killed	Vereeniging	4 Jan. 1901	E Lan R Coy, 8th M.I.
4751	Pte	Frost, S.	Severely wounded	Vereeniging	4 Jan. 1901	E Lan R Coy, 8th M.I.
5543	Pte	Smith, W.	Killed	Meyerton	5 Jan. 1901	E Lan R Coy, 8th M.I.
6023	Pte	Howarth, W. H.	Died of disease	Bloemfontein	7 Jan. 1901	
4955	Cpl	Glancey, W.	Died of disease	Bloemfontein	10 Jan. 1901	3rd Bn
8627	Pte	Hargreaves, J.	Died of disease	Vet River	16 Jan. 1901	3rd Bn
5690	Pte	Hanson, J.	Died of disease	Bloemfontein	18 Jan. 1901	
3504	Pte	Lang, J.	Died of disease	Elandsfontein	19 Jan. 1901	3rd Bn
7868	Pte	Jones, D.	Died of disease	Bloemfontein	20 Jan. 1901	3rd Bn
4687	Pte	Kammerer, L.	Died of disease	Cape Town	22 Jan. 1901	
9735	Pte	Green, A.	Died of disease	Brandfort	23 Jan. 1901	3rd Bn
6230	Pte	Green, T.	Died of disease	Johannesburg	4 Feb. 1901	
3501	Pte	Brown, S. S.	Severely wounded	Boshof	6 Feb. 1901	E Lan R Coy, 8th M.I. (detached)
6094	Pte	Dutton, A.	Died of disease	Bloemfontein	6 Feb. 1901	
9728	Pte	Giblin, P.	Died of disease	Bloemfontein	8 Feb. 1901	3rd Bn
5095	Pte	Mills, J.	Died of disease	Elandsfontein	14 Feb. 1901	
6099	LCpl	Tattersall, H.	Died of disease	Bloemfontein	17 Feb. 1901	
4476	Pte	Burton, J.	Severely wounded	Ventersburg Road	18 Feb. 1901	3rd Bn. Accident

No.	*Rank*	*Name*	*Casualty*	*Place*	*Date*	*Remarks*
694	CSgt	Wood, G	Died of enteric fever	Vet River	23 Feb. 1901	3rd Bn (Permanent Staff)
5593	Pte	McIvor, J.	Injured	Krugersdorp	10 March 1901	E Lan R Coy, 8th M.I. Accident
5717	Pte	Burns, A. J.	Died of disease	Bloemfontein	17 March 1901	
5799	Pte	Rowley, A.	Missing	Kaalkraal	18 March 1901	E Lan R Coy, 8th M.I., Court of Enquiry states 'dead'
7278	Pte	Biggins, P.	Died of disease	Bloemfontein	20 March 1901	3rd Bn
5693	Pte	Holland, J.	Died of disease	Elandsfontein	25 March 1901	
1687	Pte	Williams, H.	Severely wounded	Springs	2 April 1901	Accident
	2Lt	Wolseley, E. J.	Slightly wounded	Hartebeestfontein	18 April 1901	E Lan R Coy, 8th M.I.
2874	Pte	Gannon, J.	Killed	Cyferku, near Klerksdorp	22 April 1901	E Lan R Coy, 8th M.I.
4589	Pte	Levine, A.	Killed	Cyferku	22 April 1901	E Lan R Coy, 8th M.I.
5567	Pte	Wardley, R.	Severely wounded	Cyferku	22 April 1901	E Lan R Coy, 8th M.I. Died 24 April
5528	Pte	Brennan, M.	Severely wounded	Cyferku	22 April 1901	E Lan R Coy, 8th M.I.
1856	Cpl	Connery, S.	Severely wounded	Cyferku	22 April 1901	E Lan R Coy, 8th M.I.
2616	Pte	Cavanagh, A.	Severely wounded	TarantalKraal	20 May 1901	E Lan R Coy, 8th M.I.
6006	Pte	Murray, W. J.	Died of disease	Bloemfontein	5 June 1901	
4119	Pte	James, S.	Drowned	Boksburg	30 Aug. 1901	
4000	Pte	Davey, G.	Slightly wounded	Roodekop	5 Oct. 1901	E Lan R Sect, 1st M.I.
5885	Pte	Nuttall, F.	Slightly wounded	Roodekop	5 Oct. 1901	E Lan R Sect ,1st M.I.
3056	LCpl	Whelan, J.	Slightly wounded	Roodekop	5 Oct. 1901	E Lan R Sect, 1st M.I.
5929	Pte	Wilkin, J.	Slightly wounded	Roodekop	5 Oct. 1901	E Lan R Sect, 1st M.I.
3429	Pte	Gurkin, E.	Severely wounded	Greylingstad	13 Oct. 1901	E Lan R Coy, 8th M.I. Accident
5661	Pte	Padden, E.	Died of disease	Heilbron	14 Oct. 1901	
5530	Pte	Mitchell, W.	Died of disease	Elandsfontein	22 Oct. 1901	
5779	Pte	Hinchcliffe, G. W.	Severely wounded	Near Smaldeel	9 Nov. 1901	Accident
	2Lt	Tyndall-Staines, B. J.,	Died of disease	Heilbron	1 Dec. 1901	
	Maj	Pile, L. L.,	Died of disease	Heilbron	4 Dec. 1901	
4785	Pte	Dicks, F.	Slightly wounded	Near Frankfort	9 Dec. 1901	
3873	Pte	Marsden, J.	Slightly wounded	Near Frankfort	9 Dec. 1901	
5508	Pte	Sourbutts, R.	Dangerously wounded	Near Frankfort	9 Dec. 1901	
5682	Pte	Hudson, J.	Slightly wounded	Bethel	11 Dec. 1901	E Lan R Coy
5907	Pte	Ward, D.	Killed	Schaaprand	16 Dec. 1901	
2831	Pte	Grainger, W.	Dangerously wounded	Schaaprand	16 Dec. 1901	Died 21 Dec.
7388	Pte	Chew, J. W.	Died of disease	Heilbron	22 Dec. 1901	2nd Volunteer Coy
6020	Pte	Brown, S.	Died of disease	Bloemfontein	23 Dec. 1901	
2689	Pte	Shorrocks, S.W.	Died of disease	Norval's Point	7 Jan. 1902	
7416	Pte	Pooley, W.	Died of disease	Norval's Pont	9 Jan. 1902	2nd Volunteer Coy
6035	Pte	Caton, A.	Slightly wounded	Kafirstad	12 Jan. 1902	E Lan R Coy, 8th M.I.
5822	Pte	Taylor, J.	Died of disease	Ermelo	13 Jan. 1902	E Lan R Coy, 8th M.I.
5696	Pte	McGee, T.	Slightly wounded	Reitspruit	16 Jan. 1902	

No.	Rank	Name	Casualty	Place	Date	Remarks
3403	Cpl	Bailey, S.	Slightly wounded	Near Dundas Farm Post	24 Jan. 1902	Blockhouse attack
2846	Pte	Hannaway, J.	Slightly wounded	Near Dundas Farm Post	24 Jan. 1902	Blockhouse attack
5976	Pte	Hanson, R.	Severely wounded	Near Dundas Farm Post	24 Jan. 1902	Blockhouse attack
1450	Pte	King, T.	Slightly wounded	Near Dundas Farm Post	24 Jan. 1902	Blockhouse attack
6288	Pte	Morris, F.	Severely wounded	Near Dundas Farm Post	24 Jan. 1902	Blockhouse attack
6619	Pte	Dixon, B.	Died of disease	Norval's Pont	25 Jan. 1902	
	Lt	Parker, P. S.	Died of disease	Heilbron	1 Feb. 1902	2nd Volunteer Coy
6301	Pte	Saunders, J.	Died of disease	Wynberg	1 Feb. 1902	
1580	Pte	Hall, H.	Died of disease	Frankfort	8 Feb. 1902	
6426	Pte	Heatley, W.	Died of disease	Elandsfontein	14 Feb. 1902	
6325	Pte	Moorhead, W.	Died of disease	Heilbron	23 Feb. 1902	
4010	Pte	Pemberton, H.	Died of disease	Frankfort	1 March 1902	
	2Lt	Baines, L. O. T.	Died of disease	Heilbron	4 March 1902	
3131	Pte	Reeves, J.	Died of disease	Heilbron	12 March 1902	
7441	Pte	Pomfret, J. E.	Died of disease	Heilbron	14 March 1902	2nd Volunteer Coy
2106	Cpl	O'Reilly, A.	Missing	Klerksdorp	23 March 1902	E Lan R Coy, 8th M.I. Court of Enquiry states 'dead'
5946	Pte	Snowden, W.	Wounded	Near Bath	4 April 1902	E Lan R Sect, 1st M.I. Accident.
2839	Sgt	Smith, D.	Killed	Dundas Farm Post	8 April 1902	Accident
4965	Pte	Savage, R.	Died of disease	Elandsfontein	12 April 1902	E Lan R Coy, 8th M.I.
7395	Pte	Gray, W.	Died of disease	Heilbron	19 April 1902	2nd Volunteer Coy
2807	Pte	Ball, T.	Died of disease	Kroonstad	20 April 1902	
1446	Pte	Pickering, J.	Died of disease	Heilbron	12 May 1902	
1594	Pte	O'Neill, J.	Died of disease	Springfontein	24 May 1902	
3160	Pte	Caldwell, P.	Killed	Near Tafel Kop	29 May 1902	Accident

The South Lancashire Regiment (Prince of Wales's Volunteers)

No.	Rank	Name	Casualty	Place	Date	Remarks
4078	Pte	Cliffe, C.	Died of pneumonia	At Sea	12 Dec. 1899	
5758	Pte	Thompson, C.	Died disease	At Sea	22 Dec. 1899	
5666	Pte	Parker, T.	Died of disease	Estcourt	1 Jan. 1900	
583	Sgt	Brett, W.	Wounded	Three Tree Hill	20 Jan. 1900	Died of wounds 1 April 1900
3334	Pte	Brown, J.	Wounded	Three Tree Hill	20 Jan. 1900	
5561	Pte	Cooper, A.	Wounded	Three Tree Hill	20 Jan. 1900	
2841	Cpl	Johnston, A.	Wounded	Three Tree Hill	20 Jan. 1900	
2891	Pte	O'Neill, E.	Died	Frere	20 Jan. 1900	
3362	Pte	Dunmore, J.	Wounded	Three Tree Hill	23 Jan. 1900	
5238	Pte	Hayden, P.	Wounded	Three Tree Hill	23 Jan. 1900	
5732	Pte	Stevens, J.	Wounded	Three Tree Hill	23 Jan. 1900	

No.	*Rank*	*Name*	*Casualty*	*Place*	*Date*	*Remarks*
	Capt	Birch, C. G. F. G.	Killed	Spion Kop	24 Jan. 1900	
	Lt	Raphael, F. M.	Killed	Spion Kop	24 Jan. 1900	
2367	Sgt	Candy, J.	Died of wounds	Spion Kop	24 Jan. 1900	
3108	Sgt	Thomas, A.	Killed	Spion Kop	24 Jan. 1900	
4254	LCpl	Chinnery, J.	Killed	Spion Kop	24 Jan. 1900	
4658	LCpl	Smith, T.	Died of wounds	Spion Kop	24 Jan. 1900	
2749	Pte	Aldred, J.	Died of wounds	Spion Kop	24 Jan. 1900	Died 1 April 1900
1976	Pte	Brown, T.	Killed	Spion Kop	24 Jan. 1900	
4950	Pte	Dumbell, J.	Killed	Spion Kop	24 Jan. 1900	
5692	Pte	Ingman, E.	Killed	Spion Kop	24 Jan. 1900	
2957	Pte	Dolan, T.	Died of wounds	Spion Kop	24 Jan. 1900	Monument gives 'Nolan'
3631	Pte	Jones, E.	Died of wounds	Spion Kop	24 Jan. 1900	
5071	Cpl	Morgan, J.	Wounded	Spion Kop	24 Jan. 1900	
2499	Cpl	Norton, W.	Wounded	Spion Kop	24 Jan. 1900	
2840	LCpl	Callaghan, D.	Wounded	Spion Kop	24 Jan. 1900	
5049	LCpl	Nolan, T.	Wounded	Spion Kop	24 Jan. 1900	
3523	Pte	Banks, J.	Wounded	Spion Kop	24 Jan. 1900	
3142	Pte	Britton, A.	Wounded	Spion Kop	24 Jan. 1900	
2956	Pte	Chorley, C.	Wounded	Spion Kop	24 Jan. 1900	
2986	Pte	Dyer, E.	Wounded	Spion Kop	24 Jan. 1900	
3497	Pte	Gornell, J.	Wounded	Spion Kop	24 Jan. 1900	
3093	Pte	Hall, N.	Wounded	Spion Kop	24 Jan. 1900	
3435	Pte	Hughes, T.	Wounded	Spion Kop	24 Jan. 1900	
5108	Pte	Johnson, G.	Wounded	Spion Kop	24 Jan. 1900	
3360	Pte	Manning, N.	Wounded	Spion Kop	24 Jan. 1900	
3494	Pte	Metcalf, J.	Wounded	Spion Kop	24 Jan. 1900	
2919	Pte	O'Donnell, T.	Wounded	Spion Kop	24 Jan. 1900	
3530	Pte	Speake, J.	Wounded	Spion Kop	24 Jan. 1900	
3530	Pte	Thomas, C.	Wounded	Spion Kop	24 Jan. 1900	
2765	Pte	Tomlinson, J.	Wounded	Spion Kop	24 Jan. 1900	
3003	Pte	Weedall, J.	Wounded	Spion Kop	24 Jan. 1900	
3385	Pte	Campbell, J.	Wounded	Potgieters Drift	5 Feb. 1900	Battle of Vaal Krantz
5390	Pte	Goodier, J.	Wounded	Potgieters Drift	5 Feb. 1900	
3220	Pte	Lawson, T.	Wounded	Potgieters Drift	5 Feb. 1900	
1026	Cpl	Lapping, J.	Died of disease	Pietermaritzburg	8 Feb. 1900	
2718	Pte	Brown, R.	Died of wounds	Colenso Koppies (Hill 244)	21 Feb. 1900	Note: most of the following probably wounded 22–23 Feb. at Wynne's Hill
5643	Pte	Beech, J.	Wounded	Colenso Koppies	21 Feb. 1900	
2698	Pte	Brown, E.	Wounded	Colenso Koppies	21 Feb. 1900	
2955	Pte	Chester, E.	Wounded	Colenso Koppies	21 Feb. 1900	
4343	Pte	Cocklin, J.	Wounded	Colenso Koppies	21 Feb. 1900	
5073	Pte	Crawford, C.	Wounded	Colenso Koppies	21 Feb. 1900	
1894	Pte	Dee, G.	Wounded	Colenso Koppies	21 Feb. 1900	
2890	Pte	Duggan, J.	Wounded	Colenso Koppies	21 Feb. 1900	
3326	LCpl	Duggan, D.	Wounded	Colenso Koppies	21 Feb. 1900	
4529	Dmr	Fuller, H.	Wounded	Colenso Koppies	21 Feb. 1900	
3596	Pte	Hannah, J.	Wounded	Colenso Koppies	21 Feb. 1900	

No.	*Rank*	*Name*	*Casualty*	*Place*	*Date*	*Remarks*
5500	Pte	Hardyman, P.	Wounded	Colenso Koppies	21 Feb. 1900	
3441	Pte	Hayto, W.	Wounded	Colenso Koppies	21 Feb. 1900	
5778	Pte	Hesketh, F.	Wounded	Colenso Koppies	21 Feb. 1900	
3667	Pte	Hewitt, J.	Wounded	Colenso Koppies	21 Feb. 1900	
2628	Pte	Hoolin, P.	Wounded	Colenso Koppies	21 Feb. 1900	
2870	Pte	Hulme, J.	Wounded	Colenso Koppies	21 Feb. 1900	
5785	Pte	Jones, J.	Wounded	Colenso Koppies	21 Feb. 1900	
5717	Pte	Lavin, B.	Wounded	Colenso Koppies	21 Feb. 1900	
4595	Pte	Lavin, G.	Wounded	Colenso Koppies	21 Feb. 1900	
3689	Pte	Leclerq, A.	Wounded	Colenso Koppies	21 Feb. 1900	
5088	Pte	Martin, F.	Wounded	Colenso Koppies	21 Feb. 1900	
2348	Pte	McCombe, J.	Wounded	Colenso Koppies	21 Feb. 1900	
3713	Pte	McCormack, D.	Wounded	Colenso Koppies	21 Feb. 1900	
2464	Pte	McDowell, E.	Wounded	Colenso Koppies	21 Feb. 1900	
3240	Pte	Mellor, W.	Wounded	Colenso Koppies	21 Feb. 1900	
4185	Pte	Moore, T.	Wounded	Colenso Koppies	21 Feb. 1900	
2153	Pte	Pickering, C.	Wounded	Colenso Koppies	21 Feb. 1900	
3175	Pte	Pollard, J.	Wounded	Colenso Koppies	21 Feb. 1900	
5496	Pte	Purcel, J.	Wounded	Colenso Koppies	21 Feb. 1900	
3436	Pte	Radford, J.	Wounded	Colenso Koppies	21 Feb. 1900	
2888	Pte	Read, J.	Wounded	Colenso Koppies	21 Feb. 1900	
2931	Pte	Salmon, W.	Wounded	Colenso Koppies	21 Feb. 1900	
4103	Pte	Smith, T.	Wounded	Colenso Koppies	21 Feb. 1900	
2789	Pte	Suett, A.	Wounded	Colenso Koppies	21 Feb. 1900	
3420	Pte	Thomas, W.	Wounded	Colenso Koppies	21 Feb. 1900	
2569	Pte	Wilcockson, J.	Wounded	Colenso Koppies	21 Feb. 1900	
1821	Sgt	Orr, T.	Killed	Wynne's Hill	22 Feb. 1900	
4558	LSgt	Monks, H.	Killed	Wynne's Hill	22 Feb. 1900	
2592	Pte	Farnen, T.	Killed	Wynne's Hill	22 Feb. 1900	
5973	Pte	Heywood, L.	Killed	Wynne's Hill	22 Feb. 1900	
2391	Pte	Johnson, E.	Killed	Wynne's Hill	22 Feb. 1900	
3353	Pte	Walmsley, H.	Killed	Wynne's Hill	22 Feb. 1900	
	Lt	Kane, H. R.	Wounded	Wynne's Hill	22 Feb. 1900	
5264	Pte	Kelly, J.	Wounded	Wynne's Hill	22 Feb. 1900	
5573	Pte	Magee, J.	Wounded	Wynne's Hill	22 Feb. 1900	
5094	Pte	Waters, J.	Wounded	Wynne's Hill	22 Feb. 1900	
	Maj	Hall, R. H.	Slightly wounded	Wynne's Hill	23 Feb. 1900	
	Capt	Goren, B. R.	Wounded	Wynne's Hill	23 Feb. 1900	
	Capt	Upperton, S.	Wounded	Wynne's Hill	23 Feb. 1900	
	2Lt	Marsh, C. H.	Wounded	Wynne's Hill	23 Feb. 1900	
3531	Pte	Gillen, W.	Died of wounds	Wynne's Hill	23 Feb. 1900	
2632	Pte	Shears, C.	Wounded	Wynne's Hill	23 Feb. 1900	
2461	Cpl	Worrall, T.	Died of wounds	Colenso Koppies	24 Feb. 1900	
3317	Pte	Davies, J.	Wounded	Colenso Koppies	24 Feb. 1900	
3508	Pte	Pennington, R.	Died of wounds	Natal	27 Feb. 1900	Possibly wounded Wynne's Hill
	Lt Col	MacCarthy O'Leary, W.	Killed	Pieters Hill	27 Feb. 1900	
2502	Sgt	Wheatley, W.	Killed	Pieters Hill	27 Feb. 1900	
3533	Pte	Jones, S.	Killed	Pieters Hill	27 Feb. 1900	
3430	Pte	Jones, W.	Killed	Pieters Hill	27 Feb. 1900	

No.	*Rank*	*Name*	*Casualty*	*Place*	*Date*	*Remarks*
2633	Pte	Ryan, J.	Killed	Pieters Hill	27 Feb. 1900	
2824	Pte	Smith, A.	Killed	Pieters Hill	27 Feb. 1900	
3486	Pte	Divine, P.	Died of wounds	Pieters Hill	27 Feb. 1900	Died of wounds 28 Feb. 1900
3064	Pte	Warren, H.	Died of wounds	Pieters Hill	27 Feb. 1900	
2843	Cpl	Connolly, D.	Wounded	Pieters Hill	27 Feb. 1900	Died of wounds 9 March 1900
	Maj	Lamb, T.	Wounded	Pieters Hill	27 Feb. 1900	Lost eye
5466	LCpl	Darn, J.	Wounded (since dead)	Pieters Hill	27 Feb. 1900	
3598	Sgt	Welsh, G.	Wounded	Pieters Hill	27 Feb. 1900	
3501	Cpl	Carter, C.	Wounded	Pieters Hill	27 Feb. 1900	
2751	Cpl	Upton, T.	Wounded	Pieters Hill	27 Feb. 1900	
2555	LCpl	Jones, W	Wounded	Pieters Hill	27 Feb. 1900	
5112	Dmr	Handley, G.	Wounded	Pieters Hill	27 Feb. 1900	
5407	Pte	Bolen, J.	Wounded	Pieters Hill	27 Feb. 1900	
2544	Pte	Bowling, T.	Wounded	Pieters Hill	27 Feb. 1900	
2494	Pte	Brighouse, R.	Wounded	Pieters Hill	27 Feb. 1900	
2471	Pte	Concar, M	Wounded	Pieters Hill	27 Feb. 1900	
5253	Pte	Cowan, J.	Wounded	Pieters Hill	27 Feb. 1900	
3469	Pte	Cowan, O.	Wounded	Pieters Hill	27 Feb. 1900	
2784	Pte	Dominey, G.	Wounded	Pieters Hill	27 Feb. 1900	
2687	Pte	Draper, W.	Wounded	Pieters Hill	27 Feb. 1900	
2625	Pte	Edmonds, P.	Wounded	Pieters Hill	27 Feb. 1900	
5405	Pte	Finnan, J.	Wounded	Pieters Hill	27 Feb. 1900	
3370	Pte	Ford, W. A.	Wounded	Pieters Hill	27 Feb. 1900	
3563	Pte	Hamilton, A.	Wounded	Pieters Hill	27 Feb. 1900	
3335	Pte	Horton, J.	Wounded	Pieters Hill	27 Feb. 1900	
3162	Pte	Imrie, J.	Wounded	Pieters Hill	27 Feb. 1900	
2869	Pte	Jones, J.	Wounded	Pieters Hill	27 Feb. 1900	
4972	Pte	Jones, R.	Wounded	Pieters Hill	27 Feb. 1900	
2561	Pte	McDonald, J.	Wounded	Pieters Hill	27 Feb. 1900	
3625	Pte	McLelland, J.	Wounded	Pieters Hill	27 Feb. 1900	
3062	Pte	Powell, D.	Wounded	Pieters Hill	27 Feb. 1900	
2729	Pte	Purcell, S.	Wounded	Pieters Hill	27 Feb. 1900	
2826	Pte	Ralphson, C.	Wounded	Pieters Hill	27 Feb. 1900	
2861	Pte	Rankin, J.	Wounded	Pieters Hill	27 Feb. 1900	
2416	Pte	Richmond, J.	Wounded	Pieters Hill	27 Feb. 1900	
5685	Pte	Vause, J.	Wounded	Pieters Hill	27 Feb. 1900	
5351	Pte	White, P.	Wounded	Pieters Hill	27 Feb. 1900	
1971	Pte	Jones, R.	Died of enteric fever	Mooi River	3 March 1900	
3345	Pte	Robertson, C.	Died of wounds	Natal	4 March 1900	
4664	Pte	Gredart, C.	Died of dysentery	Pietermaritzburg	8 March 1900	
3233	Pte	Cheetham, G.	Died of wounds	Natal	9 March 1900	Wounded 'Colenso Koppies'
5756	Pte	Rylands, J.	Died of wounds	Natal	11 March 1900	
5767	Pte	Canning, A.	Died of pneumonia	At sea	12 March 1900	*S.S. Tantallon Castle*
5715	Pte	Birkenhead, H.	Died of enteric fever	Pietermaritzburg	13 March 1900	

No.	*Rank*	*Name*	*Casualty*	*Place*	*Date*	*Remarks*
340	Pte	Travers, G.	Died of disease	Naauwpoort	19 March 1900	3rd Bn. 'Travis' in Regt Records
4121	Pte	Braid, G.	Died of disease	Pietermaritzburg	21 March 1900	
986	Pte	Wood, W.	Died of disease	Naauwpoort	23 March 1900	3rd Bn
3651	Pte	Neilson, J.	Died of sunstroke	Pietermaritzburg	23 March 1900	
5624	Pte	Webster, T.	Died of enteric fever	Pietermaritzburg	25 March 1900	
3239	Sgt	Gray, G.	Died of enteric fever	Pietermaritzburg	26 March 1900	4146 Pte
5312	Pte	Leslie, J.	Died of enteric fever	Pietermaritzburg	26 March 1900	
3151	Pte	Hogan, P.	Died of enteric fever	Pietermaritzburg	26 March 1900	
4425	Pte	Garlick, A.	Died of enteric fever	Pietermaritzburg	27 March 1900	
3619	Pte	Keane, P.	Died of enteric fever	Pietermaritzburg	29 March 1900	
4876	Pte	Harding, C.	Died of enteric fever	Pietermaritzburg	1 April 1900	
3103	LCpl	Appleton, J.	Died of Wounds	Natal	1 April 1900	Late notifications from one of the Tugela battles
2339	Pte	Foy, J.	Died of Wounds	Natal	1 April 1900	
3470	Pte	Keeley, F. R.	Died of Wounds	Natal	1 April 1900	
5597	Pte	Jones, G.	Died of Wounds	Natal	1 April 1900	
6057	Pte	Mahon, M.	Died of disease	Naauwpoort	1 April 1900	3rd Bn
7034	Pte	Blackwood, W.	Died of pneumonia	Durban	2 April 1900	1st Volunteer Coy
6710	Pte	Follett, A.	Died of disease	Rondebosch	3 April 1900	3rd Bn
2298	Pte	Murther, G.	Died of disease	Naauwpoort	5 April 1900	3rd Bn
6584	Pte	Schofield, A.	Died of disease	Naauwpoort	6 April 1900	3rd Bn
1764	Pte	Mallinson, G.	Died of disease	Naauwpoort	8 April 1900	3rd Bn
5704	Pte	Jeffries, J.	Died of enteric fever	Middelburg	9 April 1900	
7022	LCpl	Fishwick, J.	Died of enteric fever	Ladysmith	18 April 1900	1st Volunteer Coy
5679	Pte	Knowles, S.	Died of disease	Naauwpoort	22 April 1900	3rd Bn
5318	Pte	Dewhurst, G.	Died of disease	Chieveley	23 April 1900	
2401	Pte	Bramwell, J.	Died of dysentery	Pietermaritzburg	27 April 1900	
3396	Pte	Jennings, T.	Died of enteric fever	Pietermaritzburg	27 April 1900	
4502	Pte	Dolan, J.	Died of disease	Wynberg	27 April 1900	3rd Bn
5454	Pte	Stubbs, R.	Died of enteric fever	Pietermaritzburg	30 April 1900	
2781	Pte	Flynn, D.	Died of disease	Naauwpoort	8 May 1900	3rd Bn
2451	Pte	McDonald, J.	Died of tuberculosis	At Sea	15 May 1900	
6712	Pte	Hilton, J.	Died of disease	Naauwpoort	15 May 1900	3rd Bn
4092	Pte	Farquhar, W.	Died of enteric fever	Mooi River	16 May 1900	
5311	LCpl	Dodd, F.	Died of disease	Naauwpoort	18 May 1900	3rd Bn

No.	*Rank*	*Name*	*Casualty*	*Place*	*Date*	*Remarks*
4507	Pte	Reynolds, J.	Died of enteric fever	Estcourt	24 May 1900	
6288	Pte	Waterworth, A.	Died of disease	Naauwpoort	24 May 1900	3rd Bn
1018	Pte	Harvey, E.	Died of disease	Cape Town	25 May 1900	3rd Bn
2214	Pte	Brown, J.	Died of disease	Deelfontein	26 May 1900	3rd Bn
5979	Cpl	Murphy, T.	Died of disease	Naauwpoort	28 May 1900	3rd Bn
2443	Pte	Casson, J.	Died of disease	Naauwpoort	30 May 1900	1st Bn
3414	Pte	Traynor, E.	Died of enteric fever	Estcourt	30 May 1900	
3596	Pte	Rigby, J.	Died of disease	Naauwpoort	31 May 1900	3rd Bn
6468	Pte	Lester, R.	Died of disease	Naauwpoort	1 June 1900	3rd Bn
5772	Pte	Elliott, A.	Died of disease	Naauwpoort	2 June 1900	3rd Bn
7067	Pte	Sudlow, T. G.	Died of enteric fever	Pietermaritzburg	3 June 1900	1st Volunteer Coy
4770	Pte	Egan, T.	Died of disease	Naauwpoort	5 June 1900	3rd Bn
6637	Pte	Prior, T.	Injured by train	Near Rensburg	5 June 1900	3rd Bn
6286	Pte	Tucker, A.	Injured by train	Near Rensburg	5 June 1900	3rd Bn
4371	Pte	Naughton, T	Died of disease	Naauwpoort	6 June 1900	3rd Bn
5621	Pte	Duffy, J.	Killed	Botha's Pass	8 June 1900	
5043	Dmr	Hackett, F.	Died of enteric fever	Estcourt	8 June 1900	
2005	Pte	Matthews, J.	Died of disease	Green Point	19 June 1900	3rd Bn
4670	Pte	Sparks, T.	Died of disease	Naauwpoort	22 June 1900	3rd Bn
3729	Pte	Spencer	Slightly wounded	Honingspruit	22 June 1900	3rd Bn
5590	Pte	Sweeney	Slightly wounded	Honingspruit	22 June 1900	3rd Bn
5075	Pte	Smith, J.	Died of enteric fever	Ladysmith	24 June 1900	
4260	Pte	McGaragle, J.	Died of dysentery	Newcastle	28 June 1900	
2498	Cpl	Neilson, W.	Died of enteric fever	Ladysmith	6 July 1900	
2446	Pte	Fowler, J.	Died of disease	Springfontein	11 July 1900	3rd Bn
3406	Pte	Lynch, J.	Died of enteric fever	Newcastle	17 July 1900	
5897	Pte	Reilly, J.	Died of enteric fever	Ladysmith	24 July 1900	
3150	Pte	Pink, F.	Slightly wounded	Near Babanango	10 Aug. 1900	
7118	Pte	Woods, F.	Died of enteric fever	Howick	15 Sept. 1900	1st Volunteer Coy
5917	Pte	Towers, A.	Died of pneumonia	Springfontein	6 Oct. 1900	1st Bn, attached 3rd Bn
	Lt	Hanbury, E. M.	Killed	Gryskop	13 Oct. 1900	3rd Bn M.I.
5343	Pte	Cantello, T.	Killed	Bankies	13 Oct. 1900	3rd Bn M.I.
6826	Pte	Morrison, J.	Wounded	Jagersfontein Rd	13 Oct. 1900	3rd Bn
4111	Sgt	Chapman, F.	Mortally wounded	Springfontein	26 Oct. 1900	1st Bn, attached 3rd Bn. Died of wounds 12 Nov.
	Capt	Lynch, N. M.	Died of disease	Mooi River	13 Nov. 1900	
4989	Cpl	Harrison, G.	Wounded in leg	Springfontein	21 Nov. 1900	3rd Bn
3871	Pte	Erlam, W.	Slightly wounded	Springfontein	21 Nov. 1900	3rd Bn
6870	Sgt	Richardson, J. J.	Wounded	Springfontein	24 Nov. 1900	3rd Bn
5757	Pte	Hughes, J.	Died of disease	Mooi River	13 Nov. 1900	

No.	Rank	Name	Casualty	Place	Date	Remarks
5366	Pte	Heron, T.	Died of disease	Mooi River	5 Dec. 1900	
5000	Pte	Forber, R.	Died of disease	Springfontein	3 Jan. 1901	3rd Bn
5807	Pte	Siggins, T.	Died of disease	Mooi River	9 Jan. 1901	
5942	Pte	Heaton, J.	Died of disease	Springfontein	12 Jan. 1901	1st Bn, attached 3rd Bn
5208	LCpl	Westwood, J.	Severely wounded	Near Gegund	29 Jan. 1901	Possibly M.I.
2847	Pte	Connor, W.	Died of disease	Mooi River	31 Jan. 1901	
4096	Pte	Monaghan, P.	Died of disease	Springfontein	9 Feb. 1901	3rd Bn
3863	Pte	Wood, C. G.	Killed	Marienthal	18 Feb. 1901	Accident
5872	Pte	Forber, W.	Died of disease	Springfontein	24 Feb. 1901	1st Bn, attached 3rd Bn
5802	LCpl	Barnfather, J.	Died of disease	Springfontein	24 Feb. 1901	1st Bn, attached 3rd Bn
5528	Pte	Rayson, A. W.	Died of disease	Norval's Pont	2 March 1901	3rd Bn
	Lt	Ewart, G. D. H.	Severely injured	Vryheid	6 April 1901	Accident
6425	Pte	Jones, J.	Died of sunstroke	Jagersfontein Rd	23 April 1901	3rd Bn
2991	Pte	McCabe, J.	Died of disease	Green Point	25 April 1901	3rd Bn
3658	Pte	Cassidy, H.	Died of disease	Norval's Pont	26 April 1901	3rd Bn
3437	Pte	McClear, J.	Slightly wounded	Near Driefontein	1 May 1901	M.I.
3678	Pte	Philbin, R.	Severely wounded	Near Driefontein	1 May 1901	M.I.
7171	Pte	Richardson, B.	Died of dysentery	Heidelberg	7 May 1901	3rd Volunteer Coy
	Maj	Heath, E. K.	Killed	America Siding	17 May 1901	3rd Bn (OC No. 6 Armoured train)
3366	Pte	Wardle, E.	Died of disease	Vryheid	17 May 1901	
1109	Sgt	Penwill, G.	Died of disease	Vryheid	19 May 1901	
5153	Pte	Green, S.	Dangerously wounded	Nr Jagersfontein Rd	24 May 1901	3rd Bn
5418	Pte	Dolan, T.	Severely wounded	Graskop	15 June 1901	M.I.
2947	Pte	Torney, J.	Died of disease	Vryheid	30 June 1901	
5863	Pte	McBride, W.	Died of disease	Vant's Drift	12 July 1901	
5837	Pte	Cantrell, A.	Died of disease	Dundee	11 Aug. 1901	5th M.I.
4221	Pte	Irwin, D.	Died of disease	Pietermaritzburg	15 Aug. 1901	
5144	Pte	Jones, T.	Died of disease	Vryheid	11 Sept. 1901	
5297	Pte	Armstrong, H.	Slightly wounded	Blood River Poort	17 Sept. 1901	Gough's M.I.
5774	Pte	Gallimore, T.	Slightly wounded	Blood River Poort	17 Sept. 1901	Gough's M.I.
5340	Pte	McLoughlin, W.	Dangerously wounded	Blood River Poort	17 Sept. 1901	Gough's M.I.
	Lt	Kane, H. R.	Killed	Itala	26 Sept. 1901	5th M.I.
5073	Pte	Crawford, L.	Killed	Itala	26 Sept. 1901	5th M.I.
3370	Pte	Ford, W.	Killed	Itala	26 Sept. 1901	5th M.I.
3299	Pte	Goulding, R	Killed	Itala	26 Sept. 1901	5th M.I.
3269	Pte	Jones, M	Killed	Itala	26 Sept. 1901	5th M.I.
5798	Pte	Keating, R.	Killed	Itala	26 Sept. 1901	5th M.I.
5544	Pte	Pennington, E.	Killed	Itala	26 Sept. 1901	5th M.I.
5654	Pte	Walker, J.	Killed	Itala	26 Sept. 1901	5th M.I.
3257	Pte	Jackson, J.	Dangerously wounded	Itala	26 Sept. 1901	5th M.I. Died 27 Oct.
3354	Pte	Bentham, E.	Dangerously wounded	Itala	26 Sept. 1901	5th M.I.
3680	Pte	Bradbury, F.	Severely wounded	Itala	26 Sept. 1901	5th M.I.
3107	Pte	Clarke, F.	Severely wounded	Itala	26 Sept. 1901	5th M.I.
5537	Pte	Fallon, J.	Severely wounded	Itala	26 Sept. 1901	5th M.I.
3972	CSgt	Duffy, M. L.	Slightly wounded	Itala	26 Sept. 1901	5th M.I.
3193	Cpl	Wintersgill, G.	Slightly wounded	Itala	26 Sept. 1901	5th M.I.

No.	Rank	Name	Casualty	Place	Date	Remarks
3310	Pte	Hughes, W.	Slightly wounded	Itala	26 Sept. 1901	5th M.I.
3193	Pte	Levy, J.	Slightly wounded	Itala	26 Sept. 1901	5th M.I.
4167	Pte	Duckworth, G.	Killed	Fort Prospect	26 Sept. 1901	
4738	Dmr	Lambert, T.	Died of disease	Vryheid	2 Oct. 1901	
5528	Pte	Hesketh, J.	Wounded	Vryheid	25 Oct. 1901	Accident
3338	Pte	Canning, J.	Killed by lightning	Vryheid	10 Nov. 1901	Signals
5264	LCpl	Kelly, J.	Injured by lightning	Vryheid	10 Nov. 1901	Signals
3346	Pte	Buckley, T.	Injured by lightning	Vryheid	10 Nov. 1901	Signals
3335	Pte	Horton, J.	Injured by lightning	Vryheid	10 Nov. 1901	Signals
3537	Pte	Hughes, P.	Injured by lightning	Vryheid	10 Nov. 1901	Signals
3887	Pte	Kennedy, R.	Injured by lightning	Vryheid	10 Nov. 1901	Signals
3080	Pte	Maypother, E.	Injured by lightning	Vryheid	10 Nov. 1901	Signals
1723	Pte	Patience, D.	Injured by lightning	Vryheid	10 Nov. 1901	Signals
4133	Pte	Roach, J.	Injured by lightning	Vryheid	10 Nov. 1901	Signals
3043	Pte	Fearnley, G.	Wounded	Vryheid	12 Nov. 1901	Accident
5422	Pte	Turton, T.	Dangerously wounded	Standerton Kop	14 Nov. 1901	24th M.I.
5503	LSgt	Heppenstall, H.	Died of disease	Vryheid	23 Nov. 1901	
4792	LSgt	Bridge, S.	Died of disease	Mooi River	28 Nov. 1901	
5895	Cpl	Bethell, J.	Slightly wounded	Near Rooikop	19 Dec. 1901	
5935	Pte	Horrocks, J.	Wounded	Vryheid	19 Dec. 1901	Accident
1698	QM Sgt	Barrow, C	Died of disease	Vryheid	2 Jan. 1902	
2280	LSgt	Kinrade, T.	Died of wounds	Pietermaritzburg	7 Jan. 1902	Self-inflicted
4879	Pte	Birkett, H.	Died of disease	Standerton	9 Jan. 1902	M.I.
5694	Pte	Hale, J.	Died of disease	Charlestown	18 Jan. 1902	M.I.
6072	Pte	Pritchard, C.	Slightly wounded	Vryheid	23 Jan. 1902	Accident
2875	LSgt	Hesketh, J.	Died of disease	Dundee	21 May 1902	
5656	Pte	Johnson, J.	Died of disease	Vryheid	21 May 1902	M.I.
3457	Sgt	Threlfall, J.	Died of wounds	Pietermaritzburg	23 May 1902	Self-inflicted

The Loyal North Lancashire Regiment

No.	Rank	Name	Casualty	Place	Date	Remarks
4075	Pte	Brandon, F.	Died	Orange River	16 Oct. 1899	Bathing accident 13 Oct.
	2Lt	Fletcher, W. J. C.	Died of sunstroke	Kimberley	18 Oct. 1899	
	Lt	Lowndes, J. G.	Wounded	Dronfield	24 Oct. 1899	Kimberley sortie
	Lt	Bingham, C. H. M.	Wounded	Dronfield	24 Oct. 1899	
3983	Pte	Lee, H.	Wounded	Dronfield	24 Oct. 1899	

No.	*Rank*	*Name*	*Casualty*	*Place*	*Date*	*Remarks*
4188	Pte	Milner, A.	Wounded	Dronfield	24 Oct. 1899	
	Lt	Wood, C. C.	Died of wounds	Near Belmont	10 Nov. 1899	M.I. Coy
5377	Pte	Beaton, J.	Wounded	Near Belmont	10 Nov. 1899	M.I. Coy
5070	Pte	Thompson, J.	Wounded	Near Belmont	10 Nov. 1899	M.I. Coy
5317	LCpl	Hall, J.	Killed	Graspan	25 Nov. 1899	M.I. Coy
5093	Pte	Cole, J. H.	Killed	Graspan	25 Nov. 1899	M.I. Coy
4679	Pte	Keeley, A.	Killed	Graspan	25 Nov. 1899	
5074	Pte	Owens, T.	Died of Wounds	Graspan	25 Nov. 1899	Died Wynburg, 28 Dec. 1899
4850	LCpl	Foulser, G.	Wounded	Graspan	25 Nov. 1899	
3568	LCpl	Yould, A.	Wounded	Graspan	25 Nov. 1899	
3857	Pte	Askew, W.	Wounded	Graspan	25 Nov. 1899	
4997	Pte	Burden, F.	Wounded	Graspan	25 Nov. 1899	
3583	Pte	Counsell, T.	Wounded	Graspan	25 Nov. 1899	
4792	Pte	Courtney, H.	Wounded	Graspan	25 Nov. 1899	
4576	Pte	Dodd, A.	Wounded	Graspan	25 Nov. 1899	
4460	Pte	Ellison, H.	Wounded	Graspan	25 Nov. 1899	M.I. Coy
4523	Pte	Ellis, E.	Wounded	Graspan	25 Nov. 1899	
3963	Pte	Foy, J. T.	Wounded	Graspan	25 Nov. 1899	
4337	Pte	Rigby, J.	Wounded	Graspan	25 Nov. 1899	
3707	Pte	Riley, T.	Wounded	Graspan	25 Nov. 1899	
5181	Pte	Rogers, G.	Wounded	Graspan	25 Nov. 1899	
3949	Pte	Speight, G.	Wounded	Graspan	25 Nov. 1899	
4514	Pte	Thompson, A.	Wounded	Graspan	25 Nov. 1899	
3964	Pte	Wilkinson, S.	Wounded	Graspan	25 Nov. 1899	
4247	Pte	Wilson, J.	Wounded	Graspan	25 Nov. 1899	
4525	Pte	Walcroft, J.	Wounded	Kimberley	25 Nov. 1899	1st Carter's Ridge sortie
965	Sgt	Richardson, F.	Killed	Modder River	28 Nov. 1899	
4486	Sgt	Wilson, F.	Killed	Modder River	28 Nov. 1899	
4316	Pte	Bell, H.	Killed	Modder River	28 Nov. 1899	
5486	Pte	Colbourne, J.	Died of wounds	Modder River	28 Nov. 1899	Died 29 Nov. 1900
5470	Pte	Johnson, J.	Died of wounds	Modder River	28 Nov. 1899	Died Wynberg, 10 Jan. 1900
	Lt	Flint, R. B.	Wounded	Modder River	28 Nov. 1899	
4558	Cpl	Throup, S.	Wounded	Modder River	28 Nov. 1899	
3930	LCpl	Bradley, W.	Wounded	Modder River	28 Nov. 1899	
5204	LCpl	Smith, E.	Wounded	Modder River	28 Nov. 1899	
4151	Pte	Burton, T.	Wounded	Modder River	28 Nov. 1899	M.I. Coy
4484	Pte	Campbell, J. W.	Wounded	Modder River	28 Nov. 1899	
4975	Pte	Degnan, O.	Wounded	Modder River	28 Nov. 1899	
5069	Pte	Gregory, G.	Wounded	Modder River	28 Nov. 1899	
4240	Pte	Harris, J.	Wounded	Modder River	28 Nov. 1899	
4070	Pte	Houghton, G.	Wounded	Modder River	28 Nov. 1899	
5050	Pte	Howell, W.	Wounded	Modder River	28 Nov. 1899	
4953	Pte	Newey, W.	Wounded	Modder River	28 Nov. 1899	
5336	Pte	Preston, J.	Wounded	Modder River	28 Nov. 1899	
4111	Pte	Shakes, G.	Wounded	Modder River	28 Nov. 1899	
5047	Pte	Witterick, R.	Wounded	Modder River	28 Nov. 1899	M.I. Coy
2393	CSgt	Heald, A.	Killed	Kimberley	28 Nov. 1899	2nd Carter's Ridge sortie

No.	*Rank*	*Name*	*Casualty*	*Place*	*Date*	*Remarks*
3746	Pte	Lutner, T.	Killed	Kimberley	28 Nov. 1899	
	Lt	Clifford, W. R.	Slightly wounded	Kimberley	28 Nov. 1899	M.I. Coy. Awarded DSO.
4045	Pte	Cooper, A. J.	Slightly wounded	Kimberley	28 Nov. 1899	M.I. Coy
4046	Pte	Edkins, G.	Seriously wounded	Kimberley	28 Nov. 1899	
4857	Pte	Kenton, J.	Seriously wounded	Kimberley	28 Nov. 1899	Regt Record states 24 Nov.
3983	Pte	Lee, H.	Slightly wounded	Kimberley	28 Nov. 1899	
4649	Pte	Neville, J.	Slightly wounded	Kimberley	28 Nov. 1899	M.I. Coy
4261	Pte	Tyldesley, T.	Seriously wounded	Kimberley	28 Nov. 1899	
4494	Pte	White, A.	Wounded	Magersfontein	11 Dec. 1899	M.I. Coy
3965	Pte	Chambers, S.	Killed	Kimberley	3 Jan. 1900	Accident
4769	Pte	Anderson, J. M.	Died of disease	Kimberley	4 Jan. 1900	M.I. Coy
5320	Pte	Lynn, H.	Died of disease	Kimberley	4 Jan. 1900	
3786	Cpl	Scott, E. G.	Died of disease	Orange River	7 Jan. 1900	
5107	LCpl	Wild, F.	Died of disease	Kimberley	15 Jan. 1900	
5048	Pte	Platt, G.	Died of disease	Orange River	19 Jan. 1900	
5112	Pte	Almond, J.	Died of disease	Orange River	26 Jan. 1900	M.I. Coy
4562	Pte	South, A.	Died of disease	Orange River	27 Jan. 1900	
4576	Pte	Dodd, A.	Died of disease	Orange River	29 Jan. 1900	
4361	Pte	Henry, C.	Died of disease	Orange River	9 Feb. 1900	
5361	Pte	Chantler, H.	Died of disease	Orange River	9 Feb. 1900	
4271	Pte	Blacow, J.	Died of disease	Orange River	10 Feb. 1900	
3356	Pte	Stanley, R.	Died of disease	Wynberg	10 Feb. 1900	
5174	Pte	Jones, T.	Wounded	Kimberley	11 Feb. 1900	Hit by 'Long Tom'
5234	Pte	Hall, S.	Died of disease	Kimberley	11 Feb. 1900	
3868	Pte	Nixon, G.	Died of disease	Modder River	12 Feb. 1900	
3752	Pte	McDermott, A.	Wounded	Kimberley	13 Feb. 1900	
5030	Pte	Graham, M.	Died of disease	Orange River	15 Feb. 1900	
5309	Pte	Haley, T.	Wounded	Kimberley	16 Feb. 1900	Sortie following Relief
2814	Sgt	Hellard, H.	Wounded	Kimberley	16 Feb. 1900	
4192	Pte	Ingram, H.	Wounded	Kimberley	16 Feb. 1900	
3984	Pte	Kirby, A	Wounded	Kimberley	16 Feb. 1900	
5485	Pte	Cooper, H.	Died of disease	Orange River	21 Feb. 1900	
3716	Pte	Charnock, J.	Died of disease	Kimberley	23 Feb. 1900	
3776	Pte	Wilcock, K.	Died of disease	Orange River	2 March 1900	
3744	Pte	Garvey, A.	Died	-	3 March 1900	Medal roll
4612	Pte	Beard, E.	Died of disease	Cape Town	4 March 1900	M.I. Coy
4680	Pte	Ellis, G.	Died of disease	Rondebosch	8 March 1900	
4004	LSgt	Morley, J.	Died of disease	De Aar	14 March 1900	
4817	Pte	Moore, P.	Died of disease	Orange River	19 March 1900	M.I. Coy
4322	Pte	Hughes, J.	Died of disease	Orange River	27 March 1900	
5150	Pte	Starkey, W.	Died of disease	Kimberley	6 April 1900	
5605	Pte	Blackburn, W.	Wounded	Jammersberg Drift	9–21 April 1900	LNLR Coy 3rd M.I.
4984	Pte	Quinn, T.	Died of disease	Kimberley	18 April 1900	

No.	Rank	Name	Casualty	Place	Date	Remarks
4181	Pte	Fewster, C.	Wounded	Near Boshof	21 April 1900	
3197	LSgt	Harrison, J.	Died of disease	Boshof	11 May 1900	
5581	LCpl	Reeves, G.	Died of disease	Kimberley	11 May 1900	
5445	Pte	Backhouse, J.	Died of disease	Boshof	14 May 1900	
3027	Pte	Woolley, J.	Died of disease	Boshof	24 May 1900	
4581	Pte	Daulby, G.	Died of disease	Kimberley	25 May 1900	
4100	Pte	Lee, A.	Died of disease	Boshof	25 May 1900	
5414	Pte	Manley, W.	Died of disease	Aliwal North	26 May 1900	
4930	Pte	Calvert, D.	Died of disease	Boksburg	10 June 1900	LNLR Coy 3rd M.I.
5209	Pte	Daniels, J.	Wounded	Bappisfontein	24 June 1900	LNLR Coy 3rd M.I.
4186	Sgt	Passmore, S.	Wounded	Serfontein	26 June 1900	O.R.S. (Orderley Room Sgt)
3153	Pte	Rouse, J.	Died of disease	Kroonstad	27 June 1900	
4348	Pte	Butler, A.	Died of disease	Heilbron	5 July 1900	
4561	Cpl	Mulcock, C.	Died of disease	Viljoen's Drift	7 July 1900	
5175	Pte	Drew, W.	Wounded & prisoner	Witpoort, near Pretoria	11 July 1900	
5068	Pte	Ward, T.	Died of disease	Kroonstad	17 July 1900	
3119	Pte	Thompson, A.	Died of disease	Kroonstad	18 July 1900	
3840	Pte	Lucey, P.	Died of disease	Boshof	22 July 1900	
4786	Pte	Stanley, J.	Died of disease	Krugersdorp	24 July 1900	
4340	Pte	Gray, J.	Died of disease	Heilbron	30 July 1900	
7360	Pte	Snailham, J.	Died of disease	Bloemfontein	1 Aug. 1900	
5453	Pte	Daw, A.	Wounded	Holfontein	2 Aug. 1900	2nd LNLR Det Malta M.I. Awarded DCM
3573	Pte	Ryan, J.	Died of disease	Norval's Pont	26 Aug. 1900	Medal roll gives 26 July 1900
3709	Pte	Baines, J.	Died of disease	Kroonstad	28 Aug. 1900	
5259	Pte	Jones, D.	Died of disease	Krugersdorp	28 Aug. 1900	
5268	Pte	Maher, T.	Killed	Cyphergat	10 Sept. 1900	2nd LNLR Det Malta M.I.
5082	Cpl	Peacock, F.	Severely wounded	Cyphergat	10 Sept. 1900	2nd LNLR Det Malta M.I.
2939	Pte	Argyle, W.	Killed	Cyphergat	14 Oct. 1900	2nd LNLR Det Malta M.I.
4875	Pte	Kenyon, G.	Killed	Cyphergat	14 Oct. 1900	2nd LNLR Det Malta M.I.
5400	Pte	Bell, C.	Dangerously wounded	Cyphergat	14 Oct. 1900	2nd LNLR Det Malta M.I.
5117	Pte	Healey, H.	Slightly wounded	Cyphergat	14 Oct. 1900	2nd LNLR Det Malta M.I.
2731	Pte	White, A.	Killed	Nooitgedacht	17 Oct. 1900	
3514	Pte	Maguire, J.	Died of wounds	Nooitgedacht	17 Oct. 1900	
4166	Sgt	Whittle, J.	Wounded	Nooitgedacht	17 Oct. 1900	O.R.C. (Orderly Room Cpl)
4429	Pte	Ashworth, R.	Severely wounded	Nooitgedacht	17 Oct. 1900	
2525	Pte	Bisson, J.	Wounded	Nooitgedacht	17 Oct. 1900	
4293	Pte	Griffin, M.	Wounded	Nooitgedacht	17 Oct. 1900	
3917	Pte	McDonough, J.	Wounded	Nooitgedacht	17 Oct. 1900	
3848	Pte	Orrell, W.	Wounded	Nooitgedacht	17 Oct. 1900	

No.	Rank	Name	Casualty	Place	Date	Remarks
3571	Pte	Fisher, F.	Wounded	Weltevreden	20 Oct. 1900	2nd LNLR Det Malta M.I.
2996	Pte	Brooks, G.	Wounded	Weltevreden	20 Oct. 1900	2nd LNLR Det Malta M.I.
4839	Pte	Whiteway, C.	Wounded	Belfast	5 Dec. 1900	LNLR Coy 3rd M.I.
4653	Pte	Hughes, R.	Wounded	Belfast	6 Dec. 1900	LNLR Coy 3rd M.I.
	Capt	Knight, G. C.	Wounded	Houwater	26 Dec. 1900	OC New South Wales M.I.
5353	Pte	Lever, B.	Wounded	Bethlehem	29 Dec. 1900	2nd LNLR Det Malta M.I.
5364	Pte	Cotterall, W.	Slightly wounded	Zeerust	7 Jan. 1901	Regt Digest gives Cottrell
2587	Pte	Gibson, J.	Slightly wounded	Zeerust	7 Jan. 1901	
3667	Pte	Kennedy, B.	Slightly wounded	Zeerust	7 Jan. 1901	
	Lt	Bingham, C. H. M.	Wounded	Zeerust	8 Jan. 1901	Accident (shot by sentry)
	Lt	Wallace, A. R.	Killed	Zeerust	13 Jan. 1901	Explosion of mine
	Lt	Macauley, K. Z. P.	Mortally wounded	Twyfelaar, near Middelburg	27 Jan. 1901	LNLR Coy 3rd M.I. Died Middelburg, 30 Jan.
5856	LCpl	Fletcher, A.	Wounded & prisoner	Twyfelaar	27 Jan. 1901	LNLR Coy 3rd M.I.
5049	Pte	Hickey, J.	Killed	Twyfelaar	28 Jan. 1901	LNLR Coy 3rd M.I.
5197	Pte	Ratcliffe, D.	Wounded	Twyfelaar	28 Jan. 1901	LNLR Coy 3rd M.I.
3595	Pte	Thompson, R.	Severely wounded	Twyfelaar	28 Jan. 1901	LNLR Coy 3rd M.I.
4198	LCpl	Schofield, T.	Dangerously wounded	Strathrae	29 Jan. 1901	LNLR Coy 3rd M.I.
5008	Pte	McConville, C.	Severely wounded	Strathrae	29 Jan. 1901	LNLR Coy 3rd M.I.
2865	Sgt	Bowman, G.	Died of disease	Middelburg	4 Feb. 1901	LNLR Coy 3rd M.I.
4343	Pte	Clarkson, W.	Slightly wounded	Bothwell	5 Feb. 1901	LNLR Coy 3rd M.I.
4516	Pte	Didsbury, T.	Slightly wounded	Bothwell	5 Feb. 1901	LNLR Coy 3rd M.I.
4714	Pte	Caine, M.	Died of disease	Zeerust	16 Feb. 1901	
5117	Pte	Healey, H.	Died of disease	Kroonstad	17 Feb. 1901	2nd LNLR Det Malta M.I.
	Lt	Creak, W. H.	Killed	Hartebeestfontein	18 Feb. 1901	
	Lt	Hewett, A. V.	Killed	Hartebeestfontein	18 Feb. 1901	
2133	CSgt	Dorey, J.	Killed	Hartebeestfontein	18 Feb. 1901	
2137	Cpl	Meade, W.	Killed	Hartebeestfontein	18 Feb. 1901	
2735	LCpl	Ousley, W.	Killed	Hartebeestfontein	18 Feb. 1901	
3012	Pte	Jenks, W.	Killed	Hartebeestfontein	18 Feb. 1901	
4277	Sgt	Wright, F.	Slightly wounded	Hartebeestfontein	18 Feb. 1901	
4171	LCpl	Moore, S.	Severely wounded	Hartebeestfontein	18 Feb. 1901	
4313	Pte	Doyle, H.	Slightly wounded	Hartebeestfontein	18 Feb. 1901	

No.	*Rank*	*Name*	*Casualty*	*Place*	*Date*	*Remarks*
3643	Pte	Duffy, P.	Severely wounded	Hartebeestfontein	18 Feb. 1901	
3849	Pte	Pownall, J.	Slightly wounded	Hartebeestfontein	18 Feb. 1901	
3438	Pte	Sweeney, W.	Slightly wounded	Hartebeestfontein	18 Feb. 1901	
2558	Pte	Walsh, J.	Severely wounded	Hartebeestfontein	18 Feb. 1901	
5044	Pte	Wright, T.	Slightly wounded	Hartebeestfontein	18 Feb. 1901	
4922	LCpl	Gerrard, J.	Died of disease	Ventersdorp	20 Feb. 1901	
3926	Pte	Holgate, J.	Died of disease	Middelburg	25 Feb. 1901	LNLR Coy 3rd M.I.
4920	LCpl	Wilder, J.	Died of disease	Bloemfontein	27 Feb. 1901	2nd LNLR Det Malta M.I.
4001	Pte	Butler, J.	Died of disease	Springfontein	28 Feb. 1901	
4182	Pte	Davies, W.	Killed	Ventersburg Road	1 March 1901	LNLR Coy 3rd M.I.
5367	Pte	Vick, W.	Killed	Ventersburg	1 March 1901	2nd LNLR Det Malta M.I.
4426	LCpl	Hawkins, W.	Died of disease	Klerksdorp	2 March 1901	
5413	Pte	Moran, M.	Died of disease	Orange River	2 March 1901	2nd Bn (possibly M.I.?)
5797	Pte	Ireland, T.	Wounded & prisoner	Near Ventersburg	6 March 1901	2nd LNLR Det Malta M.I.
	2Lt	Wiltshire, R. C.	Died of disease	Kimberley	21 March 1901	
4788	Sgt	Bower, W.	Wounded	Dewetsdorp	15 March 1901	Accident
5104	Pte	Hope, B.	Slightly wounded	Steenbokspan	31 March 1901	
5437	Pte	Shaw, G.	Shot for desertion	Ventersdorp	27 April 1901	
4962	Pte	Clarke, J.	Slightly wounded	Brakpan	5 May 1901	
4976	Pte	Slicer, W.	Slightly wounded	Uitkom	16 May 1901	LNLR Coy 3rd M.I.
5686	Pte	Hutchinson, T.	Died of disease	Wynberg	16 May 1901	2nd Bn
5347	Pte	Hayes, R.	Died of disease	Bloemfontein	21 May 1901	2nd Bn
5756	LCpl	Seymour, J.	Died of wounds	Bloemfontein	23 May 1901	
2975	Pte	Gallagher, M.	Killed	Near Kaalfontein	23 May 1901	Ventersdorp Convoy
4929	Cpl	Waterhouse, W.	Wounded	Near Kaalfontein	23 May 1901	
2890	Pte	Hanley, J.	Wounded	Near Kaalfontein	23 May 1901	
3721	Pte	Lomas, J.	Wounded	Near Kaalfontein	23 May 1901	
4809	LCpl	Merriman, R.	Killed	Witpoortje	26 May 1901	2nd Bn, probably M.I.
5600	Pte	Garvey, T. W.	Killed	Witpoortje	26 May 1901	2nd Bn, probably M.I.
5749	LCpl	Reid, J.	Dangerously wounded	Donkerspoort	26 May 1901	2nd Bn (M.I.). Lated died of wounds
	2Lt	Helme, H. L.	Slightly wounded	Donkerspoort	26 May 1901	2nd Bn (M.I.)
4834	Cpl	Perrin, G.	Dangerously wounded	Donkerspoort	26 May 1901	2nd Bn (M.I.)
6078	Pte	Roberts, C.	Dangerously wounded	Donkerspoort	26 May 1901	2nd Bn (M.I.)
2920	Pte	Alston, E.	Suicide	Zeerust	31 May 1901	
2849	Pte	Thompson, A.	Died of disease	Kimberley	10 June 1901	

No.	*Rank*	*Name*	*Casualty*	*Place*	*Date*	*Remarks*
4875	Pte	Perry, F.	Killed	Mooiband	13 June 1901	
7041	Pte	Moss, G.	Died of wounds	Mooiband	13 June 1901	
7036	Pte	Kockeshott, T.	Slightly wounded	Beyersburg	25 June 1901	
4553	Pte	Hall, C.	Died of injuries	Mafeking	19 June 1901	
2767	Pte	Maddell, A.	Died of disease	Mafeking	6 July 1901	
3833	Sgt	Nevison, C.	Dangerously wounded	Klein Jagersfontein	28 July 1901	2nd Bn (attached 17th M.I.). Died 1 Aug.
7481	Pte	Lane, J.	Died of asphyxia	De Aar	31 July 1901	Volunteer Coy
5386	LCpl	Entwistle. J.	Killed	Schietfontein	1 Aug. 1901	
2856	Cpl	Street, C.	Slightly wounded	Schietfontein	1 Aug. 1901	
4372	Pte	Allinson, J.	Severely wounded	Schietfontein	1 Aug. 1901	
4871	Pte	Ascott, E.	Severely wounded	Schietfontein	1 Aug. 1901	
7501	Pte	McKeown, J.	Died of disease	De Aar	31 Aug. 1901	Volunteer Coy
4734	Pte	Dowd, A.	Slightly wounded	Vaalkop	9 Sept. 1901	
	Col	Kekewich, R. G.	Severely wounded	Moedewil	30 Sept. 1901	
1037	Sgt Maj	Goward, W.	Suicide	Honingspruit	6 Oct. 1901	2nd Bn (attached 9th M.I.)
6782	Pte	Lord, W.	Died of disease	Aliwal North	6 Oct. 1901	3rd Bn
3562	Pte	Rigby, R.	Killed	Baakenlaagte	30 Oct. 1901	LNLR Coy 3rd M.I.
3766	Pte	Howcroft, J.	Severely wounded	Baakenlaagte	30 Oct. 1901	LNLR Coy 3rd M.I.
6475	Pte	Horwood, T.	Slightly wounded	Rondekraal	11 Nov. 1901	3rd Bn
5685	Pte	Bailey, J.	Died of disease	Kroonstad	25 Nov. 1901	Malta M.I. Coy 9th M.I.
4794	Pte	Fisher, A.	Killed	Near Stormberg	27 Nov. 1901	3rd Bn M.I.
6890	Pte	Dryhurst, J.	Severely wounded	Near Stormberg	27 Nov. 1901	3rd Bn M.I.
6039	Pte	Jones, O.	Severely wounded	Near Stormberg	27 Nov. 1901	3rd Bn M.I.
2958	Sgt	Waring, J.	Slightly wounded	Pitsani	28 Nov. 1901	Blockhouse attack
3584	Pte	Rigby, J.	Severely wounded	Pitsani	28 Nov. 1901	Blockhouse attack
3394	Pte	Watson, A.	Severely wounded	Pitsani	28 Nov. 1901	Blockhouse attack
4505	Pte	Sheppard, G.	Died of disease	Klerksdorp	17 Dec. 1901	
5243	Pte	Lawrence, T.	Died of disease	Springfontein	18 Dec. 1901	2nd Bn (attached 17th M.I.)
4105	Pte	Williams, J.	Died of disease	Klerksdorp	23 Dec. 1901	
6891	Sgt	Egan, J.	Died lacerated brain	Springfontein	27 Dec. 1901	2nd Bn (attached 17th M.I.)
4496	Pte	Taylor, W.	Died of disease	Zeerust	30 Dec. 1901	
7503	Dmr	Lowe, J.	Died of disease	Mafeking	15 Jan. 1902	Volunteer Coy
3721	Pte	Lomas, J.	Died of disease	Mafeking	18 Jan. 1902	

No.	Rank	Name	Casualty	Place	Date	Remarks
	Maj	Dowell, G. W.	Severely wounded	Klip River	12 Feb. 1902	2nd Bn (attached 28th M.I.)
	Lt	Bridges, T. McG.	Severely wounded	Klip River	12 Feb. 1902	2nd Bn (attached 28th M.I.)
	Lt	Colley, A. W.	Severely wounded	Klip River	12 Feb. 1902	2nd Bn (attached 28th M.I.)
4824	Dmr	Louis, W.	Dangerously wounded	Klip River	12 Feb. 1902	2nd Bn (attached 28th M.I.)
5761	Pte	Johnson, T.	Killed	Tweebosch	7 March 1902	
5468	Pte	Tedder, G.	Killed	Tweebosch	7 March 1902	
	Lt	Fitzpatrick, E. R.	Slightly wounded	Tweebosch	7 March 1902	
5758	Pte	Ashton, T. H.	Slightly wounded	Tweebosch	7 March 1902	
5474	Pte	Firth, W.	Slightly wounded	Tweebosch	7 March 1902	
5916	Pte	Lyness, R.	Slightly wounded	Tweebosch	7 March 1902	
5015	Pte	McGreavy, J.	Dangerously wounded	Tweebosch	7 March 1902	Died 12 March 1902
3503	Pte	Molyneaux, R.	Severely wounded	Tweebosch	7 March 1902	
5225	Pte	Taylor, J.	Slightly wounded	Tweebosch	7 March 1902	
3693	Pte	Wilson, R.	Slightly wounded	Tweebosch	7 March 1902	
2977	Sgt	Conlong, W.	Died of disease	Kroonstad	22 March 1902	2nd Bn (attached 17th M.I.)
6041	Pte	Richardson, J.	Died of disease	Harrismith	30March 1902	2nd Bn (attached 17th M.I.)
	Lt	Jackson, D. R. H.,	Slightly wounded	Boschbult	31 March 1902	3rd Bn (attached 28th M.I.?)
7455	Pte	Ashman, H.	Died of disease	Mafeking	15 April 1902	Volunteer Coy

Summary of Casualties

Casualty	*East Lancashires*	*South Lancashires*	*Loyal North Lancashires*	*Total*
Killed in action/died of wounds	22	55	41	118
Died of disease	102	98	61	261
Died by accident and other causes	3	4	9	16
Wounded in action	39	131	125	295
Accidental wounding or injury	7	13	2	22

Bibliography

Published books and journals

General

Amery, L. S. (ed.), *The Times History of the War in South Africa*, Sampson Low, Marston & Co. Ltd, London, 1906–1909 (seven volumes)

Atkins, J. B., *The Relief of Ladysmith*, 1900

Baker, Anthony, *Battles and Battlefields of the Anglo-Boer War 1899–1902*, The Military Press, Milton Keynes, 1999

Beet, A. J., and Harris, C. B., *Kimberley under Siege* (2nd edn), Diamond Fields Advertiser, Kimberley, 1950

Carver, F. M. Lord, *The National Army Museum Book of The Boer War*, Sidgwick & Jackson, London, 1999

Childs, Lewis, *Ladysmith*, Leo Cooper, London, 1998

Churchill, W. S., *London to Ladysmith via Pretoria*, 1900

Creswicke, Louis, *South Africa and the Transvaal War*, Caxton Publishing Co., London, 1901–2 (eight volumes)

De Wet, C. R., *Three Years War*, Archibald Constable and Co. Ltd, London, 1902

Doyle, Arthur Conan, *The Great Boer War*, Smith, Elder & Co., London, 1902

Harris, Col. Sir David, *Pioneer, Soldier and Politician*, Sampson Low, Marston & Co. Ltd, London, *c.* 1920

Hart's Annual Army Lists, John Murray, London, 1899–1902

H.M.S.O., *South African War Despatches*

Jones, H. M. and M. G. M., *A Gazetteer of the Second Anglo-Boer War 1899–1902*, The Military Press, Milton Keynes, 1999

Marix Evans, M. F., *The Boer War – South Africa 1899–1902*, Osprey, Oxford, 1999

Maurice, Maj.-Gen. Sir Frederick, and Grant, Capt. M. H., *History of the War in South Africa 1899–1902*, Hurst and Blackett Ltd, London, 1906–1910 (four volumes)

O'Meara, Lt.-Col. W. A. J., *Kekewich in Kimberley*, Medici Society, London, 1926

Packenham, Thomas, *The Boer War*, Weidenfeld & Nicholson, London, 1979

Ten Months in the Field with the Boers, William Heinemann, 1901

The Siege of Kimberley 1899–1900, Diamond Fields Advertiser, Kimberley, 1900

The South African War Casualty Roll – The Natal Field Force 20th Oct. 1899–26th Oct. 1900, and *South African Field Force 11th Oct. 1899–June 1902.* Haywood & Son, 1980 and 1982

Wilson, H. W., *With the Flag to Pretoria*, and *After Pretoria – The Guerilla War*, Harmsworth Bros Ltd, London, 1900– (four volumes)

With Lord Methuen from Belmont to Hartebeestfontein, H. M. Guest, Klerksdorp, 1901

Regimental

Appleton, Capt. F. M. (compiler), *The Volunteer Service Company (1st South Lancashire Regiment) in South Africa during the Boer War*, Mackie & Co., Ltd., Warrington, 1901

1st Battalion Loyal North Lancashire Regiment, South African War 1899–1902, Swiss & Co., Devonport, 1903 (printed Regimental Digest of Service)

Mullaly, Col. B. R., *The South Lancashire Regiment (Prince of Wales's Volunteers)*, White Swan Press, Bristol, 1952

Neligan, Pte. T., *From Preston to Ladysmith*, Preston

Pine-Coffin, Capt. J. E. (ed. Susan Pine-Coffin), *One Man's Boer War*, Edward Gaskell, Bideford, 1999

Records of The 3rd Battalion South Lancashire Regiment, Taylor, Garnett, Evans & Co. Ltd, Manchester, 1909

The South Lancashire Regiment in the South African War, 1899–1902, Mackie & Co. Ltd, Warrington (printed Regimental Digest of Service)
Wylly, Col. H. C., *The Loyal North Lancashire Regiment, Vol. I, 1741–1914*, R.U.S.I., London, 1933

Newspapers and Journals

XXX (journal of 1st East Lancashires)
The Lilywhites' Gazette (journal of 2nd East Lancashires)
The East Lancashire Regiment Journal
The East Lancashire Regiment Bulletin
The Regimental Chronicle of The South Lancashire Regiment
The Lancashire Lad (journal of The Loyal North Lancashire Regiment and of The Queen's Lancashire Regiment)
Black and White Budget
The Blackburn Times
The Burnley Express and Advertiser
The Daily Mail
The Diamond Fields Advertiser (Kimberley)
The Jersey Times and British Press
The Lancashire Daily Post
The Liverpool Courier
The Liverpool Daily Post
The Nelson Chronicle
The Northern Whig (Belfast)
The Preston Herald
The Times
The St Helens Advertiser
The St Helens Reporter
The Warrington Guardian

Unpublished Sources

Manuscript Letters, Diaries and Memoirs in The Queen's Lancashire Regiment Archives
Bradley, LCpl. C, 1st South Lancashires, Diary
Braithwaite, Lt. F. J., 2nd Loyal North Lancashires (Malta Mounted Infantry), Letters
Brindle, Pte. J., 1st Loyal North Lancashires, Letters (copy)
Cleaver, CSgt. H., 1st South Lancashires, Notes
Gregson, Pte. R., 1st Loyal North Lancashires, Letter
Hackett, Sgt. E., 1st South Lancashires, Memoirs
Hall, Lt. -Col. R. H., 1st South Lancashires, Letter and Notes
Hart, O., Volunteer Service Company 1st Loyal North Lancashires, Diary (typed copy)
Humphries, Pte J., 1st South Lancashires, Letter (contemporary transcription)
Kekewich, Lt. -Col. R. G., 1st Loyal North Lancashires, Kimberley Siege Diary
Kelly, LCpl. M., 1st South Lancashires, Diary
MacCarthy O'Leary, Lt. -Col. J., Letter (contemporary transcription)
Mott, Lt. G., 1st South Lancashires, Memoirs
Pegum, CSgt. J. T., 1st South Lancashires, Diary (typed copy)
Pendlebury, Pte. W. H., Volunteer Service Company 1st South Lancashires, Diary
Raphael, Lt. F. M., 1st South Lancashires, Letters (mostly contemporary transcription)
Wain, Pte G., 1st South Lancashires, Diary (copy)
Weaver, Pte F. G., 1st East Lancashires, Diary
Webster, Lt. A. Mc., 1st Loyal North Lancashires, Memoir

Other unpublished documents – all in Regimental Archives unless noted otherwise

Digest of Services XXX [1st Bn East Lancashire Regiment] South Africa 1899 to 1902
Digest of Services 3rd Bn. East Lancashire Regiment 1853–1913
Digest of Services of 1st Loyal North Lancashire Regiment October 1894 – August 1914
1st Bn. South Lancashire Regiment Digest of Service [1899–1902]
Records of 1st East Lancashire Mounted Infantry Company
South African War Medal Rolls, East Lancashire Regiment, South Lancashire Regiment and Loyal North Lancashire Regiment (P.R.O.)

Index

(Figures in bold type refer to illustrations)

Abbreviations:

E Lan R	East Lancashire Regiment
S Lan R	South Lancashire Regiment (Prince of Wales's Volunteers)
LNLR	Loyal North Lancashire Regiment
Vol Svc Coy	Volunteer Service Company

C

F

G

H

U

V

W

Y

Z